Science and Mathematics in Early-Childhood Education

Curriculum Teaching

Science and Mathematics in Early-Childhood Education

Curriculum & Teaching

Donna M. Wolfinger

Auburn University at Montgomery

HarperCollinsCollegePublishers

Acquisitions Editor: Christopher Jennison
Project Coordination and Text Design: Publisher Services, Inc.
Cover Design: John Callahan
Production: Hilda Koparanian
Compositor: Black Dot Graphics
Cover and Text Printer: Malloy Lithographing, Incorporated

Science and Mathematics in Early-Childhood Education

ISBN 0-06-501262-3

Library of Congress Cataloging-in-Publication Data

Wolfinger, Donna M.
    Science and mathematics in early childhood education : curriculum
and teaching / Donna M. Wolfinger.
        p.   cm.
    Includes bibliographical references and index.
    ISBN 0-06-501262-3
    1. Science—Study and teaching (Early childhood)—United States.
    2. Mathematics—Study and teaching (Early childhood)—United States.
    I. Title.
    LB1139.5.S35W65   1994
    372.3′5—dc20   93-30557
                                                                         CIP

93 94 95 96 9 8 7 6 5 4 3 2 1

To my mother
and all other exemplary kindergarten teachers.

BRIEF CONTENTS

CONTENTS

15 Strategies for Teaching Science   240

PART FOUR

Evaluation   255

16 Evaluation in the Early-Childhood Science and Mathematics Program   257

INTRODUCTION

In the education of the young child, there are no areas more fundamental than science and mathematics. Indeed, the questions asked by the young child often focus on questions of why and how. Why is grass green? Why is the sky blue? Why do I have to eat broccoli? How does a car work? How does a candle burn? Such questions reveal a fundamental desire on the part of the young child to understand the surrounding environment. Science is a search for understanding and so the young child is, in both questions and actions, a young scientist. But the young child's questions also reveal a desire to know how much and how many. How old am I? How many days until my birthday? How tall am I? How much does it cost? Such questions help to reveal the child as a mathematician.

To the adult interacting with a young child, such questions often are seen not only as a quest for information but also as a foundation for later understanding of more difficult topics. So science and mathematics for the young child traditionally have been viewed as preparation for far more complex understanding. Specifically, science and mathematics for the young child have been viewed as preparation for the next year of life, the next grade level, or for adulthood. Unfortunately, when science and mathematics are viewed as preparation for the future, the programs in these areas become reflections of projected adult needs rather than contributors to the education of young children. Often this point of view serves to push the curriculum downward so that four year olds are taught to add and six year olds are instructed in the molecular theory.

The young child should neither be viewed as an adult in preparation nor as a precursor to an older and somehow more educable child. Instead, the young child should be viewed as a complete person, as an individual to be educated today with a program appropriate to the young child. When the child is viewed as a child rather than as an adult in preparation, science and mathematics are no longer considered in terms of what they will contribute to the adult but are viewed in terms of what they do contribute to the education and development of the child as a child.

The role of mathematics in the education of the young child should involve three areas:

- First, mathematics should be viewed as a means of investigation. Mathematics as investigation allows the child to describe and quantify the world. In this role, mathematics is a way of answering questions about how much, how many, how long, and what shape. It is a way of describing the phenomena and experiences of a young child actively investigating the world. Mathematics as description is demonstrated whenever children try to describe the circumference of the Halloween pumpkin, the length of a Tyrannosaurus Rex, or the difference in number of children who prefer chocolate pudding to vanilla pudding. It is quantification, but it is meaningful quantification used to describe familiar events.
- Second, mathematics should be viewed as a way of problem solving. As a problem-solving strategy, mathematics includes both a means for determining an answer and a way of thinking that seeks out a variety of possible ways for finding that answer. Children find solutions to

problems such as how to determine the distance from the school to the fire station, how to find out the number of children who like one cartoon character rather than another, or how to show the children who have brothers, sisters, or both brothers and sisters. The goal of problem solving is to find a multiplicity of ways of determining answers rather than to identify a single correct answer.

- Third, mathematics is a means of computation. After young children have developed cognitively and constructed an understanding of number, they can begin to develop the algorithms necessary for computation of answers to standard problems. But even computational skills should be considered from the viewpoint of the needs and interests of the young child rather than the future needs of the mathematics student.

Like mathematics, science should be viewed for the contributions it makes to the child as a child rather than to the child in preparation for adulthood.

- Science should first be considered as a technique for investigating the world. Through investigations, children are able to construct an understanding of the environment and the way in which the parts of that environment function both separately and together. The child who plants seeds and watches them grow to produce flowers and fruit is constructing an understanding of living organisms. The child who investigates rolling objects to determine how they can be made to roll faster and farther or slower and straighter is not only learning physics but is also demonstrating science as an investigative procedure.
- The second contribution of science to the education of the young child is a direct outgrowth of science as investigation. Science should also be considered as a means of problem solving. How can we make a cage to keep insects alive so they can be observed? What could have caused some of the beans to grow well and some not to grow at all? How can we classify rocks into groups? What affects how fast a pendulum swings? What kinds of objects will a magnet pick up? It is easy to give a quick, verbal answer to questions such as these, but when science is

viewed as problem solving, children discuss methods of finding answers, look for alternate methods, and then use their methods to find out for themselves the answers to their questions.

- The third contribution of science to the education of the young child is the contribution of knowledge. Science investigation and science problem solving both result in the development of information that the child can apply in other situations. For the very young child, at preschool and kindergarten levels, scientific knowledge and general knowledge cannot be separated. Scientific knowledge comes to the very young child through investigation and through mental construction that is little affected by the teacher or by direct verbal instruction. As the child matures toward the third-grade level, science information becomes more differentiated until science is a specific branch of knowledge.

The contributions that science and mathematics make to the education of the young child are dependent on the way in which science and mathematics are presented to the young child. At the early-childhood education level, science and mathematics should be integrated, with the degree of integration dependent on the age and developmental level of the child. The reasons for integration are easily seen.

- First, the contributions of science and mathematics to the education of the young child are the same: They both help the child describe the world, solve problems, and gather content information.
- Second, in the world of science and the world of advanced instruction in science, mathematics and science are fully integrated. Indeed, physics is so closely related to mathematics that theoretical physics can be carried on with chalk and blackboard or computer and keyboard through the solutions to mathematical equations. The use of mathematics in all of the sciences, from astronomy to zoology, is a necessity.
- Third, the processes of science and the skills of mathematics overlap in many areas. For example, the science process skill of using numbers includes both counting and computation, while

the science process skill of observation includes measurement and shape identification. It is only logical to combine these two areas of study where they overlap.

- Fourth, and perhaps most important, the thinking processes of the young child do not differentiate between the two areas. In the mind of the young child, there is no compartmentalization of subject areas. Consequently, compartmentalization, which is an artificial distinction between mathematics and science, is in opposition to the natural thinking of the child. Integration is not only consistent with the nature of the child's thought process but is also consistent with the nature of science and mathematics.

It is not, however, only science and mathematics that should be integrated when teaching the young child. Indeed, language arts and reading contribute extensively to the learning of science and mathematics. The science process skills of communication, conclusion, inference, prediction, and cause and effect are also the skills of reading. Keeping records in science or mathematics requires the development of language arts skills in writing. Consequently, the curriculum is tied together not only in terms of the simultaneous consideration of science and mathematics but also in the use of language and reading to develop science information and science process skills to enhance reading and language. Again, however, the degree of integration of the subject areas should always be dependent on the developmental level and educational level of the child.

The focus of this textbook is on appropriate science and mathematics for the young child. Therefore, the source of the curriculum becomes the child and the development of the curriculum is based on the changing child.

Part One: The Unified Curriculum deals with children at the preschool and kindergarten levels. It details the curricular pattern, teaching techniques, and subject matter most appropriate for the young child in a unified approach to science and mathematics.

Part Two: The Combined Curriculum examines children at the first- and second-grade levels. It details the curricular pattern, teaching techniques, and subject matter most appropriate for the child who is beginning to differentiate subject areas.

Part Three: The Defined Curriculum focuses on children at the third-grade level. It details the changes in the curriculum that allow children to make the transition to the more differentiated curricula of the upper grades. The curricular pattern, teaching techniques, and subject matter for the third grade are discussed in terms of appropriate material for the grade level.

Part Four: Evaluation discusses the types of evaluation appropriate to the various curricular patterns.

Science and Mathematics in Early-Childhood Education

Curriculum & Teaching

PART ONE

The Unified Curriculum

INTRODUCTION

At the preschool and kindergarten level, the child is both the source and the recipient of the curriculum. The developmental and social characteristics of the very young child rather than the content of the subject matter area determine not only the information included but also the teaching techniques and the curricular pattern. When the child is the source of the curriculum, the educational setting and the teaching strategies are appropriate to the child's developing skills and cognitive abilities. It is a curriculum that fits the child rather than a curriculum to which the child must be molded.

Preschool and kindergarten should be viewed as introductory levels because children at these ages are still being introduced to the world. They are neither lacking in intelligence nor in ability but are simply novices, inexperienced in the workings of the world. As active seekers of information, preschool and kindergarten children strive to understand their world, find meaning in their experiences, and find connections between new and old experiences. The experiences selected for use at the preschool and kindergarten levels should enhance the natural learning behaviors of children as well as form a foundation for subsequent learning.

Because preschool and kindergarten form the foundation levels and because the very young child thinks in ways far different from those of the adult, the selection of content information should be based on the characteristics of young children rather than on the preferences of the teacher or on tradition. The teacher might find the mysteries and magnificence of space fascinating, but the young child is not generally prepared to comprehend the wonders of astronomy. The traditional viewpoint may consider the experience of growing crystals a topic for young children, but the young child can only think "magic" as the crystals of sugar form on the string. It is the cognitive characteristics of the child that determine what the child can comprehend. It is both the cognitive and the social characteristics of the child that determine how the child can best be taught.

The unified curriculum pattern is based on the child's cognitive and social characteristics. In the unified curriculum, no distinction is made between mathematics and science. Because there is no distinction, knowledge of both science and mathematics is constructed simultaneously by the child. The knowledge constructed is not only a part of the realm of science and mathematics but is also general knowledge. It is general knowledge that the child is able to comprehend directly but it is also general knowledge that will form the basis for later construction and explanation from a scientific or mathematical viewpoint. The difficulty lies in selecting learning experiences, not on the basis of what will be useful later in life but on the basis of what will contribute to the child's present understanding of the world and his or her place in it. Because the child is the focal point of the curriculum, both the teacher and the child select areas of investigation and study. Interests developed by individual children as a result of teacher-shaped experiences or by interactions with the environment are also a part of the unified curriculum pattern.

The unified curriculum pattern has no specific subject matter goals that all children must meet in order to avoid failure. Instead, the unified curriculum provides for the varying needs, interests, and backgrounds of the children involved. If knowledge is constructed, then that knowledge will depend on the previous experiences of the child. To expect that all young children will have had the same prior experiences is absurd. To expect that all children will construct identical concepts at precisely the same time is equally absurd. To expect that all children will gain knowledge commensurate with their interests, backgrounds, and investigations is appropriate. The unified curriculum looks for growth within the individual child rather than for growth measured against an external and predetermined yardstick.

The goals of the unified curriculum are not subject matter goals. However, that is not to say that the unified curriculum does not have goals.

Within the unified curriculum, the major goal is the construction of knowledge. The second goal is to decrease heteronomy and increase autonomy, particularly within a problem-solving format. The experiences provided within the framework of the curriculum permit the child to investigate in a variety of ways. The teacher acts as a collaborator, a facilitator, and an aid rather than as a director of events and outcomes. It is the child's initiative and autonomy that determine the direction that the activities and, therefore, the experiences will take.

Finally, the unified curriculum often involves groupings of children in which various ages are represented. Multiage groups frequently spur the younger child to different investigations and the older child to demonstrations of the "how," "what," and "when" of an activity. The young child learns from the older child and the older child is able to display competence. And, of course, the older child learns from the games, activities, and investigations initiated by the younger child.

If the unified curriculum pattern is to function at the optimal level, the teacher must understand the developmental characteristics and social characteristics of the child. The unified curricular pattern functions only as well as the teacher is able to develop teaching strategies appropriate to the young child.

CHAPTER 1

Developmental Characteristics of Three to Five Year Olds

Chapter Objectives

On completion of this chapter, you should be able to

1. list the cognitive characteristics of three- and four-year-old children,

2. describe each of the cognitive characteristics of three- and four-year-old children,

3. list the cognitive characteristics of five-year-old children,

4. describe each of the cognitive characteristics of five-year-old children,

5. compare the cognitive characteristics of three- or four-year-old children to those of five-year-old children,

6. discuss some of the tasks used to assess the developmental characteristics of children, and

7. conduct a Piagetian interview or task with a child of three, four, or five years of age.

Not long ago, a teacher was approached by a grandfather who knew that she was interested in the education of his young grandchild. He took a sheet of paper—the kind that is vanilla in color and has widely spaced blue lines—out of his pocket. The paper had addition problems on it of the type 1 + 1 = 2, 2 + 1 = 3, and 2 + 2 = 4. The problems had been written in faint, wobbly numerals that avoided the neatly printed lines and trailed off toward the bottom left. On the top of the paper was a frowning face and the notation "messy" along with a −4 because of incorrect problems. The grandfather was concerned about his grandson. The child was having so much trouble with arithmetic and he wanted to find a tutor so the child would not fail.

"What grade is your grandson in?" the teacher asked.

"He's not in any grade," the man answered.

"I don't quite understand," the teacher said. "Is he in school?"

"Yes. He goes to preschool."

"How old is he?" the teacher asked.

"Almost four."

The teacher suggested that he withdraw his grandson from that school and put him into a preschool without forced academics.

As adults, teachers no longer think as their young pupils think and so often make decisions about teaching and content that are inappropriate to the young child. Almost-four year olds are not cognitively ready for the experiences of formal arithmetic: written papers, and graded assignments. Such activities cause the child to memorize meaningless information or to reject such information and so become failures before even entering school.

If formal arithmetic—even the "easy" kind of 1 + 1 = 2—is beyond the cognitive characteristics of young children, then what is within their capabilities and characteristics? In order to answer this question, the cognitive characteristics of three, four, and five year olds must be considered.

COGNITIVE ABILITIES OF PRESCHOOL AND KINDERGARTEN CHILDREN

Reasoning in Children

Children at the preschool and kindergarten levels use similar forms of reasoning. The type of thinking available to the preoperational child is in no way inferior to the thinking patterns of adults. It is simply different and reflects differences in the child's level of experience with the world as well as in the cognitive structures developed by the child.

Children at the preschool and kindergarten levels are capable of reasoning, but their reasoning is concrete in nature. It is based on past experience, emphasizing objects and materials rather than abstract words and ideas. The child relates past experience to new experience through attention to similarities and differences among materials as well as to the reactions of those materials. The abstraction of generalizations by the young child is based on personal, concrete experiences.

One form of reasoning common to the very young child is *transductive reasoning*. Transductive reasoning generally includes two ideas.

First, the child centers on one characteristic and proceeds to draw as a conclusion from that characteristic some other perceptually connected occurrence. The child may come to a correct conclusion, but there is no certainty that the reasoning used was logical rather than transductive. In flying paper airplanes, the child may center on the trait of color and predict that red paper airplanes will fly farther than any other color of airplane. In testing the color, this may actually be shown to be a valid conclusion. The reason, however, lies in the design of the airplane rather than in the color of the paper. To the child using transductive reasoning, however, the color is the cause of the longer flight path.

Second, transductive reasoning may be considered as reasoning from specific to specific to specific without ever really coming to a conclusion that fits all of the specifics. In this case, the child confronted with a basket of different foods and asked how they are the same may reply in the following manner: "I can eat a banana. I can eat potatoes. Yesterday I had a piece of cake. Sometimes I eat bread." The child does not, however, make the single generalization "all are food" to encompass all of the items contained in the basket. The use of the term *all* in this sense is beyond the cognitive ability of many children.

A second type of reasoning used by very young children is termed *syncretic reasoning.* Syncretic reasoning causes children to connect a series of separate ideas into a single confused whole. In syncretic reasoning, almost anything can be related casually. If asked why A occurred, the child will supply B as a cause, but B is simply some element that occurred simultaneously with A in perception; the child has fused B with A in syncretism. For example, a child watches a plant turn from bright green to yellow and finally to brown. While the plant was dying, new carpet was put into the room and a new chair was purchased. Using syncretic reasoning, the child concludes that the plant died not because it was at the end of its life cycle, but because of the new objects brought into the room. Rather than looking for a true causal relation, the child connects unrelated events. For the young child, anything and everything must have a cause and so a cause is provided. This type of thinking results in an inability to form, at this age, a genuine concept of chance or probability.

Cause and Effect in Children

Cause and effect is a special case of reasoning with which young children have particular difficulty. Because a true concept of cause and effect does not develop until approximately ten years of age, young children are generally said to be using either magical or precausal forms of reasoning.

Three and Four Year Olds. Children of three or four frequently use a form of causal reasoning that is termed *magical causality.* In this case, the child can give no reason for an occurrence and so attributes the occurrence to magic. On seeing that a magnet will hold a long string of paper clips, a four year old in a preschool setting may exclaim, "It's magic!" Even though the teacher takes a great deal of time to explain the workings of magnets, the child, who considers magnets magical, will still continue to show the magnet to other children and tell them it is magic. Logical explanation of cause and effect will be meaningless to a child who has yet to develop a concept of cause and effect.

Five Year Olds. The child of five uses precausal rather than magical forms of cause-and-effect reasoning. Children using precausal forms of cause-and-effect reasoning do not relate a particular cause to a particular effect but rather reason in ways that do not require causality.

There are, according to Piagetian research, eight types of precausal thinking: motivation, finalism, phenomenism, participation, moralism, artificialism, animism, and dynamism.

Motivation is a form of precausality in which the child attributes cause and effect to some sort of divine plan. Motivation is considered a primitive type of causality because it is both causal and final. In this case, a child may explain the cause of dreams by saying that God sends them because something was done that should not be done. In another example, a child may reason that two mountains exist side by side because there must be one for adults and a second one for children. In this second example, the concept of God or of some causative agent is implied rather than stated.

Finalism overlaps with motivation to start, but gradually becomes separate from it. In finalism, things simply are; there is neither origin nor consequence. In essence, things occur because they do. What caused a glass to be lying on the floor in pieces? It just broke. Why does a river flow into the sea? It just does. Finalism does not imply any sort of psychological motivation.

Phenomenism is a frequently used form of causality that disappears between five and six years of age. In this form of causality, two things are related because of resemblance or general affinity and are considered to have something in common that enables them to act on one another at a distance. One item is considered the source of some sort of emanations and the other is the emanation of the first: a certain word causes something to happen, a certain gesture protects one from danger. This may be evidenced in a common childhood belief. Many children tiptoe to school over cracked sidewalks trying hard to avoid those cracks. The reason is simple: Step on a crack, break your mother's back. This is definitely a form of phenomenism as causality.

Moral causality uses the explanation of necessity to explain movement or a feature of an object. This is very close to both motivation and finalism, but the necessity is attributed to the object itself. Why does a car move? So it can take people to work. Why does the Sun shine? So it can give light to people. In this case, objects have intentions that participate with the intentions of human beings.

Artificialism as causality explains events or objects as the result of human creative activity or as necessary to human activity. Why do the hands of a clock move? So people can tell time. Where did the Sun come from? People made it. This type of causality is, perhaps, understandable. To the young child, adults (whether parents, teachers, or caregivers) are the source of all things. Therefore, it seems appropriate that everything should be caused by human beings.

Animism is an explanation of causality that attributes life and consciousness to all things. Children using animistic reasoning will explain the movement of clouds, cars, and the Sun by saying that they are alive. Mountains are thought to grow out of the ground because they are alive, not because of geologic changes.

Dynamism is the final type of precausal explanation. It arises once animism has vanished as an explanation. In dynamism, force is confused with life. In this case, a stream runs down a mountain not because of the force of gravity but because it is pushed by the mountain. This type of precausality continues to exist even after the period of use of precausal explanations has vanished.

Appropriate Cause and Effect.   There is one case in which the preschool or kindergarten child is able to identify cause-and-effect relationships. This case involves immediacy in time and space, which includes four factors. First, the cause and effect are so closely related in time that the cause immediately produces the effect. Second, the child's own action is the cause of the reactions. Third, the child is able to directly experience the effect. And, fourth, the cause and the effect are close to each other in space. For example, a group of preschool children discovered that a board placed over a

cylindrical block had great potential. If a sponge was put on one end and a child jumped on the other, the sponge flew into the air. Some children could get the sponge to fly up only a few feet. One boy was able to get it to hit the ceiling. The difference? As a four year old put it, "Gina is little and can't jump hard. Tommy is big and jumps real hard. If you jump hard, it goes up more." This is cause and effect, but it is cause and effect that meets the four criteria of immediacy, proximity, observability, and involvement.

Classification in Children

As a result of his investigations into children's ability to classify objects, Piaget showed that the ability to classify develops through various stages until the child is able to classify in a highly sophisticated format known as a hierarchical classification system. The hierarchical system, the type that is used in the biological classification system, is not available to the young child. In fact, the type of classification used by the young child is far different from the classification system used by the adult.

Three and Four Year Olds.   Children of three or four who are presented with a collection of squares, rectangles, circles, and triangles and asked to put these shapes into groups do not actually form a classification system. Instead, many young children will form patterns or pictures with the objects. A pattern is an arrangement of objects that is pleasing to the child. It may be repetitive. It may be a quiltlike pattern (see Diagram 1.1). To the child, it is a way of grouping objects. In forming pictures, the child uses the objects available to make things such as houses and trees, stop signs, fish, and arrows (see Diagram 1.2). Periodically, the young child will use the objects to create a representation of something else. A four year old presented with circles, rectangles, triangles, and squares in the colors of red, blue, green, and yellow quickly selected all of the circles and piled them one on top of the other. He held it out: "There." Asked what he had done, he announced that he had made a bologna sandwich: the yellow circle was the bread, the red circle was the bologna, a thin yellow circle was mustard, a green circle was lettuce, and a top blue circle was bread. Why was the top "slice of

LEARNING ACTIVITY 1

Physical Causality Interview

Purpose: The purpose of this activity is to interview children to determine their concept of physical causality.

Materials: Three children aged three, four, and five; a tape recorder or pencil and paper

Procedure:

1. Talk with each child on a one-to-one basis in a quiet area of the classroom or other setting.
2. You may use the following questions, from an interview with a four-year-old boy, to initiate a discussion with the child. Follow-up questions will depend on what the child gives as a response.

What are some things in this room that are alive?

Your glasses. The table. My new sneakers.

What is it about my glasses that make them alive?

They make you see better. Can I look through them? They make things look really funny.

What is it about your new sneakers that make them alive?

They help me run real, real fast. (His foot was extended so that the new sneakers were easily seen.)

And this table. How do you know this table is alive?

It helps you write.

The following is an example of an interview with a five-year-old girl.

What are some things that are alive?

Me and you and my daddy's car and clouds and . . . I don't know more.

How do you know that you and I are alive?

We can run and play games.

How about your daddy's car? How do you know it's alive?

'Cause it moves and brings me to school. It can drive.

How about the clouds outside?

They can move in the sky. Sometimes they're here and sometimes they aren't.

What do you think makes those clouds move?

They just do. They want to go across the sky so they do.

3. The following are some questions that can be used to initiate a discussion with a child
   a. (On a windy day) *Think about the wind that is blowing outside. What do you think causes wind?*
   b. *Have you ever gone for a walk at night and seen the moon? Where do you think the moon came from? Does the moon stay still when you walk down the street?*
   c. *Do you ever have dreams when you're asleep? Where are those dreams when you dream them? Could I see your dream if I walked into your room?*
   d. (After putting toy boats in water) *What do you think makes a boat float?*
   e. *What are some things in this room that are alive? What are some things in this room that are not alive?*
   f. *Have you ever ridden a bicycle? What makes the bicycle move?*
   g. *Think about your name for a minute. Your name is _____. Do you think you could have been named* (some name other than the child's)?
   h. *What do you think makes a shadow?*
   i. *When you go outside during the day, the sun is usually shining. Where does the sun go at night?*
   j. *Have you ever seen the ocean (or a river)? What do you think causes the ocean (river) to move?*

Cautions:

1. Be certain to give the child time to talk and to think about what he or she wants to say. Follow the direction that the child takes in the conversation rather than trying to direct it along certain lines.
2. Be careful not to laugh or to look surprised at anything a child says in answer to a question. The

LEARNING ACTIVITY 1 Continued

child is voicing his or her beliefs and they should be respected.

3. Remember that the purpose of the interview is to find out how a child thinks. This is not the time to try to "teach" the child "correct" answers. Your explanations are more likely to halt discussion than foster it.

Interpreting the Results: The resulting responses should be considered in terms of the types of causal explanations typically given by children. Try to identify the kind of causal thinking that is being exhibited by the child.

Linear Arrangement

   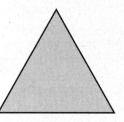 

Quilt Arrangement

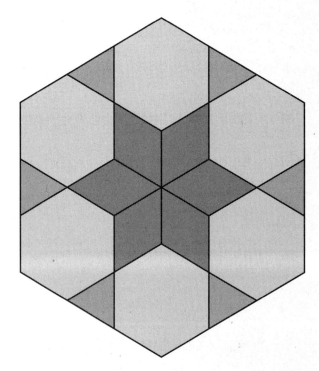

DIAGRAM 1.1 Classification by Patterns

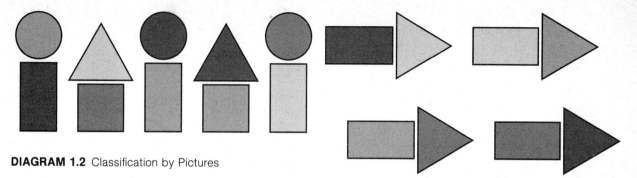

DIAGRAM 1.2 Classification by Pictures

bread" blue rather than yellow? It was whole wheat.

At its most sophisticated state, the child of three or four uses *resemblance sorting* in classification. In this case, two objects with a similar characteristic are placed together. The objects may both be red or triangular or thick. A third object, however, may be green because the child notices that the second object was triangular and the green object is triangular. Resemblance sorting places two similar objects together followed by an object that is using a different trait than that used for the first two objects (see Diagram 1.3).

Classification is a task for which the child of three or four is not yet ready. It is true that a young child can be coerced by the teacher to place all of the objects into separate piles according to color. However, the child sees little reason for the task and is unlikely to complete it without the constant attention of the teacher.

Five Year Olds. Five-year-old children are beginning to develop a concept of classification. They no longer make pictures or patterns when given a collection of attribute blocks to classify. However, the ability to classify consistently is not yet devel-

The triangle leads to a triangle with stripes. The stripes lead to a striped circle. The circle leads to a circle with dots. The dots lead to a dotted square. The square leads to a large square. The large aspect leads to a large triangle. The triangle leads to a checked triangle. The checked aspect leads to a checked square.

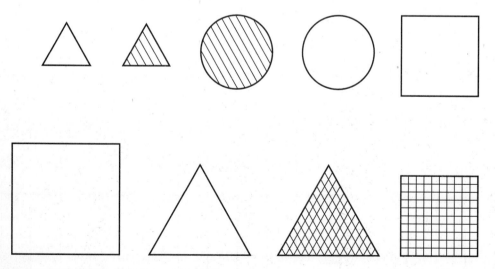

DIAGRAM 1.3 Classification by Resemblance Sorting

oped. Like the three or four year old, the five-year-old child frequently changes the trait being used for classification of objects. In general, the five-year-old child uses resemblance sorting, matching two objects and then changing the trait. The classification of objects by resemblance sorting continues until the child runs out of blocks or simply decides to end the activity. The decision to end before classifying all objects is as much a characteristic of classification as is resemblance sorting. The young child ends a task when he or she wishes to stop rather than because all of the objects have been classified. This is known as a *lack of exhaustive sorting*. Lack of exhaustive sorting can be overcome by the teacher who insists that all objects be placed into an appropriate group, but the child will see no purpose to the activity and be unlikely to comprehend the characteristics used in the classification. Lack of exhaustive sorting should never be misconstrued as not finishing a task, and so in some way naughty, but rather should be viewed as a normal characteristic of young children.

Seriation and Ordering in Children

Seriation is the ability to place objects into order on the basis of an ascending or descending value of a trait. Straws that are cut into lengths ranging from one centimeter to ten centimeters can be seriated from largest to smallest to form a stairstep (see Diagram 1.4). For the child of three or four, the task of seriation is inappropriate.

Three and Four Year Olds. The three- to four-year-old child has a global impression of a set of objects ordered by length. He or she will see the differences in length and be able to describe a completed seriation as looking like a staircase. This ability to describe indicates that the child is fully aware of differences in size and the meaning of the order shown: the arrangement is from largest to smallest. In a double seriation, the child will be able to describe the appearance of the completed seriation, again showing an ability to describe what is seen and state the relationship between the two objects at each location within the double seriation.

The three or four year old will attempt to replicate a single or double seriation but is not generally successful. Instead, the child will produce a pattern of objects that is pleasing but haphazard in terms of seriation.

Five Year Olds. The child of five has begun to seriate but the accomplishment of the task of seriation is through trial and error rather than through a coherent plan of attack. At this level in seriation, children try one object, then another until they have finally placed all of the objects into serial order.

One-to-One Correspondence in Children

One-to-one correspondence is the ability to match one object to one object. Each time a child helps to give out crackers at snack time, the child is making a one-to-one correspondence. The strategy of one for you, one for me is appropriate for the accomplishment of this task.

Three and Four Year Olds. In situations where, perhaps, the task is not so familiar as distributing crackers or cupcakes, the child of three or four has

Single Seriation

Double Seriation

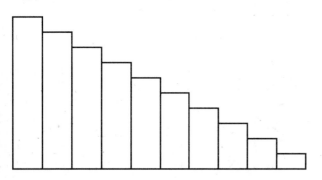

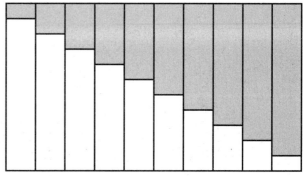

DIAGRAM 1.4 Single and Double Seriation

LEARNING ACTIVITY 2

Classification

Purpose: The purpose of this activity is to determine a child's ability to classify objects.

Materials: circles, squares, and triangles in two sizes, each size in three colors for a total of 18 shapes (The shapes should be made from heavy-weight cardboard, wood, or styrofoam.)

Procedure:
1. Mix up the shapes and place them in a pile in front of the child.
2. Ask the child to put the objects into groups so that each group contains objects that are the same in some way.
3. If the child is able to group all of the objects successfully by one criterion (like color), then mix up the objects and see if the child can do it again using a different criterion in classifying the shapes.
4. Ask the child how all the items in one group are the same.

Cautions:
1. Be careful not to give the child too many directions. You should give only enough information to present the task. Do not ask the child specifically to group the objects by color, shape, or size.
2. Refrain from making facial expressions and comments. The child's actions will give clues to his or her level of thought in terms of classification. There is no right or wrong answer to the task.

Interpreting the Results:
1. Children who have not yet reached the level where classification is possible will make pictures or patterns using the objects.
2. Resemblance sorting occurs when the child begins to group two objects together on the basis of some characteristic and then moves to a new characteristic. The child may show a lack of exhaustive sorting and not group all of the objects in the pile.
3. Children who are able to classify will generally do so on the basis of a single characteristic, either color, size, or shape. As children become more proficient in classification, they will be able to reclassify objects grouped by shape into categories based on color or size.

LEARNING ACTIVITY 3

Single-Seriation Interview

Purpose: The purpose of this activity is to investigate a child's ability to develop a single seriation.

Materials: Ten sticks or heavy cardboard strips cut to the following lengths: 10 in., 9 in., 8 in., 7 in., 6 in., 5 in., 4 in., 3 in., 2 in., 1 in.

Procedure:
1. Mix up the sticks or cardboard strips and show them to the child. Make the following requests.
   a. Show me the smallest stick.
   b. Show me a stick just a tiny bit bigger.
   c. Now, show me the smallest stick, then one a little bit bigger, then another a little bit bigger.
2. Using the first three sticks (beginning with the largest), make a staircase.
3. Ask the child to continue the staircase using the other sticks.

4. After the seriation is performed, give another stick to the child and ask where it belongs in the seriation. Once the child places the stick, ask why it belongs in that location.

Cautions:
1. Be certain that the objects are carefully cut so that there is no doubt about the differences in size. Diagonal or ragged ends can cause difficulty because they are uneven. All objects should be the same color.
2. Be very careful not to coach the child either through verbal cues or facial expressions. Praise whatever response is given. You are trying to determine the child's thought patterns, not obtain the "right" answer to a question.

LEARNING ACTIVITY 3 Continued

Interpreting the Results:

Level One: Level-one children are not able to construct a series. They can pick out a little stick and then a big one, another little one and another big one. Some children will even pick up groups of three: small, medium, large. There is, however, no coordination of the total series.

Level Two: Level-two children may construct a partial seriation or, by trial and error, an entire seriation. A complete coordination is not yet present. This lack of complete coordination can be shown by pre-

senting the child with a few more sticks and asking that they be placed in the seriation. Generally, this cannot be done.

Level Three: Level-three children are able to construct the complete seriation by selecting the sticks in the order needed and not relying on a trial-and-error procedure. These children also realize that any individual stick is shorter than the previous stick and longer than the stick that follows.

---

difficulty in making a one-to-one correspondence. When constructing a line of pennies similar to a line already constructed, the child is more likely to make a line in which the ends of both lines match rather than a line showing a one-to-one correspondence (see Diagram 1.5).

Five Year Olds. Children of five years of age are now able to develop a one-to-one correspondence among objects. This is shown in their ability to distribute objects to other children in a group and to accomplish the creation of a similar row of objects to the model row during the conservation of number task.

Conservation of Number in Children

Conservation of number is the ability to recognize that the quantity of objects in a set does not change simply because the arrangement of those objects changes.

Three and Four Year Olds. Many academic programs for three- and four-year-old children have requirements for counting and computation. Children quickly learn to say the number names in order, perhaps because of reinforcement by teachers and certainly because of the joy it gives to parents. For the three- or four-year-old child,

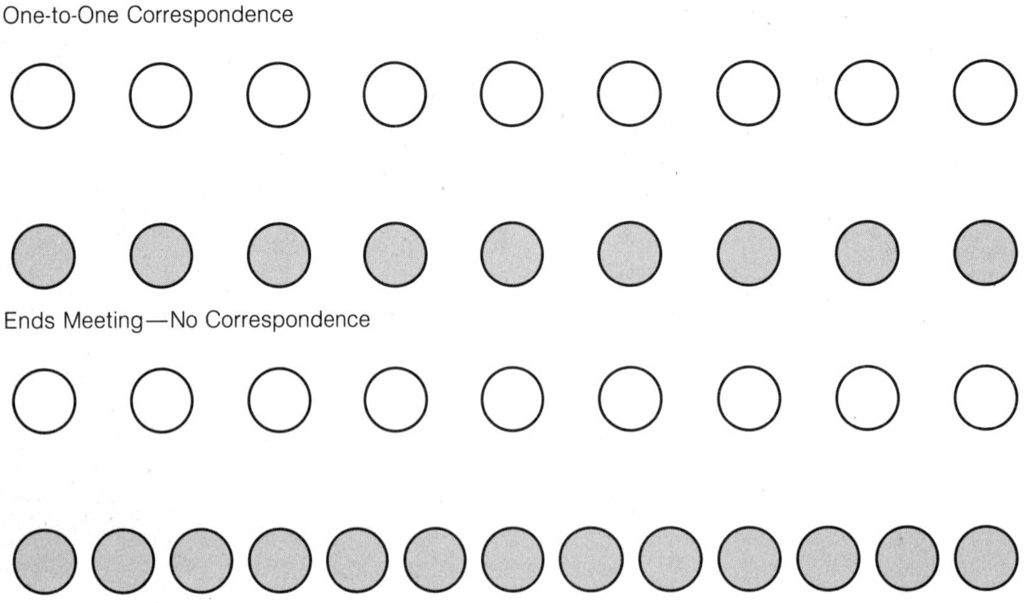

One-to-One Correspondence

Ends Meeting—No Correspondence

DIAGRAM 1.5 One to-One Correspondence

LEARNING ACTIVITY 4

Double-Seriation Interview

Purpose: The purpose of this activity is to investigate a child's ability to develop a double seriation.

Materials: Twenty sticks or heavy-cardboard strips cut so that there are two sets of the following lengths: 10 in., 9 in., 8 in., 7 in., 6 in., 5 in., 4 in., 3 in., 2 in., 1 in.

Procedure:
1. Mix up one set of ten sticks or cardboard strips and show them to the child. Ask the following questions.
    a. Show me the smallest stick.
    b. Show me the largest stick.
    c. Show me a stick just a little bit smaller than the largest stick.
2. Show the second set of ten sticks. Ask the child how the new set of sticks is the same as the first set.
3. Tell the child to watch while you arrange one set of sticks into a staircase from largest to smallest.
4. Ask the child to make a staircase with his or her set of sticks that matches her or his smallest stick to the largest stick in your staircase.

Cautions:
1. Be certain that the objects are carefully cut so that there is no doubt about the differences in size. Diagonal or ragged ends can cause difficulty. Additionally, all strips should be the same color.

2. Be careful not to coach the child with verbal cues or facial expressions. Praise whatever response is given. The purpose of the task is to investigate the child's thought processes, not elicit a particular answer considered to be "right."

Interpreting the Results:

Level One: Level-one children will be unable to construct a seriation with the sticks given to them, whether similar or opposite to the model.

Level Two: Level-two children will construct a seriation similar to the model through constant attention to the model and matching of the sticks into order.

Level Three: Level-three children will begin to construct an opposite seriation to the model but will be unable to complete the seriation. Generally, these children will return to the model and finish the seriation in a manner identical to the model.

Level Four: Level-four children will be able to construct the seriation that is opposite to the model but will probably use a trial-and-error procedure.

Level Five: Level-five children will construct the opposite seriation by selecting the appropriate sticks from the pile and placing them in the proper locations.

LEARNING ACTIVITY 5

One-to-One Correspondence Interview

Purpose: The purpose of this activity is to investigate a child's understanding of one-to-one correspondence.

Materials: 10 paper cups and 15 artificial flowers *or* 1 egg carton (separate the 2 rows so that they may be placed end-to-end, making a row of 12 spaces) and 20 plastic eggs *or* 10 small boxes and 15 small toy animals (the boxes are considered to be cages for the animals)

Procedure:
1. Place the paper cups, egg carton halves, or boxes in a row in front of the child. Give the child the flowers, eggs, or animals.
2. Depending on the materials, say one of the following statements and questions to the child.
    a. Each cup needs to have a flower. Can you make a row of flowers so that each cup will have a flower?

b. Each space in the egg carton needs to have an egg. Can you make a row of eggs so that each space will have an egg?

c. Each cage needs to have an animal. Can you make a row of animals so that each cage will have an animal?

Cautions:

1. Be careful not to give the child too many directions. You need to give only enough information to present the task. If, however, the child has no idea what to do, demonstrate the task with a different set of objects.

2. Be very careful not to make facial expressions and comments. Give praise even if a child simply

makes a row using all of the objects. The task shows how the child thinks and so all answers are correct.

Interpreting the Results:

1. A child who has not yet attained the ability to make a one-to-one correspondence will line up all of the objects or use enough to make the ends meet. It is also possible for the child who has not yet attained one-to-one correspondence to distribute all of the objects among the cups, egg carton halves, or boxes.

2. The child who has attained one-to-one correspondence will match one flower to one cup, one egg to one carton space, or one animal to one cage.

---

however, the recitation of number names is without meaning. Children of this age group do not yet conserve number. For the three or four year old, the arrangement and rearrangement of objects is seen to cause an increase or decrease in the quantity of the objects. Consequently, a string of twenty beads with wide spaces between the beads is seen as having more beads than a string of twenty beads that are closely spaced. The child's perceptions strongly influence the quantity determination that is made.

Five Year Olds. Conservation of number has not generally been attained by the five-year-old child, but there is a change in thinking at this point. The five year old is generally able to make a row of coins or counters similar to that of the adult. One-to-one correspondence is attained. The child is no longer tied to making ends meet, but is, rather, concerned with matching one object to one object.

The five-year-old child, however, is still tied to his or her perceptions. If one row of coins or counters is now extended or pushed together, the child considers there to be more or less coins in one row than in the other (see Diagram 1.6).

Without conservation of number, children can learn mathematics only through rote memorization of answers and strategies. Such learning results in rapid forgetting or frustration as the child grapples with information that has neither meaning nor purpose. The inability to conserve number means that the child of three, four, or five is still not able

to truly understand computation skills in arithmetic. Consequently, the child will memorize answers to problems or develop a finger-counting strategy to get the expected answer without developing a real understanding of the problem.

Egocentricity in Children

Egocentricity in an adult is generally not appreciated by that adult's friends or family. It is a sign of self-centeredness in adults and usually is an irritating quality. The negative connotation of egocentricity in adults should not follow the application of the term to the young child.

Egocentricity in the preschool or kindergarten child is a function of cognitive development and indicates the young child's inability to look at issues or concepts from the viewpoint of another individual. The child sees only what he or she sees and is unable to place himself or herself into the position of another person. For example, a child sitting with a teddy bear on his or her lap so that the toy is "looking" in the same direction as the child can describe what the toy "sees." If the teddy bear is turned to "look" to the left while the child remains looking ahead, the child will continue to describe what he or she sees as being identical to what the teddy bear "sees."

Language Skills in Children

Children at the preschool and kindergarten levels have the ability to speak coherently and with a

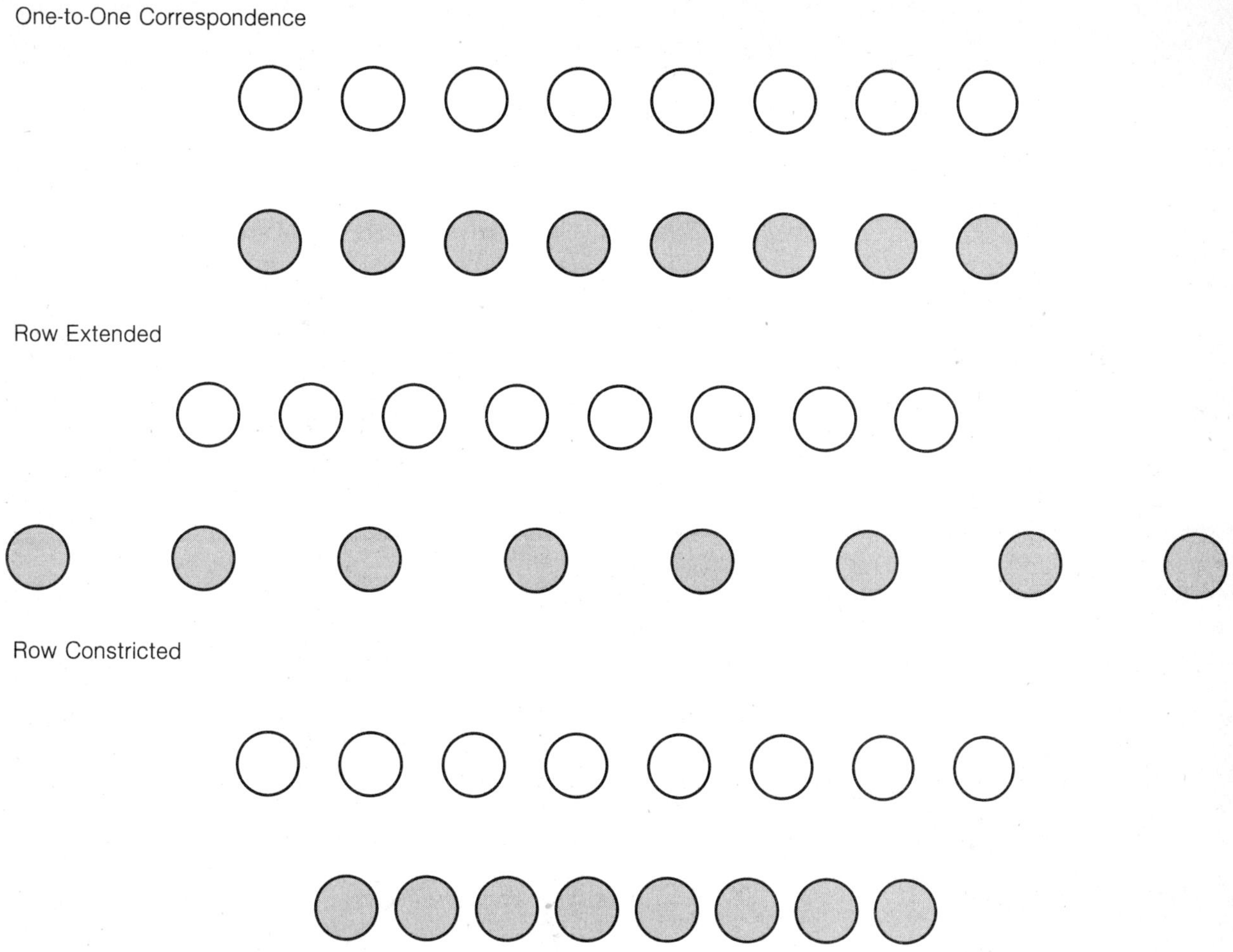

One-to-One Correspondence

Row Extended

Row Constricted

DIAGRAM 1.6 Conservation of Number

considerable, though functional, vocabulary. By the age of three or four, the child's vocabulary has reached about 2,000 words. This vocabulary is extensive enough by the age of four that preschool children are able to understand simple explanations and reasons. The ability to make a word, mental symbol, or object represent something that is not present has developed by this age. Children are now able to use one object to represent another during play. They are able to discuss something that is not currently present.

The language skills of the three, four, or five year olds, however, have a characteristic rarely found in adult speech. Because children of these ages are highly egocentric, they frequently talk to themselves whether alone or with others, and definitely talk about themselves.

In addition to talking about themselves, children of three, four, or five are unable to put themselves into the position of another individual;

the egocentricity of children causes them to believe that everything they know everyone knows. Thus, conversation with a child can be confusing to the listening adult while completely understandable to the child involved. A child may communicate that "he did it with me and her" and have the full expectation that the adult to whom it was communicated will understand the comment completely. If the child has certain knowledge, then the listening adult must have the same knowledge.

If an adult is asked to characterize the speech of young children, one characteristic is invariably mentioned: questions. The young child is a fountain of questions. Most of the questions begin with the infamous "why" so characteristic of young children. To the adult listener, "why" signals the necessity for an explanation of cause and effect. "Why is the sky blue" causes the parent, teacher, caregiver, or other adult to begin searching through the memory for an explanation of lightwaves and

LEARNING ACTIVITY 6

Conservation-of-Number Interview

Purpose: The purpose of this activity is to investigate a child's level of understanding of conservation of number.

Materials: approximately 30 coins, small blocks, or counters all the same size but not necessarily the same color

Procedure:

1. Sit at a table or on the floor with the child facing you. Explain that you are going to make a row of pennies (or whatever object) and ask the child to watch you.
2. Make a row of ten pennies (or whatever object), leaving spaces between the objects.
3. Give the child the remaining pennies (or whatever object) and ask the child to make a row just like your row.
4. Give the child a chance to make the row. Ask ''Are there the same number of pennies in your row as in my row?'' Whether the child answers ''yes'' or ''no,'' ask ''How do you know there are (are not) the same number of pennies?''
5. Tell the child to watch what you do. Stretch out or push together the pennies in one of the rows. Do not add any or take any away. Ask ''Are there still the same number of pennies in my row as in your row? How do you know they are the same (different)?''
6. No matter what response is given, praise the child for having done a good job.

Cautions:

1. Be careful not to lead the child to the answer that he or she ''should'' give. For example, do not say ''The rows are still the same, aren't they?'' after extending or squeezing together a row of coins. Also avoid asking ''Are you sure?'' Many children will immediately reverse their answers just to please you.
2. Use more total objects than are needed to construct the two rows. If the child has exactly ten objects in front of him or her, that child is likely just to use them all. Having more than ten requires the child to select just those needed to make the one-to-one correspondence.

3. If the child is unable to make the one-to-one correspondence needed in constructing the row in step three, stop after that step. There is no need to go further to determine whether the child is a conserver of number or not.
4. It is important to establish that the two rows have an identical number in them in step four. The child who indicates that there are different numbers in each row should be asked to construct rows with the same number. If a one-to-one correspondence is then used, continue with the interview.

Interpreting the Results:

Level One: Level-one children are definitely nonconservers of number. These children are unable to make a one-to-one correspondence between the two rows of objects.

Level Two: Level-two children can make a one-to-one correspondence between the two rows of objects and so are successful in constructing a row like the first row. However, when the row is stretched or squeezed, they believe the number is changed because the ends no longer meet.

Level Three: Level-three children are transitional in their thinking about number. Some children will be able to tell that the quantity of objects remains the same when the row is stretched but not when it is squeezed. In other cases, the child will need to count the objects to be certain the number is still the same.

Level Four: Level-four children are definitely conservers of number. Not only are they able to make the one-to-one correspondence, but they are able to state that the quantity remains the same no matter how the rows are changed. Children in this level tend to use one of three arguments in explaining how they know the rows are the same. Some use the reversibility argument in which they state that the row can be put back the way it was. Others use an identity argument, explaining that no objects were taken away or added so the rows must still be the same. Finally, some use the compensation argument, stating that the spaces between the objects are larger so the line just seems longer.

LEARNING ACTIVITY 7

Observation of Language and Conversation in Children

Purpose: The purpose of this activity is to observe and record conversation taking place between children or between children and adults.

Procedure:

1. Arrange to make at least two 30- to 60-minute observations of children. Make a boy the focal point of one observation and a girl the focal point of another.

2. During at least half of your observation time, record the conversations of the focal child and of other children with which she or he interacts. The conversation may be tape recorded (with permission of the teacher, caregiver, and parent) or recorded in writing. Be as unobtrusive as possible in recording the conversation.

3. During another part of the observation, record the child's verbal interaction with an adult: yourself, a teacher or caregiver, or a parent. Record exactly the words of both the child and the adult.

4. Analyze the results of your observations in terms of the kinds of verbal interactions that the child has with other children or with an adult.

---

refraction. The questioning child, however, is generally not asking for a causal explanation. Rather, the "why" of the young child is generally a request for purpose. "Why is the sky blue" may be better answered by "because it looks pretty that way" or by "what do you think" than by an explanation requiring more than a general understanding of physics.

Reversibility of Thought in Children

Reversibility of thought means that a thought process can begin at point A, move along to point B, and then turn around and return to point A. For example, water is placed into a container and then put into a freezer. The water eventually turns to ice. When the ice is taken out of the freezer, it eventually returns to liquid water. This is a reversible physical change. For the adult, it is easy to conclude that liquid water freezes when it is cold and melts when it is heated. For the young child, it is easy to determine that being in the freezer caused the change in state but it is not so easy to retrace the idea that heat will cause the ice to melt back into water.

Reversibility of thought causes the child to see the two parts of the same change as distinctly separate phenomena rather than two aspects of the same phenomenon. In mathematics, inability to use reversible thought is demonstrated by the inability of the child to comprehend that $3 + 5 = 8$ so

$8 - 5 = 3$. The child tends to see both problems as distinct from one another; therefore, both must be memorized.

Children of three, four, or five years of age have not yet attained the ability to use reversible thought processes.

Centering in Children

Children of three, four, or five years of age exhibit the characteristic of *centration*. Centration is the consideration of a single characteristic to the exclusion of all others. Children may notice the color of an object but not its shape. They may notice the size of an object but not its texture. The tendency to consider only one characteristic at a time can result in interesting conclusions from science activities.

In many textbooks and activity guides, there is an activity in which one geranium is put on a sunny windowsill and another is placed in a closet. Both plants are watered. After a week or longer, the plants are again placed side by side on a table for comparison. The plant that has been in the closet is a sickly yellowish green, has three leaves, no flowers, and is spindly in appearance. It is also twice the height of the plant that has been in the sunshine. Which plant grew better? If children center on height, the one in the closet grew better. If the teacher tries to convince students that the plant in the window grew better because of other factors, he

LEARNING ACTIVITY 8

Class-Inclusion Interview

Purpose: The purpose of this activity is to investigate a child's understanding of class inclusion.

Materials: cardboard cutouts of 3 red flowers, 2 yellow flowers, and 3 yellow butterflies

Procedure:

1. Place the cutouts in a row in front of the child in the following order: yellow flower, red flower, yellow butterfly, red flower, yellow flower, yellow butterfly, red flower, yellow butterfly.
2. Ask the child to identify the colors and the objects shown. Ask "What color is this?" and "What is this?" Point to the various objects while asking the questions.
3. Ask "Are all of the butterflies yellow?"
4. Ask "Are all of the yellow ones butterflies? Why?" or "Why not?"

Cautions:

1. Be certain in step 2 to establish the colors and names of the objects. If a child identifies one of the objects as something different, a bird rather than a butterfly or a daisy rather than a flower, use the term given by the child during the questions.

2. The question in step 4 is far more difficult than the question in step 3, so give the child time to think.

Interpreting The Results:

Level One: Level-one children are unable to answer the question in step 4 correctly because they are unable to separate the butterflies as a subset of the total set of objects. The word *all* simply means everything in the total set.

Level Two: Level-two children can separate the butterflies and the yellows from the reds but cannot logically include those objects in the total set. These children interpret the question "Are all butterflies yellow" to mean "Are the butterflies *all* of the yellows?" They are likely to give the answer "No, because there are yellow flowers."

Level Three: Level-three children can answer the question in step 4 correctly and can give a logical reason for the answer. A typical response at this level would be that only some of the yellow objects are butterflies but that all of the yellow objects include both yellow butterflies and yellow flowers.

---

or she may fail miserably. At best, the children will parrot back the teacher's conclusion. However, it is unlikely that they will truly believe that conclusion or understand why the teacher thinks the plant from the windowsill grew better.

Use of Concrete Objects in Children

Children at the preschool and kindergarten levels are strongly tied to the use of concrete materials when thinking or developing concepts. Concrete objects are generally considered to be three-dimensional objects that are the actual object or a model of the object: blocks, dolls, toy cars, magnets, beads, sand and sand toys, water and water toys, and so on. Concrete objects do not include textbooks, workbooks, worksheets, color sheets, or other pencil-and-paper materials. Children develop

many concepts informally through their play activities. It is through the manipulation of blocks that children begin to develop concepts of balance and structure. It is by putting objects in water that they discover not only what will sink and what will float, but also the characteristics of water. The manipulation of environmental objects allows children to develop concepts about the world, test those concepts, and make modifications of those concepts to bring them more in line with the true state of the world. Because of the necessity for concrete materials in the construction of concepts, verbal explanations and written materials are not effective in helping children develop an understanding of their world. Work and play that involve direct manipulation of materials and direct investigation are effective.

Class Inclusion in Children

Class inclusion is the ability to understand that the set of all objects will be larger than any of its subsets. This includes concepts of some and all. For example, a child is confronted with pictures of animals. Included in the set of pictures are five pictures of birds such as robins, sparrows, and starlings. Also included are ten pictures of ducks. It is obvious to the adult that all of the pictures are pictures of birds. And, before the question is asked, the child is helped to identify all of the pictures as birds. The question posed to the child is "Are there more birds or are there more ducks?" A child who has yet to attain a firm understanding of class inclusion will answer that there are more ducks. The subset, ducks, is larger than the set, birds. The terms *all* and *some,* which are difficult for preschool and kindergarten children to comprehend, are crucial for the development of logical thinking skills.

Topological Space in Children

The first concepts of geometry in preschool and kindergarten children are topological rather than Euclidian. In topological geometry, shape is not a rigid thing and the shapes the child sees are related to one another through change. In some cases, topological geometry is known as rubber sheet geometry because it shows shapes as changing and changeable. Figures such as squares, circles, and triangles are equivalent topologically because they can be squeezed or stretched and so transformed into one another. This is the child's view of space and shapes. The topological relations that are developing at this time are those of proximity, separation, enclosure, and order. Proximity refers to the nearness of an object so that in drawing a picture of a face, the eyes are placed near the nose. Separation refers to the distance between objects so that the child begins to separate objects from one another. Separation shows up in drawings of a face as increasing separation of the eyes, nose, and mouth. Order deals with the development of a pattern in which the objects appear in certain relation to one another. The stringing of beads in a particular pattern (red, yellow, blue, red, yellow, blue) is an example of order. The five year old can order only by constant attention to the model. Finally, enclo-

sure is the concept of surrounding an object. The terms *in, between,* and *inside* are parts of the concept of enclosure. The eyes and nose are inside the circle that forms the head; the nose is between the eyes.

SUMMARY

To say that the three-, four-, or five-year-old child thinks differently from the adult is to understate the situation. But, even with this difference in thinking skills, children of three, four, or five are capable of learning a great deal, particularly when that learning is through direct experiences. The teacher who is planning for a program appropriate to preschool children needs to take into account the child's thinking skills and perception skills. Children of three, four, and five reason transductively and syncratically. They need to be given individual and group experiences with a variety of objects and situations that will allow them to explore number, seriation, one-to-one correspondence, and cause and effect in ways that enable them to be successful. In particular, it is important that children interact with those who are older or younger than themselves so that differences in thinking ability provide a catalyst to investigation and to the development of language skills.

Vocabulary Terms

Animism: an explanation of precausality that attributes life and consciousness to all things.
Artificialism: a form of causality that explains events or objects as being the result of human creative activity or as being necessary to human activity.
Cause and Effect: the ability to sequence events so that the result of interactions between events is attributed to a previously occurring event.
Centration: the consideration of a single characteristic to the exclusion of all others.
Classification: the ability to put objects into groups on the basis of one or more common characteristics.
Class Inclusion: the ability to understand that the set of all objects will be larger than any of its

subsets; the ability to determine that some of a set is contained within all of that set.

Concrete Object: any three-dimensional object within the environment.

Conservation of Number: the ability to recognize that the quantity of a set of objects does not change simply because the arrangement of the objects changes.

Double Seriation: the ability to seriate two sets of objects simultaneously so that the object in set A having the least degree of a trait is matched to the object in set B having the greatest degree of the trait.

Dynamism: a type of precausal explanation in which force is confused with life.

Egocentricity: the young child's tendency to look at issues or concepts from his or her own point of view and the child's inability to look at issues and concepts from the point of view of another.

Exhaustive Sorting: the ability to sort all of the objects in a set into categories during a classification activity.

Finalism: a form of precausality in which events are believed simply to happen without a cause.

Heteronomy: control that originates from outside of the child.

Hierarchical Classification: classification using classes and subclasses and requiring the ability to use class inclusion as a part of the classification system.

Moral Causality: a form of precausality that uses the explanation of necessity to explain movement or a feature of an object.

Motivation: a form of precausality in which the child attributes cause and effect to a divine plan.

One-to-One Correspondence: the ability to match one object from set A to one object from set B.

Ordering: the ability to copy a pattern formed by objects.

Participation: a form of precausality in which two things are related because of resemblance or general affinity and are considered to have something in common that enables them to act on each other.

Phenomenism: a form of causality that relates events because they are perceived as being together even though no relation exists between them except time and space.

Precausal Reasoning: a type of reasoning that develops prior to an understanding of cause and effect

and that may not attribute a particular cause to its effect.

Preoperational: a developmental stage in which thought is characterized by egocentricity, precausal forms of reasoning, centration, transductive and syncratic reasoning, as well as by lack of reversibility of thought and lack of conservation skills.

Resemblance Sorting: a method of classification in which the characteristic used for grouping is changed after only two objects of the total set are classified together.

Reversibility: the idea that a thought process can begin at point A, move to point B, and then return to point A.

Seriation: the ability to place objects into order on the basis of an ascending or descending value of a trait.

Syncretic Reasoning: a form of reasoning in which a series of separate ideas is connected into a single confused whole.

Topological Space: a form of geometry in which shape is seen as constantly changing.

Transductive Reasoning: (1) a form of reasoning in which relationships that do not necessarily exist are identified between two or more objects or (2) a form of reasoning from specific to specific without drawing a conclusion.

Why of Purpose: a why question that asks for the purpose of a phenomenon rather than the cause.

Study Questions

1. What are the cognitive characteristics of three- and four-year-old children?
2. How do the cognitive characteristics of three- and four-year-old children differ from those of five-year-old children?
3. A child of four is playing with pattern blocks. The teacher determines that the child is beginning to notice the different colors and shapes of the blocks. In order to help the child discover that there are six different colors and six different shapes, she suggests that the child classify them by color and sets up categories for the child to use. As soon as the teacher walks away, the child goes back to her original play. Why did this child return to play rather than continuing to classify as the teacher wanted?

4. Many adults remember walking carefully to school to avoid stepping on the cracks in a sidewalk. The reason for the avoidance was the saying "Step on a crack, break your mother's back." What kind of reasoning is evident in this saying? Explain your answer.

5. A little girl is helping the teacher to set out plates, napkins, and cups for a birthday party. When the girl is finished, some places have more than one cup, plate, and napkin while others have only one of each and still others have no plates at all. She did, however, distribute all of the objects. Another child comes by, looks at the table and redistributes the items so everyone has one of each. What cognitive ability is demonstrated by the second child? On the basis of the actions of each child, how old do you think they were?

6. A preschool child asks the question "Why is grass green?" What would be an appropriate response to this question?

7. Give an example of the use of each of the following types of precausality: motivation, finalism, phenomenism, participation, moral, motivation, animism, and dynamism.

8. How would a lack of conservation of number affect a child's ability to learn basic addition facts?

9. One child has made a bead necklace for herself that includes four different colors of beads. Her friend wants to make one for himself that looks the same. However, he finds it very difficult to make a necklace the same as his friend's and decides instead to design his own. Why would duplicating such a design be a difficult task for a child?

CHAPTER 2

Social Characteristics of Three to Five Year Olds

Chapter Objectives

On completion of this chapter, you should be able to

1. list the social characteristics of three- and four-year-old children,

2. describe the social characteristics of three- and four-year-old children,

3. list the social characteristics of five-year-old children,

4. describe the social characteristics of five-year-old children,

5. compare the social characteristics of three- and four-year-old children to the social characteristics of five-year-old children,

6. conduct an observation of a three-, four-, or five-year-old child in order to describe the social characteristics of that child,

7. describe the two categories of at-risk children at the preschool level,

8. make suggestions for working effectively with at-risk children at the preschool level, and

9. compare the social characteristics of an at-risk child of three, four, or five years of age to the child who is not considered at risk.

Look into a preschool setting that attends to the needs of three-, four-, and five-year-old children and you see many different kinds of activities and investigations. One group of children is finger painting while another is making snakes and cookies from play dough. Across the room, children are watching hamsters run around in a cage while other children are making necklaces from beads. Some children are constructing towers and houses with blocks. In the water play area, children are putting a variety of objects into the water and watching how the water drips from some, sprinkles from others, and pours from still others. Outside, children are running, climbing, swinging, and riding. The children appear to be in constant motion. Even in the book corner, children swing their legs and turn the pages of books with large movements. Some children are alone, some are in pairs, and some are in larger groups. All these children are exhibiting the kinds of social characteristics that a preschool teacher should take into account in selecting topics and preparing activities.

SOCIAL CHARACTERISTICS OF THREE AND FOUR YEAR OLDS

Planning and Finishing

Children of three and four enjoy planning activities. They will help the teacher plan how to work with finger paints or set up the sand-and-water area. They will be enthusiastic about helping to plan a field trip. In this characteristic, the very young child is similar to the adult. Children of three and four enjoy planning activities whether with their peers, parents, teachers, or alone. The difference occurs between the young child and the adult in finishing an activity. Children enjoy planning. Children do not enjoy or even see a need for finishing an activity. Young children accomplish as much of an activity as they are ready to complete, then move on to another activity. The young child has no imperative to come to closure in activities. There is joy in planning. There is joy in doing. Finishing, at least the adult concept of finishing, is not a major factor in the life of a young child.

Investigative Behavior

To describe the three to four year old as curious is to make a serious understatement of fact. Three and four year olds are interested in everything and anything. It is easy to capture a child's attention and to get the child involved in an activity. The child is interested not only in what is happening, but also in investigating to find out what will happen. Investigating the environment is an automatic act provided the environment is one in which investigation is encouraged.

Two groups of preschool children were introduced by a guest in the classroom to a variety of small items, basins, water, and flour. In the first of the two groups, the children watched solemnly while the guest put the water and the flour into basins. They sat quietly waiting for the guest to distribute materials. They were asked what they thought would happen if a marble was dropped into the basin with the water. After they guessed that it would splash, the guest dropped a marble from shoulder height into the basin. When the water splashed everywhere, the children turned to look at the regular teacher with wide, horrified expressions and the teacher immediately ran over to clean up the mess. These children eventually did get involved in placing the items into both materials and into a variety of other self-determined investigations, but their activity was inhibited by the teacher's insistence on continually cleaning up to maintain neatness. Children often whispered to one another that they "better not" do something because it would be messy.

In contrast, the children in the second group not only helped fill the basins and give out the materials but had already begun making splashes before a word could be said to officially begin the activity. Their investigations were spontaneous, individualized, messy, and fascinating. They investigated height, angle, and force of drop in objects. They investigated the differences between dropping in water and dropping in flour. They mixed flour and water to find out how drops of paste worked. They rolled marbles and other objects from tables, chairs, and their arms, legs, and noses to find out what would happen. Their regular teacher joined in the investigations with activities of her own, demonstrating her own curiosity and willingness to be messy. Consequently, the investigative behaviors

LEARNING ACTIVITY 9

Observing Classroom Structure

Purpose: The purpose of this activity is to observe the general structure of the early-childhood setting and develop a description of the general environment.

Procedure:

1. Get a general impression of the classroom or daycare setting by taking some time to simply look around.
2. Describe the general layout of the setting, including furnishings, organizational pattern, centers, and large- and small-group areas.
3. Describe the kinds of materials that are found in the setting: puzzles, blocks, trucks, dolls, dress-up clothes, animals, plants, and so on.
4. Describe the kind of schedule that is followed during the day. Is the schedule teacher-structured, student-structured, or a combination of both? What evidence do you have for your conclusion?
5. Consider the entire room. Are there locations in the room from which the teacher or caregiver can see all of the area at the same time? Where are these locations?
6. What areas in the classroom or educational setting allow for large-group interaction? What areas allow for small-group interaction? What areas allow children some privacy?
7. What areas in the classroom or setting could be considered "cozy" areas? Explain why you describe these areas as cozy.
8. What areas in the classroom or setting are designed for multiple uses? What areas are designed for single uses?
9. Is the classroom or setting cluttered and overstimulating or uncluttered and understimulating?
10. Are there areas in which student work is displayed? What kinds of work are displayed?
11. What is the general traffic pattern in the classroom or setting? Is the pattern conducive to the activities and centers in the classroom?
12. What other observations can you make about the classroom or setting?

Cautions:

1. Always make a clear distinction between what you are actually seeing and the conclusions you are drawing. "There are nine tables" is an observation. "The tables are not arranged in the best possible order" is a conclusion.
2. Try to draw conclusions that are based on actual observation. Do not rely on hunches or on your beliefs about what should happen in a classroom.
3. Have a clear understanding of what you are trying to accomplish in the observation.
4. Be certain the classroom teacher or caregiver knows what your purpose is for observing.
5. Place yourself in as unobtrusive a location as possible.
6. Take down exact words and behaviors when possible.
7. Treat all observations with total confidentiality.
8. Be as objective as possible. Do not allow your feelings, beliefs, or preferences to cause you to make inaccurate observations.

---

of the children were extensive, contagious, enthusiastic, and uninhibited.

Children are natural investigators, but the social climate of the classroom must be such that investigation is encouraged. A teacher who models investigative behaviors encourages active involvement. A teacher overly concerned about classroom neatness inhibits such involvement.

Large- and Small-Muscle Activities

The preschool setting with three- and four-year-old children should be an active place where children freely move about and have the opportunity to use large-muscle skills more frequently than small-muscle skills. The three- and four-year-old child is better able to cope with large-muscle activities such as throwing, climbing, and running than he or she is with small-muscle activities required for pencil-and-paper activities. For three year olds, jumping is difficult. In addition, three year olds often experience periods where coordination seems to disappear and they become awkward. Four year olds, on the other hand, are strong, efficient, and speedy in their movements. Four year olds seem never to stop moving.

Large-muscle skills are often referred to as locomotor skills. These skills, such as walking, jumping, hopping, skipping, and galloping, do not, however, represent the whole picture in terms of body skills of children. Locomotor skills help the child to develop an awareness of his or her body in space. Such awareness is termed *perceptual-motor awareness* and considers body awareness and perceptual motor skills. The type of skills considered here are awareness of one's own body, time, spatial relations, and directional concepts, as well as visual and auditory awareness. For the child of three or four, such awareness is most easily seen as children attempt to mimic the actions of other children or the teacher. Children of three or four have difficulty following the movements of others.

The child's skill in the use of large-muscle skills can have ramifications for the child's social growth. Children who have good large-muscle skills are more likely to be chosen for games by other children. Consequently, children with poor motor skills may not be included in games and so self-esteem may suffer.

In the areas of science and mathematics, the use of large-muscle activities is far more appropriate than the use of small-muscle activities. In fact, activities that allow children to use throwing, hopping, pushing, or running will generally be more successful than those that require the child to cut, paste, or manipulate small objects.

Kinds of Play

Three-year-old children will often sit together as they carry out activities such as painting or bead stringing. They sit next to one another and frequently talk together as they work. At first, it appears that the children are playing together and talking with one another. With closer observation, however, it becomes evident that three year olds are not really playing together. Instead, they are playing side by side in what is known as parallel play. Three-year-old children are more likely to play simultaneously than to play cooperatively.

Among three year olds, statements of one child may not be related to the statements of another child. A question may be answered by an unrelated answer or by another question. This type of conversation is known as a *collective monologue*. A typical "conversation" may consist of an exchange between children along the lines of the following:

Tommy: "My dog had puppies."

Mary: "I have new shoes."

Tommy: "Do you have a puppy?"

Mary: "This floats and this sinks. See?"

By four years of age, children are beginning to play cooperatively so that they share materials and contribute to one another's projects. Conversation frequently takes the form of a collective monologue, but that too is beginning to show signs of more communicative speech. Four-year-old children who have had little experience with other children are likely to show parallel play and collective monologue and so will exhibit social behaviors more like those of three-year-old children.

Play activities among three- and four-year-old children are helpful in developing social competence among those children. Early experience in play groups helps children become more socially adept. At the preschool level, the ability to interact socially with other children allows for the development of cooperation and competition in an appropriate setting. Such activities also allow children to develop an ability to persuade others to assist or to play in a group situation. The greater the amount of contact that three or four year olds have with other children, the more likely they are to become socially able, learn to give and take, and avoid the use of aggression and bullying as a means to an end.

Concrete Materials

Young children enjoy talking to adults and being included in conversations with adults. They enjoy talking about themselves and about anything else that happens to come to mind. This talkativeness gives the impression that young children understand a great deal of what they hear and so learn a great deal from verbal information. Any parent,

LEARNING ACTIVITY 10

Observing Social Behavior in Children

Purpose: The purpose of this activity is to observe the social behavior of a child in a group situation and in a one-to-one situation with another child.

Procedure:
1. Select one child within the classroom or setting. Observe that child for 30 to 60 minutes on at least three separate occasions.
2. Consider the following as you make your observations:
   - Does the child play alone, with objects, or without objects?
   - Does the child play alone in pretending-type activities?
   - Does the child play parallel to others, with or without objects?
   - Does the child play parallel to others, in pretending-type activities?
   - Does the child play parallel to others, constructing or creating something?
   - Does the child play with a group, with or without objects?
   - Does the child play with a group in pretending-type activities?
   - Does the child play with a group, constructing or creating something?
   - Does the child play in a give-and-take manner with others?
   - Does the child give something of his or her own to another child? Does he or she share with others?
   - Does the child take turns with toys or activities?
   - Does the child wait for his or her turn without a fuss?
   - Does the child spend more time alone than with other children?
   - Does the child engage in inappropriate verbal or physical behaviors with other children?
   - Does the child show interest in classroom activities and in other children?
   - Does the child spend more time in some activities than in others?
   - Does the child spend more time with some children than with others?
   - Does the child exhibit impulsivity in behavior with other children?
3. Remember that even though these questions can all be answered with a yes or no, it is necessary to support responses with observations. What, when, how often, or how long should be a part of the observations and descriptions of the child and his or her interactions.

Cautions:
1. If the child who is being observed begins to realize he or she is under observation and becomes uncomfortable or distressed, STOP IMMEDIATELY!
2. Always make a clear distinction between what you are actually seeing and the conclusions you are drawing. "The child constructed a block house with two other boys" is an observation. "The boys cooperated and enjoyed their construction" is a conclusion.
3. Draw conclusions that are based on actual observation.
4. Have a clear understanding of what you are trying to accomplish in the observation.
5. Be certain the classroom teacher or caregiver knows what your purpose is for observing.
6. Place yourself in as unobtrusive a location as possible.
7. Take down exact words and behaviors when possible.
8. Treat all observations with total confidentiality.
9. Be as objective as possible. Do not allow your feelings, prejudices, or preferences to cause you to make inaccurate observations.

---

however, knows that a young child can be told the same bit of information a dozen times without effect. The young child does not necessarily comprehend the conversation or the comments he or she hears.

Because young children enjoy conversation, it appears that teaching strategies can rely on the use of verbal communication with young children. The use of verbal lessons with children, however, is generally ineffective. Both the developmental stage and the lack of competence in the use of language require that young children use concrete materials for effective learning.

This is not to say, however, that words and the development of literacy skills should not occur with young children. The development of literacy begins with the child in the preschool program and before. If words are to be used with children, then certain guidelines should be followed. First, the use of correct terminology should be meaningful to the children involved. In general, this means that the terms are used after the child has had a chance to develop an understanding of the concept that is named by the term. Meaningful learning of new vocabulary means that the terms are embedded within the total learning experience. For example, children may notice that objects roll more easily on some surfaces than they do on others. A discussion can bring out the idea that the places where objects do not roll well are bumpy when they are touched while those that allow objects to roll easily are not bumpy. Children may also notice that objects are easy to roll down a hill but not so easy to roll up a hill. Once children have seen these things for themselves and have described the conditions to adults, then the teacher can begin to use terms like "smooth," "rough," and "incline." If terms are used as a result of an activity using concrete materials, then it is far more likely that the children will understand the new words and use them appropriately.

Whether developing concepts or vocabulary terms, the use of concrete materials is a necessity for the child at the preoperational stage of development.

SUMMARY

The social characteristics of three- and four-year-old children, like the cognitive characteristics, indicate that these young children are different from older children in the early childhood program. They plan and they act, but the planning may come to be the activity and the activity may not come to closure. In working with other children, three and four year olds appear to be cooperating more effectively than they are in actuality. Parallel play and collective monologue are common characteristics. Activity is vital to the young child. It is

through activity that the child improves large- and small-muscle skills, engages in investigative behavior, and constructs concepts from experiences with the environment.

SOCIAL CHARACTERISTICS OF FIVE YEAR OLDS

Language Ability

Children of five are beginning to use language to communicate more effectively with one another. Collective monologue is no longer common in child conversation. Children now talk in order to communicate their ideas to their peers. A major difference between the conversation of five-year-old children and adults, however, does exist. Children of five make statements. They do not yet see the need to support their decisions or defend their ideas. It is enough for a five-year-old child to tell another that one plant grew better than another. There is no need in the child's mind to go beyond that statement to tell what caused him or her to conclude that one plant grew better than another.

Routine and Flexibility

Children at the kindergarten level need both the security of a routine and the flexibility to make decisions within that routine. The kindergarten routine may begin with free play, move to work within centers, go to outdoor play and snack time, continue into a nap, move on to more centers work, and end with a large-group experience. This sort of routine provides the young child with a certain sense of security. She or he knows what will happen during a day and can feel in control of the situation. Within the routine, however, choices can be included to help the student develop a sense of autonomy and a growth in a sense of control over the environment. A science/mathematics center may provide two or three choices of activities with the possibility of a variety of experiences within each activity. Investigating balls can provide experiences in rolling, bouncing, tossing, targets, and a wide variety of other experiences that the child chooses.

The problem with a routine is that it can become so inflexible that the teacher no longer sees the possibility for "teachable moments," those unexpected occurrences that allow for incidental teaching and learning. The cement truck pouring a new sidewalk provides the child with an opportunity to see how a sidewalk is made, what cement is like when it comes from the truck, how long it takes to harden, differences in consistency, and a myriad of other experiences. Children welcome some changes in routine but not so many that the school experience becomes chaotic and, perhaps, frightening.

Cooperation and Social Competence

Three and four year olds may sit together during activities, but their work and play is parallel rather than cooperative. A major distinction between the three or four year old and the five year old is in their relationships with one another. Five-year-old children cooperate in play and work. Watch a group of five-year-old children playing with blocks and it is likely that you will watch a group effort to construct a "house" rather than single children constructing various "houses" near one another. Five year olds, perhaps because of their increasing language skills, enjoy cooperative play but they should also have the opportunity to choose to work alone whenever they wish to do so.

Another aspect of cooperation among young children is the concept of social competence. Social competence is the degree to which the child is able to adapt to the school environment and to interact with other children in an effective manner. The five-year-old child needs to be given a great deal of opportunity to interact with other five-year-old children. During such interactions, children have the opportunity to play a variety of roles that they may not be able to play as they interact with adults. For example, five-year-old children rarely have the opportunity to be the leader when they are interacting with adults or older children. As a part of interactions with other children, five year olds have the opportunity to contribute ideas and to respond to the ideas and suggestions of others. As they respond to ideas and suggestions, five year olds also begin to encounter such issues as power, compliance, and cooperation.

All five year olds are not going to exhibit the same level of social competence. Some children will be well liked while others will be disliked by members of the group. Children who are well liked by their peers are generally those who are cooperative and who help other children. These socially competent children are able to recognize and respond to the emotions of other children. Socially competent, liked children know the names of the other children in their class, touch others, and establish eye contact when interacting. Children who are disliked by their peers, and who are less socially competent, are likely to be ignored when they attempt to enter a small group of children or when they attempt to join into a play group. These children often have not developed the skills needed to cooperate and so turn to conflict or aggression when they do not get their own ways. Children who are less socially competent often are heard making self-centered or self-aggrandizing comments that call attention to themselves rather than joining a group as an equal participant. Finally, these children often have difficulty in responding to the emotional needs of other children.

Poor relationships with peers at the early childhood level are correlated with difficulties at other educational levels. Children with poor social competence often develop less favorable perceptions of school, have higher levels of school avoidance, and have lower levels of school performance. Consequently, children who have difficulty being accepted by others in the classroom need to receive assistance in developing more positive social skills. One way of helping these children is to model the kinds of behaviors that are desirable. A second way is to develop a classroom atmosphere that is conducive to the development of good interpersonal relationships. A classroom in which students structure some of the daily activities, in which activities allow for child variation, and in which the teacher encourages autonomy and peer interaction fosters the development of more positive social behaviors.

Attention and Activity

Children of five are generally able to concentrate on an activity for 15 to 20 minutes or longer. The length of time for concentration depends to a large extent on the activity in which the child is engaged. Activities that are too easy or too difficult result in less attention, while those that are interesting and self-chosen often result in longer periods of concen-

LEARNING ACTIVITY 11

Observing Interactions During Play

Purpose: The purpose of this activity is to observe the kinds of interactions that occur as children play with one another.

Procedure:
1. Select one child of three, one child of four, and one child of five to observe in the classroom or setting and on the playground or other play area. Observe the child for at least 30 minutes on at least three separate occasions.
2. Consider the following questions as you make your observations.
   a. What opportunities for cooperation with other children arose during the observation period?
   b. How many children were involved in the cooperative play?
   c. What toys or other items were used during the cooperative play?
   d. What conflicts arose during play? What were the causes of these conflicts?
   e. How did the children settle conflicts over play or rules?
   f. How did the children settle conflicts over the use of space within the play area?
   g. How did the child handle verbal or physical aggression?
   h. Did the child experience rejection? How was it handled by the child?
   i. Did different children in the group react to the observed child in different ways? How?
   j. How did the child under observation react to different children in the group?
   k. How did the social behavior of the three year old compare to that of the older children?

Cautions:
1. If the child who is being observed begins to realize he or she is under observation and becomes uncomfortable or distressed, STOP IMMEDIATELY!
2. Always make a clear distinction between what you are actually seeing and the conclusions you are drawing. "The child constructed a block house with two other boys" is an observation. "The boys cooperated and enjoyed their construction" is a conclusion.
3. Draw conclusions that are based on actual observations.
4. Have a clear understanding of what you are trying to accomplish in the observation.
5. Be certain the classroom teacher or caregiver knows what your purpose is for observing.
6. Place yourself in as unobtrusive a location as possible.
7. Take down exact words and behaviors when possible.
8. Treat all observations with total confidentiality.
9. Be as objective as possible. Do not allow your feelings, prejudices, or preferences to cause you to make inaccurate observations.

---

tration. Children constructing block structures or engaged in water play will frequently work for long periods of time.

Children of five also develop the ability to leave a particular activity and later return to it. It is important to be certain that children have finished completely with what they are doing before suggesting a clean-up. Although the blocks, beads, or clay may seem to have been abandoned, the activity may be continued in the afternoon or, perhaps, the next day.

Muscle Coordination

Children of five are showing increasing small- and large-muscle coordination. Walking a balance beam is possible for a five year old but not for a three year old. In the area of large-muscle activities, speed and control are increasing and coordination is such that children of five rarely fall when running, even on uneven surfaces. Small-muscle coordination is also improving. At five, children can be expected to fold a paper on a corner-to-corner diagonal; to copy a square, triangle, or design; and to draw easily recognized letters and numerals. Children of five also enjoy rhythms, songs, and dramatic play. The fact that children of five can produce recognizable numerals and letters should not be taken as evidence that they are ready to begin written activities. The symbols produced by the child are laboriously drawn by small muscles not yet developed enough to allow smooth, easy writing.

CHILDREN AT RISK

Definition

Children at risk are those who come from impoverished backgrounds or who experience handicapping conditions that may not allow them to progress at the rate of their nonhandicapped peers. In the case of children from impoverished backgrounds, five-year-old children may have the same social characteristics as three- or four-year-old children. They often lack the experiences necessary for social development. Children with handicapping conditions, particularly those conditions that restrict the child's movement or language development, may also show the characteristics of younger children. Such children should not be stigmatized with labels of failure but should be given the opportunity for the kinds of interactions with other children necessary to develop the social skills commensurate with their chronological age. For children at risk, multiage groupings often provide the most appropriate setting for the development of social skills.

Working with Children at Risk

In working with children who are at risk because of handicapping conditions or impoverished backgrounds, certain suggestions are helpful.

1. Encourage all children in the classroom to work together. Children learn a great deal from one another, especially in the area of social skills, and so the at-risk child will gain from such interaction.

2. Accept varying levels of performance from children. Some children will be able to work easily with others while some will not yet be ready for true cooperation. Some children will investigate rolling and sliding objects for most of the morning while others will be satisfied after only a few minutes.

3. Model the kinds of behaviors you want children to show toward their peers. Model patience, sharing, helping, and other behaviors that will allow the at-risk child to interact successfully and be successful.

4. Apply the same rules to all children. Expect the child from an impoverished background to adhere to the same rules as one from an affluent background, the handicapped child to follow the same rules as the nonhandicapped child.

5. Be certain that at-risk children participate in activities even if it means partial participation or a modified version of the activity.

6. Select materials for activities that are multisensory so that children who are impaired in one or more senses will be able to use the materials effectively with a different form of sensory input. Also, select materials that encourage cooperative play so that children can interact with one another easily.

7. Always be certain to allow the child to do things for himself or herself. Children need to feel that they are competent and can accomplish a great deal on their own. Allowing the child to do for herself or himself may take longer but it is valuable to the child.

8. Always maintain a sense of humor. It can be frustrating to work with some children who are at risk and so a sense of humor is a necessity.

Although there is a tendency to consider at-risk children to be those who have handicapping conditions or backgrounds, a second category of children can also be considered at risk. These are the children at the preschool level who are classified as gifted. At the preschool level, children are developing the attitudes that will influence their later learning and so gifted preschoolers need to be encouraged. The gifted child at the preschool level is generally inquisitive and has a relatively long attention span. They generally are independent in their problem-solving skills and will often discover new problems on their own that they will then solve. Children who are gifted may demonstrate advanced ability and interest in a single area to the point that they may become uninterested in other areas. These children have the ability to remember a large amount of information and to see relationships that other children at the preoperational level may not see. Also, gifted children tend to have an advanced vocabulary, use language more easily and more competently than the average child, show great skill in ordering and classifying objects, take apart and reassemble objects, and carry out complex instructions.

The preschool gifted child is at risk not because of difficulty in learning but because he or she learns too easily. There is a tendency to treat the gifted child as if he or she can be instructed in ways more appropriate to older children: written materials and worksheets rather than concrete experiences. The preschool child who is gifted is still a child of three, four, or five years of age and needs to have a variety of concrete experiences just as do children who are not gifted. The accommodation that is needed for the preschool gifted child is an allowance for more intensive investigation using greater problem-solving skills and, perhaps, more complex materials. But, the rapidity with which a gifted child learns may not be the only reason he or she can be considered at risk. Gifted children may be advanced cognitively and emotionally, but may not be advanced or even competent socially. Gifted children need to interact with peers in order to develop the social competence that will allow them to interact effectively with other children through games, use of materials, and in problem-solving situations.

SUMMARY

Five-year-old children are both similar to and different from their three- and four-year-old peers. They are progressing in their ability to use language for communication both with adults and with other children. Language has not yet begun to serve the function of argument and debate that is characteristic of adult language, but it is used to pass information from person to person. Large and small muscles are developing and consequently there are new possibilities for movement and activity. Children of five are also growing in autonomy, but still appreciate a routine. The routine, however, should include both structure and flexibility. The flexibility allows for both the teachable moment and choice on the part of the child.

At-risk children include both those who may have difficulty learning due to impoverished backgrounds or handicapping conditions and those who are gifted, or quick to learn. Both categories of at-risk children need to be encouraged to interact with other children, investigate using hands-on materials, and develop concepts for themselves.

Vocabulary Terms

Children at Risk: children coming from impoverished backgrounds or who experience handicapping conditions that may not allow them to progress at the rate of their nonhandicapped peers. Also includes gifted children who may not have their special learning needs addressed.

Collective Monologue: conversation in which the statements of one child may not be related to the statements of the other child.

Cooperative Play: play in which children interact with one another.

Gifted Child: a child who is capable of progressing more rapidly in academic or nonacademic areas than average children.

Investigative Behavior: any behavior on the part of a child that allows for interacting with the environment and that results in the construction of knowledge.

Large-Muscle Activity: any activity that involves the use of large body muscles: throwing, climbing, running, and so on.

Literacy Skill: skills that help to develop general literacy, particularly word meanings, language, and writing.

Locomotor Skill: a large-muscle skill that helps children develop an awareness of their bodies in space.

Parallel Play: a situation in which children appear to play cooperatively but are actually playing side by side without interaction.

Perceptual-Motor Activity: activity that develops

the child's awareness of his or her own body, time, spatial relations, or directional concepts.

Small-Muscle Activity: activity, such as writing, cutting, and coloring, that requires the use of small muscles such as those of the hands.

Social Competence: the ability in children to relate effectively to one another, including such skills as cooperation, responding to others, and easily joining others in small groups.

Study Questions

1. Compare and contrast the ability to plan and carry out an activity of a child of three and a child of five.
2. Which would be a more appropriate activity for children of four: constructing a tower using blocks or constructing a model house using popsicle sticks? Why is the one you chose the more appropriate activity?
3. Compare the play activities of three and four year olds to those of five year olds.
4. How do the language abilities of preschool children differ from those of kindergarten-age children?
5. Some of the parents of the children in our kindergarten class are concerned because their children are not bringing home "papers" that they have done in school. As a teacher, you realize that worksheets and other papers are not appropriate for young children. How could you convince these parents of the need for concrete objects rather than papers for their children?
6. Discuss the social competence of five-year-old children.
7. What suggestions can you make for helping the child at risk at the preschool or kindergarten levels to succeed?
8. Why is the gifted child sometimes considered to be a child at risk?

CHAPTER 3

Curriculum for Three to Five Year Olds

Chapter Objectives:

On completion of this chapter, you should be able to

1. list the characteristics of unified curriculum experiences appropriate to three and four year olds,

2. discuss the characteristics of unified curriculum experiences appropriate to three and four year olds,

3. list the characteristics of unified curriculum experiences appropriate to five year olds,

4. discuss the characteristics of unified curriculum experiences appropriate to five year olds,

5. discuss the effect of cognitive development on the selection of unified curriculum experiences for three, four, and five year olds,

6. identify unified curriculum experiences that are appropriate to three, four, and five year olds, and

7. develop additional unified curriculum experiences appropriate to three, four, and five year olds.

Traditional science and mathematics topics for three- to five-year-old children usually reflect the topics found in textbooks or science programs for older children. Topics like plants, animals, air, weather, day and night, the four seasons, dinosaurs, and rocks are frequently found in science programs. In mathematics, children are often expected to learn to count, write numerals, or make sets of objects equivalent to a particular cardinal number. At the kindergarten level, more and more five-year-old children are being subjected to addition and subtraction in the formal manner in which these topics were formerly taught to first or second graders.

Tradition, however, is not a good criterion for the selection of content for young children. In general, the science topics included in this list are of interest to children, but they do not allow the child to become involved in his or her learning and, therefore, in the construction of knowledge. In each of the topics listed, the child is an observer of phenomena rather than a participant in the creation of phenomena. A child can observe weather conditions and chart those conditions on a daily calendar, but the activity is observational and the child's own involvement is lacking. Teachers who attempt to explain why weather changes may be met with quiet children, but the quiet is more likely to reflect the teacher's ability at classroom management than any understanding on the part of children.

Many of the science topics presented to children are not only observational in nature, but are also far beyond the child's comprehension. Consider the concept of day and night. If the differences between day and night are examined, the child is a passive observer of phenomena: At night, it is dark and you go to sleep; during the day, it is light and you go to school. If, on the other hand, the child is subjected to an explanation of the cause of day and night, she or he has no possibility of comprehending the explanation. The child needs to have previously developed the concepts of planet, star, rotation, axis, and movement through space. All of these ideas are beyond the young child's experience and comprehension. Not only is the child unable to utilize concrete materials in learning, but the child is assumed to have a sophisticated understanding of cause and effect that is far beyond his or her years.

In mathematics, teaching children to form numerals without previously developing a meaning for the symbols is a meaningless exercise in conformist drawing. Every child attempts to please the teacher by making the same marks on a piece of paper. Preoperational children have no concept of what those marks mean. When addition and subtraction are considered by children who have yet to attain conservation of number, the outcome is likely to be meaningless memorization of a sequence of words. Such memorization wastes both the child's time and the teacher's time. Inappropriate science and mathematics topics send the same message to children: They are incapable of understanding and so are incompetent in school-related tasks.

If tradition cannot be used as a guide for the selection of science or mathematics content, what can be used? In the case of the young child, the source of the curriculum in science and mathematics should be the young child and the developmental and social characteristics of that child. If the child becomes the source, then there is no distinction between science and mathematics. The curriculum becomes unified.

SELECTING UNIFIED CURRICULUM CONTENT FOR YOUNG CHILDREN

The content of the unified curriculum for three-, four-, and five-year-old children should be based on the social and developmental characteristics of the children rather than on tradition or teacher preference. The topics selected should also reflect the basic premise of the unified curriculum: the total integration of science and mathematics into a single experience.

Unified Curriculum Experiences for Three and Four Year Olds

Appropriate unified curriculum activities for three- and four-year-old children begin with the use of investigative behaviors. Children should have the opportunity to interact directly with materials in a setting that will allow them to act autonomously. This type of activity precludes the teacher-structured and -led activity in which all children do the same thing at the same time. Rather, the children usually in small groups, are presented with a variety of materials that will allow for a variety of uses. The teacher may give a starting activity or a starting question, but the children should then have the opportunity to investigate the materials following whatever direction their interests take them and their abilities allow. Autonomy increases and heteronomy decreases as the child has the opportunity to make decisions about the use of the materials. Problem solving is fostered as children determine methods of investigation for themselves.

Because there are a wide variety of possibilities and a wide variety of materials, the activities appropriate to three- and four-year-old children are open-ended. Children of three or four do not see a need for closure in activities. Consequently, the activities presented to children should allow the child to determine when he or she has investigated thoroughly enough. There is no need in this type of investigation for the teacher to draw a particular conclusion or for the children to be guided toward a particular conclusion preestablished by the teacher.

As mentioned, the materials themselves are important to the type of activity presented to three- and four-year-old children. The materials should allow the child to investigate a variety of possibilities rather than only a single idea. The greater the flexibility of use, the better the materials selection. Additionally, the materials should be familiar to the children. "Science" materials are unnecessary for the three or four year old. The microscopes, balances, test tubes, and flasks most teachers recall from science labs at the high school or college level are not only inappropriate for the young child but are also unnecessary. Squeeze bottles, funnels, blocks, plastic bottles, balls, beanbags, swings, seesaws, and other items familiar to the child and to the early childhood setting are far more appropriate.

The use of materials in the activity also leads to another criterion for activities appropriate for young children. Three and four year olds generally play or work together by proximity rather than by sharing. Consequently, individual sets of materials should be available so that each child can have his or her own materials. Proximity will allow children to cooperate if they wish or to work separately if they wish. Children will show each other their

discoveries and even show other children how they did something, but they may not be ready to work in a fully cooperative manner.

Finally, the kinds of activities selected for inclusion in the unified curriculum should reflect the natural play activities of children. Young children enjoy running, jumping, climbing, throwing, bouncing, swinging, pushing, pulling, rolling, and generally moving themselves and other objects. Such play activities are also unified curriculum experiences because they allow investigation of the environment through changes. The changes are made by the children and so become meaningful to the children as they integrate those experiences into their developing cognitive structures.

Activities for the young child, then, should allow the greatest possible interaction with the environment and the greatest possible autonomy. High degrees of structure, definite endings, and predetermined conclusions have no place in the activities of the unified curriculum.

Unified Curriculum Experiences for Five Year Olds

The types of activities appropriate for three and four year olds are similar to those appropriate for five year olds. The activities of the unified curriculum should allow children of five to actively manipulate materials. The materials, once again, should be familiar to children, unlike the more unusual and unfamiliar materials of the traditional science program. Activities should allow for the use of large-muscle skills: throwing, jumping, running, pouring, catching, swinging, and so on. Some small-muscle-skill requirements should begin to be introduced to allow for the continued development of such skills in children. The materials and the starting question of the activity should lend themselves to the active manipulation of materials, with children being able to make a variety of changes during their manipulations. Children should also have the opportunity to work with materials in a variety of ways rather than in a single teacher-determined way.

Two differences are present in the types of activities presented to five year olds as opposed to three and four year olds. The five year old is beginning to cooperate with others in activities and in play. Consequently, some activities should be presented that allow the child to cooperate with one or more other children. Planning and carrying out a joint venture should be possible in at least some of the activities. However, children of five should not be forced into cooperation with others. Rather, the possibility of cooperation should be made clear through proximity or by offering individual sets of materials or a large variety of materials from which children can choose. This allows children who are ready to cooperate with other children to do so, while those who are not yet ready or willing to cooperate to also participate effectively in the activity. Children will also have the opportunity to cooperate and then to separate as investigations proceed. The second difference in activities appropriate for five year olds as opposed to three or four year olds is the increasing use of mathematical ideas such as patterning, seriation, and classification.

The differences in thought processes of three-, four-, and five-year-old children are small enough that the same criteria for selection of topics can be used for both the preschool and kindergarten levels.

CRITERIA FOR SELECTION OF ACTIVITIES FOR THE UNIFIED CURRICULUM

Criterion One

Cause and effect should be immediate in time and space. As a consequence of the preoperational-level child's inability to work effectively with true cause and effect, topics for the unified curriculum should be selected that will allow for immediate occurrences rather than results over time or over distance. Activities should be such that the effect of an action immediately follows the cause. An activity in which children investigate how different kinds of objects roll on ramps placed at various angles is an appropriate activity while an activity dealing with the effect of fertilizers on the growth of plants is not. In the former activity, the children act on the objects and see the result immediately while in the latter, the children have no opportunity to see an immediate reaction.

Criterion Two

Children should construct knowledge rather than be taught knowledge. Children at the preoperational level of cognitive development need to construct knowledge rather than memorize words. The topics selected for the unified curriculum should allow the child direct, multisensory experience rather than vicarious, observational, or verbal experience. Activities should be selected that will allow the child to directly manipulate materials. The materials being manipulated should always be real objects rather than models or diagrams. Having children investigate the swing of a pendulum by changing the length of the pendulum or the weight of the object is far more appropriate than having children watch the teacher demonstrate the effect of heat on ice. Having children handle bones of various types is far more effective than having children observe a plastic skeleton model.

Criterion Three

Topics should allow children to investigate both the forward results of an activity and the reverse. Children at the preoperational level of cognitive development lack the ability to reverse thought processes. Consequently, the topics selected for the unified curriculum should not require children to undo processes. Children can easily observe that chocolate candy melts if placed in a warm place. To expect them to infer that the chocolate will harden if it is placed in a cool area without providing experience is inappropriate. This inference requires reversibility of thought.

If an activity is selected that requires the reversing of an action, then the child should be able to experience both the forward and reverse directions of the activity rather than be expected to make inferences. Children can observe how ice melts and how they can affect how quickly ice melts by holding it in their hands, blowing on it, or putting it in a container in the Sun. They also need to see that the water that forms from the melted ice will turn back into ice if it is placed in the freezer. Since the ability to reverse thought is not available to the young child, both the melting of ice into liquid water and the refreezing of the resulting water into ice must be shown.

Criterion Four

Activities should allow children to discuss the "what" of an activity rather than the causal "why" of an activity. If preoperational children have little ability in identifying cause and effect relationships, then it is only logical that they will also have difficulty in using cause and effect relationships to develop explanations. The topics selected for the unified curriculum should not require the child to explain the reason for an occurrence but should, instead, ask students to demonstrate effects discovered and the ways in which those effects were produced. Children should have the opportunity to talk about the "what" of an activity without having to explain the "why" of the activity. The activities of the unified curriculum should, therefore, allow the child to readily demonstrate and interact with materials. In discussions of what occurred during an activity, the materials should always be present so the child can show as well as tell about what was done and what happened.

Criterion Five

Activities should allow children to investigate ideas related to conservation in an intuitive rather than a formal manner. Children at the preoperational level of cognitive development are not yet able to conserve number, substance, length, area, weight, or volume. Consequently, topics selected for the unified curriculum should not require the child to use these concepts in a formal manner. It is inappropriate to expect the young child to measure length using a ruler, to measure weight using a balance or scale, or to measure volume using cups or liters. Rather than introducing formal concepts of measurement, the activities selected for the unified curriculum should allow students to explore these concepts. It is appropriate for children to place different objects on the pans of a balance, especially a homemade balance, to see what will happen, to pour various liquids or solids from container to container, or to find different ways of covering a certain area with a variety of objects. These kinds of activities help the child to construct a concept of weight or volume or area. Formal measurement activities expect the child to memorize a piece of information without understanding.

Criterion Six

Activities should allow children to use forms of reasoning that are cognitively appropriate. Children at the preoperational level are unable to draw conclusions from a set of data or to reason from a premise. Instead, children at this level use transductive and syncretic reasoning. Consequently, the topics selected for the unified curriculum should not require students to develop broad, specific generalizations. Students should be able to look at the results of various investigations with a set of materials and discuss those results without drawing a conclusion that ties all of the results together. Activities selected for the unified curriculum should allow children to construct ideas and information without the necessity of developing connections or conclusions specified by the teacher. It is appropriate for children to tell about the block, pencil, and plastic bottle that floated in water and the nail and magnet that sank. It is not necessary for children to generalize that wood and plastic objects float and metal objects sink or, worse, that objects light in weight for their volume float and objects heavy in weight for their volume sink.

Criterion Seven

Activities should allow for the development of written language skills but not be directed by such skills. Although children at the preoperational level of cognitive development have functional vocabularies that they can use successfully in a variety of situations, these children are not able to learn effectively from words, whether written or oral. The young child learns from experience. Consequently, topics selected for the unified curriculum should not require the use of worksheets, workbooks, or pencil-and-paper learning. Young children are neither cognitively nor socially ready for this type of learning experience. The use of written symbols is generally meaningless and the formation of those symbols is a tedious task for students who have yet to develop small-muscle coordination. Rather than pencil-and-paper learning, the activities of the unified curriculum should involve the young child in hands-on learning experiences utilizing concrete materials. Preschool and kindergarten children should learn about how objects move by moving objects, how liquids behave by playing at a water table, and how sounds are made with various objects. Preschool and kindergarten children should not learn about moving objects by looking at pictures of trucks, cars, and buses, about liquids by watching the teacher pour water and explain how water differs from clay, or about sound by listening to a written description of sounds in the environment.

The inappropriateness of written materials as a primary learning tool should not, however, be interpreted to mean that written and oral language should be omitted from the unified curriculum. The use of a language-experience approach helps develop in children the connection between written and spoken language. For example, as the children discuss their experiences with how various objects move, the teacher can record their activities and findings on chart paper. In this way, the teacher creates a permanent record of the activity and demonstrates that spoken language can be recorded in written form. Additionally, written materials can be appropriately used with the young child after concrete experiences have occurred. Children who have had opportunities to investigate water through water play should have the opportunity to interact with books and other print materials dealing with water, boats, oceans, and other aspects of water. Print materials should be used as a secondary rather than as a primary source with young children.

Criterion Eight

Activities should encourage appropriate oral-language development. Children at the preoperational level of cognitive development may not learn effectively through the use of oral and written language but they are developing language skills and vocabulary at a rapid rate. Consequently, language use and vocabulary are important in the unified curriculum. Language allows the child to communicate activities and results to others. Vocabulary allows the development of a common language. Language development through vocabulary development should be a natural rather than artificial part of the unified curriculum, with words being introduced informally during and after activities. The purpose of the activities in the unified curriculum should not be to develop specific vocabulary terms or language skills but to develop the concepts on which vocabulary later can be built. Consequently, an activity in the unified curriculum would never begin with the introduction of new vocabulary followed by an activity in which children are expected to demonstrate the meaning of that vocabulary. For example, children can investigate how well objects roll on various kinds of surfaces. As a result of their investigations, they discover that objects roll farther on the tile floor than on the concrete sidewalk. As they talk about what they have done, the children mention that the tile was smooth and the concrete was bumpy. As the teacher responds to these observations, he or she may say, "The tile was smooth and the sidewalk was rough." In this situation, a new term is used in a natural way. Children are not expected to remember the term, but if the word is understood, it will appear often in conversation. Similarly, after listening to children talk about objects that stayed on top of the water and objects that fell to the bottom, the teacher may use the words *sink* and *float* in her or his comments. Vocabulary comes last, not first. New vocabulary terms should appear in the language-experience records developed by the teacher and children, but only when the terms are used by the children in their contributions to that written record. The teacher should refrain from forcing new terms into the record simply because they have been used by the teacher.

ORGANIZATION IN THE UNIFIED CURRICULUM

Effective organization is important in any teaching situation no matter what the age or grade level of the students. When hands-on activities using a wide variety of materials are a major part of the program, organization becomes particularly vital. In the case of the unified curriculum, organization involves three factors: materials, classroom, and parents.

Organization of Materials

Organization of materials begins with the determination of the activities that will be used in the classroom. Until the activities have been selected, it is impossible to know what materials will be needed. This is not, however, to say that every activity for the school year must be known prior to the start of school, only that some are known so that the materials can be collected. For example, the teacher may decide to use Investigating Bouncing Objects, Investigating Sound Makers, and Investigating Balancing as the first three activities for the year. As soon as those are known, the teacher can begin to collect the needed objects.

Collecting the necessary objects is the second step in organizing materials. The list of materials included with each of the unified curriculum activities mentioned above gives only some of the materials that can be used and it should serve as a starting point rather than as a complete list. As objects such as styrofoam packing bits, buttons, balls, and rhythm instruments are collected, the teacher may think of related items that can also be added to the collection. This original collection of items should be considered the starting point. As children investigate, the teacher should notice which items are not used and what kinds of items are requested by the children that were not originally provided. In this way, some items can be deleted and some added.

Packing the items is the third step in organizing materials. Small items in large quantities such as buttons, beads, bottle caps, or pasta shapes can be packaged in recycled margarine tubs or in sealable plastic bags. This helps to prevent loss and also makes it easy for children to locate objects they need. The items for a single activity should be packaged in a larger container; plastic storage boxes, cardboard boxes, and recycled ice cream tubs available in ice cream stores make good storage bins. It is a good idea to wait until the objects are collected before selecting a storage container, otherwise you may end up with a great storage box into which nothing will fit. For some activities, standard classroom items such as blocks are also needed. To help with organization, include a list of these standard items in the container with the other materials. The list can quickly refresh the memory of the hurried and harried teacher.

As materials are used, the fourth aspect of organizing materials comes into play: maintenance. Small items such as beads and beans are going to be lost. Materials such as paint and food coloring or paper are going to be used up. Popsicle sticks can break. Obtain extras of inexpensive and consum-

able materials so that those that are used or lost can be quickly replaced without disrupting the activity. It is far better to quickly add a handful of new beans to a set of materials than to waste valuable investigation time searching for lost beans.

Finally, organization includes clean-up after an activity is concluded. Three-, four-, and five-year-old children are not only capable of cleaning up but generally enjoy the clean-up as much as the activity. The children should be responsible for the majority of cleaning, with the teacher assisting as necessary. Children can dry off materials and return them to the appropriate containers. The teacher should lift and empty basins filled with water.

Organization of the Classroom

Organization of the classroom for use of the unified curriculum must consider two factors: space and time. Space includes the physical space available for activities and the location of that space. Time involves the length of time permitted for interaction as well as the time of day during which activities are presented.

The amount of physical space allocated for a unified curriculum activity is strongly dependent on the activity. An activity that focuses on a water table or large basin of water requires far less physical space than one that involves the children in constructing towers and then knocking them over with beanbags or balls. In the case of an activity that is localized, the teacher can easily designate the area to be used for the activity. If the activity is water play, the area can be designated indoors with a colorful plastic drop cloth indicating where water can be splashed. An activity involving balances can have its space delineated by placing the balances and objects on a particular set of tables. It is not so easy to designate an area for an activity involving tossing objects at targets or for an activity dealing with ramps and rolling objects. The most efficient way of determining the space needed is to provide a large area of the classroom and watch to see if more or less space is actually needed. Although it is easier to say that children can use all of the space they need for activities involving materials such as targets or ramps, consideration must be given to those children not participating in the activities and who may be engaging in quiet, solitary activities. It is better to designate an area than to allow an activity to take over the entire classroom, unless all children are involved.

Space also involves the location of activities. Once again, this will be strongly dependent on the activity. Some activities will not require high levels of teacher supervision to assure child safety. Activities involving water play, shadows, or rolling and sliding can be put in locations where teacher observation is possible but not necessarily continuous. Some activities do require high levels of teacher supervision and need to be placed in locations conducive to continuous observation. These activities would include bubbles (because of the use of detergent or soap), mixing (because of the use of a variety of "tasteable" materials), and targets (because of the tossing of objects). And, finally, some activities are best located outside so that children can feel free to make as much "mess" as they wish. Making bubbles and splashes are both good outdoor activities.

Time is an additional consideration in organizing the classroom for unified curriculum activities. Time limits on investigations are both unnecessary and undesirable at the preschool and kindergarten levels. Children will investigate to the extent of their interests and abilities, then move on to other interesting tasks within the classroom. Time limits are undesirable because one purpose of the unified curriculum is to enhance autonomy and decrease heteronomy. The setting of specific time limits works against this purpose.

The time of day allocated for activities is dependent on the type of classroom situation. In an open classroom situation, materials can be continuously available for use by the children in their investigations. In a more structured situation, one that includes centers and large-group experiences, a unified curriculum activity can be one of the choices during the time for centers.

Informing Parents

Parents should be informed about the intention to use a unified curriculum approach to the mathematics and science areas for two reasons. First, many parents look for evidence of the academic subject areas even at the preschool and kindergarten levels. Since the unified curriculum does not have a specific science program and a specific mathematics program, parents will need to be informed about how their children are working in these areas, but in a way that is appropriate to the children. Involve parents by including them in unified curriculum activities, sending out a newsletter, or making a verbal presentation. Second, parents can be an excellent source of materials and so should be informed of activities and the kinds of materials that will be needed. Parents are generally happy to help by donating their "junk": margarine tubs, buttons, egg cartons, unused aquariums, bottle caps, jar lids, soft drink bottles, tin cans, empty boxes, oatmeal boxes, cardboard cores from paper towel rolls, and milk cartons.

APPROPRIATE TOPICS FOR THE UNIFIED CURRICULUM

Appropriate topics for the unified curriculum should reflect not only the cognitive necessities of the young child but also the unified nature of the curriculum. Science and mathematics are undifferentiated in the mind of the preoperational child and so should be undifferentiated in the curriculum. Appropriate topics, then, cut across the boundaries artificially set by adults for mathematics and science.

The following topics are some of those appropriate to the unified curriculum. Each topic is followed by some of the kinds of materials that could be provided and by a starting question or activity.

Investigating Motion
Materials: balls, rollers, plastic soft drink containers, empty soft drink cans, empty milk cartons, straws, boards, blocks, clay or play dough, marbles, etc.
Getting Started: What ways can you find to make these move?

Investigating Pouring
Materials: cardboard, plastic, and metal containers of various sizes and shapes; water, salt, sand, sugar, baby oil or cooking oil, sieves, colanders, etc.
Getting Started: Pour some sand from one container to another. Ask students if all the things will pour the same way that sand pours.

Investigating Balancing
Materials: large pan balances either purchased or constructed from milk cartons and string, various sizes of cereals, beans, styrofoam packing bits, small and large stones, paper clips, bottle caps, buttons, rice, beads, etc.
Getting Started: Put some beans or stones on one side of the balance. Ask students to find ways to make the balance even again.

Investigating Ramps and Inclines
Materials: cardboard, styrofoam, boards (to make ramps), blocks, chairs, balls, cylinders, toy cars and trucks, empty soft drink cans, sand, salt, sugar, etc.
Getting Started: Make a ramp and roll a can down it. Ask students if some of the other things will roll as well as the can.

Investigating Bubbles
Materials: commercial bubble mixture or detergent-based bubble mixture, bubble blowers and bubble pipes, keys, sieves, colanders, straws, cardboard tubes, small rectangular boxes, whisks, fly swatters, large and small containers, water, additional liquid and solid detergent. (Caution: This activity should be closely supervised because of the use of soap or detergent.)
Getting Started: Blow some bubbles. It is unlikely that children will need more encouragement than that.

Investigating Pinwheels
Materials: pinwheels of different sizes, materials, and types; construction paper, light-weight cardboard, aluminum foil, notebook paper, butcher paper, scissors, tape, glue, straws, etc.
Getting Started: Ask students how many ways they can find to get a pinwheel to turn. What other things can they make that will move?

Investigating Mixing
Materials: water, oil, syrup, soft drink, powdered drink mix, powdered milk, sand, salt, sugar, flour, gelatin powder, food coloring, powdered paint, styrofoam beads, corn starch, powdered detergent, etc. (Caution: This activity should be closely supervised so that children do not taste the various materials or mixtures.)
Getting Started: Put salt into the water. Ask students what else will disappear like the salt did.

Investigating Swinging Objects
Materials: string, twine, rope, 35 mm film cans, gallon milk cartons (bottom half), plastic buckets, blocks, empty plastic soft drink bottles, oatmeal or other cylindrical boxes, balls, etc.
Getting Started: Prepare a variety of differently sized pendula including some hanging from the ceiling and from lower structures. Ask children what they could do with the swinging objects and the other materials.

Investigating Bouncing Objects
Materials: rubber balls of different types and sizes, baseballs, basketballs, footballs, golf balls, wiffle-balls, empty cans, blocks, boards, etc.
Getting Started: Ask students to find out if all of the things bounce the same way.

Investigating Sinking and Floating
Materials: basins of water or water table, small objects that sink, small objects that float including plastic squeeze bottles and other objects that can be filled with water, transparent and opaque plastic tubes, etc.
Getting Started: Ask students to investigate what happens when they put the objects in water.

Investigating Targets
Materials: different types of balls, beanbags, empty boxes, plastic soft drink bottles, tin cans, etc.
Getting Started: Construct a tower of boxes to act as a target. Toss one of the beanbags at the target so that it falls over. Challenge children to see if they can do the same thing.

Investigating Rolling and Sliding Things
Materials: various wheeled and nonwheeled toys, empty cans, plastic containers with lids, blocks, boards, aluminum foil, cardboard, sand, water, rectangular and cylindrical boxes with and without lids, heavy string or twine, etc.
Getting Started: Ask students what ways they can find to get the objects to move.

Investigating Ice
Materials: ice cubes in various sizes and shapes, water, salt, sand, etc.
Getting Started: Challenge children to find ways of getting the ice cubes to melt or not melt.

Investigating Sound Makers
Materials: various rhythm instruments, rubber bands, boxes, pencils, bottle caps, beads, sand or

gravel, plastic boxes, unsharpened pencils or dowel rods, etc.

Getting Started: Ask students what sounds they can make with the objects.

Investigating Shadows

Materials: sunny window or other light source including an overhead projector, various objects of different shapes and sizes, screen or wall

Getting Started: Demonstrate some of the shadows that can be made with the objects. Ask children to see what kinds of shadows they can make.

Investigating Volume

Materials: large and small boxes and other containers of differing sizes and shapes, various sizes of cereals, beans, styrofoam packing bits, small and large stones, paper clips, bottle caps, buttons, rice, beads, etc.

Getting Started: Put some beans or stones in one of the containers and pour them into a smaller or larger container. Ask students which of the containers holds the same amount.

Investigating Towers and Constructions

Materials: boxes, blocks, straws, cardboard strips from boxes, tongue depressors, popsicle sticks, clothespins, masking tape, styrofoam blocks and balls, clay, string, unsharpened pencils or dowel rods, etc.

Getting Started: Challenge children to see what they can build from the materials.

Investigating Splashes

Materials: basins of water, basins of flour, basins of sand, any small objects that can be dropped into the basins without breaking

Getting Started: Ask students what they think will happen if the objects are dropped into the basins.

Keep in mind two notes of caution when supervising each of the activities listed here. First, the Getting Started questions and challenges are given only to help initiate the activity. Children should be encouraged to investigate as many other questions as they wish. If an activity becomes "messy" according to adult standards, take it outside or place a plastic drop cloth in the area. The only real limitation on the investigations of chil-dren should be safety. If children begin to take a dangerous course of action, stop the activity and discuss the reasons for stopping at that point. Then, help the children find alternatives to the dangerous action and allow them to return to the activity. Children do not learn to exercise appropriate behaviors by having things taken away. They learn appropriate behaviors through discussion and modeling, and then applying the behavior. Second, the activities are not designed with a specific objective or outcome in mind. Since the children will learn from the activities depending on what they choose to investigate and according to their previous experiences, it is inappropriate to specify what will be learned from an activity. Allow children at the preschool or kindergarten levels to explore freely.

SUMMARY

Traditional topics in science and mathematics are generally inappropriate for the very young child. The inappropriateness of topics such as the four seasons, what causes objects to float, or what causes day and night stems from the cognitive abilities of the children. Explanations of cause and effect are generally inappropriate. Other topics, such as the four seasons, are inappropriate not because children cannot learn about them, but rather because children have no control over the phenomena under study. The child can only act as a passive observer and parrot back information presented by the teacher. Learning computation skills such as adding and subtracting, writing numerals, or measuring objects using standard measurement systems are inappropriate because of the young child's lack of conservation skills.

The unified curriculum erases the artificial boundaries between science and mathematics. The child is able to participate in experiences that develop general knowledge rather than knowledge specifically related to either science or mathematics. This general knowledge lays the foundation for later understanding of traditional science and mathematics topics.

Appropriate activities for the unified curriculum allow the child to directly interact with

LEARNING ACTIVITY 12

Designing a Unified-Curriculum Activity

Purpose: The purpose of this activity is to design a unified-curriculum activity based on the characteristics of children at play.

Procedure:

1. Design an activity based on outdoor play.
   a. Observe a group of three-, four-, and/or five-year-old children at play outdoors and make notes about the kinds of activities in which they engage.
   b. Select one or more of the kinds of activities observed among the children.
   c. Design a unified-curriculum activity that includes observed play activities.
   d. Include in your designed activity materials that could be used, a starting question, and a description of how you would follow up the activity.

2. Design an activity based on indoor play.
   a. Observe a group of three-, four-, and/or five-year-old children at play indoors and make notes about the kinds of activities in which they engage.
   b. Select one or more of the kinds of activities observed among the children.
   c. Design a unified-curriculum activity that includes observed play activities.
   d. Include in your designed activity materials that could be used, a starting question, and a description of how you would follow up the activity.

LEARNING ACTIVITY 13

Using Traditional Topics in Unified-Curriculum Lessons

Purpose: The purpose of this activity is to develop open-inquiry activities that are based on traditional activities for the preschool and kindergarten levels.

Procedure:

1. Select a physical-science activity that is traditionally advocated for the preschool-level child.
   a. Describe the activity as it is traditionally done with the preschool child.
   b. Discuss the appropriateness of the activity in terms of the cognitive and social abilities of preschool children.
   c. Using the activity as a basis, develop an open-inquiry activity for use with three and/or four year olds.
   d. Try the unified-curriculum activity with a small group of children. Discuss the results of the activity and the kinds of modifications you might make as a result of watching the children participate.

2. Select a physical-science activity that is traditionally advocated for the kindergarten-level child.
   a. Describe the activity as it is traditionally done with the kindergarten child.
   b. Discuss the appropriateness of the activity in terms of the cognitive and social abilities of kindergartners.
   c. Using the activity as a basis, develop an open-inquiry activity for use with kindergarten children.
   d. Try the unified-curriculum activity with a small group of children. Discuss the results of the activity and the kinds of modifications you might make as a result of watching the children participate.

materials, make changes, and see the immediate results of those changes. Appropriate activities for the unified curriculum also allow the child to describe experiences rather than expect the child to explain those experiences in terms of cause and effect. In one case, however, the use of cause and effect is appropriate: when cause and effect are immediate in time and space and when the child directly causes the change through his or her action.

Vocabulary Terms

Autonomy: self-directed and self-directing behavior.

Construction of Knowledge: idiosyncratic development of conceptual knowledge through interaction with the physical environment and persons in the environment and resulting from cognitive consideration of those interactions.

Interaction: direct manipulation of concrete materials.

Oral-Language Development: development of an ability to communicate effectively through words, including the use of sentences and appropriate vocabulary.

Traditional Mathematics: mathematics that focuses on the development of basic computation skills: addition, subtraction, multiplication, and division.

Traditional Science: science that focuses on the acquisition of scientific information and that often focuses on the development of scientific vocabulary.

Undifferentiated: not separated into specific subject-matter areas.

Unified Curriculum: a curriculum pattern that allows for the full integration of science and mathematics into a single experience.

Study Questions

1. What are the characteristics of an appropriate unified-curriculum experience?
2. How are the cognitive and developmental characteristics of the young child incorporated into the unified curriculum?
3. How do unified-curriculum experiences differ from traditional experiences in science or mathematics?
4. Why is it inappropriate to consider science and mathematics separate subject-matter areas at the preschool and kindergarten levels?
5. A preschool teacher provided her students with a water table and many objects to put into the water so that they could investigate sinking and floating. When the children began to share the results of their investigations, they talked about splashes, pouring, filling containers, making bubbles, and pretending to have boats. Because not one child mentioned the idea of sinking and floating, the teacher was disappointed with the outcome of the activity. What could you say to this teacher to help her overcome her disappointment?
6. You have been using unified curriculum activities in your kindergarten classroom for nearly four months and have considered the activities successful. Another teacher comes to you, takes you aside, and suggests that you stop wasting so much time in your classroom. She explains that her children can already write their names, count to twenty, name the kinds of vertebrate animals, and even solve simple addition problems. How would you defend your classroom practice to this teacher?
7. What differences exist between a unified curriculum activity and either a science or a mathematics activity?

CHAPTER 4

Teaching in the Unified Curriculum

Chapter Objectives

On completion of this chapter, you should be able to

1. list the characteristics of open inquiry as a teaching strategy for the unified curriculum,

2. describe the roles of the teacher and the student in an open-inquiry teaching strategy,

3. describe the benefits of open inquiry for children,

4. plan an open-inquiry lesson that is appropriate for the child of three, four, or five years of age,

5. list the problems that may be encountered in using the open-inquiry strategy with young children, and

6. discuss the role of questions in open-inquiry teaching.

Teaching in the unified curriculum presents a different type of problem for the teacher than teaching in any other curricular pattern. The traditional view of teaching and learning demands that subject-matter areas be considered as discrete entities from which specific bits of content information are selected. This view also requires that the teacher function as the determiner and conveyer of those specifics to children. This idea that discrete bits of knowledge can be conveyed to students is contrary to the concept of the young child as an active constructor of information. It is also contrary to the concept of the child as seeing the world as a unified whole rather than as a series of individual pieces of information.

In the unified curriculum, the teacher is the designer of experiences that will allow the young child to determine the direction of investigations and conceptualize from those investigations knowledge that can be integrated into the individual child's cognitive framework. In order for this child-dependent and child-specific construction of knowledge to occur, the child must be placed into a setting of active involvement with materials. The investigations that are carried out by children cut across traditional subject-matter areas so that science and mathematics are unified and integrated with other areas. The teaching strategy that is suited to this type of investigative learning is known as open inquiry.

OPEN-INQUIRY TEACHING

A group of preschool children is given blocks, boxes, boards, cylinders, and toy cars and trucks. One of the children notices that the cars can be made to run along the boards. The children begin to get interested in making tracks for the cars. While they work, the teacher joins into the activity. As part of what the teacher investigates, she constructs a ramp that allows the car to travel not only on a board but to continue rolling across the floor. "I wonder," the teacher muses aloud, "how far I could get my car to travel across the floor? I wonder if I could get it to go as far as the reading corner?" Her musings immediately provide a challenge to the children who spend considerable time and effort in investigating cars and ramps. They even discover that they can mark the distance traveled by each car with a block and so can see which car travels farthest. The crowning achievement is when one child's car rolls past the reading corner and collides with the door on the opposite side of the classroom!

This is open inquiry. Open inquiry is a free-form teaching strategy in which students are active investigators of the environment. In open inquiry, the teacher presents a starting problem, provides the materials that could be used to solve the problem, then allows the students to use any method they wish to arrive at a solution. The term *problem* is loosely interpreted to mean a challenge as simple as "can you do this." The method is so unstructured that students can investigate the problem presented at the starting point or can use the materials to investigate a question of greater personal interest.

Characteristics of Open Inquiry

The first characteristic of open inquiry is that it is not used to teach specific bits of information to the child. Rather than teaching predetermined information, open inquiry places the child into an investigative situation in which she or he is able to investigate freely and, thereby, construct knowledge of the environment. Such construction is idiosyncratic to the child and so is, by its nature, developmentally appropriate. The content of an open-inquiry activity is, therefore, specific to the child rather than to the experience. For example, in the activity with the ramps and cars, one child may discover that the steeper the ramp is, the farther the car will travel, another child may construct the concept that distance can be measured, and yet another child will simply notice that cars and trucks can be made to roll on boards.

The second characteristic of open inquiry is that the teacher's role is different from that of the teacher in the traditional classroom setting. In the traditional setting, the teacher is the authority figure within the classroom. He or she develops the activity, determines the direction of the investigation, and specifies the outcome. The image of the teacher developed within the traditional setting is that of a director of learning. The open-inquiry teaching strategy places the teacher in the role of aid and assistant. The teacher develops the activity or expands on an on-going activity, accumulates any materials that could be used in the investigations derived from the starting point, and then steps back to observe. As an observer of child activity, the teacher is placed in the role of assisting when asked, helping students to continue an investigative behavior, and acquiring additional materials as needed.

The third characteristic of open inquiry is its emphasis on problem solving and decision making through active investigation. Active investigation leads the child to observe the outcomes of his or her actions. Because of these observations, children will often begin a new investigation that has little resemblance to the original course of action. Consequently, students make decisions about what and how they will investigate. This decision making is autonomous and inherent in both the child and the teaching strategy. The child decides which avenues of investigation to pursue and which problems to solve. The child has the opportunity to grow in both autonomous behaviors and in problem-solving skills.

The fourth characteristic of open inquiry is that the teacher models investigative behaviors for the children. The teacher becomes involved in investigations, demonstrating those qualities of curiosity, inquiry, and investigation that are desired of the children. The teacher can become more than a model—he or she can become a co-investigator. A common difficulty that arises when the teacher becomes a co-investigator is that the teacher also becomes a director. As a co-investigator, the teacher need do no more than say "I wonder what would happen if . . ." followed by an investigation of that question. If some of the children become interested in the question posed, fine. But, the teacher as co-investigator should make no attempt to direct the children into a particular investigation through questions or demonstrations.

While the teacher can be both a model and a co-investigator, the teacher cannot be a purveyor of knowledge. Children will gain from their investigations information that will allow them to construct new ideas. At times, these new ideas will reflect the child's level of cognitive functioning and so will be incorrect according to adult standards. The teacher should not attempt to correct these ideas either through verbal explanation or demonstration of the

"right" idea through concrete materials. Verbal explanations are likely to result in meaningless verbalism on the part of the young child. Demonstrating correct ideas using materials may result in a "correct" response but is not likely to be incorporated into the child's cognitive structure. Rather, the child should be allowed to express his or her ideas without judgment from the teacher. Further interactions with the environment will allow the child to refine and develop ideas in a developmentally appropriate way.

The final characteristic of open-inquiry teaching is that it is child directed. As a child-directed technique, open inquiry allows children to pursue individual investigations, move from one type of investigation to another, and conclude an investigation at a personally appropriate time. The starting point of open-inquiry teaching is the same for all children in a class. But once that starting point has passed, the individualized investigations begin. What begins as a single area of investigation moves into such a variety of individualized activities that it is possible no two children will be investigating the same problem. This individualization of activity extends from the initiation of an activity to its conclusion. The young child has the opportunity to conclude the investigation whenever he or she is satisfied and ready to move on to something else. Once again, the child's feelings of autonomy and competence are enhanced.

Benefits of an Open-Inquiry Approach to Teaching

The benefits of the open-inquiry experience for three- to five-year-old children stem directly from the nature of open inquiry as a teaching strategy.

First, open inquiry allows children to directly manipulate objects in ways that cause changes or variations in behavior of the objects. This manipulation of objects results in the construction of knowledge through direct sensory and cognitive experience. Manipulation to cause change also develops the child's sense of control over the environment. Children at play at the water table quickly discover that some objects will hold water and some will not. Of those that hold water, some allow it to sprinkle out and some do not allow it to run out at all. Children involved in such an activity learn a great deal about their environment without ever having to listen to an adult explanation. The children construct their own concepts.

The second benefit of open inquiry is that it develops a child's autonomy by utilizing decision-making and problem-solving skills. The child exerts increasing control over the environment and over his or her learning. For example, while investigating what happens when objects are placed in water, the fact that some objects cause water to splash out of the containers may lead one child to investigate which object produces the biggest splash. The child involved in this activity decides what line of investigation to follow and then uses problem-solving skills to decide how to carry out the investigation. Additionally, while investigating, the child begins to learn that some factors can be controlled and, therefore, begins to develop the concept that she or he has control over the environment.

The third benefit of open inquiry is that it promotes creativity by allowing students to pursue a variety of possibilities beginning with the original problem or challenge. Children are limited only by their imaginations and abilities. The greater the variety of possibilities inherent in the open-inquiry activity, the greater the value of the activity and the more appropriate the activity in terms of knowledge construction and creativity. Children who are working with pattern blocks may begin by making simple, repetitive patterns but will soon develop more creative patterns, build towers with blocks, or even engage in fantasy play in which the blocks become substitutes for food, people, or animals. Such creative uses of materials enhances the ability of children to think creatively.

The final benefit of open inquiry is that it is based on child competence and success. There is no failure in the open-inquiry approach. Children investigate to the limits of their own abilities and interests, learning their own capabilities and extending them as they experience success. As a result, children develop self-confidence and self-concept. It is only when young children are forced to attain goals determined by the adult in the classroom that young children fail. Because open inquiry is based on the capabilities of the child and is directed by the child, there is virtually no possibility of failure. Open inquiry is truly "no-fail" in its methodology.

Planning an Open-Inquiry Experience

Step One in planning for an open-inquiry activity is to select the type of experience that will be initiated. Chapter 3 gives a variety of possible activities. In developing your own activity, the major criterion should be the child's experience. Good open-inquiry experiences allow the child to produce movement in objects in a variety of ways or to manipulate objects in ways that will allow for changes in the objects themselves: Mixing, pouring, spreading, and molding all fall under this latter category. The greater the flexibility in child action on the objects, the better the activity.

A good starting place for the development of activities is an observation of the children as they play. Children run, jump, kick, throw, hop, slide, roll, bounce, and toss in never-ending motion. These kinds of movements are frequently good starting places for open-inquiry activities. Additional ideas for activities can be found by watching children as they play at the sand and water tables, use art materials, or ask questions about their environment. Other ideas can be found by looking at the materials that are generally available in the preschool classroom. The possibilities for active exploration of blocks, water, balls, and rolling toys are endless. And, finally, open-inquiry activities may begin with a question asked by a child. Whatever the point of origin, the key to open-inquiry experiences is in the activity of the child. The place to begin in determining new open-inquiry experiences is with the child.

Step Two in planning an open-inquiry experience is to collect the kinds of materials that may be useful in investigating the starting problem or challenge. Trying to anticipate the kinds of things children will do as they carry out their investigations may be the hardest part of planning. If possible, it is helpful to attempt to think as a child thinks. Another way of determining the kinds of materials that may be needed is to try the activity and see what kinds of problems you are led to investigate. If thinking or investigating like a child is too difficult, try watching young children as they play. The materials children use in play may give clues as to the kinds of materials your students will use. In general, the greater the variety of materials, the better. Familiar materials are better than unfamiliar materials. Simple materials are better than complicated materials. Items that are unusual or items that are placed in conjunction with unrelated materials may spark a child's imagination. But, if the materials are too unusual, the young child will probably give more attention to investigating the materials than to investigating the problem presented by the teacher. In open inquiry, this is really not a difficulty, but it may be disconcerting to the teacher. In any case, whether familiar or unfamiliar, the materials should be safe for children to use: unbreakable, rounded at the corners, large enough so as not to be swallowed or stuck into small ears, and nontoxic. In some cases, it will be better to put out some of the collected materials, observe the students as they use those materials in their investigations, and then add additional materials for the students to use in extending and developing their activities. Be ready to accommodate requests for other materials or to suggest substitutes for materials requested but unavailable. And, be ready for children to drop, bend, roll, or otherwise investigate the materials before they become involved in the problem.

Step Three is to determine the starting point for the activity. There are a variety of ways to initiate an open-inquiry activity. The most successful activity initiations are open-ended and nondirective. Here are strategies for beginning an open-inquiry activity.

1. Provide materials and ask students what they can do with those materials.
2. Demonstrate one thing that can be done with the materials and ask students to see what else they can do with them.
3. Do something with the materials yourself and invite students to join in your activity. After the students become involved, move away from the activity to allow them to diversify the activity.
4. Provide a challenge for students and have them respond to the challenge.
5. Remind students of something that they observed at an earlier time and provide materials that will allow investigation of the phenomenon observed.
6. Have a child demonstrate something he or she has discovered and have other students see if they can do the same thing or something even better than the original.

Step Four is to determine the follow-up that will occur after the activity. Remember that the point of an open-inquiry investigation is not to learn a particular piece of knowledge or vocabulary term but rather to construct knowledge that will be individual to the child. Consequently, the follow-up of an activity cannot focus on one particular piece of information. Instead, the follow-up can be a large- or small-group experience in which children tell what they did and how they did it. Children should be encouraged both to describe and to demonstrate their activities for other children. For example, children who have been investigating the kinds of things that splash could be encouraged to demonstrate their findings to the rest of the children in the group and then describe what they saw. Children of three, four, and five can be expected to show what they have done or to tell about what they discovered. Children of this age cannot, however, be expected to discuss the cause-and-effect relationships in an activity unless the relationships are immediate in time and space. A child may notice that the harder the ball is thrown, the bigger the splash. That same child may not notice that styrofoam splashes farther than sand if the two materials are used with a long time interim between them. Children can draw a particular conclusion from the results of a variety of activities, but that conclusion should be specific to the child and to the activity, not one that has been predetermined by the teacher. The expectation that all children will learn the same thing at the same time is inappropriate to the open-inquiry technique.

Problems in Using Open Inquiry

There is no teaching strategy that is foolproof or that will work perfectly for every child in a group on every day of the year. Children vary in their abilities, backgrounds, and learning modalities. Interests of young children are often intense but fleeting. The teacher needs to be aware that problems can occur in a teaching strategy and should be aware of some of the possibilities for circumventing or ameliorating those problems.

In some cases, the activity that is chosen by the teacher may not strike the children as something interesting to try. The activity is soon abandoned by the children and the teacher is left with a pile of materials and no investigations. In this case, the teacher may simply allow the children to go off to other activities and leave the set of materials available. Children may return to the materials with an activity of their own to try and investigative behavior may quickly escalate. If the materials simply go unused, let them go unused. The open-inquiry technique rarely results in this type of behavior on the part of children, but it may be a signal that the activity or the materials or both are developmentally inappropriate for the children in the group. Allow the children to move to a different activity within the educational setting.

A second problem may result when the activity chosen or the challenge issued is too difficult for the children and they have no idea how to pursue the investigation. Paper airplanes may be great fun for older children, but small children have neither the skill nor the small-muscle coordination to pursue this type of investigation. When the task is too difficult for young children, frustration and dependence rather than autonomy are likely to follow. In the case of an activity that is too difficult for children, drop back, restart the activity with a question such as "what can you do with these materials?" or "what else can we do with these materials?"

Teachers select the materials for use in an activity with adult eyes and adult possibilities in mind. Sometimes the materials that are selected are too adult for the young minds that will use them. Once again, rather than increasing autonomy and investigative behavior, the activity increases dependence on adults for direction, help, and ideas. In cases like this, a good strategy is to listen to the children and watch what they are doing, then quickly gather additional materials. The additional materials, because they are based on observations of children, are more likely to reflect the abilities and needs of the children. The key is to have a variety of materials available in the classroom that may be useful in child investigations.

Time can sometimes become a problem in open-inquiry activities, but only in those situations where the educational setting is highly structured and children must move from activity to activity. Because the investigations are highly individualistic, time limits cannot easily be set on the children's investigations. Some children will need only a few minutes to investigate to their satisfaction.

Others will continue to investigate or return again and again to their investigations. A reconsideration of the way time is managed in a highly structured setting may result in allocating additional investigation time within the program.

Parents or administrators may constitute a problem of their own. Open-inquiry teaching is far different from the traditional perception of teaching and learning found in parents who recall their own school experiences and in administrators who are not attuned to developmentally appropriate practices. Open inquiry frequently resembles free play, and should resemble free play in many of its characteristics. Play is often seen as a "waste of time" in the educational setting where young children are more and more likely to be pressured into reading, writing, and mathematics at the four- and five-year-old level. In order to ameliorate this problem of perception, parents and administrators should be educated in the technique through conferences and presentations. An effective presentation for parents or administrators is one in which the parents or administrators are involved in an open-inquiry experience followed by a discussion of the kinds of concepts being developed during the experience.

Questions in the Open-Inquiry Experience

In the traditional setting, the role of the teacher is to ask questions that will direct the students toward a particular bit of content information. Since open-inquiry does not strive to teach particular bits of content, the use of questions in the traditional sense does not suit the teaching strategy. The use of questions in open inquiry is important, but the use of questions must be appropriate.

The role of questions in the open-inquiry experience is to provide the child with an opportunity to communicate what is being done or what was done in the investigation. The teacher should encourage the child to talk about what is happening through questions and requests such as the following:

- "This looks interesting. What are you trying?"
- "Tell us about the kinds of things you did with the squeeze bottles."
- "What did you use to get this to happen?"

- "Show us some of the ways you got the blocks to move."
- "What did you mix together? What happened?"

A second role for questions in the open-inquiry strategy is to guide children into other possible investigations without dictating what should or must be done. In this case, questions and requests such as the following can be used:

- "How could I use the string to move these objects?"
- "I wonder what would happen if . . ."
- "How else could I use these blocks?"
- "What could we do to the clay to get it to float?"
- "Let's see who can . . ."

Questions are also used in open inquiry to get children to convey to others what has been done and what has been discovered. This use of questions should not be misconstrued to mean that students should be expected to draw a particular conclusion but rather that they should be able to tell others one or more interesting things they did with the materials or that they found as a result of using the materials.

In order to facilitate discussion of activities that have been completed, the teacher can sequence questions in a way that develops and extends ideas. In this case, there are four stages in questioning.

Stage One: Asking for the Obvious. At this stage, the teacher is trying to have the children recall what was done or what senses were used. Sample questions include

- "What is _____?"
- "What do you (smell, taste, hear, feel, see)?"
- "How many _____?"

Stage Two: Making Associations. At this stage, the teacher is trying to develop the child's ability to see relationships among and between objects or ideas. Sample questions include

- "What else is like this?"
- "What other objects float like the block?"
- "Where have you seen something like this before?"

Stage Three: Considering Cause and Effect. At this stage, the teacher is beginning to direct the attention of the students toward ideas of cause and effect that are based on the activities and the experiences of the children. Sample questions include

- "What could cause _____?"
- "How could we find out?"
- "What are some other ways we could do it?"

Stage Four: Developing Imagination. At this stage, the teacher is asking the children to extend the activity into new areas by having students make predictions for new activities. Sample questions include

- "What would happen if _____?"
- "What would we need to do to make these _____?"
- "How could we make something different happen?"

This is a good time to begin a written record of what children are doing. Children of three, four, and five may not be able to read the written record, but such a record demonstrates the connection between the spoken and written word and also indicates that the teacher values the communications of the students. A written record also provides an invaluable record of the kinds of activities carried out by the children. Such a record can be used to plan additional activities and materials or to show parents the accomplishments of their children.

Questions should not be used in open inquiry to direct children to causal explanations beyond those of direct experience and immediacy in time and space. The ability of young children to identify cause-and-effect relationships beyond these limited boundaries is virtually nonexistent. Consequently, cause-and-effect explanations have little, if any, meaning for the young child. The explanation of "why" is the explanation of the adult. The explanation of "what" is the explanation of the child. A young child can tell you what happened when a marble was dropped into a container of water but cannot be expected to tell why the water splashed higher when the marble was tossed into the container than when the marble was gently dropped from an inch above the water.

LEARNING ACTIVITY 14

Teaching with Open Inquiry

Purpose: The purpose of this activity is to carry out an open-inquiry activity with a group of three-, four-, and/or five-year-old children including both implementation of the activity and evaluation of the success of the activity.

Procedure:

1. Select an open-inquiry activity, either one of your own design or one from this text.
2. Collect the materials that will be needed.
3. Decide on how you will initiate the activity with a group of children.
4. Do the activity with the children, including a follow-up discussion.
5. Evaluate the activity and the follow-up. What do you think worked particularly well? Why do you think that worked so well? What problems did you encounter while conducting the activity? How did you overcome those problems? What could you have done differently so as to avoid the kinds of problems encountered?

LEARNING ACTIVITY 15

Comparing Open-Inquiry and Traditional Teaching

Purpose: The purpose of this activity is to provide a comparison of traditional teaching to open-inquiry teaching at the preschool or kindergarten levels.

Procedure:

1. Select a traditional physical science activity that is used at either the kindergarten or the preschool level.
2. Develop an open-inquiry activity that is based on the traditional activity, including the introduction, activity, and follow-up ideas.
3. Try the traditional activity with a small group of children. Describe the reactions of the children to the activity and your own reaction to the activity.
4. Wait at least three days, then try the open-inquiry activity with the same group of children. Describe the reactions of the children to the activity and your own reaction to the activity.
5. Compare the two activities in terms of developmental appropriateness and student interest. Draw a conclusion about which of the activities was most successful.

Finally, questions should not be used with open-inquiry activities in order to force children to parrot back some fact or vocabulary term predetermined by the teacher. This is not to say that new vocabulary cannot be used as the teacher talks with the children. The words *force* and *energy* may be used naturally by the teacher as he or she talks with children about the investigations they conducted. But each time the new terminology is used, a definition, preferably in the form of an illustration using materials, should be included. At no time should the teacher expect all children to use the terms or to use them correctly and concisely. It is, however, surprising how quickly children will pick up on the new words and begin to use them. The children will use new terminology when that terminology is understood. They will simply repeat words when those words are not understood.

SUMMARY

Open-inquiry experiences are developmentally appropriate for the young child in terms of both cognitive and social development. The open-inquiry activity, because of its flexibility, allows the young child to investigate materials and phenomena at a level that is commensurate with the level of ability of the child. The child selects the activity. The child pursues the investigation. The child determines which problems will be solved and which will be ignored. The child constructs the knowledge for which he or she is developmentally ready. The use of open inquiry, then, becomes a no-fail approach to teaching the young child that is based on four steps of planning. The teacher must decide (1) what is to be done, (2) what materials are to be used, (3) how to initiate the activity, and (4) how to follow up the activity. The teacher is instrumental in developing the initiating activity, but the child is the focal point and sole determinant of the direction and outcome of the activity.

Although open inquiry is no-fail for the child, it is not a no-fail situation for the teacher. Problems can occur in open-inquiry teaching. The most common of these problems are selecting an activity that is unappealing to children, selecting too difficult a starting point, selecting inappropriate materials, time constraints, and interference from parents or administrators. Each of these problems, however, can be solved so that the open-inquiry experience is successful for both teacher and student.

Vocabulary Terms

Action on Objects: a child's interaction with concrete materials as part of the learning experience.
Co-Investigator: a role played by the teacher in the open-inquiry approach in which she or he investigates along with the children without directing the activity.
Decision Making: a property of open-inquiry teaching that allows for self-determination on the part of the child.
Investigative Behavior: any activity, usually involving the use of concrete materials, on the part of a child that permits inquiry into a particular phenomenon.
Open-Inquiry Teaching: a free-form teaching strategy in which students are active investigators of the environment.

Problem Solving: a way of thinking and investigating that results in a solution appropriate to a particular situation or in an answer to a child-posed question.

Study Questions

1. What are the characteristics of open inquiry as a teaching strategy?
2. How does open-inquiry teaching differ from traditional teaching of science and mathematics?
3. What are the benefits of open-inquiry teaching?
4. Describe the way in which an open-inquiry lesson is planned.
5. What kinds of problems can occur in using open-inquiry teaching? What suggestions can you make for overcoming each of these problems?
6. What is the role of questions in an open-inquiry lesson? How does this role differ from that of questions in a traditional teaching approach?
7. Children have been investigating how objects and water react to one another. As the teacher, how could you use this activity to enhance the language skills of children?
8. A teacher tells you that he likes to use open inquiry in his kindergarten class but has one concern. He introduces new vocabulary words before the children begin an activity but finds that when they are involved in or discussing the activity, they do not use the new words. What suggestions would you make to this teacher?
9. You begin an activity designed to give students experience bouncing objects. Some children decide to see if they can knock down a tower made from foam blocks. Your classroom aide goes to the children knocking down the tower and tells them to put away the blocks and get back to what they are supposed to be doing. What is wrong with the way your aide handled the situation? What would be a better reaction to this unexpected activity?

PART TWO

The Combined Curriculum

INTRODUCTION

At the first- and second-grade levels, the child continues to be the focus and source of the curriculum. Six- and seven-year-old children, through their social and developmental characteristics, provide the foundation for the pattern of curriculum advocated at this level.

The child of six or seven is similar to and yet different from the preschooler or kindergartener. Consequently, as the child changes, so too should the curriculum change. A major change in the curriculum should begin to directly address the areas of science and mathematics but should not yet fully differentiate between the two areas. By providing some differentiation, children can begin to develop the skills and concepts particular to each area. But, by continuing to combine the areas, students can continue to develop the problem-solving and critical-thinking skills that are common to both areas. Additionally, the later preoperational, or early concrete operational, child does not fully differentiate between subject areas. Consequently, combining the areas of science and mathematics rather than fully differentiating between the two is more developmentally appropriate than the traditional discrete subject-matter approach.

The content selected for the curriculum at the first- and second-grade levels should be based on the characteristics of the first- and second-grade child rather than on tradition or on adult perceptions of what is considered "easy content." The topics should, first of all, allow children to develop concepts rather than simply memorize unrelated facts or definitions of new vocabulary terms. Instead, the topics selected should allow children to see the interrelationships within content and relate the facts and words to one another as understanding of the world develops. For example, students might be involved in working with the topic of classification. Some activities involve leaves, rocks, and shells while others deal with the classification of objects by shape, weight, or number of objects in a set. In the first case, science concepts about the structure of leaves or the constitution of rocks are being developed; in the second case, solid shapes and numbers are being considered. This concept of developing understanding through combining the areas of science and mathematics leads to the second consideration in the selection of content. The selection of content should always be based on what the child is able to comprehend rather than on what the child can memorize or on what will be needed at some future time. Young children, with their ability to acquire new words easily, can give the appearance of learning by parroting back words like molecule, atom, electron, extinction, or even plate tectonics. Since these words appear in chemistry, biology, and geology texts, the child seems to be receiving background information that will assure later success in the sciences. Unfortunately, the ability to recall and repeat the appropriate word in answer to a question does not indicate understanding. To develop understanding, the first- and second-grade child needs to develop relationships between subject matter areas. The development of relationships must be deliberately fostered through the curriculum. When attention is given to relationships and understanding, the curricular pattern that emerges is the combined curriculum.

The combined curriculum is based on the child's social skills and changing cognitive characteristics. The combined curriculum begins to differentiate between mathematics and science but does not fully separate the two subject-matter areas. In order to facilitate the combining of the two subject-matter areas, the combined curriculum is concerned with the development of science process skills rather than science content and the development of mathematical concepts rather than arithmetical computation. In this curricular pattern, observation, classification, communication, using numbers, using space relations, and investigating operational questions become more important than identifying plant parts, knowing the categories of vertebrate animals, or describing changes in the moon over a month. Likewise, the mathematics ideas of patterning, comparing, classifying, graphing, and problem solving are more important than computing answers to addition, subtraction, multiplication, or division problems. The combined curriculum does have specific outcomes, but those outcomes are designed to be developmentally appropriate to the children participating in the curriculum. Developing a graph of the shapes of leaves found on the playground and then using the graph to solve a problem such as which leaf shape is the most common can have a definite outcome that can be evaluated by the teacher. Not only is there a particular outcome to the activity, but graphing is developmentally appropriate. And, finally, because selection of content and teaching strategies for the combined curriculum are based on the cognitive and social characteristics of the child, the combined curriculum focuses on success for all children.

CHAPTER 5

Developmental Characteristics of Six and Seven Year Olds

Chapter Objectives

On completion of this chapter, you should be able to

1. list the developmental characteristics of six and seven year olds,

2. discuss the developmental characteristics of six and seven year olds,

3. compare the six- or seven-year-old child to younger children,

4. discuss the term *at risk* as it applies to the young child,

5. discuss some of the characteristics of children who are considered to be at risk, and

6. discuss the appropriateness of the combined curriculum format for children at risk.

Preschool and kindergarten children come to school eager to play, investigate, and interact verbally and physically with other children and the teacher. They have opportunities during the day to climb, build, paint, listen, and talk. Preschool and kindergarten classrooms are busy, active, often noisy places.

Then, as that same active, noisy, self-organizing child leaves kindergarten and moves into first grade, the environment changes. There are little desks placed in neat rows, each desk with its own chair so that only one child may occupy the desk at a time. Books, papers, and pencils replace toys and materials. The small, flexible, child-organized groups of kindergarten are replaced by individual work, usually done while seated behind one of those little desks on one of those individual chairs. The teacher expects quiet. The clock dictates what is to be done and when. The consistent praise for accomplishments is replaced by grades based on criteria determined by someone, somewhere. Suddenly, the child is expected to conform to the environment as it is established by the school and the teacher.

By the end of first grade, the child has generally learned to sit still, do the assigned work, be quiet, and leave investigation of the world for play time rather than school time.

The entrance into second grade holds few surprises. The child knows what is expected during the school day and, with the usual sort of reminders, works within those expectations.

The traditional classroom at the first- and second-grade levels is generally closer in appearance and practice to a sixth-grade classroom than to a kindergarten classroom. Is this the direction that should be taken or should the first two grades of school more closely resemble kindergarten? The developmental characteristics of the six or seven year old can help answer this question.

SIX AND SEVEN YEAR OLDS

Children of six or seven years of age are generally in the early concrete operational stage of development. This generally means that children are likely to use concrete operational thought processes to solve one problem and preoperational thought

processes to solve another. In some ways they are very much like the younger children at the kindergarten level, but in other ways they are far different.

Developmental Similarities Among Kindergarten, First-Grade, and Second-Grade Children

The child of six or seven is generally still egocentric in his or her thought processes. Like the younger child, the six or seven year old continues to see a single point of view and to center that point of view around herself or himself.

Although egocentricity is decreasing, it is still manifested in a variety of ways, one of which is the tendency to center on one characteristic or trait and to exclude others. The six or seven year old, in classifying, may notice that all of the buttons have four holes but may not notice that some are plastic and some wood until attention is called to the materials from which the buttons are made.

The six or seven year old is also similar to the younger child in his or her ability to think in a forward direction but not to reverse that thought pattern. Children will see that six pieces of candy plus five pieces of candy results in a total of eleven pieces of candy but will generally not immediately understand that eleven pieces of candy minus five pieces of candy will result in six remaining pieces.

In terms of reasoning ability, the early concrete operational child continues to use transductive reasoning and precausal forms of cause and effect. Cause and effect remains accessible to the child as long as the cause is related to the effect by immediacy in space and time. Precausality is, however, declining as the search for true cause and effect strengthens in the child.

The six or seven year old is also similar to the young child in considering the concepts of some versus all. Because class inclusion has not yet developed, the six or seven year old may consider part of a set of objects to be greater than the total set. For example, given a set of pictures of fifteen vehicles comprised of ten cars and five trucks, the six or seven year old is likely to respond that there are more cars than vehicles. The part is seen as greater than the whole.

Also like the younger child, the six or seven year old views space in a topological form where squares can become triangles and triangles can become circles if they are stretched in the proper manner.

Finally, the six and seven year old is similar to the younger child in terms of need for concrete materials if learning is to be meaningful. Children at the early concrete operational level need to be involved in an active investigation and manipulation of the environment. In fact, when a child no longer manipulates materials, learning becomes more and more verbalistic and less conceptualistic. Children learn words that they can repeat at the appropriate time, but do not have an understanding of the meaning of those words.

If all of these characteristics are similar to those of younger children, how does the six or seven year old differ from younger children?

Developmental Differences

A striking difference between the child of six or seven and a younger child lies in the development of conservation of number. Indeed, the attainment of conservation of number is the signal of the entrance into concrete operations. The attainment of conservation of number also indicates the attainment of additional thinking skills including one-to-one correspondence, order, and hierarchical inclusion. One-to-one correspondence, present in six and seven year olds, is demonstrated easily by the child who conserves. The creation of a row of objects identical to the teacher's is now easy for the child. Order is simply the ability to count each object within a large set of objects once and only once. Hierarchical inclusion is the concept that the quantity 1 is included as a part of the quantity 2 and that the quantity 3 includes both 1 and 2. The attainment of conservation of number means that the child is no longer tied to perceptions but is able to determine that the pattern of arrangement of objects can change without causing a change in the quantity. The child is now able to explain that the change in arrangement of objects in conservation-of-number tasks does not affect quantity. In general, this explanation takes three forms: reversibility argument, compensation argument, and identity argument. The reversibility argument is used when the child says, "The rows are the same because you can put this one back the way it was." The identity argument is used when the child explains, "You didn't take any away or add any so they must be the

same." And, the compensation argument occurs when the child states, "This row looks like more because the spaces between are bigger." Whichever argument is used, the child realizes that quantity and arrangement are distinct from each other.

A second difference between six and seven year olds and younger children is in the ability to classify. While younger children are using patterns or pictures, the six or seven year old is classifying more consistently by a single trait. The ability to classify by color or smell or texture develops. However, children of six may be less consistent in the use of a trait than will seven year olds. The six year old may begin by classifying according to color and then move within the same classification system to shape or texture, while the seven year old will use color as the sole criterion within a particular system.

Children of six or seven are able to develop a seriation based on a single characteristic. However, the successful completion of this seriation is based on trial and error rather than on a logical pattern of development.

Six and seven year olds still frequently talk for themselves alone without trying to gain the attention of others. Monologue is still important at this age and the child will often carry on a soliloquy even in the company of others. However, conversation and the ability of children to converse with others is also developing beyond the level of skill shown by the younger child. Although the child's egocentricity still makes conversation with others difficult, there is a greater attempt on the part of the six or seven year old to make others understand what is being said. Child-to-adult conversation is developing rapidly as the adult tries to fully understand what is being said by the child. However, children still appear to understand a great deal more than they actually comprehend. Children have a wide variety of ways of pretending to understand including the use of facial expression, nodding, and simply answering "Yes" when asked if they understand. In the classroom, it is unusual for a first-grade child to respond to the question "Does everyone understand?" with anything other than a "Yes." At about seven or seven and a half, children do begin to ask for clarification if they do not understand what is said. However, both six and seven year olds may complicate the situation by pretending not to understand. They may, for example, invent answers to questions for which they really do know the answer.

Also changing is the meaning of the ubiquitous "Why." No longer is "Why" used to ask purpose. "Why" is now used to request causality. The "why" is turning from a why of purpose to a why of cause. Now, children who ask, "Why is the sky blue?" are actually asking for an explanation of the cause rather than for the purpose of the blue sky. However, all why questions are not asking for causality. Whys of justification are also beginning to be used. The child who asks, "Why do I have to wear good shoes to church?" is asking for the justification behind the required mode of dress. These justification questions are a sign of the child's curiosity about a whole set of customs and rules that are imposed from outside, seemingly without motive, and for which he or she would like to find a reason.

Finally, genuine argument and collaboration are beginning to develop. Before seven years of age, children's arguments tend to be simple clashes of statements without any justification or delineation of respective points of view. In fact, until approximately seven years of age, children make no effort to stick to one opinion on any given subject. They do not believe what is self-contradictory, but they adopt successive opinions, which if compared, would contradict one another. For example, a child who comes into the cafeteria with a lunch box containing a tuna sandwich may have been looking forward to lunch all day. Tuna sandwiches are her favorite kind of sandwich. She sits down with a group of children who are discussing lunches and who all agree that the absolutely worst thing to find inside a lunch box is a tuna sandwich. Suddenly, the child who was so happy with her lunch hates tuna sandwiches and tells the others that she must have gotten her brother's lunch by mistake. This child does not both love and hate tuna sandwiches. Instead, she loved them at the start of lunch but hated them as soon as she heard the conversation. Thus, the opinions are successive rather than simultaneous.

The child of six or seven is far more like the child of five than the child of twelve. The developmental traits of the first- or second-grade child indicate that teaching and classroom atmosphere or structure should be more similar to that of kindergarten than sixth grade.

CHILDREN AT RISK

Children are said to be at risk when they have been exposed to certain adverse factors. In general, three categories of at-risk children are identified. Children at established risk include those with diagnosed medical disorders such as mental retardation, physical or growth deviations, or Downs syndrome. Children at biological risk include those who were exposed to toxic chemicals, born prematurely, or who have infections. Children at environmental risk include those who are in an unhealthy environment or who had early experiences that are a threat to their developmental or physical well-being. Children who are living in unnurturing, depriving, or substandard environments are more likely to develop slowly and show depressed intellectual, language, and academic performance.

Disabilities also put children at risk. A disability refers to any of a variety of conditions that can interfere with a child's ability to perform like an average child. Disabilities include sensory, physical, speech or language, cognitive, behavior, or developmental deficits.

School demands make a child's strengths and weaknesses more apparent. At school, children must be independent. Many children who are at risk because of disabilities do not possess the degree of independence necessary for school success. In addition, children in school are expected to adhere to certain time-frame expectations. Children at environmental risk, especially those from impoverished backgrounds, may never have been required to follow a particular routine and so will find working on particular tasks at particular times unfamiliar, making adaptation to the new routine difficult. A child with motor problems that makes use of hands difficult may previously have been given all of the time necessary to complete a task. Along with the necessity of adhering to a particular set of time expectations is the requirement of completing particular tasks. Once again, the at-risk child may find certain tasks more difficult and less meaningful than children who are not at risk. And, finally, the school environment expects mastery of particular concepts. Those concepts may be at odds with the perceptions that an at-risk child has gained from the home environment. Children who are continually told that good luck or bad luck cause things to happen may have little understanding that they have control over their environment and even less understanding of cause and effect. It is also more than possible that the at-risk child may not be ready for those concepts. Children who have had no experience with growing plants are unlikely to be ready to consider how different kinds of seeds grow.

Children at Environmental Risk

Children at environmental risk are most frequently those who come to school from impoverished backgrounds. Such homes are often chaotic, disorganized, and noisy. Children from such an environment are overstimulated with a barrage of disorganized and unmeaningful information or experiences. But all impoverished homes are not overstimulating or disorganized. Some impoverished homes understimulate children. Such understimulating environments lack toys, educational materials, paper, crayons, books, and other items that promote learning. Materials such as blocks and clay that allow for constructive play are also lacking. And the kind of intellectual interaction with adults that promotes language development and thinking at increasingly sophisticated levels often does not occur in impoverished homes. There are often fewer adults and more children. Parents are often missing so children are left with grandparents or older siblings. Even when parents are present, language stimulation is often low. Parents of low socioeconomic status are less likely to interact verbally with children than are parents of higher socioeconomic stature.

The result of these impoverished environmental conditions is children who are not prepared to benefit from the traditional school program. The verbal orientation of school is inappropriate for children of low verbal ability. The very orderliness of school may cause it to seem foreign, even frightening, to the child from an impoverished background. Because children from impoverished homes lack certain kinds of experiences, their developmental level may differ from that of average children. The combined curriculum is especially appropriate for children from impoverished backgrounds because it is based on interaction with the environment, the development of concepts, and has a certain amount of structure without seeming foreign to the child.

Children at Sensory Risk

Hearing Impairments. Hearing impairments result in a reduction of the sensory input received by the child. The most obvious way in which this reduction affects the child is in the area of language development. And because language is a vital component of thinking, there may also be an impairment in the child's ability to reason or use problem-solving skills. As children progress in school, learning and teaching become more and more verbal so that the child with a hearing impairment and its concomitant language development problem may fall further and further behind his or her classmates. The emphasis on activity combined with meaningful communication enhances the hearing impaired child's conceptual and language development.

Delays in speech and language development, however, are not the only result of hearing impairments. Children who experience difficulty with language often have been socially isolated at a time when working with other children and peer group membership is becoming important.

Visual Impairments. Visual impairments often result in impairments in three areas: language, motor skills, and cognitive development. Language development is impaired because it takes longer for visually impaired children to acquire concepts of concrete objects and so longer to acquire names for those objects. A child who has never seen a tiger at a zoo or a photograph of a tiger in a book has great difficulty in developing the concept behind the word *tiger*. Blind children, in addition to having difficulties in acquisition of concrete terms, may be a year behind average children in working with words and phrases out of context. Motor development is impaired because visually impaired children are delayed in reaching, crawling, and walking. Because of impaired motor development, spatial concepts are commonly deficient. Finally, cognitive development is slowed because visually impaired children are more likely to deal with the environment in concrete rather than abstract

LEARNING ACTIVITY 16

Teacher Interview: Children with Varying Cultural Backgrounds

Purpose: The purpose of this activity is to interview a first- or second-grade teacher who works with children from various cultural backgrounds.

Procedure:

1. Prepare a series of questions for a classroom teacher at the first- or second-grade level that examine the following areas:

   a. the various cultural backgrounds that are represented by the children in the classroom,

   b. the effect of the various cultures on the way in which the children learn,

   c. the benefits to the teacher and to the class of having children in the group who come from a variety of cultural backgrounds,

   d. the difficulties that arise from having children in the group who come from a variety of cultural backgrounds,

   e. changes that the teacher has made in order to accommodate the program to children from differing cultural backgrounds, and

   f. sources that the teacher uses to obtain more information about the various cultures represented by the children in the classroom.

2. Interview a teacher using the questions and record the responses.

3. Summarize the responses in writing.

Cautions:

1. If you plan to tape record the interview, be certain to ask permission from the teacher in advance.

2. Accept responses as given without making any judgments.

3. Use follow-up questions to help clarify responses to the interview questions.

4. Do not use the teacher's name in your written report or identify the teacher or school in any way.

---

terms. Because the combined curriculum emphasizes interaction with concrete materials and active investigation of the environment, it is particularly appropriate to the visually impaired child.

Visual impairments place the child at risk because of the deficit in background experiences on which the young child can build. Learning requires more time, more practice, more verbal mediation, and more encouragement from adults.

Orthopedic or Neurological Impairments. The impact of orthopedic or neurological impairments is that motor functioning is delayed. Children in this category often have been hospitalized for lengthy and repeated periods of time. Because of hospital stays, some orthopedically or neurologically impaired children have difficulty in forming attachments to adults or to other children. They may appear unresponsive. Other children in this category will show excessive dependency on adults.

The main result of orthopedic or neurological impairments is the interference that occurs in mastery of motor skills. This impairment results because movement patterns, including voluntary-gross and fine-motor actions, are restricted. Interference may also result from delays in physical growth.

In the classroom, orthopedic handicaps may result in the child having difficulty in participating in some activities. The small-muscle manipulations necessary for using mathematics manipulatives or science materials may not be available to the child. The child who is wheelchair bound may not be able to reach materials easily or approach the kinds of surfaces necessary for activities; table tops, sand tables, water tables, sinks, or shelves may be too high or low or may be unapproachable because of their location in the classroom.

Health Disorders. Health disorders can put a child at educational risk. Among the health disorders that can place a child at risk are leukemia, cystic fibrosis, congenital heart defects, and sickle cell anemia.

The impact of health disorders affects both the child and the parent. The child becomes more and more insecure and dependent and so does not develop the autonomy and independence of his or her peers. The child also has less chance to participate in early learning experiences. Parents may withdraw from the child, overindulge the child, or over-accommodate to the child thus causing difficulties with interpersonal relationships.

The tendency toward dependency puts the child at risk because of the emphasis on independence in the classroom. However, the emphasis of the combined curriculum on child autonomy promotes independence and so is appropriate for the child delayed in this area. Additionally, the lack of full participation may result in developmental delay or in lack of general background knowledge. Once again, the combined curriculum provides for the full participation in learning that is necessary for the construction of knowledge.

Speech or Language Impairments. Speech and language impairments include articulation difficulties such as omissions, substitutions, additions, and distortions, as well as problems with the fluency, volume, or pitch of the voice. Delayed language may be due to the child having little chance to use language. The child may be ignored or neglected but he or she may also have had all wishes anticipated and so have never acquired the communication skills so easily learned by the typical child.

The impact of such deficits can put the child at risk for a variety of reasons. The child may lack a functional or age-appropriate communication system and so be unable to communicate effectively with peers or adults. Such difficulty with communication interferes with social interactions and often has an adverse effect on interpersonal relations. Speech or language impairments also place limitations on ability to communicate needs or ideas and may have a negative effect on self-image. And, because most cognitive tasks are verbal in nature, the speech- or language-impaired child may appear to have deficits that do not actually exist: A concept may actually exist in the child's mind, but she or he may not have the language to express it. However, the emphasis in the combined curriculum on meaningful vocabulary development can assist the speech- or language-impaired child in developing necessary vocabulary. Communication also can be enhanced through the use of alternative methods of communicating ideas, including written, pictorial, or computer-aided techniques. And the use of open-ended activities and emphasis on success make this curriculum pattern particularly appropriate.

Children at Cognitive Risk

Mental Retardation. Children who are classified as mentally retarded are frequently mainstreamed into the regular classroom. Although most children are mainstreamed only if classroom placement is appropriate, there will still be some differences between the retarded child and the average child. The retarded child, of course, has a reduced ability to learn. Attention deficits and language deficiencies contribute to this reduced ability. Additionally, mentally retarded children often show deficits in the functional skills needed for daily living as well as in social skills. Children who have difficulty in interacting with other children often find themselves on the edge of the social arena.

The mentally retarded child in the regular classroom will probably be at a cognitive developmental level different from that of the average child. Such students will often be preoperational when the majority of average children have made the transition to concrete operations. As a result, some activities of the combined curriculum may need to be modified in order to take into account the different level of cognitive functioning. The mentally retarded child also may need extra help in following or interpreting directions. Finally, the mentally retarded child may need simplification when a variety of materials or choices are offered.

Academically Gifted. Although at-risk children are generally considered to be those with impairments, the gifted child may also be at risk. Gifted children are too often seen as miniature adults capable of putting aside the materials of childhood and taking on the verbally oriented techniques of adult learning. However, gifted children are still children who are actively involved in investigating their environment. Indeed, the gifted child needs to explore with concrete materials as much, if not more, than the average child. The gifted child not yet ready for abstract learning is just as likely as the average child to resist learning. The gifted child can also experience frustration and boredom when

LEARNING ACTIVITY 17

Teacher Interview: Children Mainstreamed into the Classroom

Purpose: The purpose of this activity is to interview a first- or second-grade teacher who works with children with handicapping conditions who have been mainstreamed into the regular classroom.

Procedure:
1. Prepare a series of questions for a classroom teacher at the first- or second-grade level that consider the following areas:
   a. the handicapping conditions that the mainstreamed children have,
   b. the effect of the handicapping conditions on the ways in which the children learn,
   c. the benefits to the teacher and to the class of having children in the group who have handicapping conditions,
   d. the difficulties that arise from having children in the group who have handicapping conditions,
   e. changes that the teacher has made in order to accommodate the handicapped child, and
   f. sources that the teacher uses to obtain more information about the handicapping conditions of the students.
2. Interview a teacher using the questions and record the responses.
3. Summarize the responses in writing.

Cautions:
1. If you plan to tape record the interview, be certain to ask permission from the teacher in advance.
2. Accept responses as given without making any judgments.
3. Use follow-up questions to help clarify responses to the interview questions.
4. Do not use the teacher's name in your written report or identify the teacher or school in any way.

---

confronted with tasks that are too easy or repetitive. The gifted child needs to be challenged to demonstrate and extend her or his abilities. The combined curriculum, with its emphasis on open-ended, student-directed activity, is especially appropriate for the gifted child.

WORKING WITH CHILDREN AT RISK

The following is a list of suggestions for working with the at-risk child in the regular classroom.

1. Arrange the classroom to allow for activities for individual children, small groups, or pairs.
2. Arrange space for flexibility so that a variety of activities appropriate to all kinds of children are possible simultaneously. Accommodate wheelchairs, walkers, or other devices to allow orthopedically handicapped children participation and mobility.
3. Plan storage of manipulatives and concrete materials so that all items can be easily obtained by all investigating children. If orthopedically handicapped children are wheelchair-bound, put materials on low, easily accessible shelves. Labels showing pictures, color coding, or use of braille may also assist in accessibility.
4. Use visual cues, verbal prompts, pictures, and other assists to allow all students the opportunity to participate fully. Assign partners when necessary to facilitate interaction.
5. Allow for a variety of modes of response to questions and other activities including words, pictures, signs, or signals or any format appropriate to the child.
6. For children who are easily distracted, remove some of the distractions from the materials or limit the choices provided.
7. Make the materials used in the classroom familiar. When possible, use common everyday materials. If unfamiliar materials are to be used, allow time for children to investigate and become familiar with them.
8. Allow for open-ended activities in which children can work successfully at their own ability

LEARNING ACTIVITY 18

Teacher Interview: Gifted Children in the Classroom

Purpose: The purpose of this activity is to interview a first- or second-grade teacher who works with gifted children in the regular classroom.

Procedure:
1. Prepare a series of questions for a classroom teacher at the third-grade level that consider the following areas:
   a. the characteristics of gifted children in the regular classroom,
   b. the effect of a child's giftedness on the way in which the child learns,
   c. the benefits to the teacher and to the class of having gifted children in the classroom,
   d. the difficulties that arise from having gifted children in the classroom,
   e. changes that the teacher has made in order to accommodate the gifted child, and
   f. sources that the teacher uses to obtain more information about working with gifted children in the classroom.
2. Interview a teacher using the questions and record the responses.
3. Summarize the responses in writing.

Cautions:
1. If you plan to tape record the interview, be certain to ask permission from the teacher in advance.
2. Accept responses as given without making any judgments.
3. Use follow-up questions to help clarify responses to the interview questions.
4. Do not use the teacher's name in your written report or identify the teacher or school in any way.

---

levels. Activities can be structured so that children at both the preoperational and concrete operational levels of development can succeed.

9. Emphasize appropriate vocabulary but be certain the vocabulary is meaningful to the children. Introduce proper terms after students have had a chance to develop concepts through the use of materials.
10. Establish a set of positively phrased work rules and adhere to those rules. Children need to know what is expected of them and usually like the security of knowing the limits. For children who are insecure due to health impairments, the establishment of rules provides a feeling of safety. For the child from a disorganized, chaotic background, the rules help the child know what is expected and allow him or her to begin to make sense of the environment.
11. Develop activities that are multisensory in nature. Children who are visually impaired or hearing impaired should be able to successfully approach an activity through other appropriate senses.

SUMMARY

The child of six or seven has characteristics that are both similar to and different from younger children. Children at the first- and second-grade level are similar to younger children in that they are still egocentric, lack reversible thinking, use transductive and precausal forms of reasoning, consider space from a topological viewpoint, and require concrete materials to learn well.

Children of six or seven differ from younger children in that they are able to conserve number, use a single trait to classify objects, and use simple seriation. They are also beginning to converse rather than use monologue, are changing the meaning of "why" questions from the "why of purpose" to the "why of causality" or "why of justification," and are beginning to carry on arguments in which points of view and reasons are exchanged.

The child who is at risk is one who may not be able to fully benefit from the school program. Children at environmental risk often come from impoverished homes where the type of stimulation

LEARNING ACTIVITY 19

Community Resources for the at-Risk Child

Purpose: The purpose of this activity is to research your community in order to develop an understanding of resources available for working with at-risk children.

Procedure:

1. Research the problem of children at risk particularly at the early-childhood education level, as it relates to your own community.

2. Develop a file of community resources that you, as a teacher, could call on for assistance in working effectively with children who are at risk.

LEARNING ACTIVITY 20

Resource File

Purpose: The purpose of this activity is to develop a resource file of ideas and activities for working with children who are at risk.

Procedure:

1. Develop a resource file of ideas and activities for working with children at risk in the regular classroom.

2. Include the following areas:

   a. hands-on activities for vocabulary development,

   b. suggestions for adapting hands-on activities for children with visual, hearing, or orthopedic handicaps,

   c. ideas for enrichment activities,

   d. suggestions for showing the contributions made by people from various cultures to science and mathematics,

   e. ideas for teaching children about careers that use science and mathematics, and

   f. ideas for showing the relationship of science and mathematics to daily living.

and experiences needed for school success are lacking. Children at sensory risk are those who have impairments that delay their development. Children who are hearing impaired, visually impaired, orthopedically or neurologically impaired, deficient in speech or language, or have continuing health problems would be placed in this category. Finally, there are children who are at cognitive risk. These children fall into two categories: mentally retarded and gifted.

Vocabulary Terms

Academically Gifted: a characteristic in some children that enables them to learn at a more rapid rate than average children.

Biological Risk: a risk of academic failure in some children due to exposure to toxic chemicals, premature birth, or infection.

Class Inclusion: the ability to determine that a subset is included as a part of the total set of objects; includes the concept of some versus all.

Cognitive Risk: a risk of academic failure in some children due to differences in rate of learning.

Combined Curriculum: a curricular pattern that results from the combining of science process skills and mathematics concepts through activities and investigations.

Compensation Argument: an explanation used by children who conserve number that states that one set of objects appears larger than another because of larger spaces between the items in the set and not because there is a change in quantity.

Concrete Operational Stage: a stage in cognitive development of children characterized by the development of operations and the continuous development of the ability to conserve various quantities.

Conservation of Number: the ability to determine that the quantity of a set of objects remains constant even if the arrangement of the set of objects changes.

Egocentric: a characteristic of being able to look at issues or concepts from one's own point of view and not from the point of view of others.

Environmental Risk: a risk of academic failure in children with impoverished backgrounds.

Established Risk: a risk of academic failure in children diagnosed with medical disorders.

Health Disorder: any health problem, including leukemia, cystic fibrosis, heart defects, and sickle cell anemia, that puts a child at risk of academic failure.

Hearing Impairment: a condition that results in the reduction of aural sensory input and that generally affects language development.

Identity Argument: an explanation used by a child who conserves number that states that the quantity remains constant because no objects were added or taken away.

Language/Speech Impairment: any impairment that puts a child at risk of academic failure because of articulation difficulties or delayed language development.

Mentally Retarded: a characteristic in some children that makes them learn at a slower rate than average children.

Neurologic/Orthopedic Impairment: an impairment involving large- or small-muscle use that affects the development of motor functioning.

Reversibility Argument: an explanation used by children who conserve number that states that quantity remains the same because the set can be returned to its original appearance.

Reversible Thought: the ability to trace one's thought processes in a forward direction to an end point and then back to the point of origin.

Visual Impairment: an impairment that results in the reduction of visual sensory input and often affects language, motor skills, and cognitive development.

Why of Cause: a why question that asks for an explanation based on cause and effect.

Why of Purpose: a why question that asks for an explanation based on purpose rather than cause and effect.

Study Questions

1. What are the similarities and differences between the unified curriculum and the combined curriculum?
2. On what characteristics of first- and second-grade children is the combined curriculum based?
3. What are the developmental characteristics of six and seven year olds? How do six and seven year olds differ from each other?
4. How do children of six or seven differ from children at the preschool-kindergarten level?
5. What is meant by the term *at risk*?
6. What are the characteristics of children at risk at the first- and second-grade levels?
7. What are some modifications that can be made to accommodate at-risk children in the classroom?
8. How does the first- or second-grade child's understanding of number differ from that of younger children?
9. How does the meaning of "why questions" change from preschool to the first- or second-grade levels?
10. How does the six- or seven-year-old child's ability to converse with others differ from the ability of younger children to converse?

CHAPTER 6

Social Characteristics of Six and Seven Year Olds

Chapter Objectives

On completion of this chapter, you should be able to

1. list the social characteristics of six- and seven-year-old children,

2. describe the social characteristics of six- and seven-year-old children, and

3. compare the social characteristics of six- and seven-year-old children to those of younger children.

A first-year teacher was at his wits end as he described his first day of class with first graders. Two children who liked to draw cried most of the day because they could not be best friends anymore with another child in the class who had lost interest in drawing. During the science activity, the small groups broke apart into individual pursuits. And the mathematics activity was a disaster because the teacher's explicit directions about how to play the game had been changed so much by the players that the outcome was entirely unexpected. With those events as the starting point, the day deteriorated as two children got into a ten-minute argument consisting of "Did so—did not" shouted back and forth. And, finally, as the children lined up to go home for the day, everyone jockeyed to be first in line. The teacher ended the day with two aspirin and a quiet moment alone in his classroom, now empty of wiggling children chewing on pencils and talking to themselves even when asked to be quiet. He felt himself envying the second-grade teacher and wondering why he couldn't have had that group of children as first graders. They were perfect.

But are any students really perfect? Were these first graders really as troublesome as they seemed, or were they simply exhibiting the natural characteristics of six or seven year olds placed into the traditional school setting?

The six-year-old child arrives at first grade in the fall and finds a setting very different from that of kindergarten. There are desks and chairs. There are books and pencils. There are papers and crayons and scissors. The child is suddenly faced with a situation in which he or she is expected to sit still, be quiet, finish each task in a certain period of time, and reach a certain level of quality that is determined by the teacher or the school. The demands of first grade are far different from those of kindergarten and the demands of second grade are different from those of first grade.

How ready is the child of six or seven for the traditional first or second grade? The physical and social characteristics of the child can help in determining whether traditional classroom practice is appropriate.

SOCIAL CHARACTERISTICS OF SIX YEAR OLDS

Physical Activity

The six-year-old child is a bundle of activity. Because motor skills are developing, the child is restless, continuously lugging, tugging, digging, dancing, climbing, pushing, and pulling. Even when seated and supposedly quiet, the six year old bites his or her lips, chews on pencils and other objects, and wiggles. Although the six year old is rapidly developing large-and small-muscle skills, he or she can be quite awkward. This awkwardness may be the result of trying out new-found abilities and often finding the limits of those abilities. Six year olds are the children who swing too high in a swing, run too fast to stop easily, or build a tower of blocks too tall. These children need to be encouraged to keep testing rather than urged to adopt adultlike caution. Also within the area of physical activity is the development of small-muscle skills. By the age of six, handedness is well established and first graders have a definite preference for the use of the right or left hand. However, there is still some difficulty with concepts of left and right in terms of direction.

Social Interaction and Peer Groups

Six-year-old children enjoy working with other children and peer groups quickly form. The peer groups formed by six year olds tend to be small and loosely organized. Because the groups are generally based on common interests, as the interests change so do the peer groups. But, even though the composition of the peer group can change quickly, the peer group is important to the young child. It is through the supportive network of the peer group that children often receive answers to questions that adults may not understand or wish to answer. The peer group allows the transmission of information from one child to another, bypassing adults. The peer group aids in the development of autonomy and independence as the child distances himself or herself from parents in order to become a part of the group. Although it is the social aspect of peer groups that is usually emphasized, peer groups can also affect the cognitive development of a child. The peer group enhances cognitive development by functioning as a social support system and thereby fostering individual enthusiasm and curiosity. Unfortunately, children with special needs are often excluded from the peer group because they are seen as different and, therefore, undesirable. Consequently, these children may not receive the beneficial cognitive and social development that comes with belonging to a group.

As children interact more frequently with one another, particularly in situations where sharing or taking turns is required, arguments begin to occur. The arguments of six-year-old children are generally a clash of opinions without any attempt at elaboration or justification. The stereotypical child argument of "Did—did not, did—did not," is typical of this age. The argument style of the young child results from a lack of concept of causality. Without a concept of cause and effect, there is no way to justify a particular point of view. The causal terms of "because" and "since" are not used by the six year old during arguments. Arguments among six-year-old children need to be mediated by the teacher.

Withdrawal

Six-year-old children want to be the best at mathematics. They want to be the first in line. They want to have the most jelly beans. Consequently, six year olds often will withdraw from a social situation when unable to get their own way. The desire to be best in all things, however, is only one part of the reason for a child's withdrawal. A second reason for withdrawal from social situations in which a child cannot get his or her own way is that the six year old sees rules as something that can be changed unilaterally. A child who is engaged in a game suddenly may decide that one of the rules should be different and may make the change in rules without conferring with the other players. If the rule is not accepted by others or if a change in rule is made by another child, then one player may decide to go and play by his or her own rules. A third reason for a child's withdrawal may arise from the six year old's tendency to consider the process of doing something more important than the final product. An individual child's explorations may lead him or her into areas not being considered by others. Thus, a child may withdraw from a social situation in order to continue with an individual pursuit. Finally, a child's withdrawal may simply be a part of his or her egocentrism. Since the child views herself or himself as the center of all things, withdrawing may make more sense to the child than sharing or waiting for a turn.

Responsibility in Children

As six-year-old children gain autonomy and independence, they also wish for more responsibility. Six-year-old children want responsibility but tend to want that responsibility within an established routine. Children enjoy distributing papers, napkins, pencils, or cupcakes. They enjoy helping to clean up after an activity, helping younger children, or being considered responsible enough to take a note to the school office. Although they can be helpful and bubbly one moment, they can also be uncooperative and quarrelsome the next. Six year olds move from one extreme to another with great rapidity. Thus, the child who enjoyed helping to clean up after an art activity on Monday may stubbornly refuse to assist in cleaning up on Tuesday. And, on Wednesday, the same child may have difficulty deciding whether to help clean up or paint his or her arms yellow. The key in dealing with such behavior is to remember that the young child is developing and has not yet reached a level where he or she can be consistently responsible or autonomous.

Competition in Children

Competition is important for six-year-old children. As mentioned earlier, they want to be first and they want to be best. The rules used in competition are considered to have been handed down by some authority: parents, older children, teachers. Consequently, rules are something that must be obeyed. But, as anyone who has played board games with a child or who has watched children playing together knows, rules may also change. Changes in rules occur unpredictably and often are made to put the rule changer into a more favorable position. A child who is losing at a board game suddenly may decide that children wearing green shirts get an extra turn. Amazingly enough, the child making the "green shirt rule" is the only one in the game wearing a green shirt.

When unable to effect a change in rule in order to come out the winner in a game, the six year old may resort to a simple solution: cheating. Pushing a checker into a better location or counting more than one space at a time on a game board is a child's solution to the possibility of losing a game.

Finally, criticism is difficult for the child to handle. The child of six wants to be best and perceives himself or herself as best in all things. Consequently, to have one's efforts criticized as being imperfect can be devastating to the child of six.

By six and one half, the child is beginning to calm down and become more comfortable in his or her abilities. With the passage of a few more months, the child becomes a seven year old with characteristics differing from those of the younger child.

SOCIAL CHARACTERISTICS OF SEVEN YEAR OLDS

Physical Activity in the Seven Year Old

The seven-year-old child is far less restless and active than the six-year-old child. By age seven, the child calms down and begins to take life at an easier pace. Children of seven are still reckless and active in their physical activities, but their fine-motor and large-motor skills are more fully developed and their reaction times have improved. Seven-year-old children will continue to test their abilities, but their muscle control is such that they are no longer so awkward. Seven year olds are also more able than six year olds to judge their abilities. In addition, seven year olds are consistent in their application of the terms left and right to their own bodies.

Interaction and Communication

Peer groups continue to be of great importance to the child of seven. Children at this age base peer groups on mutual interests, but usually those mutual interests involve same gender grouping. For example, a peer group may form that includes boys who are interested in miniature cars. A girl interested in the same hobby may not be permitted to join the group. Similarly, girls may form a group around drawing ability and not permit a boy artist to be a member of the group.

The peer group is especially important because the seven year old is a talkative individual. The talkativeness of the seven year old may be due to the child's increasing ability to communicate effectively with other children. True conversations are possible but discussions of a causal nature are still difficult for children of this age because of their lack of a true concept of cause and effect. Conversations tend to orient around statements of fact, including elaborate descriptions of objects and events. Seven year olds also are prone to exaggerate as they tell stories and break silence more frequently than adults when working at a task.

The development of conversation also signals the beginning of true arguments in children, usually at about seven and seven and one-half years of age. The true argument occurs when children begin to confine themselves to stating their opinions instead of teasing, criticizing, or threatening one another. In addition, children engaging in arguments begin to give motives for their respective points of view. Although the teacher still needs to mediate such arguments, the purpose of the mediation is to assure that both sides are heard and a decision is made rather than to settle the argument from an adult perspective.

Independence

Children of seven are rapidly gaining in independence. As they strive to become more independent and mature, seven year olds will both stand up for their rights and turn to adults for assistance. In order to assist them in developing independence, adults need to provide a secure environment in which children can try new-found social skills without fear of serious repercussions. For example, seven year olds need to be able to argue with one another without having to be concerned that they will automatically be punished for arguing. On the other hand, seven year olds have a real desire to please adults, which can result in dependence at an age when independence should be the goal. Teachers can help children to become more independent by providing choices. For example, teachers can

LEARNING ACTIVITY 21

Observing Social Interactions Among Children

Purpose: The purpose of this activity is to observe the social interactions of six- and seven-year-old children during play.

Procedure:
1. Observe a small group of six- to seven-year-old children in a play situation for 30 to 60 minutes on at least three separate occasions.
2. Consider the following questions as you make your observations.
   a. What opportunities for cooperation arise during the play period?
   b. How does the group of children react to those opportunities for cooperation?
   c. Does the group appear to have a single leader? What are the characteristics of that leader?
   d. Are there any opportunities for rule-governed play? How do the children react to the rules?
   e. Does the small group interact with other groups during the play period? What is the result of this interaction?
   f. Is there any occasion when a child attempts to join the group in play? What is the result of this attempt?

g. Do conflicts arise during the play period? How are conflicts settled?

Cautions:
1. Always make a clear distinction between what you are actually seeing and the conclusions you are drawing. Saying there was a shoving match between two children is an observation, while saying one child is a bully is a conclusion.
2. Draw conclusions that are based on actual observations.
3. Be certain that the classroom teacher or the parents know what your purpose is for observing.
4. Place yourself in as unobtrusive a location as possible.
5. When possible, take down exact words and behaviors.
6. Treat all observations with total confidentiality.
7. Be as objective as possible. Do not allow your feelings, prejudices, or preferences to cause you to make inaccurate observations.

LEARNING ACTIVITY 22

Observing Children's Interactions in the Classroom

Purpose: The purpose of this activity is to observe the way in which children of six and seven interact with one another in the classroom.

Procedure:
1. Observe a first- or second-grade classroom for a period of 30 to 60 minutes on three separate occasions, being certain to observe a variety of subject-matter areas.
2. Consider the following questions as you make your observations.
   a. Do the children react differently to different subject-matter areas? What differences are there?

b. In what kinds of tasks are the children involved in the classroom? Do they react differently to various kinds of tasks?
c. What opportunities for cooperation are found in the classroom? How do the children react to those situations?
d. How do the children in the classroom interact with those children who are at risk in some way?

ask children whether they would prefer to clean up first or to have a snack first, whether they would prefer to work with others in a small group or to work alone. Both choices are appropriate from the viewpoint of the adult, but independence from adult authority is enhanced, along with decision making, by asking the child to make the actual choice.

Rules are important to the seven-year-old child. For such a child, the most appropriate rules are those they develop for themselves rather than those that are imposed by an outside source. Consequently, seven year olds will often define a set of acceptable rules for a game and then play cooperatively according to those rules. The rules the children develop may not be the standard rules, but they are purposeful and sensible to the players. This does not mean, however, that rules cannot be changed. In reality, rules used on Monday may be changed when the same game is played on Tuesday. Such changes in rules tend to be unilateral and unpredictable, but they are followed by the group.

Closure

Seven-year-old children are still more concerned with the process of doing an activity than they are with closure of an activity. As a result, seven year olds are likely to leave a task unfinished, at least according to an adult view of unfinished. The child ends because she or he has accomplished a sufficient amount and sees no need for further development. Children working with magnets to determine what a magnet will or will not pick up may decide, after trying a dozen objects and finding that all are picked up, that enough has been done. He or she knows what a magnet will pick up and, at that moment, is not concerned with the other side of the issue. Open-ended activities allow children to work to their satisfaction.

Differences

There are differences among children in just about any group. One child may be in a wheelchair while another uses a walker. One child may need hearing aids and another glasses. One may be Navaho, another Japanese, and still another Kenyan. Children of six years of age seem to accept such differences without difficulty and often find them interesting, though unimportant, facts. By seven,

however, differences among children are noticed and are not always treated with such acceptance. This noticing of differences can affect peer-group interactions in the classroom. Children of seven need to be assisted in understanding and accommodating differences.

SUMMARY

Children of six and seven exhibit some characteristics that are similar but also have many that are different. Because the six year old is beginning to work with other children, the first peer groups develop at about the first-grade level. These groups are loosely organized but provide the kind of support necessary for children who are trying out their newly acquired abilities and moving toward independence. As children begin to work with one another, conflicts arise. Part of the reason for the conflicts is the six year old's desire to be first and best. When children of six engage in conflict, they may withdraw or engage in arguments of the "Did —did not" variety.

By seven, peer groups are more organized but still shifting. Seven-year-old children are looking for greater autonomy and independence, but they want the approval of the teacher as well. When seven year olds reach points of conflict, their growing conversational abilities allow them to argue about their perceptions of what occurred and to begin to develop reasons and express opinions.

At the first- and second-grade levels, children begin to notice differences between themselves and other children. For the child of six, such differences tend to be unimportant, but for the seven year old, differences often are viewed as undesirable. This negative view of difference can lead to the exclusion of children from the peer group.

Vocabulary Terms

Closure: reaching a specific end-point of an activity.

Competitiveness: a form of social interaction among children in which one child tries to show greater competence than another.

Independence: the ability to function easily through self-directed behavior.

Peer Group: the age group or social group to which a child belongs.

Responsibility: the desire and ability to take control of a situation and complete a task effectively.

Social Interaction: interaction, including conversation, play, and cooperative problem solving, between and among children in a social setting.

Withdrawal: a child's voluntary removal of himself or herself from a group situation.

Study Questions

1. What are the social characteristics of six- and seven-year-old children? How do six and seven year olds differ from one another?

2. Compare and contrast the social characteristics of six and seven year olds to those of younger children.

3. What are the functions of peer groups in the lives of six- and seven-year-old children?

4. What are some reasons that six year olds choose to withdraw from an activity?

5. How does a six year old tend to view rules that are established for a game?

6. Describe the ability of seven year olds to communicate with one another and with both adults and children of other ages.

CHAPTER 7

Curriculum in the First and Second Grades

Chapter Objectives

On completion of this chapter, you should be able to

1. identify the criteria used in the selection of topics for the first- and second-grade curriculum in science and mathematics,

2. differentiate between science process and science content,

3. differentiate between mathematics and arithmetic,

4. discuss the relative appropriateness of science content, science process, arithmetic, and mathematics for the first- and second-grade child,

5. identify the science process skills that are appropriate to the first- and second-grade child,

6. identify the mathematics concepts that are appropriate to the first- and second-grade child,

7. discuss the kinds of topics that are appropriate for the first- and second-grade child, and

8. discuss how traditional topics from mathematics and science textbooks can be made more appropriate for the first- or second-grade child.

It is eight-fifteen in the morning. The children in first grade come into the classroom, go quietly to their assigned desks, pick up pencils, and begin the "morning work" that they find on their desks each day. They are silent as they work out the answers to addition problems. Any whispering is immediately silenced by the teacher who is busy taking attendance and making certain that all of the worksheets needed for the day are ready. By nine o'clock, the class is restless but it is time for math and the teacher is ready to teach the children to subtract. She writes the problem $7 - 3 =$ _____ on the chalkboard, followed by $7 - 3 =$ _____ and $3 + ? = 7$. The teacher asks, "What do I need to add to three to get seven?" A few children begin to work the problem out on their fingers, but fingers in math are forbidden and they are admonished to "think." Finally, Tanya raises her hand and tells the teacher that the answer is four. With that out of the way, the teacher returns to $7 - 3 =$ _____ and asks for the answer to that problem. No one responds. Finally, she explains that if three plus four equals seven, then seven minus three must equal four. A few more problems are demonstrated and then the children are given a worksheet of subtraction problems to do. Talking is not permitted. Students must work alone. After the math problems are completed, the children are told to get out their science books. They look at the pictures and identify the animals shown. The teacher calls on students to read the limited text that discusses how animals move. After reading about the ways animals move, the students are asked to draw pictures of an animal that crawls, an animal that hops, an animal that swims, and an animal that flies.

Across the hall from this classroom is a second first-grade classroom. Children also begin to arrive at eight-fifteen but there are no worksheets waiting on the desks and there is no silence. Instead, the children find a variety of activities for them to try. On the floor in the open area used for the reading circles are board games that involve counting. On one cluster of desks are magnets and piles of objects. At another cluster of tables are water, food coloring, and clear plastic containers. And on the floor away from the board-game area are blocks, straws, string, popsicle sticks, clay, and styrofoam along with a challenge to "Build the tallest tower in the classroom!" Some children are working in small groups. Some children are working alone.

One starts out working with a friend but decides to go off on her own to do something different. And, in the midst of the noise of discussion and sharing, one child sits quietly at a desk and looks at the pictures in a *National Geographic.*

Which of these scenarios is most appropriate for children of six or seven? The characteristics of the child will help in determining the answer.

CRITERIA FOR SELECTING TOPICS FOR THE FIRST AND SECOND GRADES

Certain principles can be applied to the selection of content for the combined curriculum for children at the first- and second-grade levels. These principles are based on the cognitive and social characteristics of the six- and seven-year-old child and are outlined as follows.

1. *Topics selected for the first- and second-grade levels should allow for the direct manipulation of materials.* The child in the later preoperational stage or early concrete operational stage of development needs concrete objects in order to construct concepts that are understood rather than merely memorized. Working with simple machines such as levers and pulleys is appropriate; looking at pictures and reading about stars and planets is not. In the area of mathematics, exploring the arrangement of popsicle sticks to determine that the quantity five can appear in a variety of forms is appropriate; memorizing addition tables so answers to problems can be written within a certain period of time is not. Although pictures, books, and other printed materials are ineffective as a primary source of information, these sources can be effectively used after hands-on activities to further develop concepts that the children have already investigated.

2. *Topics selected for the first- and second-grade levels should be open ended and without the necessity of closure.* The child of six or seven is interested in the process of investigation but not necessarily interested in reaching a conclusion, particularly some predetermined conclusion. Hence, the topics selected for inclusion in the combined curriculum should focus more on the investigation of phenomena than on the

elucidation of some particular scientific fact, law, or principle. An activity investigating the kinds of sounds that objects make and how those sounds can be varied is more appropriate within the combined curriculum than is an activity designed to develop the definition of sound as the result of vibration. In mathematics, it is more appropriate to have children investigate size in terms of number of steps or body lengths than it is to insist on accurate measurements in feet or inches, meters or centimeters.

3. *Topics selected should gradually include more small-muscle skills.* Children of six still have difficulty in manipulations involving small-muscle skills. They do love to color, cut, paste, and work with paint and clay. Their drawings are becoming more recognizable and they can print letters and numerals as well as copy a square, cross, rectangle, or diamond. The use of small muscles is, however, fatiguing to the six year old and, therefore, should be minimized. By seven, children are in better control of small muscles and can accomplish more over a longer period of time. In both six and seven year olds, girls tend to have better control of small muscles than boys. Activities must be selected that will allow for the use of both small- and large-muscle skills. In mathematics, patterning using pattern blocks is more appropriate than drawing a pattern with a pencil. In science, classifying large leaves is more appropriate than classifying small seeds.

4. *Topics selected for the combined curriculum should permit both group and individual use of materials with the option of single-child activity or small group-activity.* As activities are selected, enough materials and work space should be provided so that children can choose to work alone, work with a group, or begin as a part of a group and then move to individual work. Expecting the six- or seven-year-old child to consistently share or consistently work in a small group is unrealistic and developmentally inappropriate. As children approach seven years of age, activities can be selected that will allow children to interact more frequently on both physical and verbal levels.

5. *Topics selected for the combined curriculum should permit the investigation of a variety of changes that can be easily and directly observed.* This is of particular importance for topics that are selected for their contribution to the science component of the combined curriculum. Children should have the opportunity to investigate a variety of changes in objects or conditions. The topic of levers within the general study of simple machines is appropriate. Within this topic, children can investigate the effect of type of material, placement of fulcrum, type of load, amount of force, or anything else within the limits of safety. The topic of levers is inappropriate, however, if the child is directed to find the effect of the placement of the fulcrum on the amount of force needed to move an object. In the former case, the child is able to investigate a variety of changes, while in the latter case, the child is directed into a single avenue of investigation in which closure is expected with a particular conclusion.

6. *The topics selected for the combined curriculum should allow for discussion of results without explanation of results based on logical causality.* Children of six and seven are becoming more adept in their use of language skills. Consequently, discussion of activities in which children describe what they investigated and the results of their investigations to other children are appropriate. Such discussion develops the child's ability to use language effectively to communicate information to others. Additionally, the follow-up discussion allows the development of new vocabulary, which children of six and seven enjoy. The key to such vocabulary, however, is the development of understanding prior to terminology so that words are used with meaning. Children who have had the opportunity to plant radish seeds, watch them mature, eat some of them, and watch others produce seeds are more likely to understand the concept of a "life cycle" than are children who have the term defined for them by a teacher or text without an accompanying activity.

7. *Topics selected for the combined curriculum should be adaptable to the requirements of children with special needs.* A topic selected for the science component of the curriculum that allows only for the use of touch is inappropriate if there is a child in the class who is unable

to use his or her hands for investigation. The selection of a mathematics topic that requires a blind child to visualize objects without touching them is inappropriate. Any topic selected should be considered in terms of the children in a particular classroom. Adaptations for disabled children should be a major consideration during planning stages. For example, an activity in which an object is placed in a sealed "mystery box" and children are asked to investigate to figure out what is inside can be modified to allow the deaf child to feel the object or the orthopedically handicapped child with little hand control to work with a partner. Such modifications should be easy to make if an activity is appropriate.

8. *Topics selected for the combined curriculum should permit the integration of science and mathematics skills in a natural manner.* Many of the topics of mathematics overlap with the processes of science. This makes the task of topic selection easier. Rather than selecting a topic and determining how two disparate areas can be combined, the teacher's role is to select a topic that can act as a vehicle for classification, graphing, number, or measurement. The key to combining the areas of mathematics and science is to combine the topics purposefully. For example, classifying leaves, graphing classification categories, and determining how many leaves fall into each category shows the purposeful integration of observing, classifying, graphing, and counting. Each mathematics/science skill results in the gathering of additional information about leaves. On the other hand, investigating the characteristics of rocks and then solving contrived addition problems such as "Maria has three rocks and Lee has five rocks—how many rocks do they have all together?" does nothing to advance an understanding of the topic of rocks.

9. *Topics selected for the combined curriculum should be relevant to and take into account the interests of a particular group of children.* In many cases, children can be a source of topics that will be appropriate. The questions and materials children bring to school or the observations they make during the school day can be an indication of what is of interest to them. When observations or questions lend themselves to investigation or to incorporation into a broader area of content, they should be used by the teacher in developing a combined curriculum activity.

SCIENCE PROCESS SKILLS APPROPRIATE TO THE FIRST AND SECOND GRADES

The developmental characteristics of first- and second-grade children determine the science process skills that will be appropriate for the combined curriculum.

Definition

Process skills are techniques that can be used to gather information about the environment. Frequently, science process skills are considered to be those skills that are used by the scientist in the laboratory as he or she investigates some phenomenon. Another way of looking at what is meant by process skill is to consider process as the "doing" of science. The use of processes as the basis for the science component of the combined curriculum requires an orientation to science that is different from the traditional orientation.

In the traditional orientation, science is considered to be a collection of facts, laws, principles, and theories. The teacher chooses from this collection what he or she thinks should be taught to students at a particular grade level. Often, the teacher is expected to select topics from the physical sciences, earth-space sciences, and biological sciences in order to present a balanced curriculum. The topics selected generally reflect one or more biases. One bias may be that of the teacher toward certain areas of science. Many early childhood teachers are comfortable teaching about plants and animals, uncomfortable teaching about matter and energy, and consider rocks and soil utterly boring. Consequently, the child is presented with a great deal of information about plants and animals by an enthusiastic teacher and a little information about rocks and soil by a teacher who would prefer to omit the entire topic. A second source of bias in topic selection is tradition. Some topics traditionally have been taught to young children: the five senses, the four seasons, dinosaurs, and water come immediately to mind. Some topics traditionally are not taught to young children: simple machines, energy, and soil and so are omitted from the program. There also is bias in terms of adult perceptions of what is easy information and what is difficult information. For the adult, the distinction between solids, liquids, and gases is easy. For the young child, solids and liquids are indeed easy but gases are a problem when air is used as the prototype. The child is tied to sensory experiences with objects and air is odorless, colorless, tasteless, soundless, and "touchless." The senses do not detect this invisible material. In fact, even adults designate a glass as empty even though it is completely filled with air.

The selection of content information is difficult. The selection of process skills, because that selection can be based on the developmental characteristics of children, is far easier. And, because process skills are used in the pursuit of content information, the selection of appropriate process skills results in the concomitant selection of appropriate content information. In general, there are nine process skills that are appropriate for use by the first- and second-grade child.

APPROPRIATE SCIENCE PROCESS SKILLS

Observation

Observations are pieces of information that are learned through direct use of the five senses. Observations do not require interpretation in order to make the information meaningful to the child. The object is red is an observation. The object is a sweet, delicious, red apple is an interpretation that requires past experience with apples for it to be meaningful.

Observations can be made through the use of each of the five senses: sight, touch, hearing, taste, and smell. Using the sense of sight, one can observe color, luster, relative size, surface markings, and object location. Using the sense of touch, one can observe the texture and relative temperature of an object. The sense of hearing allows for observation of similarities of sounds, considering pitch and

loudness through comparison of one sound to another. The sense of taste gives information about the sweetness, sourness, bitterness, or saltiness of an object. And, through the sense of smell, one can detect the similarity of one smell to another or the relative strength of one smell over another. Because our ability to use the senses of taste and smell is limited by our adjectives for describing these sensations, observations of taste and smell are often worded in the form "It smells like . . ." or "It tastes like . . .". The use of the word *like* immediately signals an observation.

Children in the first and second grades, as well as preschoolers and kindergartners, can use the process of observation effectively. At the first- and second-grade levels, observations should be a routine part of any activity. Children can gain a great deal of information through their senses, information that is gained firsthand rather than through listening to the teacher or reading from the textbook. For example, children can be told that leaves differ from one another by their colors, sizes, shapes, odors, and textures. It is easy to speak of such characteristics, perhaps accompanied by an example held up by the teacher. However, it is far more effective to give children a variety of different types of leaves that they can see, touch, and smell, collect their observations, and use those observations in coming to a conclusion about whether leaves are all alike or whether they differ in some ways.

Communication

Communication is defined as any means used to pass information from one person to another. All too frequently, communication is considered to occur only through words. For the child at the first- and second-grade level, communication through oral or written language alone may not be effective. Communication as a process skill can include such nonverbal forms as drawings, models, and movement.

When involved in activities, children will naturally communicate with one another. They communicate by telling other children about what they have done as well as by demonstrating what happens when particular changes are made or particular operations are performed. It is through these kinds of communications that children confront new phenomena and ideas. As they see what others are doing and hear what others are describing, children get additional ideas for activities. For this reason, children should not be expected to be quiet during activities. In fact, talk and excitement are signs that children are effectively using the process skill of communication.

In order to foster communication as a process skill, the teacher needs to consider several ideas. First, because children of six and seven years of age are just beginning to develop written communication skills, the teacher also should keep a record of the activities performed and the children's comments about those activities. An experience chart is an effective way of fostering written communication. Student journals and logs should be used as soon as children are able to work with them. Second, children at the first- and second-grade levels can begin to develop drawings of their activities. Such drawings, along with the experience-chart text or children's own text, help to foster written communication skills. Third, children should have the opportunity to show and tell other students about what they have been doing. This oral communication is aided by having the materials used by the children present or by having the child tell about a drawing he or she made of the activity. Having concrete materials or drawings helps the child recall what occurred. The use of materials is also helpful for the shy child who will have some of the attention drawn away from himself or herself and onto the object. Finally, communication should be made an integral part of the activity rather than a follow-up occurring after the activity has ended. Have children talk about what they are doing as the activity progresses, draw pictures of interesting things while those things occur, demonstrate for others their activities as they find interesting effects, and keep written journals discussing their activities.

Classification

Classification is the ability to place objects into groups on the basis of characteristics that those objects either do or do not possess.

For the first-grade child, the process of classification may be difficult. Classification for the first grader should be based on a single characteristic that is identified by the child. The child will be able to classify leaves as smooth around the edge or not smooth around the edge. If, during the classification process, first graders seem to lose interest in putting all of the leaves of a particular type into a category, remember that many first graders will not have reached exhaustive sorting. At this point, it might be best to ask children how the leaves in each pile are the same and how the two piles are different, record the responses on an experience chart, and switch to a different way of classifying the leaves so that another characteristic can be pinpointed.

For the second-grade child, classifying on the basis of a single characteristic and expecting all objects to be classified is appropriate. The second-grade child will be able to find numerous ways to classify objects. A challenge for second graders is to see how many different ways they can classify the same objects.

Using Numbers

Using numbers is defined as the use of counting and computation skills during an activity for the purpose of gaining additional information. For the first- and second-grade child, the use of numbers focuses on counting, intuitive addition and subtraction, and finally using any formal computation skills that have been acquired.

The key to the process of using numbers is that the process skill be used in natural rather than contrived ways. Determining how many seeds are found in various kinds of fruits is an appropriate use of counting skills because it advances the child's understanding that fruits contain different numbers of seeds. Counting how many leaves each child collected on a nature walk to see who has the most is not only an invalid use of number since it does not advance an understanding of leaves, but is also ecologically unsound because it reinforces the child who caused the greatest amount of damage by plucking leaves. Adding together the number of times a gerbil visits the water container in the morning and afternoon is an appropriate use of addition because it answers the question of how many times a gerbil drinks during a school day. Using subtraction to determine how many more times the gerbil drinks during the morning than in the afternoon is also a valid use because it gives information about water use. Setting up contrived problems such as "Tommy has three gerbils and Mary has four gerbils—how many gerbils do they have altogether?" is a way of getting children to add but it is not an appropriate use of number as a process skill since it does nothing to advance an understanding of gerbils.

Using Space Relations

Using space relations as a process skill is defined as the ability to use words to describe the shape or location of objects in space. This involves the use of plane and solid geometric shapes, informal measurement, and terms such as *over, under, near, far, above,* and *below.*

Solid Shapes.   In identifying and describing solid shapes, children should be allowed to handle cubes, prisms, spheres, ovoids or ellipsoids, cylinders, cones, and pyramids. A soup can is a cylinder, a box is a prism, an ice cream cone is a cone, and a baseball is a sphere. Children of first- and second-grade levels can learn to recognize these solid shapes and utilize the proper terminology.

Plane Shapes.   The plane shapes should be introduced after the solid shapes because the solid shapes are easily identified by students. The reason for this is that the solid shapes are concrete and can be handled by the students, whereas the plane shapes are two dimensional and must be approached by students as drawings or shadows that cannot be handled.

Care must be taken to prevent confusion on the part of children in terms of the two categories of shapes. Don't call a ball a circle or a cube a square. The shadow cast by a ball is indeed a circle and the side of a cube is a square, but the objects themselves are spheres and cubes.

Spatial Terms.   The terms *over, under, above, below, near,* and *far,* among others, can be developed through natural conversation with children. Concepts of spatial relations are developed as children extract relationships among and between objects rather than through formal lessons.

Measurement.   Finally, measurement can be used with the child at the first- and second-grade level, but it should be informal. Since children of these age levels do not conserve length, weight, or volume, formal measurement has little meaning for them. Determining that a tree is twenty steps from the school or that a plant is as tall as a pencil are informal measurements that are meaningful for children. Keeping a record of plant growth by cutting strips equal in length to the height of the plant and pasting them to paper in sequence is a more appropriate use of measurement than having children measure in units such as inches or centimeters.

Cause and Effect

Cause-and-effect reasoning is the ability to observe actions between objects and then to sequence those actions so that the resulting action is seen as having a particular cause. For the first- or second-grade child, logical cause-and-effect relationships can be determined when the actions are on concrete objects and the result is immediately observable. A first grader has little difficulty in determining that the harder one end of a lever is pushed, the higher a sponge or block placed on the other end will fly in the air. That same child may have difficulty determining that the fertilizer put on a plant caused it to grow better than its nonfertilized companion on the windowsill because it takes a great deal of time for the effect to occur and because the fertilizer is no longer visible as an agent in causing better growth.

Inference

Inferences are interpretations of observations. A child can observe an object that is red, yellow, green, blue, and orange on the outside. If the object is a rectangular prism (a shoebox shape), that same child can observe that the prism is heavy and a noise occurs when it is shaken. All of these are observations because they are based on direct sensory experiences. If, however, children are asked what they think the object is, there can be a variety of possible answers. The object may be a block, a present wrapped in colorful paper, a box of cereal, or even a lump of plastic that has been colorfully decorated. These guesses are interpretations of observations. As soon as the child tries to decide what an object is on the basis of observations, he or she is making an inference. For any set of observations, there is a wide variety of possible inferences.

Conclusion

Conclusions are a special type of inference. Conclusions are interpretations of observations. A conclusion takes into account both observations and inferences. Often the conclusion is what is left after some of the inferences have been ruled out on the basis of new evidence.

Going back to the previously mentioned prism, there were several inferences about its identity: a box of cereal, block, present, or lump of plastic. Now, a child picks up the object and finds that the surface is slightly bumpy. Since plastic would probably be smooth to the touch, the lump of plastic inference is ruled out. On shaking the object, there is a thumping sound rather than a rattling sound. The child decides there must be only one thing inside rather than lots of things. The box of cereal can be ruled out. Since the sound indicated that there was something inside the object, the inference that it is a block can also be ruled out. There is now only one inference left: a present wrapped in colorful paper. At this point, there is a conclusion. If a child now discovers that the colorful layer can be removed to show a box beneath it, the conclusion is strengthened. And, if the box is opened to reveal a ball, the conclusion is confirmed.

Prediction

A prediction is also a type of inference. A prediction is an inference, based on past experience, about what could happen at some future time. A child who has observed butter and chocolate melt on a windowsill may infer that it was either the bright light or the heat that caused the melting. He or she may then predict that chocolate will also melt if it is put into a pan placed on a hot plate.

A prediction is not a guess. Predictions are based on past experiences with objects or events. A child who has had experience putting a variety of objects into water can predict that a sponge will float or that a nail will sink. The predictions may not be correct, but they will be logical because of the experience. On the other hand, a child asked to predict where he or she should go to look for an Okapi can only guess. It is unlikely that first- or second-grade children will have experience with the Okapi and so they can only guess where one should go to look for an Okapi. Making guesses can be fun, but the terms *guess* and *prediction* should not be used as synonyms.

Finally, predictions are inferences about what could happen at some future time. Whenever possible, predictions should be tested to determine their validity. A child may predict that a small nail will float because it is small or because it is light in weight. Only by testing that prediction can the child actually discover what will happen.

The process skills of science should be emphasized with first and second graders. It should always be remembered, however, that process skills cannot be divorced from content information. Classifying shapes for the sake of classification can be done, but classification becomes more meaningful to children if they classify leaves and also begin to observe the differences among those leaves. Children can observe an object for the sake of honing their observational skills, but it is more beneficial to observe differing kinds of soil and draw conclusions about the similarities and differences in soil types. The key to the use of processes is to focus on the process skill rather than on specific content information. Children may decide to classify on the basis of a characteristic that is different from what the teacher would have selected. The teacher's role in this situation is to determine whether the characteristics selected will contribute to the children's understanding of the world. The teacher may have wanted students to classify animals by whether they have fur. The children instead may have classified the animals by their means of movement. The children's use of movement as the classification criterion is appropriate because it advances an understanding of animals. To classify the animals on the basis of whether they are pretty or ugly really does not advance the understanding of animals. Children should be encouraged to come up with a variety of possibilities for classifying animals. An appropriate classification category not only allows for the use of classification as a process skill but also advances the child's understanding of a particular topic.

MATHEMATICS AT THE FIRST- AND SECOND-GRADE LEVELS

The developmental characteristics of first- and second-grade children point to one inescapable conclusion. Most first and second graders are not ready to understand arithmetic as it is traditionally and formally taught. The major reason for this conclusion is that conservation of number, the foundation for understanding in formal arithmetic, is generally reached at approximately seven and a half years of age. Prior to conservation of number, the learning of arithmetic is through rote memorization of meaningless bits of information that frequently are forgotten.

If traditional formal arithmetic is inappropriate to the first and second grader, what, then, is appropriate? The answer to this question is based on a distinction that can be made between mathematics and arithmetic.

Everyone is familiar with arithmetic. In arithmetic, one adds, subtracts, multiplies, or divides. As well as learning to compute more difficult problems such as $67 + 89 = $ _____, one also has the task of memorizing tables of basic facts. Arithmetic is concerned with memorizing facts and getting correct answers to problems. For the most part, it makes little difference whether one understands what one is doing. As long as the right answer is forthcoming, one is on safe ground. In arithmetic, the teacher is a director of learning. He or she presents the technique to be used in solving a problem, provides practice, tests, and remediates. The teacher's role is that of a diagnostician and remediator.

Mathematics generally is used as a synonym for arithmetic, but a differentiation between the two terms should be made. Mathematics is concerned with the concepts that underlie and make meaningful computation skills. Rather than being concerned with the fact that $3 + 5 = 8$, mathematics is concerned that children understand the concept of addition. In mathematics, the teacher's role is to provide experiences that will allow the children in the class to develop such concepts. Because concepts are being developed, there is no need for diagnosis or remediation. There is no particular right or wrong answer. Each child's concept may differ even for as well-defined a term as subtraction. Subtraction may mean "You take something away" or "You have to find out if somebody has more" or "You start with a lot of candy and then you eat some" or even "It means you lost some things and so you don't have as many as you did." All of these are concepts of subtraction and all indicate that the young child understands the underlying idea. Mathematics does not require the child to have attained conservation of number because number is treated as a concept to be developed rather than as an established prerequisite. Many times, mathematics is termed *prenumber skills*. A better term would be *prenumber concepts*.

Mathematics Concepts

The concepts used in mathematics are frequently the same as the science process skills. Mathematics consists of classification, counting, number, measurement, and geometry. Because these skill areas have already been discussed under the category of science process skills, we will consider only brief definitions here, highlighting the differences between the mathematics skills and the science process skills.

1. *Classification* is the ability to put items into groups on the basis of a single characteristic. In mathematics, this extends to the idea of a set of objects and to the use of sets in developing concepts.
2. *Counting* involves the development of a one-to-one correspondence between a numeral and an object. In mathematics, children develop the ability to count forward and backward and use skip counting—counting by twos, fives, tens, and so on. The ability to count is put into practice in the science process skill of using numbers.
3. *Number* is the development of a concept of quantity so that the numeral applied to a set of objects is meaningful to the child. This is included within the science process skill of using numbers. Once again, mathematics develops the concept of number, while science asks children to use that concept within their activities.

4. *Measurement* is the quantification of size through informal means. In mathematics, the child is introduced to the concept of measurement and the variety of possible ways of measuring, while in the science process skill, students use their ability to measure.
5. *Geometry* is the topological consideration of shapes, including an informal and intuitive introduction to weight, volume, and area. The mathematical consideration of geometry is a part of the science process skill of using space-time relations and is used to describe or locate objects.

There are some additional mathematics concepts that are not found within the process skills of science. That is not, however, to say that they are completely divorced from the science processes. The first two mathematical concepts rely heavily on the ability to observe.

Comparing and Contrasting

Comparing and contrasting is the ability to use observations to determine similarities and differences among and between objects. By working with the mathematical skill of comparing and contrasting, children begin to develop concepts such as same, different, size relationships, and other order concepts based on the characteristics of objects.

Graphing

Graphing is the ordering of objects to determine quantity relationships. The use of graphing among young children begins with graphs using real objects, proceeds to graphs that use pictures, and finally moves to graphs using symbols. Graphing helps children conceptualize relationships such as more, less, and equal. As number and counting concepts develop, children extend the relative terms of *more, less,* and *equal* and then to actual quantities of objects.

Patterning

Patterning is the perception and identification of regularities. Patterning is considered to be the underlying concept of all of arithmetic and of mathematics in its more complex forms. Place value is a pattern and so are the algorithms that are used in solving computation problems. Even the formation of the various numeral symbols can be considered patterning. The ability to identify, replicate, and construct patterns is also a thinking skill that helps children develop concepts about the world in general. Patterning begins with perception of regularities in concrete examples and proceeds to perception and recording of abstract patterns.

Problem Solving

Problem solving is the application of thinking skills to new situations. Frequently, problem solving is considered in terms of word problems in which numerals are manipulated in order to determine an answer that either is judged as correct or incorrect. The more general skill of problem solving assumes thinking to be a flexible process in which many possible solutions to the same situation (problem) can be determined. Rather than focusing on a single right or wrong answer, problem solving in its general form looks for variety in answers, rewards creativity, and looks at the solution from a viewpoint of what works, what does not work, what nearly works, and how what nearly works can be changed so that it does indeed work.

For most children at the first- and second-grade levels, the concepts of mathematics will be the most appropriate form of number or prenumber work. However, children of seven and one half will often conserve number. As soon as conservation of number occurs, children can begin to develop formal arithmetic skills with understanding through a foundation in concrete models. The introduction of arithmetic should be a natural progression from prenumber skills to number skills. Counting forward and backward can be used to approach addition and subtraction in a natural progression. The use of sets of objects can form the foundation for all four of the basic computation skills. The use of counting and patterning is a means for introducing place-value concepts. At the second-grade level, some children will be ready for true arithmetic. This does not mean, however, that those children are ready for the rote memorization and rote computation that is found in many traditional classrooms. Rather, computation should be based on understanding through the use of manipulative materials.

APPROPRIATE TOPICS FOR THE FIRST- AND SECOND-GRADE LEVELS

The following list is by no means exhaustive, nor is it meant to be. One thing that will be noted is that the topics are frequently couched in terms that are science oriented rather than mathematics oriented. If it is kept in mind that the content of the combined curriculum is not differentiated, but that the two areas are combined within an exploration, then the wording of the topics should not be troublesome. Each topic is accompanied by a brief description of a starting point and a list of the mathematics topics and science process skills that are most frequently used.

1. *Investigating Growing Plants.* Children plant seeds of various types and keep records of the growth of the resulting plants. Children could also plant a class garden or observe plants that have already begun growing. This activity develops the science process skills of observing, communicating, inferring, predicting, using space relations, and using numbers, as well as the mathematics skills of measuring, classifying, counting, and problem solving.
2. *Investigating an Aquarium, Vivarium, or Terrarium.* Children construct one of the listed habitats and investigate the effect of varying conditions on the organisms in the habitat. Care must be taken that nothing is done to harm the living organisms. This activity develops the science process skills of observing, communicating, inferring, concluding, using space/time relations, cause-and-effect reasoning, and using numbers, as well as the mathematics skills of comparing and contrasting, counting, using number, measuring, and problem solving.
3. *Investigating Magnets.* Children are given various types of magnets to investigate the effect of magnets on different materials, on other magnets, and through different kinds of materials. This activity develops the science process skills

of observing, inferring, predicting, concluding, classifying, cause-and-effect reasoning, and communicating, as well as the mathematics skills of counting, using number, graphing, and problem solving.
4. *Investigating Simple Machines.* Children use materials to investigate inclined planes, levers, pulleys, and wheels and axles. This activity develops the science process skills of observing, communicating, cause-and-effect reasoning, predicting, using space relations, and classifying, as well as the mathematics skills of measuring, counting, using number, using geometry, and problem solving.
5. *Investigating Reflection of Light.* Children use unbreakable mirrors and several sources of light to investigate reflections. This activity develops the science process skills of observing, communicating, predicting, inferring, concluding, cause-and-effect reasoning, and using space relations, as well as the mathematics skills of comparing and contrasting, using geometry, patterning, and problem solving.
6. *Investigating Weather.* Children establish a weather station in which they can take air temperature; look at wind direction and speed; and determine precipitation amounts, cloud cover, and changes in weather during a school day. This activity uses the science process skills of observing, communicating, using space/time relations, and predicting, as well as the mathematics skills of using number, counting, measuring, and graphing.
7. *Investigating a Mini-environment.* Students use string to mark off a square-meter environment and then investigate it. This activity develops the science process skills of observing, communicating, using space/time relations, and using numbers, as well as the mathematics skills of classifying, comparing and contrasting, counting, using number, and problem solving.
8. *Investigating Melting and Freezing.* Children investigate simple materials, including both solids and liquids, to determine the conditions under which the materials will freeze or melt. This activity develops the science process skills of observing, communicating, cause-and-effect reasoning, predicting, and inferring, as

LEARNING ACTIVITY 23

Observation

Purpose: The purpose of this activity is to investigate the use of the science process skill of observation among first- or second-grade children.

Definition: Observations are pieces of information that are obtained through direct use of the five senses: taste, touch, sound, smell, or sight. Additionally, observations may be any kind of measurements or may identify shapes. A key to observation is to describe an object without actually naming it.

Procedure:

A.

1. Choose any three of the objects listed below. Write at least fifteen observations of each of the three objects you select. Include in your observations the use of all appropriate senses, measurements, and shapes.
   a. another adult person
   b. a hamburger
   c. a rose bush
   d. an old shoe
   e. a burning candle
   f. a cake
   g. a dog or cat
   h. your own hand
   i. a box of crayons
   j. a cup of coffee or tea
   k. a can or bottle of soft drink
   l. a baby or child
   m. an insect
   n. a book
   o. a piece of jewelry

B.

1. Select two or three children of first- or second-grade level.
2. Ask each child individually to describe through observations two of the objects you selected.
3. Record all of the children's observations.
4. Compare your observations with those of each child.
   a. What similarities and differences do you find between your observations and those of the children?
   b. What similarities and differences do you find among the observations made by the children? How would you account for these similarities and differences?

---

well as the mathematics skills of comparing and contrasting, patterning, measuring, classifying, and problem solving.

9. *Investigating Evaporation.* Children investigate a variety of liquids and conditions. This activity develops the science process skills of observing, communicating, predicting, inferring, and cause-and-effect reasoning, as well as the mathematics skills of classifying, graphing, and problem solving.

10. *Investigating Things That Make Sound.* Children are given a variety of objects and investigate the ways in which they make sounds and how those sounds can be changed. This activity develops the science process skills of observing, communicating, cause-and-effect reasoning, predicting, and inferring, as well as the mathematics skills of comparing and contrasting, patterning, measuring, classifying, and problem solving.

11. *Investigating Mixing Colors.* Children use red, blue, and yellow food coloring in water, paint, and colored clay to investigate what happens when the colors are mixed together in various ways. This activity develops the science process skills of observing, inferring, predicting, concluding, classifying, cause-and-effect reasoning, and communicating, as well as the mathematics skills of counting, using number, graphing, and problem solving.

12. *Investigating Liquids.* Children are given various familiar liquids, differing surfaces, and objects that can be used to stir, pour, or drop into the liquids. They investigate the behavior of the liquids under different conditions. This activity develops the science process skills of

LEARNING ACTIVITY 24

Communicating

Purpose: The purpose of this activity is to investigate the use of the science process skill of communication in children at the first- or second-grade level.

Definition: Communication is any means that can be used to pass information from one person to another. Communication can include written or oral presentations, pictures, models, or movement.

Procedure:

1. Consider the following activity for children at the first- or second-grade level. List and describe as many ways as possible that could be used to help the children communicate the results of the activity to one another, the teacher, and parents.

2. The children are given drawing paper; brushes; sponges; straws; cotton balls; and red, blue, and yellow paint. They are asked to use the materials to make whatever pictures they want. By the time they are finished, each child has made at least three pictures. Some pictures are realistic and some are designs. Many of the pictures have not only red, yellow, and blue but also orange, green, purple, brown, and black.

3. Now, conduct the activity with a small group of children and have them use one or more of your means for communicating. Which of the methods that you tried was most successful? How could you change the less successful methods to make them more successful?

---

observing, communicating, cause-and-effect reasoning, predicting, and inferring, as well as the mathematics skills of comparing and contrasting, patterning, using number, counting, classifying, and problem solving.

13. *Investigating Dissolving.* Children are given various familiar solids and liquids and are encouraged to investigate what happens when the solids and liquids are combined. This activity develops the science process skills of observing, inferring, predicting, concluding, classifying, cause-and-effect reasoning, and communicating, as well as the mathematics skills of counting, using number, graphing, and problem solving.

14. *Investigating Things that Float and Sink.* Children are provided with a basin of water or water table and a variety of objects that float, sink, or do both. They are encouraged to investigate how the objects behave when placed in water. This activity develops the science process skills of observing, inferring, predicting, concluding, classifying, cause-and-effect reasoning, and communicating, as well as the mathematics skills of counting, using number, graphing, and problem solving.

15. *Investigating Growing Molds.* Begin with a par-

tial loaf of bread that has been allowed to get moldy. Have children use nonmoldy bread to investigate the conditions under which mold will grow best. This activity develops the science process skills of observing, inferring, predicting, concluding, classifying, cause-and-effect reasoning, and communicating, as well as the mathematics skills of counting, using number, graphing, and problem solving.

16. *Investigating a Worm Farm or Ant Farm.* Children construct either a worm farm or an ant farm and then observe the actions of the animals as they develop the farm. This activity develops the science process skills of observing, communicating, using space/time relations, and inferring, as well as the mathematics skills of using number, counting, and problem solving.

17. *Investigating Soil.* Students are given a variety of soil samples to investigate the kinds of materials found in different types of soil. This activity develops the science process skills of observing, classifying, and communicating, as well as the mathematics skills of classifying, comparing and contrasting, counting, graphing, and problem solving.

18. *Investigating Rubbings.* Children make rub-

LEARNING ACTIVITY 25

Classifying

Purpose: The purpose of this activity is to investigate the use of classification as a science process by first- or second-grade children.

Definition: Classification is the ability to place objects into groups on the basis of the characteristics that those objects either do or do not possess.

Procedure:

A.

1. Obtain a crayon and twenty-five pieces of white construction or typing paper that are approximately 14 cm by 22 cm. Using the paper and crayon, make rubbings of the objects by placing the paper over the object then rubbing the side of the crayon against the paper.
2. Look at the rubbings you made and then make a list of their characteristics.
3. Classify the rubbings according to one of the characteristics you have listed. Identify any problems that made it difficult to classify according to the given characteristic.
4. Repeat step three two more times using a different characteristic each time.

B.

1. Have a small group of first- or second-grade children make at least twenty different rubbings.
2. Ask the children to help you make a list of some of the ways the rubbings are the same and some of the ways they are different.
3. Ask the children to classify the rubbings according to one of the characteristics they listed. Then, ask them to classify the rubbings in a different way.

C.

1. Describe the ways in which the children classified the rubbings.
2. How do the children's methods of classifying compare to the methods you used?
3. What problems did the children encounter as they classified the objects?
4. Were the children's problems in classification similar to or different from those you encountered?

---

bings by placing a piece of paper over an object and rubbing the paper with the side of a crayon to form a pattern. Children are encouraged to make rubbings of a variety of objects and surfaces. This activity develops the science process skills of observing, classifying, predicting, and communicating, as well as the mathematics skills of comparing and contrasting, counting, classifying, graphing, and problem solving.

19. *Investigating Rocks and Minerals.* Students collect rocks and minerals from outdoors. This collection is supplemented by the teacher so that there is variety in the materials. The students then investigate the rocks and minerals. This activity develops the science process skills of observing, classifying, using space/time relations, inferring, and communicating, as well as the mathematics skills of counting, comparing and contrasting, graphing, classifying, and problem solving.

20. *Investigating Leaves.* Students collect different types of leaves, taking only one or two leaves from any plant. They investigate the leaves by observing them and making rubbings of them. This activity develops the science process skills of observing, communicating, using space/time relations, using number relations, classifying, and concluding, as well as the mathematics skills of counting, using number, comparing and contrasting, classifying, patterning, graphing, and problem solving.

LEARNING ACTIVITY 26

Using Number Relations

Purpose: The purpose of this activity is to investigate the use of the science process skill of number relations with first- or second-grade children.

Definition: Using number is defined as the use of counting and computation skills during an activity for the purpose of gaining additional information.

Procedure:
1. Collect a knife and a variety of fruits including an apple, orange, peach or plum, cantaloupe, cucumber, and green pepper. Also obtain a sheet of experience chart paper and a marker.
2. Conduct the following activity with a small group of first- or second-grade children.
   a. Ask the children to make observations of the fruits. Ask them what they will find if they cut

open each of the fruits. Focus their attention on the idea that there are seeds inside.
   b. Cut open the fruits and have the children locate the seeds. Help them count the seeds inside each of the fruits. Record the number of seeds found in each fruit.
   c. Ask the children what they have found out about the number of seeds in different kinds of fruits.
   d. Note: Cucumbers and green peppers scientifically are fruits because they contain the seeds of the plant.
3. Describe the reactions of the children to the activity, focusing on their use of number relations.

LEARNING ACTIVITY 27

Using Space Relations

Purpose: The purpose of this activity is to investigate the use of the science process of space relations among first- and second-grade children.

Definition: Space relations is defined as the ability to use words to describe the shape or location of objects in space. It involves the use of plane and solid geometric shapes, informal measurement, and terms such as *over, under, near, far, above,* and *below.*

Procedure:
1. Select two first-grade children and two second-grade children. Do the following activity separately with each child.
2. Set up a tableau for children consisting of a stuffed toy on a chair, a ball on the floor in front of

the chair, a book behind the chair, a block beside the chair, and a toy car beneath the chair.
3. Ask children to describe what they see. Note any use of the spatial terms *above, behind, in front of, beside, on, beneath,* and so on.
4. After the child describes the tableau, ask the child to move some of the objects. For example, have the child put the doll beneath the chair, or put the block in front of the chair. Record the responses of the child.
5. Describe the children's use of space relations in the activity. Compare the use of space relations of first-grade children to that of second-grade children.

LEARNING ACTIVITY 28

Cause-and-Effect Reasoning

Purpose: The purpose of this activity is to investigate the use of the science process of cause-and-effect reasoning by first- or second-grade children.

Definition: Cause-and-effect reasoning is defined as the ability to observe actions among and between objects and then to sequence those actions so that the resulting action is seen as having a particular cause.

Procedure:

1. Collect a container for water and a paint brush. The brush should be at least 2.5 cm across. Working with a small group of first or second graders, have the children "paint" pictures using the water on either a chalkboard or a sidewalk.

2. After the children paint with the water, have them watch as the water evaporates. Ask the children what happened to the water. Use follow-up questions to help the children give the fullest possible explanations.

3. Ask the children to paint another "picture." Then, have them fan the "picture" so the water evaporates more quickly. Ask them what caused the water to evaporate more quickly than last time. Use questions to further pursue the children's ideas.

4. Describe the children's use of cause-and-effect reasoning in this activity.

LEARNING ACTIVITY 29

Inferring

Purpose: The purpose of this activity is to investigate the science process of inferring among children in the first or second grade.

Definition: An inference is an interpretation of observations. There can be many inferences for the same set of observations.

Procedure:

1. Present a small group of first- or second-grade children with each of the following problems. Record the children's responses. Use follow-up questions to elicit further explanations.

2. *Problem A.* Present the children with two paper cups, one containing a growing bean plant and the other containing seeds that were planted at the same time but that are not growing. Ask the children what could have happened to cause seeds in one cup to grow and seeds in the other not to grow.

   a. Encourage the children to come up with a variety of possible ideas.
   b. Ask the children to explain the reasoning behind their ideas about the seeds' behavior.

3. *Problem B.* Tell students that a boy named Enrico built a tower of blocks. When he turned away from his tower to talk to his friend Judy, the tower fell down. What could have caused the tower to fall down?

   a. Encourage the children to come up with a variety of possible explanations.
   b. Ask the children to explain the reasoning behind their ideas about why the tower fell down.

4. Compare the children's responses to Problem A to those of Problem B. How does the use of concrete objects in Problem A affect the children's ability to make inferences?

LEARNING ACTIVITY 30

Concluding

Purpose: The purpose of this activity is to investigate the use of the science process of conclusion among first- and second-grade children.

Definition: A conclusion is a special type of inference that typically takes the form of an explanation or generalization about data gathered in an activity.

Procedure:

1. Collect a plastic basin, water, newspaper, a crayon, and a small object such as a ball, block, or rock. Fill the basin with water and place it on the floor in the center of a layer of newspaper.
2. Work with a small group of first- or second-grade children.
   a. Have one child drop the object into the water.

Locate and circle with a crayon the farthest splash.
   b. Have the children brainstorm a list of factors that could affect how far the water splashes.
   c. Have them test two of the factors to determine how they affect the distance the water splashes. Circle the most distant splash of each factor.
   d. Based on the results of the activity, ask the children to draw a conclusion about how to get the water to splash the farthest distance.
3. Consider the children's conclusions. How accurate are they? How does the children's use of cause-and-effect reasoning influence the conclusions they draw?

LEARNING ACTIVITY 31

Predicting

Purpose: The purpose of this activity is to investigate the use of the science process of prediction in first- or second-grade children.

Definition: A prediction is a type of inference. Predictions are based on past experience and define what will happen at some future time.

Procedure:

1. Present a small group of first- or second-grade children with the following problems. After discussing each situation, compare and contrast the children's ability to use prediction.
2. *Problem A:* Ask the children to answer the following question. What do you think would happen if

the Sun did not come up tomorrow morning? Ask for the children's reasoning.
3. *Problem B:* Present the children with a magnet and four or five objects that the magnet will pick up. Have the children pick up the objects with the magnet. Present the children with six new objects, three that are attracted by the magnet and three that are not. Before they explore the new objects, ask the children to predict which objects will be picked up by the magnet. Ask for the children's reasoning.
4. Compare the children's responses to Problem A to those of Problem B. How does the use of concrete objects in Problem B affect the children's ability to make predictions?

LEARNING ACTIVITY 32

Counting

Purpose: The purpose of this activity is to investigate the use of the mathematical concept of counting in first- and second-grade children.

Definition: Counting involves the development of a one-to-one correspondence between a numeral and an object. Counting includes counting forward, counting backward, and skip counting.

Procedure:

1. Collect fifty popsicle sticks, pipe cleaners, or toothpicks and at least twenty-five rubber bands.
2. Choose two first-grade children and two second-grade children and do the following activity separately with each of the four children.
3. Place the objects in front of the child and ask him or her to count them. After the child has counted to at least twenty-five, stop the child and ask if he or she can think of an easier way to count the objects.
4. If the child makes no suggestions, ask if the objects can be counted by groups of two. Have

the child bundle the objects into groups of two and then ask the child to count how many objects there are altogether. If the child counts each bundle as one, remind the child that there are two sticks in each bundle and demonstrate counting by two, four, six, and so on.

5. Repeat step three, bundling by fives and then by tens.
6. If the child suggests ways of counting that involve bundling and counting, use the child's methods before suggesting others.
7. Describe each child's use of counting. How are the counting abilities of first- and second-grade children similar and different?

LEARNING ACTIVITY 33

Using Number

Purpose: The purpose of this activity is to investigate the understanding of the mathematical concept of number in first- and second-grade children.

Definition: Number is a concept of quantity that gives meaning to the numeral attached to a set of objects.

Procedure:

1. Select two children from first or second grade, one who conserves number and another who does not. (See Learning Activity 2 for Conservation of Number Task.)
2. Collect a box of colored toothpicks, white drawing paper, and glue.

3. Show the child a set of eight toothpicks of the same color set in a single row. Ask the child to count how many toothpicks are in the set.
4. Now, give the child the rest of the toothpicks and ask the child to use them to show eight in as many ways as possible. Have the child make a record of the arrangements by gluing them to the paper.
5. Compare and contrast the results of the activity for each of the two children. Were there any differences between the performance of the conserver and the nonconserver?

LEARNING ACTIVITY 34

Measuring

Purpose: The purpose of this activity is to investigate the use of the mathematical concept of measurement in first- and second-grade children.

Definition: Measurement is the quantification of size through informal means.

Procedure:

1. Present the following problem to a small group of first- or second-grade children:

   All of the rulers in the world have suddenly disappeared and I need to know how long

LEARNING ACTIVITY 34 Continued

our classroom is. What are some ways I could find out how long the classroom is?

2. Collect the children's ideas for solving the problem and write them on a piece of experience chart paper.
3. Have the students try out some of their ideas. Involve all of the children in the activity. Record the results on the chart paper.
4. Discuss with the children what could cause the "measurements" to differ from one child to another. For example, if children solve the problem by counting the number of steps, ask why one child said the room was twenty steps long and another said it was twenty-five steps long. Record their ideas.
5. Discuss the results of the activity in terms of the understanding of measurement shown by the children.

LEARNING ACTIVITY 35

Using Geometry

Purpose: The purpose of this activity is to investigate the use of the mathematical concept of geometry, particularly weight, by first- or second-grade children.

Definition: Geometry is the topological consideration of shapes as well as an informal and intuitive introduction to weight, volume, and area.

Procedure:
1. Collect a balance and several different objects of varying weight: styrofoam packing pieces, rocks, blocks, pennies, crayons, beans, paper clips, beads, macaroni, and so on.
2. Working with a small group of first- or second-grade children, place the heaviest of the items on one side of the balance. Then ask the children what they could do to make the balance even. Allow them to experiment with the materials to make the balance even.
3. Give the children time to investigate other objects and how to balance the objects against one another.
4. After the children have had a chance to investigate the objects, ask them the following questions.
   a. What do you have to do to make the balance even if there is a heavy rock on one side?
   b. What do you have to do if the balance is even and you want to make one side go up?
   c. What do you have to do if the balance is even and you want to make one side go down?
   d. If the balance is even, what does it tell you about the objects on each side of the balance?
5. Describe children's investigations and responses.

LEARNING ACTIVITY 36

Comparing and Contrasting

Purpose: The purpose of this activity is to investigate the use of the mathematical concept of comparing and contrasting by children in first or second grade.

Definition: Comparing and contrasting involves the ability to use observations to determine similarities and differences among and between objects.

Procedure:
1. Seat a group of six or seven first or second graders with you in a circle on the floor. Place an experience chart where it can be used easily.
2. Have each child put one of her or his shoes into the circle. Put one of your shoes into the circle as well.

LEARNING ACTIVITY 36 Continued

3. Ask the children to look carefully at the shoes and to name some ways the shoes are the same.
4. Use the experience chart to keep a record of the students' responses.
5. Now ask the children to look at the shoes again and name ways that the shoes are different.
6. Record the responses on the experience chart paper.
7. Describe the similarities and differences listed by the children.

LEARNING ACTIVITY 37

Graphing

Purpose: The purpose of this activity is to investigate the use of the mathematical concept of graphing among first- or second-grade children.

Definition: Graphing is the ordering of objects to determine quantity relationships.

Procedure:
1. Work with a class of first or second graders in developing an object graph.
2. Obtain a large bag of candies in various colors (gumdrops, jellybeans, candy-covered chocolate, etc.). Separate the candy so that only four of the colors are used. Place the candy of each color into a separate container.
3. Make a graphing board from a piece of plastic at least six feet in length. Draw four colums, each divided into 12 blocks (see diagram below).

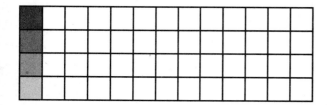

4. Ask the children to name the colors of candies. Then ask, "If everyone picked his or her favorite color of candy, which color do you think most of the children in the class would pick?" Write the students predictions on the board or on experience chart paper.
5. Have each child come up and select one piece of her or his favorite candy, keeping the color selected a secret.
6. Graph the candy pieces selected by having the children place the piece of candy on the graphing board, one piece to a square.
7. After the graph is completed, ask the following questions.
   a. Which color was chosen the most times? How do you know?
   b. Which color was chosen the fewest times? How do you know?
   c. Were any colors not chosen at all? How do you know?
   d. Were there any colors chosen the same number of times? How do you know?
8. Describe the graphing abilities the children demonstrated during the activity and the discussion.

LEARNING ACTIVITY 38

Patterning

Purpose: The purpose of this activity is to investigate the use of the mathematical concept of patterning in first- and second-grade children.

Definition: Patterning is the perception and identification of regularities.

Procedure:
1. Collect or construct a set of pattern blocks consisting of squares, trapezoids, hexagons, diamonds, and triangles. Each type of shape should be a different color; for example, all triangles are green, all diamonds are blue.

LEARNING ACTIVITY 38 Continued

2. Working with a small group of first- or second-grade children, construct a repeating pattern using only two of the shapes. For example, create a pattern of a triangle followed by a square:

3. Have the children copy the pattern using their own blocks.

4. Make three or four additional patterns using two or three different shapes. Have the children repeat each pattern.

5. Now ask each child to construct a pattern of his or her own design and then have the child describe the pattern in words.

6. Keep a record of children's patterns and descriptions.

7. Describe the results of the activity in terms of the patterning abilities shown by the children.

LEARNING ACTIVITY 39

Investigating Appropriate Science Topics

Purpose: The purpose of this activity is to analyze a first- or second-grade science textbook for the appropriateness of its content.

Procedure:

1. Select three chapters from a first- or second-grade-level teacher's edition of a science textbook. One chapter should cover biological science, one should cover physical science, and one should cover earth-space science.

2. List the concepts covered in each of the three chapters. The concepts are generally found at the start of the chapter but may also appear at the beginning of each separate lesson.

3. Using the criteria listed in this chapter for appropriate learning experiences, determine whether the listed concepts are appropriate to the first or second grader's cognitive ability.

4. Discuss any changes that could be made to make the concepts more appropriate to the first- or second-grade child.

LEARNING ACTIVITY 40

Analyzing Science Activities

Purpose: The purpose of this activity is to analyze the use of process skills in science activities found in a first-grade textbook and a second-grade textbook.

Procedure:

1. Select two hands-on activities from a first-grade science textbook and two from a second-grade science textbook. Choose activities dealing with biological science, physical science, and earth-space science.

2. Analyze the use of process skills in each of the activities.

3. Describe the grade-level appropriateness of the use of process skills in the activities. If the activities are inappropriate, describe what could be done to make them more appropriate.

LEARNING ACTIVITY 41

Investigating Appropriate Mathematics Content

Purpose: The purpose of this activity is to analyze a first- or second-grade mathematics textbook for the appropriateness of its mathematics content.

Procedure:

1. Select two chapters from a first- or second-grade-level teacher's edition of a mathematics textbook. One chapter should deal with a computation skill and one with a noncomputation skill.
2. List the concept included in each of the two chapters. The concepts are generally found at the start of the chapter but may also appear at the beginning of each separate lesson.
3. Using the criteria listed in this chapter for appropriate learning experiences, determine whether the listed concepts are appropriate to the first- or second-grade-level child's cognitive ability.
4. Discuss any changes that could make the listed concepts more appropriate.

LEARNING ACTIVITY 42

Developing a Combined-Curriculum Activity

Purpose: The purpose of this activity is to develop a combined-curriculum activity that focuses on the science process skills.

Procedure:

1. Consider the criteria, outlined in this text, for a combined-curriculum activity.
2. Select one or more of the science process skills and develop a combined-curriculum activity that will allow students to develop their abilities to use those process skills.
3. After creating the activity, look it over to determine whether it also develops mathematics concepts. If it doesn't, revise it to include mathematics concepts.
4. Try the activity with a small group of children.
5. How would you rate the success of your activity? What could you do to make the activity even more successful?

LEARNING ACTIVITY 43

Developing a Combined-Curriculum Activity

Purpose: The purpose of this activity is to develop a combined-curriculum activity that focuses on mathematical concepts.

Procedure:

1. Consider the criteria, outlined in this text, for a combined-curriculum activity.
2. Select one or more mathematical concepts and develop a combined-curriculum activity that will allow students to develop their abilities to use those concepts.
3. After creating the activity, look it over to determine whether it also develops science process skills. If it doesn't, revise it to include science process skills.
4. Try the activity with a small group of children.
5. How would you rate the success of your activity? What could you do to make the activity even more successful?

LEARNING ACTIVITY 44

Collecting Materials

Purpose: The purpose of this activity is to develop a collection of materials that can be used to develop in children science process skills and mathematical concepts.

Procedure:

1. Develop a file of activities that could be used to teach science processes or mathematical concepts to children at the first- or second-grade level.

2. Select ten of the activities and collect the materials needed to use those activities in a classroom.

3. Using your file and the collected materials, develop a resource kit in which the materials are organized for easy use in the classroom. Since materials often are lost or broken by children, they should be inexpensive and easily replaced. Also keep in mind that classroom storage space is limited and, therefore, the packaging of the kit should reflect wise use of space.

SUMMARY

At the first- and second-grade levels, the characteristics of the children are used to determine the content of the curriculum. These characteristics show that the traditional content of the curriculum may not be as appropriate as it could be.

The development of appropriate content for the combined curriculum requires, first, differentiation between mathematics and arithmetic. Because meaningful arithmetic is based on conservation of number, the teaching of computation to the first grader and many second graders may not be appropriate. Instead, the child of first- and second-grade level should be involved in developing the concepts of mathematics: classifying, counting, using number, measuring, using geometry, comparing and contrasting, graphing, patterning, and problem solving.

Many of the traditional concepts of science are based on a logical understanding of cause and effect. Since this understanding is not fully developed in young children, the combined curriculum focuses on the process skills of science rather than on the content of science. The process skills that are most appropriate to the young child are observing, classifying, communicating, using numbers, using space relations, inferring, predicting, con-

cluding, and cause-and-effect reasoning that is immediate in space and time.

The combined curriculum considers the separate existence of science and mathematics but combines the two areas in meaningful ways so that both the processes of science and the concepts of mathematics help the child develop an understanding of the world as it exists.

Vocabulary Terms

Arithmetic: the aspect of quantification that deals with computation skills.

Cause-and-Effect Reasoning: the ability to observe actions among and between objects and then to sequence those actions so that the resulting action is seen as having a particular cause.

Classifying: placing objects into groups on the basis of the characteristics that those objects either do or do not possess.

Communicating: passing information verbally or nonverbally from one person to another.

Comparing and Contrasting: using observations to determine similarities and differences among and between objects.

Concluding: summarizing observations and inferences based on observations of a particular object or event.

Counting: developing a one-to-one correspondence between a numeral and an object.

Graphing: ordering objects to determine quantity relationships.

Inferring: interpreting a set of observations.

Mathematics: the aspect of quantification that deals with the underlying concepts that make computation and other arithmetic skills meaningful.

Number: a concept of quantity that allows a numeral applied to a set of objects to be meaningful.

Observing: any piece of information learned through the direct use of the five senses. Observations do not require interpretation to make them meaningful.

Open-Ended Activity: an activity that allows for child-determined and child-developed investigations and, therefore, does not result in a single, predetermined outcome.

Patterning: perceiving and identifying regularities.

Problem Solving: applying thinking skills and conceptual knowledge to new situations.

Predicting: inferring based on past experience and stating what could occur at a future time.

Science Content: any of the facts, laws, theories, principles, or concepts that make up the body of knowledge in science.

Science Process Skills: techniques, often used by scientists in laboratories, of gathering information about the environment.

Using Number: using counting or computation skills during an activity for the purpose of gaining information.

Using Space Relations: using words to describe shape or location of objects in space.

Study Questions

1. What criteria are used to choose appropriate topics for the combined curriculum?
2. How does science content differ from science process? What relationship exists between these two areas?
3. How does mathematics differ from arithmetic? What relationship exists between these two areas?
4. List and define the science process skills most appropriate to the first- and second-grade levels.
5. List and define the mathematics concepts most appropriate to the first- and second-grade levels.
6. A second-grade teacher decides to integrate mathematical skills into a science experience with plants. The children have learned the parts of a typical flowering plant, investigated the characteristics of various kinds of seeds, and grown lima bean seeds and marigold seeds. Now, the teacher decides to incorporate mathematics into the unit and hands out a worksheet of problems of the type "Miko had thirty-five seeds and Jane had seventeen seeds. How many do they have altogether?" Is this an appropriate use of mathematical skills? Why or why not? How could you incorporate greater use of mathematical skills into the investigation of plants?
7. A first-grade teacher completes a unit of study with his class that deals with stars and planets. Although the children were interested and attentive, the evaluation of the unit shows that they learned little of the information even though they made models of the planets, watched a film on the Sun and planets, and even listened to a former astronaut talk about going into space. What could you tell this teacher to help him understand why minimal learning took place?
8. What can be done to make a traditional science or mathematics topic more appropriate to the combined curriculum?

CHAPTER 8

Teaching Techniques for the First and Second Grades

Chapter Objectives

On completion of this chapter, you should be able to

1. list the characteristics of a centers approach to teaching in the first and second grades,

2. discuss why a centers approach is appropriate to the developmental needs of the first- and second-grade child,

3. discuss the role of the teacher in a centers approach to teaching,

4. discuss the use of questions in a centers approach to teaching,

5. plan for the use of a centers approach in a self-contained, open, or traditional classroom,

6. plan for the use of a centers approach in an open setting,

7. plan for the use of a centers approach in a departmentalized situation,

8. plan and carry out an activity appropriate for the combined curriculum,

9. discuss the integrated approach to teaching in the combined curriculum,

10. plan an integrated-approach teaching strategy that has a focal topic in the area of science, and

11. plan an integrated-approach teaching strategy that has a focal topic in the area of mathematics.

Teaching in the combined curriculum requires that the teacher shift his or her focus away from discrete bits of information that can be taught, tested, and graded to concepts that cut across science and mathematics as well as other subject-matter areas. Conceptual development means that the child is directly and actively involved in the learning experience and that the learning experience is designed to allow the child to investigate broad ideas rather than narrow facts. The teacher and the child together help to determine the direction of learning.

Within the combined curriculum, the teacher can either establish certain mathematical or process-centered goals and construct learning experiences around those goals or can select broad conceptual areas and provide experiences that will allow the child to construct concepts. The child as an inquirer within those experiences directs the learning process through the background experiences he or she brings to the activities, the variations imposed on the activities, and the concepts constructed as a result of the activities. It is the teacher's role as a guide and facilitator to see that the concepts embodied in the activity are developed by the child. The teacher's role is to develop the activities and then to follow up on those activities after the children have finished their investigations.

In order to allow for the combining of mathematics with science process skills and the incorporation of other subject-matter areas as a part of science- or mathematics-oriented investigations, the combined curriculum utilizes a variety of teaching strategies. The emphasis in all cases is on the development of the child's thought processes and problem-solving abilities. The teacher's role is not that of a purveyor of information but rather that of an assistant. The teacher assists learning by developing activities for the children, providing materials that may be requested as a part of individual investigations, and directing interaction following completion of center-based activities or integrated-approach activities.

TEACHING IN THE FIRST AND SECOND GRADES

Teaching the first- and second-grade child is traditionally seen as the same as teaching the sixth-grade child. If modifications are made in the traditional program, it is often to have shorter time periods for a subject-matter area, to include a rest period at the first-grade level, and to use more verbal instruction rather than reading materials. But, as the child reaches the end of the first grade and moves into second grade, he or she is frequently expected to observe the same school conventions as older children: sit still, be quiet, keep on task, pay attention, and pass the tests and quizzes. Such teaching methods and expectations do not match the preoperational and transitional child's cognitive abilities nor do they take into account the child's social and physical development. Open-inquiry teaching, centers-based teaching, and integrated-approach teaching are all far more appropriate for children at these levels.

Open-Inquiry Teaching

The use of open inquiry as a teaching strategy was extensively discussed in Chapter 4. The techniques of open inquiry are highly appropriate for the first- and second-grade child. At the beginning of the first-grade level, the child should participate in a variety of open-inquiry activities because he or she will probably still be at the preoperational stage of development. But, as the year progresses and as the child moves into the second-grade level, more attention should be given to the centers approach and less to the open-inquiry approach.

The Centers Approach to Teaching

Definition. A centers approach is effectively used with the combined curriculum of the first- and second-grade levels. This approach provides a variety of activities from which children select those in which they wish to participate. A center, then, is a means for organizing materials and instruction that allows the child to decide on the area to be investigated and the time to be spent on that investigation. The center is based on the concept of child choice within established parameters. The parameters are established by the teacher because it is the teacher who determines the activities that are used. Within the center, the teacher establishes the sequence of activities and the amount of information presented at any one time. The center activities may focus on the development of a single process skill or mathematics concept, but more frequently combine mathematics and science to allow for the simultaneous investigation of both areas. A center then, is a means of organizing for learning that allows the child maximum freedom of choice within an area limited by the teacher.

Appropriateness.   A centers approach is an appropriate means for working with children at the first- and second-grade levels. This appropriateness is founded in the cognitive and social characteristics of children.

First, the centers approach is appropriate because it matches the attention spans of young children. Young children vary greatly in the amount of time they can attend to a task. If a child selects the task and finds it interesting, the time span increases. If a child is required to complete a task for which he or she sees no purpose, the time span decreases. Because the centers approach allows the child to select from a variety of possibilities, it is more likely that he or she will select a task that is interesting and appropriate. Because of this self-selection, the child's attention span increases.

Second, the centers approach allows for the child's growing sense of responsibility, but retains the structure needed if particular goals are to be accomplished. Young children are reaching toward autonomy but need to feel secure within the setting. The centers approach provides a sense of security through its structure and yet enhances the development of autonomy because the child is able to select from a variety of activities.

Third, the centers approach allows for natural-ability groupings. Children using a centers approach often work together in small groups. Often some of these groups are based on similar interests and so cut across levels of ability. Children who are

interested in finding out what objects float will join with others of similar interest regardless of the academic ability of the children. In other cases, the groupings will be based on the perceptions children have of peer ability. Children who are attempting to construct the highest possible tower will look for other children who are good at constructing towers. In either case, the groupings form naturally and change according to the nature of the task.

Fourth, the centers approach allows the child to decide whether to work with others or not. As children develop in their ability to communicate effectively with one another, they choose to work with other children on a more frequent basis. A centers approach allows children to choose whether they will work with others, next to others without interacting, or alone. Such a format allows one child to decide to make unilateral changes in activity directions and procedures while also allowing children who are working in small groups to make group modifications in directions so that its investigation is extended and enhanced.

Fifth, the centers approach allows the child to decide when closure should occur. The young child often does not see the need to reach a certain preestablished end-point before concluding an activity. The use of centers gives the child the opportunity to continue a particularly interesting investigation longer than the teacher may have planned or conclude an activity within a few minutes. The child is often the best determiner of how much can be assimilated from an activity. When that level is reached, the child concludes. Thus, the centers approach develops child autonomy and considers developmental appropriateness.

Sixth, the centers approach allows the child to act directly on materials. The preoperational child and the child who is making the transition to concrete operational thought both are strongly tied to concrete materials for learning and conceptual development. Because the centers approach provides for hands-on investigation, this developmental characteristic is taken into consideration.

Establishing Centers in the Classroom

A centers approach can be used in any type of classroom setting in order to enhance children's learning experiences.

The Traditional Classroom. The traditional classroom setting usually focuses on learning from written materials in a teacher-directed format. The children are expected to complete certain activities within a specific time frame and to a certain level of accuracy. Those activities, which usually focus on textbooks, worksheets, and pencil-and-paper tasks, are geared toward teaching certain predetermined pieces of information from the various and discrete subject-matter areas. In many cases, the subject-matter areas are kept fully distinct from one another through time schedules or separate textbooks. In this setting, the use of classroom centers can provide for individualization of the program and for the introduction of developmentally appropriate practices. Centers can be used in the traditional setting in four ways.

1. *Introducing a textbook topic.* In this case, a textbook unit on magnets can be introduced prior to beginning the unit by setting up a center dealing with magnets that children can use as time allows.
2. *Providing background experiences that will allow the written or spoken word to be more meaningful.* In this case, the unit that has been started can be enhanced by having the activities of the center available for children to use after the text has been considered.
3. *Providing individualized learning experiences.* In this case, the center is used to provide students with opportunities to investigate the textbook content in individually developed activities.
4. *Providing experiences to conclude or extend a textbook-based topic.* In this case, the center is used to add to the content of the textbook by providing activities dealing with concepts that are developmentally appropriate but that may not have been included in the textbook.

Departmentalized Classroom. A departmentalized setting generally involves the differentiation of the curriculum into separate subject areas. Usually, different teachers teach each subject area, further separating the areas and decreasing the possible overlap. A departmentalized program may use traditional teaching strategies such as textbooks, worksheets, workbooks, and other written materials or it may use manipulative-based teaching strategies. Within the departmentalized classroom, centers can be used in three ways.

1. *Demonstrating how separated subject-matter areas are interrelated.* In this case, arithmetic skills learned during the arithmetic section of the curriculum can be utilized in activities dealing with science or writing skills or as part of science or mathematics activities.
2. *Providing introductory or individualized experiences related to the established curriculum.* In this case, the center provides children with integrated experiences that allow for individualized activities related to the topics of the separated curricular areas.
3. *Enriching the experiences of the departmentalized program.* In this case, the centers approach allows students to pursue investigations of topics that may not have been included within the standard curriculum and to integrate the diverse subject-matter areas through their investigations.

Open Classroom. An open-classroom setting generally allows a great deal of child decision-making because the program often revolves around interests, themes, or units. The teaching found in an open setting usually integrates the various subject areas into a variety of hands-on activities.

In the open-classroom setting, the centers approach forms the basis for learning in the areas of mathematics and science. The open setting allows for full implementation of the concept of the combined curriculum. In the open setting, the centers approach allows for a variety of purposeful activities to be going on simultaneously.

Developing Centers for Classroom Use

Step One: Decide on the purpose of the center. In order to develop a classroom center, the teacher needs to have a clear idea of what the center is to accomplish. The center should have one central purpose. If the center is to help children develop their ability to observe, that is considered the purpose of the center. If the center is to help children develop a concept of number, that is the purpose of the center. The purpose provides the focus for the selection of activities.

Step Two: Establish the objectives of the center. Knowing that the purpose of the center is to

LEARNING ACTIVITY 45

Classroom Planning for Center Use

Purpose: The purpose of this activity is to plan for the use of centers in an actual classroom setting.

Procedure:

1. Observe a first-grade classroom and a second-grade classroom. Make any measurements or sketches of the classroom that will help you gain a clear picture of the classroom arrangement.
2. Decide how you could arrange each of the classrooms in order to allow for the use of a centers approach.
3. Make a drawing of the arrangement that would be necessary for the use of centers in the classroom, including not only the placement of the centers but also the way in which materials would be stored, the organization of traffic to and from the centers, the location of collection boxes for activity results that are to be given to the teacher, and the arrangement of follow-up discussions of center activities.

---

develop the child's ability to observe is not enough to allow for selection of appropriate activities. In order to select activities that will contribute to the purpose of the center, specific objectives should be written. In general, an objective should be established for each of the activities of the center. If the purpose of the center is to have children develop a concept of number, the following objectives may be appropriate.

1. Each child will be able to use toothpicks to show a variety of arrangements, all of which include seven toothpicks.
2. Each child will be able to make sets of eight objects using at least three different types of materials.
3. Each child will be able to count out the number of unifix cubes equivalent to the quantity shown on a single die.
4. Each child will be able to construct towers of wooden blocks to show the quantities six, seven, and eight.
5. Each child will be able to record on a worksheet the number of pink beans and the number of white beans shown in the "toss the beans" game.

As can be seen in each of these objectives, the child is engaged in a concrete learning activity. Each activity is geared toward the child's concept of number and allows for a variety of responses among different children. In all cases, the child can work on the tasks alone, parallel with other children, or with other children. Also, each objective indicates that the child may stop the activity when he or she reaches closure rather than at a particular ending point established by the teacher.

Step Three: Select the activities that will be included. Once the purpose and objectives are established, then the task for the teacher is to determine which activities will be used in the center. There are many sources for finding activities. If there is a textbook series or program in use for mathematics and science, the series can give some ideas for center activities. In many cases, such text activities have a single outcome and a specified closure point and, therefore, will need to be rewritten to allow for more appropriate use. Activities may be found in magazines and journals for teachers. These activities can be directly incorporated or modified as needed so that they are appropriate for students. Ideas for activities may come from the many activity books that are available for teachers. Once again, such activities are often narrowly directed toward a single outcome and may need to be rewritten to allow for open-ended investigation and child closure. Activity ideas may also come from watching children as they play with one another. You may get an idea for modifying a board game by watching how children playing the game change it to make it more interesting or more fun. Finally, ideas for activities may come from the teacher. Teachers are highly creative individuals who know their classes better than anyone else. The important point is to know what it is that you want to accomplish through the activity before you select the activity. A wonderful activity that does not contribute to the purpose of the center is not a productive activity.

Step Four: Write the activity directions. For the first- or second-grade level, writing directions can be difficult. The reading skills of children at this age may not be developed enough for them to read and follow a set of directions. For some activities, a tape recording of the directions is effective. In other cases, directions can be written in rebus form where pictures are used in the place of some words. Directions also can be written with accompanying illustrations. And, never underestimate the ability of one child to tell or show another child how to do an activity. In classrooms where children who use English as a second language are a part of the group, include directions in the child's first language as well as in English. For blind children, include braille formats. Finally, be prepared to give directions orally when needed. A child should never be unable to participate in an activity simply because he or she can't read the directions for it.

Step Five: Collect and package the materials needed for each activity. The activity directions should tell what materials can be used during the activity. In many cases, an activity found in a book or other source will focus on a narrow outcome or a single method and the suggested materials may be quite limited. If this is the case, decide how the activity can be made more open ended and expand the list of materials. For example, an activity may ask that children arrange five tiles in a variety of ways. The list of materials (five tiles per child) easily can be expanded to include other small objects that children can arrange in a variety of ways: toothpicks, beads, gumdrops, beans, unifix cubes, colored wooden blocks, styrofoam packing "peanuts," plastic paper clips, and anything else that comes to mind as fun to arrange. The greater the variety of materials, the greater the chance that children will become involved in the activity and find a variety of possibilities.

A primary concern in the selection of materials for a center should be in the variety of materials and the variety of actions possible with the materials. However, three other factors need to be considered in the selection of materials. First, select materials with a view toward safety. Although first and second graders are able to use small objects, be careful that those objects do not look like something that can be mistaken as edible.

Caution children never to taste or eat anything that has not been specifically designated for eating. If gumdrops or other small candies are being used, provide children with some for eating and others for working. There is one caution about cautions. Giving children specific directions about not doing something can actually act as a catalyst to do it. For example, telling children never to put beans in their ears or up their noses may act as such a catalyst. Children who never thought of such an act will decide to try it in order to see what will happen! Second, select materials that are inexpensive and easy to replace. No matter how careful children are, if small objects are used over a long period of time by many different children, they will eventually get lost. It is easy and inexpensive to replace toothpicks and lima beans, styrofoam packing bits and straws. It is not easy or inexpensive to replace counters shaped like teddy bears, small toys, or other toy-store items. Third, select materials that can be used in a variety of different ways rather than materials that only may be used for limited purposes. For example, tiles can be arranged in a variety of ways because they are nothing more than square-inch pieces of ceramic. Teddy bear counters, on the other hand, have a tendency to be used as teddy bears rather than as multiple-use counters.

Finally, package the materials so that they can be easily stored, unpacked, and repacked. Plastic margarine tubs, ice cream tubs, and shoe boxes work well for packaging. The child should be able to open and close the storage package easily. Also, the containers should be small enough that they can be easily stored in small or crowded classrooms. Finally, the containers should be labeled so that their contents can be easily identified. Glue one of the stored objects or a picture of the object to the top of the container.

Step Six: Establish a method that allows the teacher to see the results of at least some of the activities. In many activities, the teacher sees the results as he or she interacts with the students in an informal manner. However, some activities lend themselves to the production of a worksheet, drawing, written item, or other material that can be turned in to the teacher as evidence of the child's activity. For example, if children are growing plants and keeping a record of the height of the plants each day through drawings, then the drawings provide the teacher with a record of the child's activity. Similarly, if the child is developing a pattern using construction-paper pattern blocks, the child can glue the construction paper to another sheet of paper as a copy of his or her patterning activities. It is not necessary to have the child hand in something as a record of every activity. The teacher can use a checklist or an anecdotal record to keep track of the kinds of activities in which the child has participated.

Step Seven: Organize the activities into a total center. The center needs to be organized so that the child is given a clear idea as to the purpose of the center. This can be effectively done through the use of a backdrop of some kind. A bulletin board should clearly show the activity's purpose through words and pictures. A backdrop also can be made from the tri-fold materials so frequently seen as the backdrop for a science-fair project. In this case, the backdrop becomes a mini bulletin board that is used to attract attention to the center. Finally, the backdrop can be a picture or poster that directs the student's attention to the activities.

Within the center, the materials should be organized so that the directions are attached to the backdrop or to the surface on which the children will work. This prevents the directions from being separated from the center. Color code the directions to the set of materials to be used for each activity. This will eliminate any doubt about which materials are to be used for each activity.

Finally, organize the materials so that there is plenty of room for children to work. This means providing space for the materials and also for the child to be able to work alone or with others.

Step Eight: Establish the procedures for using the center. As you introduce the center to the class, clearly establish the number of children who may work in the center at one time. If you intend to have students rotate from one center to another during a certain period of time, establish how the rotation occurs: clockwise, counterclockwise, or at random. If students are to be allowed to move freely from one center to another, tell them that this is appropriate behavior. And, if the centers are to be used as a part of the traditional or departmentalized program, establish when children can and cannot go to the centers.

It is also important to establish some way of keeping a record of which child uses which center. Children who are able to write easily can simply

sign in when they go to a center. Children who have difficulty in writing can put a name card into an envelope or basket at the center.

Be certain to establish rules for behavior at the centers. Rules should be kept to a minimum and worded as positively as possible; for example, "Talk quietly in the center" rather than "No loud talking."

Establish a method for gaining the attention of students so that you can give directions to the class even when the children are scattered among a variety of centers and activities. Clapping, ringing a bell, flashing the lights, or whistling all can be effective methods. Establish the signal for attention and then practice what should happen a number of times so that children react quickly.

Finally, know what to do if children use the center materials improperly. Be aware that some kinds of inappropriate behaviors are to be expected. For example, whenever children are given new materials to work with, they need an opportunity to play with those materials before they will work with them in the expected manner. Give children a chance to play with materials. Children can also be expected to shoot rubber bands or to play at sword fighting with rulers or other kinds of sticks. Head off the inappropriate behavior, not by talking about the dangers, but by allowing the behavior in a safe way. Shooting rubberbands at a wall becomes very boring after a few minutes and, by making the misbehavior into an appropriate pastime, the teacher takes all of the fun out of the action.

When children persist in using the materials inappropriately, two actions are generally helpful. First, if the behavior is dangerous, discuss with the entire class why that behavior is dangerous. Have the children determine reasons why it is not a good idea to sword fight with rulers. Have the children decide why it is not a good idea to put the colored blocks in their pockets and take them home. Children will come up with reasons that make sense to them while the reasons you have as an adult may not. Second, some children will disobey even the most positively stated and established rules for center use. In this case, an effective strategy is to remove the child from the center. Have a place where the child can sit, apart from the other children but where he or she can see what is going on. It is far more fun to be involved than to be watching. Be certain that the child knows why he or she has been removed from the center and then tell the child that he or she can return when ready. Put the responsibility for returning to the center on the child. Do not be afraid to remove the child again and again until appropriate behavior can be maintained. Also, do not be afraid to praise the child who has had difficulty in the center for appropriate behavior. However, be careful of the type of praise given. Telling a student, "You are behaving so well in the center" indicates that it is so unexpected that you have to make note of it. It also sends the message that you expect good behavior today but not necessarily tomorrow or even later on that day. Instead, use productive praise that focuses on the child's performance in the center. "You have a lot of different, colorful patterns," "These drawings really show what your plant is like," or "You have a method for showing how fast things roll that I never would have thought of" all praise the child's work rather than behavior. Example 8.1 provides a checklist for evaluating a center that has been developed for classroom use.

The Integrated Approach to Teaching

Definition. Integrated teaching is a method of organizing for teaching in which any appropriate subject-matter area is utilized in developing concepts selected by the teacher. The integrated approach not only combines mathematics and science into a single area but also may involve reading, language arts, social studies, art, and music in the learning process. The major criterion for the integration of the subject areas is that they be used purposefully in the investigation and development of a particular topic or concept within the topic. The integrated approach can utilize centers as part of the total teaching sequence.

Basis for the Integrated Approach. The integrated approach is based on three concepts about the learning process in children. The first concept is that young children do not differentiate among and between subject-matter areas. Instead, they view the subject-matter areas as an interrelated totality. Since the integrated approach also considers the subject-matter areas to be a totality rather than separate entities, the approach is effective with children. Second, the integrated approach is based on the concept that the various subject-matter

areas can be used to enhance learning. From this viewpoint, reading can be used to broaden the information learned in a hands-on approach, mathematics can be used to investigate size relations or to graph information so that conclusions can be drawn, language arts can be used in record keeping, and art can be used as a means of conveying information. Subject-matter areas are treated not only as subjects in themselves but also as means for obtaining information. Finally, the integrated approach to teaching is based on an inductive teaching method in which a variety of activities related to a particular topic are integrated into a single whole. For example, the concept of a mammal is developed through activities dealing with the ideas that mammals have fur, are warm-blooded, give birth to live young, feed their young with milk, and have a backbone. The concept of a mammal develops as all of these specifics are tied together.

Benefits of an Integrated Approach. There are five major benefits of using an integrated approach with first- and second-grade children.

First, the integrated approach allows children to utilize the skills that are developed in the specific subject-matter areas in purposeful ways. Rather than using contrived experiences such as having children read to find information in a paragraph written specifically for that purpose, the integrated approach has children reading information on a particular topic and using their reading skills to find information pertinent to the topic.

Second, because subject-matter areas overlap, the integrated approach has the benefit of using that overlap in investigating a particular concept. Skills learned in reading and language arts are useful in recording and developing new information within the areas of mathematics or science. Consequently, children benefit by seeing how the skills and concepts of one area are useful in learning in all areas. The key to this particular benefit of the integrated approach is in the purposeful use of subject matter. For example, using graphing skills when considering the topic of plants to determine whether plants with flowers or plants without flowers were more common on a nature walk is a purposeful use of a mathematical concept. Finding the total for a problem like "Mary has four plants and Tommy has three plants. How many plants do

EXAMPLE 8.1

Checklist for Centers

A center that focuses on either the mathematics area or the science area can be evaluated on the following criteria.

1. Is the learning center attractive in a way that will appeal to children? yes no

2. Are the objectives for the center clearly stated? yes no

3. Are the objectives for each activity clearly stated? yes no

4. Are the directions for each activity clearly written and easy to follow? yes no

5. Can each activity be done with a minimum of attention by the teacher? yes no

6. Is there provision for the teacher to see at least some of the activity results? yes no

7. Is the center durable and well-made? yes no

8. Does each activity relate to the center focus? yes no

9. Is the topic for the center developmentally appropriate? yes no

10. Are there provisions that allow children with handicapping conditions to use the center? yes no

11. Are mathematics concepts and science process skills combined within the center? yes no

12. Are the materials simple and easily replaced? yes no

13. Have procedures been established for center use, including number of children and time limits? yes no

14. Are the materials and activities appropriate for a variety of developmental levels of children? yes no

15. Are some of the activities open ended to allow for individual problem solving or the pursuit of individual investigations? yes no

When "no" is circled, use the space below to make suggestions for improvement.

LEARNING ACTIVITY 46

Developing a Learning Center: Science

Purpose: The purpose of this activity is to develop a learning center that focuses on the science process skills that are appropriate for the first- or second-grade level.

Procedure:

1. Choose a topic for a learning center that focuses on science process skills that are appropriate to the first- or second-grade level.

2. Develop a learning center that includes
   a. the purpose of the center;
   b. the objectives for the center;
   c. five to seven hands-on activities with clearly written directions, all materials needed for a class of children, and a method for seeing the results of at least some of the activities;
   d. a backdrop for the center that will be attractive and motivational to children; and
   e. procedures for using the center.

3. Describe the kinds of questions that you might use with the class to follow up on the activities that were done within the center.

4. Describe how mathematics concepts are included even though the focus of the center is on science process skills.

5. Construct the entire center exactly as it would appear in a classroom.

LEARNING ACTIVITY 47

Developing a Learning Center: Mathematics

Purpose: The purpose of this activity is to develop a learning center that focuses on mathematical concepts and is appropriate for the first- or second-grade level.

Procedure:
1. Choose a topic for a learning center that focuses on mathematical concepts and is appropriate for the first- or second-grade level.
2. Develop a learning center that includes
   a. the purpose of the center;
   b. the objectives for the center;
   c. five to seven hands-on activities with clearly written directions, all materials needed for a class of children, and a method for seeing the results of at least some of the activities;
   d. a backdrop for the center that will be attractive and motivational to children; and
   e. procedures for using the center.
3. Describe the kinds of questions that you might use with the class to follow up on the activities that were done within the center.
4. Describe how science process skills are included even though the focus of the center is on mathematical concepts.
5. Construct the entire center exactly as it would appear in a classroom.

---

they have all together?'' is a contrived problem that does not enhance the concept of plants.

The third benefit of the integrated approach is that problem solving and critical thinking are developed through use of skills in real situations. Children engage in purposeful problem solving during classification activities and in critical thinking as they try to determine which way of graphing gives the most information.

The fourth advantage of teaching through the integrated approach is that children's retention is aided by encountering topics in a variety of situations and through a variety of modalities. As students make more and more connections within and between subject-matter areas, they are able to process information in ways that are appropriate to their modes of thought and that allow the development of a network of concepts. Writing develops beyond a means for developing a story and into a way of recording and communicating ideas. Mathematical skills such as counting and graphing become ways of gaining and organizing information. Science processes such as observation and classification become ways of looking at similarities, differences, and relationships.

Finally, transfer of learning occurs when the situations in which skills are learned are as close to real-life situations as possible. Children may learn to read through skills learned in a basal reader, but until the value of reading as a means of gaining information is demonstrated, it may remain an isolated skill. Children may learn classification as part of science, but the benefit of classification as a problem-solving skill is not shown until it is applied in other areas. And, so long as mathematics remains the "stuff" found in a mathematics textbook, the power of mathematics as a problem-solving tool is not seen.

The integrated approach, then, allows children to learn through the various subject-matter areas rather than learning about the various subject matter areas. The integrated approach is not meant to be a way of teaching children to write, read, count, measure, graph, or classify. It assumes that these concepts and skills have been developed and that the child is now ready to use these ideas in other situations.

Organizing for an Integrated Approach to Teaching. *Step One: Select the topic to be studied as a part of the integrated approach.* The topic selected should be broad so that students can investigate a variety of related concepts. The topic "Leaves" is a better topic than "Characteristics of Leaves" because it is broader in scope. Also, "leaves" would take in the characteristics of leaves as a part of the investigations. The topic selected should be developmentally appropriate. The teacher should take into account the cognitive and social characteristics of children, as well as the science processes/mathematical concepts appropriate to the grade level. "Classification" is an appropriate topic provided the type of classification selected for use is developmentally appropriate: classification by single traits rather than by multiple traits. "Cause of Weather" would not be a developmentally appropriate topic because it requires an understanding of cause and effect.

Step Two: Decide on the concepts to be developed through the integrated approach. The concepts should be listed in statement form to determine exactly what is to be learned. This listing serves as a check for the teacher about exactly what is being learned and is also a starting point for the selection of an activity. The concepts selected should be directly related to the topic and should enhance an understanding of the topic. At this point, the teacher does not need to think in terms of reading, mathematics, science, social studies, art, or music, but rather in terms of what is to be learned. The following is a list of concepts for the topic "Liquids."

1. Liquids can be poured from one container to another.
2. Liquids take the shapes of their containers.
3. Liquids can be classified by their characteristics.
4. Some liquids are thicker than others.
5. Liquids are used in many different ways.
6. Some materials dissolve in liquids and some do not.

Step Three: Decide on the activities that will be used to investigate the listed concepts. In deciding on the activities to be used, give careful attention to the science process skills and mathematics concepts needed in the activity. Selecting activities that require only those processes and concepts appropriate to the grade level will help to assure the success of the activities. In addition, each concept should have one or more activities associated with it. The following is a brief description of activities that could be used to develop the concepts previously listed.

1. Liquids can be poured from one container to another.
    a. Provide students with water and a variety of various sized containers. Have children pour the water from one container to another,

then write a few sentences or draw a picture to tell what they did.
    b. Provide children with liquids other than water such as syrup, milk, soft drink, vinegar, shampoo, conditioner, and oil. Have them pour the liquids into various sized containers. Children should look for similarities and differences in the ways liquids pour. They can write about or draw pictures to show their investigations.
2. Liquids take the shapes of their containers.
    a. Provide children with water and variously shaped containers, all of which hold approximately the same amount. Have the children pour the water from container to container, nothing what happens to the water's shape as it is poured. They can draw pictures or write about their investigations.
    b. Provide children with various liquids and variously shaped containers, all of which hold approximately the same amount. Have them pour the liquids from container to container, noting changes in the liquids' shapes. The children can draw pictures or write about their investigations.
3. Liquids can be classified by their characteristics.
    a. Ask children to classify samples of liquids of various colors in sealed, clear plastic containers. Use liquids such as coffee, tea, cocoa, water, vinegar, lemon juice, orange juice, orange soft drink, lemonade, cooking oil, cola, milk, and white shampoo. Students can draw pictures or write sentences to describe how they classified the liquids.
    b. Ask children to classify liquids by their aroma, using containers with a small opening through which the aroma can be detected. Use liquids such as coffee, tea, cocoa, water, vinegar, lemon juice, orange juice, orange soft drink, lemonade, cooking oil, cola, milk, and white shampoo. Have them draw pictures or write sentences to describe how they classified the liquids.
    c. Ask children to classify liquids by their appearance (clear, cloudy, etc.) using liquids in sealed, clear plastic containers. Use liquids such as coffee, tea, cocoa, water, vinegar, lemon juice, orange juice, orange soft

drink, lemonade, cooking oil, cola, milk, and white shampoo. Have them draw pictures or write sentences to describe how they classified the liquids.

4. Some liquids are thicker than others.
   - Provide children with cardboard covered with plastic wrap, medicine droppers, and a variety of liquids including water, oil, maple syrup, vinegar, shampoo, and soft drink. Have drop races in which children place drops of liquid on the plastic, tilt the cardboard, and determine which of the liquids is the winner. Children should describe which is the fastest, slowest, and so on, of the liquids they tested.

5. Liquids are used in many ways.
   - Have the class brainstorm ways in which they and other people use liquids everyday. Make a master list of students' ideas.

6. Some materials dissolve in liquids and some do not.
   a. Provide children with water, cups, spoons, and a variety of familiar solids such as salt, sugar, pepper, gravel, paper confetti, plastic confetti, and epsom salts. Have them find out which ones dissolve and which do not. Written records can be kept of the investigations conducted.
   b. Provide children with cups, spoons, and a variety of familiar solids and liquids. Use liquids such as water, oil, vinegar, shampoo, soft drink, and milk. Use solids such as salt, sugar, pepper, gravel, paper confetti, plastic confetti, and epsom salts. Have them find out which solids will dissolve in the various liquids. Written records of the investigations conducted can be kept by the students or the teacher.

Step Four: Determine which subject-matter areas are used as a part of the activities and draw a diagram to show the subject-matter areas and their concepts. The diagram provides a visual record of the planning to this point. Using the diagram, it is easy to determine whether all of the activities relate to the main topic, whether activities have been planned for each concept, and which subject-matter areas are being used (see Diagram 8.1).

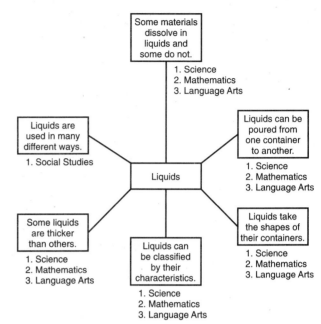

Diagram 8.1 Tentative Integrated-Approach Diagram: Liquids

Step Five: Review the activities and the subject areas being incorporated into the integrated approach. First, review the activities to determine if effective and purposeful use of the subject-matter areas is being made. For example, when considering uses of liquids, the activity planned involves only brainstorming a list. The subject-matter areas included are science and language arts. This activity can be made more effective by extending it to include classifying the list into categories, drawing pictures to illustrate the various uses of liquids, and then graphing the categories to show which category had the most uses or fewest uses. Additional information can be gained through reading and adding to the list developed. Second, review the activities to determine if a variety of kinds of activities are included. Activities should allow for work by individual children, pairs, small groups, and the class as a whole. After reconsidering the planned activities, the chart can be revised to show the results of the brainstorming activity and how many children worked on an activity at one time (see Diagram 8.2 for the revised chart).

Step Six: Organize the materials for ease of distribution and use. Look first at whether the activity is designed for individuals, small groups,

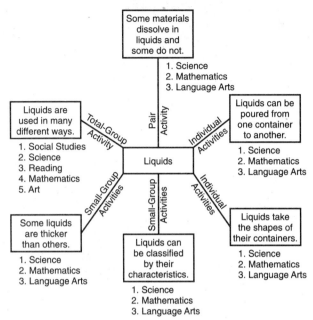

Diagram 8.2 Completed Integrated-Approach Diagram: Liquids

pairs, or the whole class as a single group. The amount of materials needed will depend on the number of children working with a single set of materials. Package what is needed for an activity in a plastic bag, box, or other container that can be easily distributed. Second, decide where children will work. Pouring activities need a large space and a location where mess will not be a problem. Activities dealing with classification by smell or with drop races need close teacher supervision and so should be located where the teacher can easily maintain that supervision.

The materials for the activity dealing with pouring water can be placed in a tub next to a water table or other large basin. The materials for the activity involving pouring a variety of liquids can be placed in a second tub and placed atop or beside the area where the activity will be conducted. The classification activities can be made into center activities with the materials for each activity placed in a container at the center. For the drop races, put the liquids in baby food jars, fasten a dropper to each jar with a rubber band, and place the jars on the cardboard for ease of distribution to small groups. For the investigation of dissolving, place

the solids into labeled, sealed plastic containers, the cups and spoons in plastic bags, and the liquids in labeled baby food jars. Since the concept "liquids are used in many different ways" is a large-group brainstorming activity, no materials are necessary.

Step Seven: Determine the sequence in which the activities are to be presented to the class. In general, sequencing from known to unknown or familiar to unfamiliar is best. The behavior of pouring water is familiar to most children, but how other kinds of liquids behave when poured may not be as familiar. Children know, either because of a school activity or a home experience, that some liquids pour faster than others. However, they may not know that rate of pouring is related to the thickness of the liquid and that the rate of flow can be determined by how the liquids move down an incline.

One appropriate sequence for the activities listed in this example is as follows.

1. pouring water
2. pouring other liquids
3. water in variously shaped containers
4. other liquids in variously shaped containers
5. drop races
6. classification of liquids by color
7. classification of liquids by appearance
8. classification of liquids by aroma
9. dissolving materials in water
10. dissolving materials in other liquids
11. uses of liquids

This sequence is appropriate because it begins with a familiar activity: pouring. The sequence then moves to formal consideration of one of the effects of pouring liquids: they take the shape of the container into which they are poured. Drop races focus on another characteristic of liquids as they are poured: some will pour faster than others. By asking children to note characteristics such as color, aroma, and clarity, classification further develops the idea that liquids have their own characteristics. Dissolving materials in water and other liquids begins to develop an idea of liquids being used for a particular purpose. Finally, brainstorming ways in which liquids are used further develops the idea that liquids can be used in many different ways.

Step Eight: Provide a follow-up discussion. The discussion that follows the activities and the total presentation of the integrated approach should encourage children to describe what they have done and help them draw conclusions about their activities. The teacher can collect their observations and the results of their investigations on the chalkboard, overhead, or chart paper and then lead a discussion of what occurred in the activities. Remember that at the first- and second-grade level children are able to easily describe what occurred in an activity but are not able to discuss why particular phenomena occurred. Therefore, the discussion should focus on what happened rather than on why it happened.

Although the eight steps in developing an integrated-teaching approach were utilized with a science topic as the focus, mathematics topics can also be used as the focus. Diagram 8.3 shows an integrated approach that utilizes the topic of measurement as its focus.

Whether using a centers approach or an integrated approach, the role of the teacher is to assist the children in understanding what was accomplished in the activities. The teacher can do this by talking with children as they work or through a follow-up discussion.

THE ROLE OF QUESTIONS IN THE CENTERS APPROACH AND THE INTEGRATED APPROACH TO TEACHING

Although independent work both by individual children and in small groups is important in the centers and integrated approach, the teacher still has a major role to play. The role not only involves the development of the centers or integrated activities, but also includes the use of questions and questioning strategies to enable children to develop the concepts inherent in the selected activities. A discussion will often help children understand ideas that were not clear to them as they worked on their own. In addition, some of the science process skills and mathematics concepts, such as classification and graphing, lend themselves well to group activities that are organized around questions. The basic role of questions in both the centers and integrated approach is to help children discuss their activities and investigations in terms of their development of problem solving skills, process skills, and content information.

Uses of Questions

Questions should, first, help children focus on the skills and concepts that they used in a particular center or integrated learning experience. After doing a series of activities with leaves, for example, you might ask children questions like the following:

"What were some observations you made of your leaves?"

"How were some of your leaves the same as other leaves?"

"How did your leaves differ from one another?"

"How many leaves did you have that had smooth edges?"

"What ways did you find to classify your leaves?"

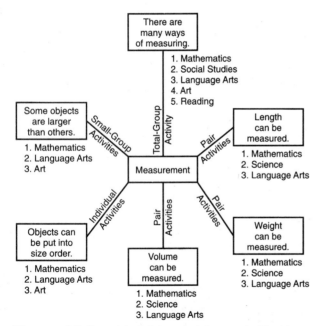

Diagram 8.3 Completed Integrated-Approach Diagram: Measurement

LEARNING ACTIVITY 48

Developing an Integrated Approach: Science

Purpose: The purpose of this activity is to develop an integrated approach that has as its topic an area selected from science content.

Procedure:

1. Choose a topic for the integrated approach based on a science content that is appropriate for the first- or second-grade level.
2. Develop an integrated approach including
   a. a selected topic;
   b. concepts to be developed;
   c. activities to be used for investigating the concepts in an appropriate sequence, including the materials needed, the directions for accom-plishing the activity, and the subject-matter areas that will be explored;
   d. a diagram showing the integrated approach topic, including the activities, number of students involved (individuals, pairs, small groups, total group), and subject-matter areas; and
   e. a description of how the materials for the activity will be packaged and how the activities will be placed in the classroom.
3. Describe the kinds of questions that you might use with the class to follow up the activities that were included in the integrated approach.

LEARNING ACTIVITY 49

Developing an Integrated Approach: Mathematics

Purpose: The purpose of this activity is to develop an integrated approach that has as its topic an area selected from mathematics content.

Procedure:

1. Choose a topic for the integrated approach based on mathematics content that is appropriate for the first- or second-grade level.
2. Develop an integrated approach including
   a. a selected topic;
   b. concepts to be developed;
   c. activities to be used for investigating the concepts in an appropriate sequence, including the materials needed, directions for accom-plishing the activity, and subject-matter areas that will be used in the activity;
   d. a diagram showing the integrated approach topic, including the activities, number of students involved (individuals, pairs, small groups, total group), and subject-matter areas; and
   e. a description of how the materials for the activity will be packaged and how the activities will be placed in the classroom.
3. Describe the kinds of questions that you might use with the class to follow up the activities that were included in the integrated approach.

"What could we do to determine whether we have more leaves with smooth edges or more leaves with rough edges?"

"What were the shapes of your leaves?"

"Were all the leaves the same size? How could we find out which leaf was the largest and which was the smallest?"

The second purpose of questioning is to help children communicate the results of their activities to others. Although children will definitely talk to one another while they are working in the centers or with integrated approach activities, they also need to be encouraged to discuss their activities with the group as a whole. In this case, you could ask questions such as the following after children have worked with simple machines.

"What were some of the interesting things you learned about simple machines?"

"What did you find that happened differently than you expected?"

"What methods did you find to get the pulley to pick up heavy objects?"

"What ways did you find to get a lever to move objects?"

"What was the funniest way you found to use an inclined plane to move a book?"

"What were some ways you used the blocks and rollers to make a lever?"

Questions such as these encourage children to talk about what they did during their activities and investigations. There are a few tips that can help make such questions successful in the classroom.

- First, ask the question in a way that will allow anyone who wishes to answer to do so. Rather than designating a name before the question, call on children who indicate that they would like to answer after the question is asked. In other words, ask the question and then call on the respondent rather than asking the question in the form "John, what did you find out about levers?"

- In order to facilitate child responses, have the materials from the center ready so that children can use them to illustrate what they are saying. Young children often need to have the materials available so that they can use gestures and actions to supplement their spoken explanations.

- Be accepting of all answers given, even answers that are not what you expected. An answer from the "class clown" may be given in a way that is intended to elicit laughter from other students and a rebuke from the teacher. Accept the answer as if it were given like any other response, ask questions that might help to develop the idea contained in the answer, and show respect for it. For example, Mary answers a question about the inclined plane by describing an orange that rolled down and "went splat all over everything" followed by great detail. The image causes laughter, and should. Rather than commenting on silly answers, ask children if they can think of other fruits or objects that could "go splat." Classify them into groups that either "go splat" or "smash." Have chil-

dren try to think of ways they could prevent the "splat" or the "smash." It is even better if you can try some of the ideas and see if they will work.

- Refrain from calling on children for responses who prefer not to respond. Such children may feel uncomfortable in sharing their ideas and will be made more uncomfortable if forced into the role. Children who are shy or uncomfortable have often been made that way by the way their teachers and peers have responded to their answers. If they begin to see that all answers are accepted, then they too will begin to respond.

- Finally, show that you respect and value the answers given by the children. You can show your respect by really listening. Nod. Smile, Keep your attention focused on the child. If something occurs that must take your attention from the child's response, ask the child to stop for a moment and then to begin again when you can give your full attention once more. Show that you value the child's response by including it in an experience chart or other written record of the activities and the follow-up discussion.

Many activities involve the science process/ mathematics concept of classification. When this process/concept is included, there generally are many methods for classification that can be used. In this case, use questions to help students determine other ways of classifying the objects. Alternative methods of classification should be used so that students develop not only classification skills, but also flexible thinking and an understanding that there are many ways to classify the same group of objects. For example, if children are investigating rocks and minerals, they may classify them by color. Alternative classification systems can be based on luster, hardness, shape, weight, marks that can be made with the rock or mineral, or size of particles making up the rock or mineral. As with classification, when graphing is used with activities, there are often alternative ways of graphing. Questions can be used to assist children in identifying and constructing these graphs. For example, children may graph the number of children who like each kind of fruit. They could, however, also graph fruits by whether they grow individually like apples or in bunches like grapes, by the number of seeds, by whether the rind is eaten or not, or even by how the fruit is used—apples and pumpkins make great pies but watermelons and cucumbers do not.

Finally, questions can help children identify new questions for investigation. It may be enough to ask "What else would you like to find out about ants?" By asking questions, new investigations can be developed and hands-on activities can be extended so that a wide variety of subject-matter areas are incorporated into learning experiences. In incorporating learning experiences from the reading area, be certain that the written sources of information are used either as supplements to an activity or when a hands-on activity is not possible. For example, a question such as "What do ants eat?" can be answered by having children try different types of food in their ant farm and then reading to find additional information that cannot be learned through hands-on activities. However, a question such as "What are the biggest trees in the world?" can be answered effectively by using a book on trees that shows and discusses various types of trees and their sizes.

Asking Appropriate Questions

In a centers approach or an integrated approach, the role of questions is to help children discuss their activities and extend their ideas beyond those activities into other areas. Questions help children develop concepts and processes and help them learn to use that information in a variety of ways. In order to help children use skills, develop concepts, and generalize to other areas, the following techniques for questioning are helpful.

1. Ask more divergent questions than convergent questions. Convergent questions ask for a particular piece of information. They have only one answer and so it is very easy to be wrong. Divergent questions, on the other hand, have a variety of possible answers, making it quite easy to be right. In addition, because of the wide variety of answers to a divergent question, there is less chance that the questioning strategy will focus on a particular piece of content information. Instead, it is likely to focus on thinking skills, particularly on flexibility in thinking.

2. Use more questions that require the child to describe and explain than questions that ask for recitation of information conveyed by the teacher. An appropriate question is "What are some of the ways we have used to measure our classroom?" An inappropriate question is "Yesterday we measured our classroom. How long was the classroom in feet?"

3. Use more open than closed questions. Open questions encourage children to speculate and to suggest possible ways for investigation, whereas closed questions require a "scientific" or "mathematical" explanation. For example, an open question is "One group found that apples have more seeds than oranges, while another group found that oranges have more seeds than apples. What could be some reasons that we have two different ideas?" This focuses on problem solving as children try to think of a variety of possibilities. An example of a closed question is "One group found that apples have more seeds than oranges, while another group found that oranges have more seeds than apples. Which group do you think is right?" In this case, the focus is on right versus wrong, rather than on the reasons for differences. By trying out some of the possible reasons for the differences, it is possible to determine if there is a right or wrong answer, but that is not the focus.

4. Ask more questions that allow for investigation than questions that assume that all answers are known. For example, "Is a cucumber a fruit or a vegetable?" is a question that indicates that there is a particular correct answer that can be learned in some way. Rephrasing the question as "How can we determine whether a cucumber is a fruit or a vegetable?" focuses on process skills such as observation, classification, conclusion, and comparing and contrasting. The answer, by the way, is that a cucumber is a fruit.

5. Ask questions that allow children to demonstrate their discoveries. In this way, children who have difficulty with the use of language as a way of communicating their discoveries will be able to effectively participate in the discussion.

6. Ask questions that will allow children to present a variety of responses. Consider an activity whose purpose is to determine how objects

LEARNING ACTIVITY 50

Using a Learning Center in the Classroom

Purpose: The purpose of this activity is to use a learning center within a classroom and then analyze the results to make the center more effective.

Procedure:

1. Arrange with either a first- or second-grade teacher to develop and set up a learning center in the classroom.
2. Observe children's use of the center, as well as the results of their investigations.
3. Conduct follow up discussions with the children.
4. Analyze children's use of the center and describe the aspects of the center that were especially productive and those that were troublesome. Make suggestions for improving the troublesome areas.
5. Discuss the center activity with the classroom teacher and incorporate suggestions for improving the center into the actual center.

LEARNING ACTIVITY 51

Activity File of Centers

Purpose: The purpose of this activity is to develop a file of activities for learning centers in the classroom.

Procedure:

1. Develop a file of ideas for learning centers that could be used to develop science process skills and mathematical concepts.
2. With each idea for a center, include the following information:

   a. materials that would be needed,
   b. the focus of the center,
   c. the objectives for the center,
   d. questions that could be used during a follow-up discussion of the center's activities, and
   e. a sketch of the backdrop for the center.

LEARNING ACTIVITY 52

Using an Integrated Approach in the Classroom

Purpose: The purpose of this activity is to use an integrated approach within a classroom, analyze the results of the approach, and make changes based on the analysis.

Procedure:

1. Arrange with either a first- or second-grade teacher to present an integrated approach to teaching in her or his classroom.
2. Work with the classroom teacher to develop and present an integrated approach that is appropriate to the children.
3. Following the presentation and follow-up of the activities, discuss the strategy with the teacher.
   a. Describe the aspects of the strategy that were most successful.
   b. Describe the aspects of the strategy that were least successful.
   c. discuss what could be done to improve the areas that were found to be least successful.
4. Revise the strategy to make it more successful.

LEARNING ACTIVITY 53

File of Activity Ideas

Purpose: The purpose of this activity is to develop a file of activity ideas for use in the integrated approach to teaching.

Procedure:

1. Develop a file of activity ideas that could be used as a part of an integrated approach to teaching.
2. Organize the file so that both mathematics concepts and science concepts are included.
3. Include with each activity idea
   a. the concept to which the activity is related,
   b. the materials needed,
   c. the subject-matter areas that can be utilized in investigating the activity,
   d. whether the activity is meant to be done by individuals, small groups, or the whole class, and
   e. directions for the activity.

---

behave on an inclined plane. The teacher may consider appropriate responses to be those that deal with how quickly the objects roll down different degrees of incline. The children may also find it interesting to consider how far objects roll after they reach the bottom of the incline, whether they can be caused to roll into a bucket, which will win a rolling race, which wiggle as they go down the incline, which stop before they get to the bottom, or whether the inclined plane can be suddenly moved so that the object starts to roll up the plane rather than down it. Once again, keep in mind that the content of the activity is of less importance than the investigations of the children.

SUMMARY

Teaching in the combined curriculum focuses on three distinct teaching strategies: open inquiry, centers, and an integrated approach. The centers approach can be utilized in a traditional, departmentalized, or open-classroom setting. It is in the open classroom that the combined curriculum and the centers approach can be most fully implemented.

The use of centers in the classroom allows the children to investigate particular topics but in a framework that accommodates independent as well as structured investigations. The teacher's role is to develop and maintain the center and then follow up on the children's investigations through group discussions.

The integrated approach to teaching at the first- and second-grade levels provides for purposeful use of a variety of subject-matter areas while investigating a science or mathematics topic. Through the use of an integrated approach, children investigate concepts within a broad topic area by means of related activities.

The discussions that follow up the use of the centers or integrated approach allow children to share the results of their activities with others. Through the use of appropriate questions, the teacher can enhance student investigations. The secret to good follow-up discussions is to gear those discussions toward the actual investigations and their results rather than toward particular bits of science or mathematics content. The discussions should allow children to show how they used science process skills or how they worked with concepts from mathematics. In addition, the questions used within the integrated approach should allow children to consider the concepts that were developed through the activity.

Vocabulary Terms

Center: a means of organizing and instructing that allows a child to choose the area to be investigated and the time to be spent on the investigation.

Centers Approach: a teaching/learning format, based on the use of centers, that allows the integration of mathematical concepts with science process skills.

Departmentalized Classroom: a departmentalized setting generally involves the differentiation of curriculum into separate subject areas, often with different teachers for each subject area.

Integrated Approach: a teaching/learning strategy that allows for the development of concepts through application of a variety of subject-matter areas.

Open Classroom: a classroom setting that generally allows a great deal of child decision making and that usually revolves around interests, themes, or units.

Traditional Classroom: a classroom setting that focuses on learning from written materials in a teacher-directed format.

Study Questions

1. What are the characteristics of a centers approach to teaching at the first- and second-grade levels?
2. How can a centers approach be used in an open classroom, departmentalized classroom, and traditional classroom?
3. Why is a centers approach appropriate to the combined curriculum?
4. How is a center developed for use in a classroom?
5. What is the role of questions within a centers approach at the first- and second-grade levels?
6. How does the integrated approach to teaching compare with a centers approach to teaching?
7. What are some advantages of an integrated approach to teaching as compared to a traditional approach or a centers approach?
8. A teacher at the second-grade level has discovered that her students are able to use science process skills and mathematical concepts effectively but do not see the connection between science and mathematics and other subject-matter areas. Which of the following teaching strategies would you recommend to this teacher in order to help her students see the connections: open-inquiry approach, centers approach, or integrated approach? Explain your answer.

PART THREE

The Defined Curriculum

INTRODUCTION

At the third-grade level, students are beginning to differentiate between mathematics and science and so the curriculum makes the distinction between the two subject-matter areas. Consequently, third grade can be viewed, in part, as an introduction to science and mathematics as specific subject-matter areas. This does not mean, however, that all overlap and correlation between the two areas should be eliminated. Rather, the defined curriculum at the third grade focuses on content areas but utilizes the concepts of science to advance the skills of mathematics and the skills of mathematics to elucidate the concepts of science.

Because subject-matter areas now become important to the curriculum, it is vital that the content information selected is appropriate to the cognitive functioning of the child. Although traditional science topics may be included in the course of study or in the textbook, the textbook cannot be considered an authority on appropriate topics for third-grade children. Traditional mathematics topics also are included in textbooks and programs in mathematics, but they may not necessarily be appropriate to the developmental level of the child. Part of the reason for this lack of appropriateness is in the use of tradition as a guide for content

selection. Because children have always studied classification of vertebrate animals in third grade, teachers continue to teach classification of vertebrate animals in third grade. Because children have always worked with area in third grade, teachers continue to teach area. A second reason why content may be inappropriate, as it is found in the textbook, is the tendency toward downward movement in the curriculum. At one point, atoms and molecules were introduced at the seventh-grade level, now some textbooks are including it at the second- or third-grade level. The topic has not become more appropriate, it has simply been pushed lower. Fractions, once reserved for the fifth or sixth grades, now appear in first-grade mathematics textbooks. Again, the ability of children to comprehend fractional quantities has not changed, only the placement of the topic. In the defined curriculum, then, it remains important to consider the cognitive characteristics of the child when selecting and implementing content information.

Finally, in the defined curriculum, all that has come before remains important. The students in the third grade and above build on the previous explorations of preschool through second grade. Consequently, students should come to the third grade having experienced the investigations that are the hallmark of both the unified and the combined curriculums, having devel-

119

oped the science process skills and mathematics concepts that underlie the content of the defined curriculum, and having constructed concepts that can be used as bases for further understanding.

It is in the defined curriculum that the child takes his or her first steps into differentiated learning and discovers that, although there are separate subject-matter areas, those areas need not remain separated.

CHAPTER 9

Developmental Characteristics of Eight and Nine Year Olds

Chapter Objectives

On completion of this chapter, you should be able to

1. list the cognitive characteristics of eight- and nine-year-old children,

2. discuss the cognitive characteristics of eight- and nine-year-old children, and

3. compare the characteristics of eight- and nine-year-old children to those of younger children.

One of the more common classroom questions from third grade on upward through high school is "Does spelling count?" Generally, this question is asked in science, mathematics, or social studies; anyplace but spelling. The question indicates that students have so fully differentiated subject-matter areas that they no longer see one subject area as being important to another. Social studies questions need not be answered in full sentences, science papers need not be grammatically correct, essays for language arts need not have correct science content, and spelling most certainly does not count in mathematics. In fact, language itself seems unimportant in mathematics as students record numerical answers to numerical problems and even to word problems. Prior to the third-grade level, the "does spelling count" question does not usually occur. Younger children simply assume that they should spell correctly no matter what the subject-matter area.

But, the "spelling question" is only a reflection of other changes found at the third-grade level. The outward appearance of the classroom frequently changes at third grade. Students are more likely to be found in individual desks rather than at tables and those desks are more likely to be arranged in rows all facing the same direction. The arrangement of desks into a formal classroom pattern may be a reflection of the arrangement of the curriculum into a more formal pattern. Not only are subject-matter areas distinct from one another, but so are the textbooks and the times designated for those subject-matter areas. Even the thematic approaches so often used with unit plans keep the subject areas separated.

The third-grade classroom is a reflection of the classrooms found for older children. This reflection is partly due to the change in the child's thinking as he or she begins to move closer in thought processes to those of older elementary-age children. The unfortunate tendency is to treat eight- and nine-year-old children, third graders, as if they were eleven or twelve. Textbooks, worksheets, and verbal teaching strategies predominate. Such strategies, although predominant and traditional, are not necessarily the most appropriate.

Although the third-grade child is more like the older child in terms of thinking skills, there are still differences that need to be considered as the final stage of the early childhood education program is developed. The developmental characteristics of the eight and nine year old must be taken into account as programs are planned.

COGNITIVE ABILITIES OF EIGHT- AND NINE-YEAR-OLD CHILDREN

General Developmental Stage

In general, the child of eight or nine years of age will be in the concrete operational stage of development. This stage of development encompasses the elementary school years, generally beginning in second grade and continuing through sixth grade where some children will begin to make the transition to formal operational thought. The essential activity of this stage of development is the physical manipulation of the world. Children in the concrete operational stage of development utilize objects in their thinking and in their conceptual development. The manipulation of symbols, such as the formula for determining the area of a rectangle, is not yet a meaningful activity for the child. But, although the use of a formula to develop area may not be meaningful, the use of centimeter squares or a grid to count the area of a rectangle is meaningful. The formula requires the use of abstractions, while using the grid or squares involves the manipulation of real materials. The concrete operational child needs to have concrete materials at hand in order to make an accurate judgment or to develop a meaningful concept.

Egocentricity in the Concrete Operational Child

While the egocentricity of the preoperational child does not totally disappear, the concrete operational child is far less egocentric than the younger child. Evidence of this change in egocentric thought is the child's growing ability to decenter, that is, to look at a variety of characteristics when viewing an object rather than at only a single characteristic. The child who is confronted with the conservation of number task notices not only that the row that has been stretched out is longer, but also that no coins have been added. Because the child looks not only at the end result, but also at the transformation that caused that result, he or she is decreasing in centration and egocentricity. Children notice and remember the transitional points that resulted in the final appearance of the objects.

Cause and Effect in the Concrete Operational Child

The concrete operational child no longer reasons from a basis of precausality but has not yet attained a true understanding of cause and effect. From about seven through nine years of age, the child interprets events in a way that begins to show an understanding of actual cause and effect. This is a transitional period. Piaget determined four types of child explanations during this developmental period.

Reaction of Surrounding Medium.   This is the first type of causality in which the child recognizes the need for contact as a cause and so uses the surrounding medium (air or water, for example) as that cause. The child explains the motion of clouds as being started in some mysterious way after which the air behind the cloud causes the motion of the cloud to continue.

Mechanical Causality.   The need for motion on the part of one object to cause motion of a second object is recognized in this type of causality. However, the child does not recognize that contact between the two objects is needed. For example, the movement of pedals on a bicycle causes movement: no chain is needed to transmit the action of the pedals to the rear wheel.

Condensation and Rarefaction.   In this form of causality, the child believes that the matter that makes up objects is more or less condensed, depending on its type. A stone, for example, sinks in water because the stone is made of condensed matter and the water is made of rarefied matter.

Atomistic Composition. Atomistic concepts of causality in children are based on the idea that objects are made of tiny particles packed tightly or loosely together. Consequently, ice becomes water because the particles are no longer so tightly packed.

One characteristic of child thought at this stage of development is the inclusion of an explanation of cause and effect factors that may have no bearing on the results of an activity. For example, in an activity in which paper airplanes are tested to see which of four planes will fly farther, a child may insist that the plane that flew farther did so because it was red. The color of the plane has no real bearing on the distance, but the child who is just beginning to comprehend logical cause and effect may insist that it does. In situations where children identify characteristics that are not true factors, the child should be encouraged to use materials to test the effect of the identified characteristic. Telling a child that a factor is not important has little impact on the child's thought. Allowing the child to test the factor causes the child to reconsider and to revise a concept. Children are most successful in working with concepts of cause and effect if they can cause and see the immediate effect operating on concrete materials.

Conservation in Concrete Operational Children

The child who has entered the concrete operational period of development is able to conserve number. In addition to conserving number, the child of eight or nine is generally also able to conserve substance, area, length, and time.

Conservation of Substance typically occurs at approximately seven or eight years of age. Conservation of substance means that the child realizes that a change in the shape of an object does not mean a change in the quantity of the object. For example, two clay balls are presented to the child. After the equality of the balls is established, one of the two is rolled out into a "snake." The child who has attained conservation of substance will realize that there is still the same amount of clay in the snake as in the ball. The transformation of the ball into a longer but thinner object is seen as a transformation and not as a change in quantity.

Conservation of Area generally occurs somewhere between eight and eleven years of age. Consequently, some children at the third-grade level will have a concept of area, while others will have difficulty with this concept. Conservation of area is most easily assessed with two identical pieces of construction paper. After establishing that both pieces are identical, one is cut on a diagonal and the two pieces rearranged to form a triangle. The child who conserves area will be able to see that the area,

LEARNING ACTIVITY 54

Conservation-of-Substance Interview

Purpose: The purpose of this activity is to assess a child's ability to conserve substance.

Materials: 2 balls of clay identical in size

Procedure:

1. Show the two balls of clay to the child. Ask, "Is there the same amount of clay in each of the balls?" If the child does not think there is the same amount of clay in each of the balls, ask the child to make them the same.
2. While the child watches, flatten one of the two balls into a "pancake" that is at least three inches in diameter.

3. Ask the child, "Is there as much clay in the ball as there is in the pancake?" Point to the two objects while asking the question.
4. Ask, "How do you know they are still the same?" or "What makes you say the pancake (ball) is greater than the ball (pancake)?"

Cautions:

1. Be certain that the child considers the original balls of clay to be identical in size before beginning the interview.
2. Be careful not to coach the child with verbal cues or facial expressions.
3. Praise whatever response is given. The purpose of the task is to investigate the child's thought processes and not to elicit a particular answer considered "right."

Interpreting the Results:

Level One: Level-one children think that the amount of clay changes because of the change in shape. These children do not conserve substance.

Level Two: Level-two children are uncertain whether the change in shape causes a change in quantity. They may answer that there is a change in one case and that there is not a change in another case. They may also say that there is no change in quantity but be unable to explain how they know there is no change.

Level Three: Level-three children are not only able to answer the question correctly, but are able to give a logical reason why no change in quantity occurs.

---

or space, covered by the triangle is identical to that covered by the rectangular piece of paper from which the triangle was formed. The triangle only looks as if it is larger.

Conservation of Length generally is attained at approximately eight years of age. Conservation of length is most easily assessed with two sticks of equal length. After the equality of length is established, one stick is pushed forward of the other although still parallel to the first. The child who conserves length will immediately realize that the length of the stick has not changed but that the perceived difference in length is due to the fact that the opposite ends do not meet.

Conservation of Time typically occurs at approximately nine or ten years of age. Prior to gaining the ability to conserve time, children often perceive time in terms of size. The child who is

taller is considered to be older simply because of size differences. This means that a child with a younger brother can believe that the younger child could become older if he becomes taller than the child. The concept of conservation of age differences, the idea that if I am five years older than my sister now I will always be five years older, occurs at about eight years of age. Conservation of time also includes the concept of time as stable in all activity, neither speeding up nor slowing down. This understanding, known as isochronism, develops at about eight years of age. Synchronicity also develops at approximately nine years of age and is the understanding that all clocks must tell the same time. The development of synchronicity, isochronism, and an understanding of time as independent of size are all needed if the child is to understand the concept of telling time.

LEARNING ACTIVITY 55

Conservation-of-Area Interview

Purpose: The purpose of this activity is to assess a child's ability to conserve area.

Materials: scissors, 2 pieces of 9 × 12 construction paper, 1 piece with a diagonal line dividing it into halves

Procedure:

1. Place the two pieces of construction paper on the table in front of the child. Ask, ''Are the two pieces of paper the same size? Is there the same amount of paper in each piece? Follow up by asking, ''How do you know they are the same size?''

2. As the child watches, cut the ruled piece of paper along the diagonal line. Arrange the resulting two triangles into a single large triangular shape.

 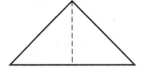

3. Pointing to the two shapes, ask, ''Is there still the same amount of paper in the rectangle as there is in the triangle?'' Ask, ''How do you know there is the same amount of paper in both shapes?'' or ''How do you know there is more paper in the rectangle (triangle) than there is in the triangle (rectangle)?

Cautions:

1. Be certain that the child considers the original pieces of paper to be identical in size and to contain the same amount of paper before beginning the interview.

2. Be careful not to coach the child with verbal cues or facial expressions.

3. Praise whatever response is given. The purpose of the task is to investigate the child's thought processes and not to elicit a particular answer considered ''right.''

Interpreting the Results:

Level One: Level-one children do not conserve area and so consider the triangle and rectangle to have different quantities of paper. No explanation is given of the reason for the perceived difference.

Level Two: Level-two children generally consider one of the two figures to be larger than the other. The explanation given is that the paper was cut or that it was turned around.

Level Three: Level-three children do conserve area. Such children can use logical reasoning to explain that the amount of paper remains the same.

LEARNING ACTIVITY 56

Conservation-of-Length Interview

Purpose: The purpose of this activity is to assess a child's ability to conserve length.

Materials: 2 1' × ½" pieces of wood or heavy paper

Procedure:

1. Show the child the two sticks placed parallel to each other so that the ends are opposite and about four inches apart.

2. Ask, ''Are the sticks the same length or is one longer than the other?'' If the child considers one to be longer than the other, move the sticks closer together until the child is certain they are the same length.

3. Move one stick about an inch to the right.

LEARNING ACTIVITY 56 Continued

4. Ask, "Are the sticks still the same length or is one longer?"
5. If the child considers one stick to be longer than the other, ask, "How do you know one is longer than the other?" If the child considers both sticks to still be of the same length, ask, "How do you know they are still the same length?"

Cautions:
1. Be certain that the child considers the original sticks to be identical in length at the beginning of the activity.
2. Be careful not to coach the child with verbal cues or facial expressions.
3. Praise whatever response is given. The purpose of the task is to investigate the child's thought processes and not to elicit a particular answer considered "right."

Interpreting the Results:

Level One: Level-one children are nonconservers of length who consider the lengths of the two sticks to change because of a change in position. The child's opinion is perceptual and she or he is not able to explain the reason for the change in length.

Level Two: Level-two children often answer that the length changes but will put the sticks back in their original places and then conclude that they were incorrect. The question dealing with whether the length changes or not is sometimes answered correctly and sometimes answered incorrectly.

Level Three: Level-three children will answer that the sticks are still the same length and will be able to give a logical reason why they are still the same.

LEARNING ACTIVITY 57

Conservation-of-Time Interview

Purpose: The purpose of this activity is to assess a child's ability to conserve time.

Materials: 2 toy cars, 3-minute egg timer, stopwatch

Procedure:
1. Put the two cars side by side on the table as if they were going to be in a race. Ask the child to start the race by saying "go" and to stop the race by saying "stop."
2. When the child says "go," move the cars along the table, keeping them side by side. When the child says "stop," ask, "Did the two cars start and stop at the same time?"
3. Tell the child that you are going to run the race again. This time, move one of the cars more quickly so that one goes farther along the table before the child says "stop."
4. Ask, "Did the cars start and stop at the same time?" If the child answers that they did not, ask, "How do you know they did not start and stop at the same time?"

Cautions:
1. Be careful not to coach the child with verbal cues or facial expressions.
2. Praise whatever response is given. The purpose of the task is to investigate the child's thought processes and not to elicit a particular answer considered "right."

Interpreting the Results:

Level One: Level-one children usually think that the car that went the farthest took more time. These children do not conserve time.

Level Two: Level-two children will answer that the cars started and stopped at the same time. However, they will answer that the duration of time for the two cars was different, with the car traveling the longer distance taking a longer period of time.

Level Three: Level-three children will answer that the starting and stopping times were the same and that the time interval was the same for both cars. They realize that one car moved faster than the other.

Logical Thought Processes in Concrete-Operational Children

The child in concrete operations can think through a situation and draw a logical conclusion based on direct observations and manipulations. The type of logic used in developing such a conclusion is based on concrete manipulation of the environment and is characteristic of concrete operations. In other areas of logical thought, however, the child at the level of concrete operations experiences difficulty. Logical thought processes such as propositional reasoning, control of variables in an experiment, probability, and the consideration of many sides to the same issue are generally not available to the child at the concrete operational level. In the science area, this generally means that the third-grade child is not yet ready for the true experiment in which control of variables is a necessity and in which propositional reasoning may be the basis for the development of a hypothesis.

Classification in Concrete Operational Children

Eight-year-old children are able to classify well and use exhaustive sorting in their classifications. The child at the third-grade level is able to select a characteristic, successfully use it to classify all objects, and then find another characteristic to use in classifying those objects in a different manner. The child who is using concrete operational thought will be able to classify the same set of objects in a variety of ways.

As the eight-year-old child becomes the nine-year-old child, the ability to classify develops from successfully using a single trait to successfully using multiple traits. The child can now classify all shiny black rocks into one grouping and shiny gray rocks into a second category. In this type of classification, two traits must be successfully coordinated. Additionally, the child of eight or nine has developed the some/all relationship. No longer is a subclass seen as larger than the total class. For example, a child of six who is confronted with nine buttercups and five white roses will say that there are more yellow flowers than flowers while a child of nine will correctly state that there are more flowers than yellow flowers. And, the child of eight or nine will be able to use the concept of multiple class membership. In this case, the child is able to state that he or she is not only a member of the family, but also of the school class and of the category girl (or boy). The ability to use multiple class membership is the foundation for more complex classification skills. For example, children are asked to classify animals into the categories of animals with backbones and animals without backbones. This is a simple classification system. In order to meaningfully classify animals with backbones into the groups fish, amphibians, reptiles, birds, and mammals and then to place a cat into the category of "mammal," the child must be able to use multiple classes. The use of multiple classes allows the child to understand that "cat" belongs to the category "mammal," which belongs to the class "animal with backbone," which in turn belongs to the class "animal."

Concepts of Number and Computation in Concrete Operations

By eight or nine years of age, children have developed the concepts of addition, multiplication, and subtraction. This occurs without direct instruction as a result of the child's interaction with objects in the environment and with adults and other children. The child constructs these concepts as a part of natural development. In addition, children of eight or nine have also developed the commutative and transitive properties that are integral to an understanding of mathematics. The commutative property is simply the idea that $9 + 8 = 8 + 9$, while transitivity is the concept that if 9 is greater than 6 and 6 is greater than 3, then 9 is greater than 3.

Reversibility of Thought in Concrete Operations

Reversibility of thought is present in children of eight or nine years of age. Indeed, it is the presence of reversible thought that allows the child to accomplish the conservation tasks, comprehend the commutative property, and develop the natural understanding of subtraction that is present at this age level. Children of eight or nine have no difficulty reversing the direction of thought and so cannot only determine that the cold temperature of the freezer caused the water to turn to ice, but also that heating the ice would cause it to become liquid again.

Using Models in Concrete Operations

Models of the Solar System, the human body, or the internal structure of the Earth are often used in the science class with greater or lesser success. The degree of success in using models will be determined by two factors: the authenticity of the model and the background experience of the child. The eight or nine year old can use models successfully in order to develop scientific understandings. The probability of success in the use of a model will be enhanced if the child has some background experience on which to base his or her understanding. The concept of planets orbiting through space around the Sun is unlikely to be understood because of children's inability to relate the concept to something known or experienced. There is no concrete experience that can serve as the foundation for this particular concept. A model of the structure of the Earth may be more successful because children can relate the idea of cutting through the Earth and finding different layers to the idea of cutting through a cake and finding different layers. However, the second factor in the successful use of models comes into play here. The model must be as close to reality as possible. A model of the internal structure of the Earth is not going to be completely realistic because of differences in size, material, color, and texture. On the other hand, a model of the human torso constructed to the actual size of a child or adult and showing the internal organs in their proper locations and size relations is an appropriate model.

Mental Models in Concrete Operations

Mental models might be thought of as concepts that provide mental pictures of objects or events and their causes. Children are able to construct such models at the age of eight or nine, provided that they have had direct experience with the object or event and that only simple concepts of classification and seriation are needed. For example, a child who resides in southern Florida has a difficult time constructing a concept of the arctic or antarctic regions of the Earth, while a child from northern Minnesota has a far easier time with this mental picture. Similarly, it is easier for a child who has traveled by airplane and seen the great vistas from the window to construct a concept, a mental model of the size of the Earth.

SUMMARY

The developmental characteristics of the eight- or nine-year-old child can be used to determine the content information that will be most appropriate at the third-grade level. Children of this level are generally in the concrete operational stage of development and so are still in need of concrete materials if they are to think logically or develop understanding. In general, the third-grade child can be expected to conserve number, substance, area, length, and time. Additionally, the child at the third-grade level has developed reversibility of thought and has an understanding of addition, subtraction, multiplication, transitivity, and commutativity. The ability to classify is well-developed at this age level. However, the third-grade child will continue to find cause and effect difficult and may have difficulty with the use of classroom models in some contexts.

Vocabulary Terms

Atomistic Composition: causality based on the concept that objects are made of tiny particles packed tightly or loosely together.

Commutative Property: a property of addition and multiplication in which the order on which factors are operated makes no difference to the final answer: $5 + 6 = 6 + 5$.

Condensation and Rarefaction: a type of causality in which the matter that makes up objects is seen as more or less condensed depending on the type of material.

Conservation of Area: the ability to determine that the amount of space covered by a material does not change because the material is rearranged into a different shape.

Conservation of Length: the ability to determine that the length of an object does not change because of its placement or its rearrangement.

Conservation of Substance: the ability to determine that a change in the shape of an object does not result in a change in the quantity of material in the object.

Conservation of Time: the concepts that size and passage of time are not related and that time remains stable in its rate of passage, neither slowing down nor speeding up because of the type of activity being done.

Control of Variables: in an experiment, the ability to manipulate a single factor while keeping all others the same.

Formal Operational Stage: a developmental stage characterized by the ability to use logical reasoning.

Hypothesis: a statement that forms the basis for an experimental procedure and that includes a prediction of the effect of one variable on another.

Traditional Classroom: a classroom setting in which the teacher determines the activities and outcomes and the subject-matter areas are generally kept separate from one another.

Isochronism: the understanding that time is stable in its rate of flow and neither speeds up nor slows down depending on an activity.

Mechanical Causality: a concept of causality that recognizes the need for motion on the part of one object to cause motion in a second object.

Mental Model: a concept that provides a mental picture of an object or an event and its cause.

Multiple-Trait Classification: classification based on the simultaneous consideration of more than one characteristic of an object at a time.

Physical Model: a concrete representation of a physical object: for example, a globe is a physical model of the Earth.

Propositional Reasoning: reasoning based on possibilities such as "what would happen if the Sun suddenly stopped shining?"

Reaction of Surrounding Medium: the first type of causality in which a child sees the need for contact as a cause and so uses the surrounding medium, air, or water.

Single-Trait Classification: classification that is based on consideration of only one characteristic of a set of objects.

Synchronism: the understanding that all clocks should reflect the same time.

Transitive Property: the concept that "if A is greater than B and B is greater than C, then A is greater than C."

Study Questions

1. What are the cognitive-developmental characteristics of eight-year-old children?
2. What are the cognitive-developmental characteristics of nine-year-old children?
3. How do eight-year-old children differ from nine-year-old children in their cognitive characteristics?
4. What changes in developmental characteristics occur between the ages of three and nine?
5. How do the thought processes of eight and nine year olds differ from those of adults?
6. A chapter in your third-grade science textbook suggests using a model of the human heart constructed from styrofoam cups and plastic tubing to demonstrate how blood circulates through the heart. Using what you know about third-grade children, is this an appropriate model? Why or why not?
7. A child in third grade is having difficulty understanding the idea that the area of a rectangle is equal to its length times its width ($A = l \times w$). What could be causing this difficulty? What would you do to determine if you have pinpointed the actual cause?

CHAPTER 10

Social Characteristics of Eight and Nine Year Olds

Chapter Objectives

On completion of this chapter, you should be able to

1. list the social characteristics of eight- and nine-year-old children,

2. discuss the social characteristics of eight- and nine-year-old children,

3. compare the child of eight or nine to the younger child at the early-childhood education level, and

4. discuss the concept of children at risk at the eight- and nine-year-old level.

A new teacher once attempted to punish a third-grade child for writing on the top of the lab tables in the science room by having her come after school to wash all of the tables. The word *attempted* is used here for a reason. The little girl arrived to clean the tables with four friends to help. They had such a wonderful time cleaning the tables and chattering to one another that they also went on to dust the rock collection, rearrange the books on the shelves, wash all of the glassware, and arrange the chairs so that the various colors of plastic were in a pretty pattern. This was not what the teacher had in mind!

These third-grade girls were, however, showing such typical third-grade behavior that this result could have been predicted. At the third-grade level, the characteristics of children are different from those of younger children not only in terms of cognitive development but also in terms of social characteristics. The third grader is trying to establish himself or herself as a competent worker, a friend, and a skilled person.

SOCIAL CHARACTERISTICS OF THIRD-GRADE CHILDREN

The social characteristics of children at the third-grade level can help the teacher determine the kinds of activities and classroom arrangements that will be most positive for organizing science and mathematics lessons.

Use of Reading and Writing in Learning

Children at the third-grade level are better able to work with small-muscle activities. The use of small-muscle skills often means that activities that require reading and writing become more accessible to the child.

The ability of children at the third-grade level to read and write with some ease is often translated into an emphasis on reading and writing as a means for learning. Children at the third-grade level may be able to accomplish these tasks with some ease, but they are still concrete operational in their thought processes and so need to have first-hand, hands-on experiences. In fact, children with learning disabilities that cause them to have difficulties with the processing of visual symbols such as letters and numerals will be put at a distinct disadvantage through over-attention to reading and writing skills.

Relationships with Other Children

Third-grade children are social creatures. Their decrease in egocentricity allows them to see other viewpoints and, as a result, they are better able to look beyond themselves and into the general environment, including the other children in the class. The third grader becomes better able to recognize different emotions in children and to determine the causes of those emotions.

Perhaps because children are reaching out more into the environment and striving for greater autonomy, the peer group gains in importance as children progress through the third-grade level. The peer group has a variety of functions for the child of eight or nine. The peer group helps the child establish independence by providing a support network as the child tries out new ideas and new roles. As a part of the peer group, a child may try out being a leader, follower, or agent of change. The peer group also helps the child establish independence by learning a variety of responses to a situation. A child who has consistently learned to be passive in a threatening situation may learn from the peer group to be assertive or even aggressive. Unfortunately, this learning of new behaviors may put the child at odds with parents. When conflicts between a peer group and parents occur, the child is more likely to defend the peer group than the parental point of view.

Almost as a contradiction, the peer group emphasizes conformity while also encouraging independence. Members of a particular group perform certain actions, use certain words, and wear certain articles of clothing. They identify with the trappings of the peer group. The conformity concept of the peer group may also extend to conformity to sex-role behaviors. The peer group encourages girls to be girls and boys to be boys without considering the possibility that behaviors can cross gender boundaries.

At times, the peer group of a child will seem to exert undesirable influence over the child. There are two factors that should be remembered here. First, the groups formed by third graders, although strong, are generally strong for only a short period of time. Up to about nine years of age, the structure of the groups frequently changes. Second, children generally will imitate peers who they perceive as warm, rewarding, powerful, high in status, and similar to themselves. For the teacher, this means that those children exhibiting appropriate behaviors should be given status within the classroom. Children model the kinds of behaviors they see as desirable.

Group Play and Work

Perhaps because the peer group is becoming more important to the child, group work and group games become popular with children. For the first time, finishing an activity becomes as important as starting and planning. For the first time, reaching closure is necessary to the child. Since planning and completing an activity are important to the child, it is not surprising that third graders are able to plan and complete activities with little assistance from adults. They are capable of sustaining activities on their own with little supervision.

Group activities in the classroom are important, as are group activities at play. Third-grade children are interested in playing organized, rule-oriented games. Organized sports such as baseball, soccer, swimming, gymnastics, and tennis interest children of eight or nine. The problem is that this interest is often translated by parents and teachers into organized sports that overemphasize competition and winning. Children of eight or nine are establishing themselves as competent people. They enjoy playing. They are generally not yet ready for the adult emphasis on winning by having only the best members of the team play or for the criticism that comes from other players, coaches, and parents when an error is made by the less-than-star player. Rules, organization, and playing are important to the child; winning and competition by the best players is neither important nor desirable.

But, the new emphasis on the group as a means of work and play does not simply mean the use of games and the use of small groups during science and mathematics activities. Because of their growing ability to relate to others, third-grade children

enjoy group discussions. The group discussion allows the third-grade child to see the viewpoints of others and to discover that differences in opinion do exist. Because children at the third-grade level are interested in the opinions of others, they begin to ask for additional information if there is something that they do not understand.

The child of eight and nine is beginning to ask a new kind of "why" question. The question is now asking for justification rather than cause. Why's of justification indicate that the child is curious about the reasons for the entire set of customs and rules that have been imposed from without. They want justification for these rules and so ask for it. The word *because* begins to be an important term in explaining feelings, opinions, or emotions.

Responsibility

Eight- and nine-year-old children frequently want to show their growing abilities through increased responsibility. The desire for increased responsibility can include such activities as running errands, caring for pets, caring for younger siblings, and helping to wash the car, as well as other simple chores. For the child to be successful and more autonomous, it is often helpful to allow her or him a choice in what to do. In the classroom, this may mean giving the choice of handing out the papers or collecting the mathematics materials. It is also helpful for the child of eight or nine to have reasonable and consistent guidelines for an activity. Rather than establishing the rule that there will be no talking at a particular time, establish the guidelines that talking will be allowed when help is needed or when additional materials are needed. For children of this age, guidelines are helpful in establishing a sense of security without stifling initiative.

Even though a sense of responsibility is growing, it is important to remember that third graders are still children and children cannot be expected to assume adult responsibilities or act in a consistently adult manner. Children of eight and nine need to know that it is all right to fail in a task. If they cannot finish a task, they need to know that someone will be there to assist and bring the task to an end. A child may volunteer to water all of the plants in the classroom, but, when faced with the hanging baskets, may end up needing some assistance. However, responsibility also means completing a task before going on to something else and so children need to be kept gently on task rather than told "go ahead, I'll finish for you."

THE AT-RISK CHILD IN THE THIRD GRADE

The child who is at risk at the third-grade level, is at risk not only for academic failure but also for social failure.

Physical Differences and the At-Risk Child

At the third-grade level, children are becoming more aware of differences among the children in the classroom. Because of this growing awareness, they see the child who is different not only as different but often as unacceptable. Physical differences from orthopedic handicaps to obesity can cause a child to be viewed as less attractive and, therefore, less desirable as a friend or co-worker. The child who is so labeled may be ignored or may ricochet from one group to another in an attempt to find a stable and accepting peer group. Such interactions may cause low self-esteem, resulting in shyness or aggressiveness. The development of low self-esteem can lead a child into a cycle of failure. The low self-esteem child expects to fail in interpersonal or academic situations. The expectation of failure causes the child to try a little less hard in that situation. And when the child does indeed fail, the expectation of failure is strengthened. The teacher's role in such a situation is to show the child that he or she can succeed by helping the child develop strategies that assure increasing success.

Cultural Differences and the At-Risk Child

Children from culturally different backgrounds may be at risk because their backgrounds do not mesh with the environment of the school. The classroom is generally a self-contained example of the middle class. Children coming from backgrounds that do not reflect middle class values may

find the classroom routine unfamiliar or uncomfortable.

Cultural differences, therefore, may mean that the classroom provides an experience very different from the home environment. It is possible that the family will not encourage success in school. The parent who continually questions the value of education or who has little education and seems to take pride in that fact is unlikely to encourage the child to succeed. In fact, in order to emulate the parents, the child may purposely fail. The family that fails to see the relevance of classroom assignments may also influence the child's performance in the school setting. Parents who question the importance of mathematics beyond basic addition, subtraction, multiplication, and division may transmit to the child the message that success is not important. And, parents from different cultural backgrounds may feel alienated because they do not themselves understand school assignments. Rather than show their lack of understanding, the parent denigrates the school and the value of education. Parents from certain cultural backgrounds may find particular subject-matter areas—for example, science and social studies—to be in conflict with their religious beliefs and, therefore, may encourage their child to reject the teachings of the school.

This is not to say, however, that cultural differences mean failure. Children from Asian cultures tend to succeed very well in schools even when their cultural backgrounds are far different from those of the children in the classroom. And, children from all cultural backgrounds can succeed if they have teachers who are patient and encouraging, expecting quality work at the same high level they expect from children of the dominant culture. In addition to having high expectations for all children, the teacher needs to show the value of education, assist parents in how to work with their children, and demonstrate the contributions of people from many cultural backgrounds to the information that children are learning.

Academic Differences and the At-Risk Child

The main purpose of the school is to impart to children information and skills that will allow them to function in a variety of different situations,

LEARNING ACTIVITY 58

Classroom Observation

Purpose: The purpose of this activity is to observe a third-grade classroom in order to determine the social characteristics of children at that grade level.

Procedure:

1. Observe the third-grade classroom on at least three separate occasions for a total of three or more hours.
2. As you observe the classroom setting, give particular attention to
   a. the arrangement of the classroom including the location of the teacher's desk and the arrangement of the students' desks;
   b. the rules for interaction established by the classroom teacher;
   c. the grouping practices used by the teacher;
   d. the kinds of interactions that occur among and between children;
   e. the peer groups that are present in the classroom and the ways in which the children in those groups associate with one another;
   f. the interactions between and among children who are mainstreamed or culturally different and those who are the majority of the class;
   g. behavior problems that occur and how those problems are handled by the classroom teacher; and
   h. the effect of various teaching practices on the children, particularly on their social interactions and communication with one another.
3. Prepare a written report of your observations.

Cautions:

1. Be certain that you do not use the name of the teacher or school in your written report. Try not to identify the observation site in any way.
2. Do not mention the children in the classroom by name in the written report.

---

whether in the pulpit, science laboratory, or assembly line. Academics are the focus of the school. Children at risk academically are at greatest overall risk because their futures are at risk as well.

The academically at-risk child may be at risk because of a handicapping condition such as a visual or auditory disability. Children with these difficulties may be somewhat behind their peers in terms of vocabulary or concept development. In these cases, techniques designed especially for such children are necessary to close the gap. Children with vocabulary deficits may find the science or mathematics classroom particularly frustrating because vocabulary is an important aspect of the subject matter. The vocabulary of science or mathematics is not only important, but it is different from that of everyday life. Terms like molecule, photosynthesis, obtuse angle, or prime number are not generally found in basal readers or daily conversation. Consequently, teaching science or mathematics vocabulary to visually or auditorially handicapped children requires special attention.

Also problematic for some children will be the use of science laboratories or mathematics manipulatives. Children with visual or orthopedic handicaps may experience difficulties in manipulating materials. These children can be assigned a laboratory partner who will assist in investigations or manipulations. The key is to assign a lab partner who will assist rather than do the activity for the handicapped child. The visually handicapped child should be able to do most of the actual manipulation of materials. The auditorially handicapped child can be assisted through written directions so that aural difficulties do not interfere with the child's success in activities.

The academically at-risk child may also be at a developmental level different from those of the other children in the class. While children of eight or nine years of age are generally concrete operational in their thought processes, some children, especially those from impoverished backgrounds, with intellectual handicaps, or with severe sensory impairments, may be functioning at the preoperational level. Children who are having particular difficulty with mathematics should be assessed for conservation of number and other prenumber skills.

The academically at-risk child may have a learning disability that makes it difficult for him or her to learn from symbols, interpret the intent of problems, or form solutions to problems. Children who are of average or above average intelligence and who perform well in some areas but not in others should probably be assessed for learning disabilities and appropriate teaching techniques should be instituted.

The academically at-risk child may also be the gifted or talented child. Talented children may not see the necessity for academic success, especially when their talent is in instrumental music, art, or dance. For these children, performance rather than academics is the goal. Gifted children may also be at risk. They are at risk when the academic program is too limited and they become bored. Boredom can lead quickly to disruptive behavior or to mental absence. But, the gifted child may also be at risk from teachers who assume that the child no longer needs to interact with concrete objects and can learn strictly from written materials. Gifted children need to use materials just as do their nongifted peers. The gifted child constructs concepts just as the average child constructs concepts and that construction begins with direct experience.

Finally, the at-risk child is the child who is average or more in all ways except one: due to illness, moving, or other factors he or she has gaps in knowledge. Those gaps mean that the child does not have the foundation needed for new information and so falls more and more behind as he or she progresses through school. The child who is having difficulty with information that is sequential and cumulative should be diagnostically tested to determine whether the background material is present or not. In this case, remediation works wonders in making an at-risk child no longer at risk.

The at-risk child comes in a variety of different formats. The two commonalities of at-risk children are that they are likely to fail in the typical academic program if they are not given attention through variations in teaching strategies or additional attention to the value and purpose of education. The

second commonality is that at-risk children may be easily swayed or ignored by their peers. With the peer group becoming more important, this can be a major problem for the child who is trying to become a person in his or her own right.

SUMMARY

Children at the third-grade level are socially different from children at the preschool through second-grade levels. Third graders tend to be more socially oriented than ever before. As a result of this social orientation, the peer group becomes more important and more influential. The peer group functions to develop both the child's autonomy and conformity to peer expectations. The third-grade child's growing social awareness is also evident in the interest the child takes in the opinions of others as well as in the reasons behind social conventions.

At the third-grade level, some children are at risk of academic failure. These at-risk children may exhibit various handicapping conditions, may be from culturally different backgrounds, or may be gifted or talented. No matter what the risk factor, the teacher needs to be aware of the factor and make appropriate modifications to the classroom program.

Vocabulary Terms

Culturally Different Children: children coming from home environments that are significantly different from the school environment and so may experience academic and social difficulties.

Peer Group: the age group and/or social group to which a child belongs or with which a child identifies.

Why of Justification: questions indicating that a child is curious about the reasons for customs and rules that seem to have been imposed from without.

Study Questions

1. What are the social characteristics of eight- and nine-year-old children?

LEARNING ACTIVITY 59

Children at Risk

Purpose: The purpose of this activity is to interview a third-grade teacher and a special-education teacher about children who are mainstreamed or who are at risk from other environmental or personal factors.

Procedure:

1. Arrange to interview two teachers who work with children at the third-grade level. One teacher should be a classroom teacher who has children mainstreamed into the classroom or who has other at-risk children in the classroom. The other teacher should be a specialist in special education.

2. Develop a series of questions dealing with the following topics:

   a. the characteristics of mainstreamed children or at-risk children,

   b. areas in which these children find particular success,

   c. areas in which these children have difficulty,

   d. similarities and differences between these children and the other children in the classroom,

   e. modifications that the teacher has made to allow for full participation by mainstreamed or other at-risk children,

   f. areas in which the teacher feels particular success in working with at-risk children, and

   g. areas in which the teacher feels inadequate in working with at-risk children.

Cautions:

1. If you plan to tape record the interview, be certain to ask permission from the teacher in advance.

2. Accept responses as given without making any judgments.

3. Use follow-up questions to help clarify responses to the interview questions.

4. Do not use the teacher's name in your written report or identify the teacher or school in any way.

5. Do not identify any of the children discussed by name or in any other way.

---

2. How do the social characteristics of eight and nine year olds differ from those of younger children?

3. What effect does each of the following have on a child's ability to learn?

   a. cultural differences
   b. visual handicaps
   c. auditory handicaps
   d. health problems
   e. learning disabilities
   f. giftedness

4. How could the functions of the peer group have a positive effect on children in the classroom?

5. A group of first graders found it difficult to discuss a class activity. Now, in third grade, the same children find discussion not only easy but also fun. What could account for such a difference?

6. One third-grade teacher assigns housekeeping tasks to children and uses the success with which they complete the task as a basis for grades in conduct. Another third-grade teacher has children select tasks and decide how and when they will complete them. Which teacher is accommodating the social characteristics of children more effectively? Why?

CHAPTER 11

Curriculum in the Third Grade

Chapter Objectives

On completion of this chapter, you should be able to

1. discuss the meaning of the term *defined curriculum*,

2. discuss the differences between the defined curriculum and the combined curriculum or the unified curriculum,

3. discuss the criteria on which content should be selected for the defined curriculum, and

4. discuss the characteristics of teaching strategies that are appropriate to the defined curriculum.

The third-grade level marks the end of the early childhood years and the entrance into the middle childhood years. Just as it is a transition from level to level in terms of age, it is also a transition in terms of educational expectations. The third grade marks the beginning of a traditional approach to curriculum and to teaching.

The transition to a traditional educational format does not mean a transition to inappropriate educational practices; within the traditional curriculum approach, there is room for a variety of content areas and instructional strategies. In order to allow for a curriculum that is as developmentally appropriate as possible, the subject matter and teaching techniques of the defined curriculum need to be carefully selected.

The third-grade level begins to expose children to a subject-matter-oriented curriculum. The selection of content information specific to each subject-matter area defines each subject area and so contributes to the definition of the curriculum. The term *defined* truly reflects the nature of the curriculum at the third-grade level.

In the defined curriculum, subject-matter areas are treated as distinct entities. For the first time, the program in the school looks like the typical elementary-school program. There is a particular time for reading, language arts, social studies, science, and mathematics. Students not only have specific times for the various subject-matter areas, they also have specific textbooks that are used for each area. This is not, however, to say that the subject-matter areas must be treated as if there are lines between the areas that must never be crossed. Rather, the distinct skills and concepts of the subject-matter areas should be utilized appropriately from one area to another. Good writing and spelling skills are not deleted because the child is working in science. No more should appropriate use of computation be deleted from science or science concepts, from word problems in mathematics, or from stories in reading and language arts. It is certainly important for children to learn to read well, but they are reading stories and articles that deal with specific topics. A child who has encountered information about volcanoes in the science area is going to find it much easier to read and comprehend a social studies passage about Hawaii. Similarly, a child who is familiar with the idea that different countries have different languages and systems of numeration will have a basis for understanding other bases and other kinds of numerals in mathematics. The connections are still there and are still demonstrated to children, but the focus is more on content specific to the various subject-matter areas. The focus is indeed on the content of the specific areas, but the specific areas need to be addressed in a balanced manner.

Children need to have an education that is well rounded rather than top heavy in one area or another. Within the science area, it is important for children to gain knowledge in the biological, physical, and earth-space sciences. It is very easy for a teacher who really enjoys gardening to spend a great deal of time on plants and little on animals. It is even easier for the teacher who is interested in biology to ignore rocks and minerals, magnets, simple machines, energy, or stars and planets. The science curriculum needs to be balanced within itself. In the mathematics area, it is also easy to develop a curriculum that is out of balance. Giving an inordinate amount of time to computation skills while quickly "going over" measurement, time, money, or geometry easily puts too much emphasis on one area to the detriment of others. Additionally, balance in the curriculum means giving equal attention to all subject-matter areas. A curriculum that devotes half a day to reading sends the signal that all other subject-matter areas are unimportant. A teacher who finds it easy to skip science or social studies when time runs low sends the message that these areas of knowledge have little worth. Balance is both an internal and an external feature of the defined curriculum. Finally, in the defined curriculum there are specific objectives that the child is expected to master and so remediation is provided in order to assure mastery. Because mastery of specific content is expected at this age level, the content of the defined curriculum must be carefully selected.

In general, content should be selected on the basis of the cognitive abilities of students, while teaching methodologies should be based on the nature of the subject matter, the social abilities of the students, and the requirements of time and environment. Because subject matter is now defined, a combination of hands-on and reading-oriented techniques is possible and desirable.

SELECTING CONTENT FOR THE DEFINED CURRICULUM

Since children are expected to master certain pieces of content information as a part of the defined curriculum, it is important that content information be selected so that understanding on the part of the child is possible. Memorization of content so that children can parrot back bits of information on a test is not important. Understanding is what is needed. Anyone can memorize a piece of information. The difficulty is that such memorized information is easily and quickly forgotten. Standardized tests that test for rote recall of facts after a lengthy period of time may give teachers surprises. The children who knew how to find the volume of a cube in January may by May have no idea what to do to solve such a problem. If information has no meaning to children when it is presented, it is quickly lost.

Selection on the Basis of Cognitive Characteristics

Content information should be selected on the basis of the cognitive characteristics of children. By the third-grade level, most children have entered the concrete-operational period of development. By the third-grade level, children have developed an intuitive understanding of addition and multiplication. Because they have developed reversibility of thought, these children are also capable of understanding subtraction as the inverse of addition, and division as the inverse of multiplication. Consequently, all of the computation skills can now be taught to children with understanding as well as skill development. Third-grade children are also able to understand the commutative property as it applies to both addition and multiplication, as well as the transitive property. The associative property, however, is not generally understood until about eleven or twelve years of age. Also, children are able to understand fractions such as halves, thirds, and fourths. Children at the third-grade level are able to use both single and double seriations and to conserve number, substance, length, and time.

Selection on the Basis of Concrete Materials

Although all of these characteristics are helpful in selecting topics for study, there are two additional traits that are of particular importance in determining whether or not a topic will be understood by children. First, children need to be able to interact with concrete materials if they are going to understand content information rather than simply memorize it. Consequently, those content topics that can be approached through a hands-on method that involves real objects are highly appropriate for children while those that can be approached only through reading and discussion are generally inappropriate. In the science area, it is easy to see that magnets is an appropriate topic while planets is not. In mathematics, this means that the topic should be able to be shown through concrete materials: Measurement in the Metric System is an appropriate topic when children use meter sticks, gram masses, and liter containers, but an inappropriate topic when children only use worksheets and textbooks. Second, the child should have some direct experience with the topic. The science topic of types of soil is appropriate because it involves both hands-on experience and is familiar to the child. The topics of volcanoes in Alabama, oceanography in Kansas, and snow in Hawaii are inappropriate for young children.

Topics, then, need to be selected so that the child has an opportunity not only to master the topic, but to master the topic with understanding. Understanding begins when children are able to explore a topic concretely and relate the new information to something that has already been directly experienced.

SELECTING TEACHING METHODOLOGIES FOR THE DEFINED CURRICULUM

Selection on the Basis of Student Characteristics

The selection of teaching strategies should be based on the characteristics of the children and of the subject-matter area. The teaching techniques selected should allow for a variety of instruction, from large group to individual. In the area of mathematics, providing students with a large-group experience working with measurement can then lead to small-group work in which groups go on scavenger hunts to locate objects or locales of specified lengths. Finally, the child can work as an individual to measure his or her own height, nose length, wrist circumference, or leg length. Techniques and activities selected should allow for a variety of possibilities.

Selection on the Basis of Student Development

Teaching techniques should also allow for student input in the development of activities and investigations. In the science area, this could mean having students decide which factors will be tested in determining how to get seeds to grow well. It is easy for the teacher simply to tell the students that they will test the amount of water and the temperature. It is more interesting and more appropriate in terms of thinking-skill development for students to be involved in deciding what could affect the growth of seeds and then in deciding which of the alternatives they will test. Student input in the math area could mean having the children help to decide what objects to weigh or which method of graphing to use.

Selection on the Basis of Varying Abilities

Teaching techniques should also allow for the varying abilities and learning styles of students. Some children learn easily through oral instruction, while others see oral instruction as a time for daydreaming and doodling. Some children are more visual or more tactile in their learning than others. Instructional strategies that take into account the differing needs of students will be more successful than those that simply assume that all children learn in the same way. Instructional strategies that allow for the use of a variety of senses in a variety of settings need to be selected. For example, in studying about rocks and minerals, students can be involved in reading, collecting, classifying, breaking rocks open to see the insides, constructing structures, making rock animals, or determining the differing sounds made by various types or sizes of rocks. In mathe-

matics, students can construct the various solid shapes from straws and clay, make string art objects, make mobiles or stabiles, or bake cakes in different shaped pans. In each case, instruction involves a variety of different senses and activities.

Selection on the Basis of Variety of Investigations

Teaching strategies should allow students to pursue a variety of explorations. This is especially true for the science area, but can also be put into practice in mathematics. In the science area, students interested in what kinds of materials dissolve can investigate not only what materials will dissolve in water, but also what materials will dissolve in other liquids such as soft drinks, oil, rubbing alcohol, orange juice, and syrup. Investigations of dissolving can lead to investigations of mixtures or of materials that do not mix with one another. In the mathematics area, children use a variety of investigations when they look for different ways to solve a particular word problem, discuss those ways, and finally make a decision about which of those ways is easiest to use.

Selection on the Basis of Materials

Teaching techniques should allow for experiences with concrete materials and written or other verbal materials. A combination of hands-on and verbal techniques is desirable. Using concrete teaching strategies should precede reading textbook content information. By seeing and doing before reading, children develop the background information they need in order to fully comprehend the textbook. Without the background information that is developed by the activity, the textbook may be incomprehensible to children. Additionally, many textbooks will tell what is to happen in the activity before the activity is performed. This takes most of the fun out of the activity and it sets the stage for the children to doubt what they are seeing. If their results do not look like or agree with what is "supposed to happen," children often assume they have done something wrong. Children quickly learn to doubt their abilities rather than to observe, draw conclusions, discuss results, and determine accuracy. The use of activities also should come before the development of new vocabulary. Many terms in science are operational definitions. That is, they are terms used to name some observed phenomenon. The red, orange, yellow, green, blue, indigo, violet pattern formed when white light is passed through a prism is called the spectrum. By seeing that pattern form on the wall when light comes through a prism, the children develop a concept that can then be named. Some terms, however, cannot be as easily developed through activity as the term *spectrum.* In this case, pictures, discussion, and familiar examples should be used prior to introducing a definition from a textbook glossary. Similarly, mathematics textbooks can be used to develop definitions after students have developed a concept. Students can develop the idea of a cube through observing a number of cubic objects, discussing their common characteristics, and developing a definition. The often inelegant definitions of students then can be compared to the definition in the textbook for a more formal statement. Once again, the experience should come before the formal definition of the textbook.

The hands-on experience is fundamental to teaching children at the early-childhood education level, but it is not the end to teaching or learning. The hands-on activity is the starting place, but the techniques chosen for teaching should require the teacher to extend the understanding students gain through the hands-on experience. One cannot assume that because a child has participated in an activity that he or she will automatically grasp the concept. The teacher consistently needs to follow up on the activity and, through questioning and discussion, help the students to understand the concepts that underlie it. For example, in the science area there is an activity in which four different colors of toothpicks are scattered in a grassy place. The children are given a time limit and asked to pick up as many toothpicks as they can find. Generally, the yellow and red toothpicks are easily found. The blue are more difficult to find and the green are nearly impossible to locate. The purpose of the activity is to show that color can camouflage animals and make it harder for predators to find them. One child, however, after doing this activity, concluded that the activity showed that if you dropped toothpicks on grass you better drop yellow ones because they would be easy to find. Children do not always interpret activities in ways that are expected by adults. The teacher's role

is to assist the students in developing the desired concept.

Selection on the Basis of Problem-Solving Skills

Teaching techniques should promote the development of problem-solving skills and critical-thinking skills. The method that involves reading, answering questions, and taking a test simply requires children to recall information printed on a page and to regurgitate that information when asked. It does not call for thinking—least of all critical thinking—and generally the only problem to be solved is how to answer the questions as quickly as possible. Teaching strategies should encourage students to think, draw conclusions based on evidence, develop rules for solving mathematics problems, evaluate ideas, and question material and information. Hands-on activities, especially those that involve student input and follow-up discussion, develop thinking skills.

Selection on the Basis of Language Development

Finally, teaching techniques should promote development of language skills, both oral and written. Discussions following hands-on activities help to develop oral communication and the ability to convey ideas clearly and concisely to another person. Keeping records of activities and explorations in a free-form notebook, rather than on the stilted record sheets often given to children as part of activities, help to develop writing skills. Teaching strategies should always encourage the use of reading, speaking, and writing in both the science and the mathematics areas.

SUMMARY

The selection of teaching strategies for use in the defined curriculum should follow certain guidelines. The topics should be developmentally appropriate to the children: They should involve the use of concrete materials and should build on students' prior knowledge.

Teaching strategies for the defined curriculum should show variety. In addition, the teaching

LEARNING ACTIVITY 60

Mathematics-Textbook Analysis

Purpose: The purpose of this activity is to analyze a mathematics textbook for the third-grade level in order to determine the teaching techniques advocated by the textbook.

Procedure:

1. Select two chapters from the third-grade-level teacher's edition of a mathematics textbook. One chapter should deal with the teaching of computation and the other with a noncomputation skill or concept.
2. Read the teaching suggestions for the two chapters of the textbook.

3. Describe the kinds of techniques suggested and how frequently each technique is suggested.
4. Critique the advocated teaching strategies according to the teaching principles presented in this text.
5. Describe any differences in teaching strategies advocated in the two chapters.
6. Discuss how the teaching strategies could be made more effective.

LEARNING ACTIVITY 61

Science-Textbook Analysis

Purpose: The purpose of this activity is to analyze a science textbook for the third-grade level in order to determine the teaching techniques advocated by the textbook.

Procedure:

1. Select from the third-grade-level teacher's edition of a science textbook three chapters: one on biological science, one on physical science, and one on earth-space science.
2. Read the teaching suggestions for each of the three chapters of the textbook.

3. Describe the kinds of techniques suggested for each of the three chapters and how frequently each technique is suggested.
4. Critique the kinds of techniques suggested according to the teaching principles presented in this text.
5. Describe how the teaching strategies differ among the chapters.
6. Discuss how the teaching strategies could be made more effective.

LEARNING ACTIVITY 62

Teacher Interview: Mathematics

Purpose: The purpose of this activity is to conduct an interview with a classroom teacher about mathematics teaching.

Procedure:

1. Prepare a series of questions for a classroom teacher at the third-grade level. Your questions should address the following areas:
   a. the kinds of teaching techniques used in teaching mathematics;

   b. the amount of time allowed each day for instruction in mathematics;
   c. mathematics areas that children enjoy and/or find easy;
   d. mathematics areas that children dislike and/or find difficult;
   e. the teacher's perceptions of the mathematics textbook currently in use; and

LEARNING ACTIVITY 62 Continued

f. suggestions the teacher would make for improving mathematics teaching, including improving the textbook series.

2. Interview a teacher, using the questions and recording the responses.

3. Summarize the responses in written format.

Cautions:

1. If you plan to tape record the interview, be certain to ask permission from the teacher in advance.

2. Accept responses as given without making any judgments.

3. Use follow-up questions to help clarify responses to the interview questions.

4. Do not use the teacher's name in your written report or identify the teacher or school in any way.

LEARNING ACTIVITY 63

Teacher Interview: Science

Purpose: The purpose of this activity is to conduct an interview with a classroom teacher about science teaching.

Procedure:

1. Prepare a series of questions for a classroom teacher at the third-grade level. Your questions should address the following areas:

   a. the kinds of teaching techniques used in teaching science;

   b. the amount of time allowed each day for instruction in science;

   c. science areas that children enjoy and/or find easy;

   d. science areas that children dislike and/or find difficult;

   e. the teacher's perceptions of the science textbook currently in use; and

   f. suggestions the teacher would make for improving science teaching, including improving the textbook series.

2. Interview a teacher, using the questions and recording the responses.

3. Summarize the responses in written format.

Cautions:

1. If you plan to tape record the interview, be certain to ask permission from the teacher in advance.

2. Accept responses as given without making any judgments.

3. Use follow-up questions to help clarify responses to the interview questions.

4. Do not use the teacher's name in your written report or identify the teacher or school in any way.

---

strategies for the defined curriculum at the third-grade level should allow for student input in investigations, accommodate varying abilities of students in the classroom, provide for a variety of explorations, combine concrete experiences with written materials and follow-up discussion, and develop problem-solving, critical-thinking, and language skills.

Vocabulary Terms

Concrete Technique: teaching strategy that focuses on the development of skills and concepts through the use of concrete materials and hands-on teaching strategies.

Defined Curriculum: a curricular pattern in which the subject-matter areas are discrete but in which integration of the areas is encouraged whenever appropriate.

Teaching Strategy: a set of behaviors used by teachers in presenting a total lesson to children.

Verbal Technique: a teaching strategy—including lecturing, reading, discussing, and oral questioning strategies—that focuses on the use of language to convey information.

Study Questions

1. What are the characteristics of the defined curriculum?
2. How does the defined curriculum differ from the unified curriculum and the combined curriculum?
3. On which cognitive and social characteristics of children is the defined curriculum based?
4. What are the characteristics of teaching strategies appropriate to the defined curriculum?
5. What is the role of written materials and oral discussion in an activity-based curriculum at the third-grade level?
6. Which of the following topics would be more appropriate for children at the third-grade level. Why?
   a. Science: the circulatory system *or* classifying kinds of leaves
   b. Mathematics: beginning multiplication *or* the associative property in addition

CHAPTER 12

General Teaching Strategies

Chapter Objectives

On completion of this chapter, you should be able to

1. develop a unit plan for teaching at the third-grade level,

2. develop a lesson plan for teaching at the third-grade level,

3. discuss the use of open discovery as a teaching strategy,

4. plan an open-discovery lesson for mathematics,

5. plan an open-discovery lesson for science,

6. describe the role of the teacher, materials, and students in open-discovery teaching,

7. discuss the use of guided discovery as a teaching strategy,

8. describe the role of the teacher, materials, and students in guided-discovery teaching,

9. plan a guided-discovery lesson for mathematics,

10. plan a guided-discovery lesson for science,

11. discuss the use of demonstration teaching at the third-grade level,

12. describe the role of the teacher, materials, and students in demonstration teaching,

13. plan a demonstration lesson in science,

14. plan a demonstration lesson in mathematics,

15. discuss the use of field trips and resource persons at the third-grade level,

16. plan for a resource person in the third-grade classroom, and

17. plan a field trip for the third-grade level.

Watching a master teacher is like watching a skilled performer. Each movement, each word seems to flow, with the entire sequence of events and words so seamlessly put together that it looks easy. The beginning teacher soon learns that the skill of the master teacher is not so easy to emulate. The master teacher's ability to move gracefully between subject-matter areas, handle difficult children in the classroom while simultaneously handling the rest of the class, and ask exactly the right question at the right time is as much the result of skillful planning as anything else. The basis for good teaching in the defined curriculum is prior planning. Once the teacher has planned the procedures, activities and questions, he or she can feel more confident in presenting the planned lesson or in deviating from the plan to address student interests and questions.

UNIT PLANNING IN THE DEFINED CURRICULUM

Within the defined curriculum, the first step in planning for teaching is the development of a unit plan. The unit plan is a long-range-planning device that allows for total development of a single subject-matter area and for integration of many other subject areas into the main area. The unit approach allows the teacher to plan for a wide variety of hands-on activities, student interests, and student abilities. Thorough planning at the start of a unit enables the teacher to see how various concepts may be interrelated and how different teaching techniques may be integrated into the total learning experience. Advance planning also allows the teacher to prepare for activities that require a lengthy period of time for completion.

Two types of unit plans can be developed. The resource unit offers a wide variety of activities and experiences relating to a single topic area so that the teacher can select from those activities or experiences those that will be utilized during teaching. The resource unit provides far more than can be used so that the teacher can select activities that best meet the needs of his or her classroom. The resource unit, with its wide variety of activities and ideas, forms the basis for the teaching unit. The teaching unit implements the activities and ideas

selected from the resource unit through specific lesson plans. The teaching unit is ready to use in the classroom exactly as it is, without any modifications. Although the teaching unit provides details about exactly what will be done during the unit, it also accommodates student-initiated activities and questions. Whether a resource unit or a teaching unit, the unit plan has four major sections.

Section One: The Unit Objectives

The objectives of a unit point out what students will learn by participating in the activities and experiences of the unit.

The Resource Unit. In a resource unit, the objectives are often written in general terms. For example, the following objectives might be found in a resource unit.

1. As a result of this unit, students will develop an understanding of addition and its uses in solving real-world problems.
2. As a result of this unit, students will develop a variety of problem-solving strategies that can be applied to problems in which the solution is not readily apparent.
3. As a result of this unit, students will develop a concept of energy and of the difference between energy and fuels.
4. As a result of this unit, students will develop an understanding of basic principles of ecology.

The objectives of a resource unit must give enough information to allow the teacher to ascertain the topic for which the activities in the unit have been selected. The objectives should be brief and do not state the specific information that will be learned.

The Teaching Unit. In a teaching unit, the objectives are typically written in specific terms, usually in a behavioral format. The following are examples of specific objectives.

1. After conducting the activity about the kinds of materials that dissolve in water, each student will be able to list four materials that will dissolve and four materials that will not dissolve.
2. After observing a variety of plants, each student will be able to draw a diagram of a plant

and label the roots, stem, leaves, flowers, and fruit.

3. After participating in an activity dealing with the characteristics of triangles, each student will be able to describe a triangle as a closed figure having three sides and three angles.

4. While working with Cuisenaire Rods and a fraction wall, each student will be able to identify the rods that show the fractions 1/2, 1/4, 1/3, 1/6, and 1/8 by naming the color of the appropriate rod.

The objectives of the teaching unit are the objectives of the daily lessons. These specific objectives guide the teacher in selecting appropriate activities as well as appropriate forms of evaluation.

Thus, in summary, the objectives for the resource unit describe the broad categories of knowledge that will be gained by the student as a result of participation in the unit, but do not give examples of the specific pieces of information that the student will learn. The objectives of the teaching unit, on the other hand, detail exactly what information the student is to master, the conditions under which the student will perform, and the level of expectation for student performance.

Section Two: Prerequisites for the Unit

When selecting a unit of work, it is always necessary to consider the student's background information. Two types of prerequisites need to be considered.

First, the teacher must consider the cognitive-developmental demands of the unit. If the unit is appropriate to the children, then there should be a match between the cognitive capabilities of the age group and the cognitive prerequisites of the unit. For example, children who are beginning a unit on multiplication should have developed an understanding of the commutative property and also have a concept of multiplication. Both of these concepts generally develop by the time the child is in the third grade. A unit that requires students to have a concept of volume so that computation of the volume of various solid shapes can be taught is a cognitive mismatch for the third-grade level. Conservation of volume does not generally occur until 11 to 15 years of age. This does not mean that a slight mismatch cannot occur in teaching. For example, a slight mismatch would be when children of eight are introduced to concepts of time. Conservation of time generally occurs at about nine years of age, so children who are in third grade generally have either developed this concept or are close to it. This slight mismatch is appropriate. An example of a gross mismatch is third-grade children being taught a unit on experimentation that involves developing hypotheses, controling variables, and carrying out experimental procedures from which they must draw conclusions based on numerical data. These concepts belong to the formal operational period of thought and are not appropriate for the early-concrete-operational child.

The second type of prerequisite in choosing a unit of work is the content information that children need to have acquired prior to beginning the unit. This is a particularly important consideration when using a spiral curriculum pattern—one in which a topic is introduced at one grade level and reintroduced and expanded on at other grade levels. Such a pattern assumes that children have certain background information and the success of the unit depends on that background. For example, students asked to classify vertebrate animals as fish, reptiles, amphibians, birds, or mammals must have an understanding of the five classes of vertebrates, as well as an understanding of classification. Without these prerequisites, students will not succeed in the new unit. Similarly, in the mathematics area, students who are working in a unit on addition with regrouping need to have developed an understanding of place value and of regrouping from ones to tens and from tens to hundreds. When children do not have the necessary prerequisites, the stage is set for failure rather than for success.

Once the prerequisites are determined, the teacher should assess the students to determine if the necessary foundation skills and concepts are present. If such a background is not present, the teacher should provide students with the necessary knowledge before starting the unit. In situations where some children are prepared for the new unit and some are not, the teacher should consider grouping students so that one group begins the new work and the other is provided with experiences that will allow the development of background information.

LEARNING ACTIVITY 64

Evaluating a Science Textbook for Prerequisites

Purpose: The purpose of this activity is to analyze a chapter of a third-grade-level textbook for the cognitive and content prerequisites assumed by the textbook.

Procedure:

1. Select a single chapter from a science textbook for the third-grade level.
   a. Determine the chapter objectives. These are usually listed at the start of a chapter or are found on the pages of the teacher's edition at the start of each chapter section.
   b. Look for the scope-and-sequence chart in the introductory pages of the textbook. What topics are studied in the first and second grade that lead into the topic at the third-grade level?
   c. Locate the selected chapter in the textbook. Is it at the start of the text, toward the middle, or at the end? What chapters come before the selected chapter? What chapters come after the selected chapter?

2. Read the chapter, including the teaching suggestions and the student text.
   a. What cognitive-developmental prerequisites are assumed by the authors? For example, is an understanding of cause and effect assumed?
   b. What content prerequisites are assumed by the authors? For example, is it assumed in a chapter on plants that students already understand the conditions under which plants will grow best?

3. Return to the information in part one, sections b and c. How well does the textbook series develop the prerequisite content information?

4. How well does the chapter match the cognitive-developmental characteristics of children?

5. Assess the appropriateness of the chapter on the basis of the prerequisites assumed by the authors.

LEARNING ACTIVITY 65

Evaluating a Mathematics Textbook for Prerequisites

Purpose: The purpose of this activity is to analyze a chapter of a third-grade-level, mathematics textbook for the cognitive and content prerequisites assumed by the textbook.

Procedure:

1. Select a single chapter from a mathematics textbook for the third-grade level.
   a. Determine the chapter objectives. These are usually listed at the start of a chapter or are found on the pages of the teacher's edition at the start of each chapter section.
   b. Look for the scope-and-sequence chart that is included within the introductory pages of the textbook. What topics are studied in the first and second grade that lead into the topic at the third-grade level?
   c. Locate the chapter in the textbook. Is it at the start of the text, toward the middle, or at the end? What chapters come before the selected chapter? What chapters come after the selected chapter?

2. Read the chapter, including the teaching suggestions and the student text.

   a. What cognitive-developmental prerequisites are assumed by the authors? For example, is an understanding of the commutative property assumed?

   b. What content prerequisites are assumed by the authors? For example, is it assumed in a chapter on multiplication that students already know the basic multiplication facts?

3. Return to the information in part one, sections b and c. How well does the textbook series develop the prerequisite content information?

4. How well does the chapter match the cognitive-developmental characteristics of children?

5. Assess the appropriateness of the chapter on the basis of the prerequisites assumed by the authors.

Section Three: The Body of the Unit Plan

The body of the resource unit differs greatly from the body of the teaching unit. The resource unit consists of activities and ideas that can be used in teaching a unit, while the teaching unit consists of the lessons that will be used in teaching the unit.

The Resource Unit.   The body of the resource unit includes suggestions for introductions to the unit, teaching activities, resource persons and field trips, and culminating activities. In general, far more activities are included in the resource unit than could possibly be used. The purposes for so many activities are easy to see. First, the teacher can select those activities that will be appropriate to a particular class. Second, the teacher can select activities at differing levels so that average, slower, and gifted children in the same classroom all have activities that are appropriate. Third, the teacher can select several activities to illustrate or develop a single concept in different ways or from different points of view. One activity is rarely enough to allow students to develop a particular concept. And, fourth, the teacher has the option of providing additional ideas for those students who would like to pursue certain ideas of the unit further than classroom time will allow.

The Teaching Unit.   The body of the teaching unit includes introductory, teaching, and culminating activities organized into specific teaching plans.

Within the teaching unit, the plans should be sequenced so that they are in an appropriate order for teaching. Sequencing means making certain each plan builds on the information from previous lessons so that children are not suddenly introduced to a concept for which they have had no preparation. The plans in a teaching unit should include a variety of age-appropriate teaching techniques. Because children learn in a variety of ways, teaching should show variety. Spending time each day reading from a textbook or working on problems in a textbook is not only instructionally boring for both the teacher and the students, but is also inappropriate in terms of child development and the nature of science and mathematics. Finally, the lesson plans should be well organized and clearly developed. A lesson that is unorganized and unclear teaches nothing. In fact, it wastes both the teacher's and the student's time.

   To assist with the problem of clarity, the teacher might begin by developing an outline of the information to be taught. Once the outline has been developed, the teacher should look back at the sequencing within the outline and determine whether a different sequence might be more appropriate. Once the most effective sequence has been determined, the teacher should decide which teaching strategy will allow the most effective communication of the content to the student. And, finally, the teacher should reconsider the entire format, attempting to look at the sequence and the strategies from the viewpoint of someone who knows little or nothing about the topic.

Section Four: Evaluating the Unit

Evaluating the total unit is important both in assessing whether students have learned the information that was planned and in determining the success of the unit. Specific evaluations for each teaching activity should be included in the evaluation section of the unit plan. The evaluations help the teacher to determine whether or not the activity has actually taught the desired information. In general, the evaluations should be an integral part of the activities of the unit rather than separated from the activities. Also, the unit should include a method for assessing the learning that took place as a result of the total unit. Students may be able to answer questions or demonstrate knowledge about specific lessons and activities, but, until the entire unit is evaluated, the teacher does not know whether the students retained information, made connections between various topic areas, or confused pieces of information. In any case, the final unit evaluation gives the teacher an idea of the total success of the unit. The teacher should always keep in mind that the end of the unit evaluation is not synonymous with a unit test.

A means for assessing the appropriateness and success of the unit itself should be included in the unit plan. A part of this evaluation should be to review the lesson and unit evaluations. Activities that were not successful in relating content to students can be replaced or modified. Areas that students did not understand can be determined from the evaluation of the total unit, and then can be appropriately modified.

The teacher also needs to assess the unit in terms of its total operation in the classroom. Did the children enjoy, as well as learn from, the area of study? Did the unit spark curiosity on the part of the students or did it cause boredom and apathy? Did the children want to continue with the area of study even though the time allotted for the unit was up? These kinds of questions can help the teacher modify a unit to make it more successful the next time it is taught. Example 1 on page 151 provides a format for a resource unit and Example 2 on page 152 provides a format for a teaching unit.

LESSON PLANNING IN THE DEFINED CURRICULUM

The lesson plan is the second stage in planning for teaching in the defined curriculum. The lesson plan serves three functions in the classroom. First, the lesson plan organizes information in an effective manner. It requires that the teacher give attention to sequence in presentation and to variety in teaching. Second, the lesson plan specifies the methods and activities that will be used in the lesson, including the questions that the teacher will ask. Third, the lesson plan provides a check on the developmental appropriateness of the subject matter. As the lesson is being planned, the teacher should constantly assess the appropriateness of the content and the activities for the group of children being taught.

Although there are a variety of formats for lesson plans, the following is a format that includes the basic areas of any lesson plan and can be worked with easily.

Preliminary Information

Any lesson plan should include certain preliminary information. This typically includes the grade level, subject-matter area, and amount of time that should be devoted to the lesson. This information is more important for others who might be reading the plan than for the teacher, but it does provide a check on one aspect of teaching: time. By considering the amount of time being given to a particular lesson, the teacher can be confident that an appropriate amount of time is budgeted for a lesson or subject area.

Topic

The topic of the lesson plan briefly describes the content information to be covered in the lesson. The topic of the lesson typically should take no more than a few words to describe, but the use of only a few words does not necessarily mean that the topic is appropriate for a single lesson. For example, a topic might read: The poles of a magnet are

EXAMPLE 12.1

Unit-Plan Format: Teaching Unit

A unit plan is a device for long-term preparation in any subject area. The material included in a unit plan is outlined below. In general, the teaching unit is assembled in the following order:

1. Cover Sheet
2. Overview
3. Objectives
4. Lesson Plans
5. Evaluation
6. Appendix
7. References
   a. teacher references
   b. student references

The following information details what is found in each of the main sections of the unit plan.

1. *Cover Sheet*
   a. topic of the unit
   b. grade level for which the unit was prepared
   c. duration of the unit
2. *Overview*
   a. list of the concepts, skills, and processes to be included in the unit
   b. a brief discussion of the importance of the area of science or mathematics to the children being taught
   c. a discussion of the prerequisite knowledge that the children should have before they begin the unit
3. *Objectives*
   a. List all of the specific objectives for the unit in behavioral format.
   b. List the objectives in the order in which they should be taught.
   c. In general, no more than two or three objectives should be included per lesson.

4. *Lesson Plans*
   a. The lesson plans should be detailed enough that a substitute teacher would be able to use them.
   b. The individual lesson plans should include the topic, objectives, procedure, materials, and method of evaluation.
   c. Order the lesson plans in the sequence in which they will be taught.
5. *Evaluation*
   a. Include with each lesson, as a part of the lesson plan, the means by which you will evaluate each of the lessons taught to the class.
   b. At the end of the unit, include a statement describing how you will evaluate the quality of the unit after it has been taught to the children in order to decide whether to revise the unit before teaching it again.
6. *Appendix*
   a. List all of the materials that you may need to teach the unit.
   b. Include a copy of any handouts, worksheets, evaluation forms, or other materials that you may need in teaching the unit.
   c. Include a diagram of any bulletin boards that you may use for the unit.
7. *References*
   a. Include a list of all materials you used in preparing the unit plan.
   b. Include a list of any materials that would be helpful in teaching the unit, particularly trade books and other materials for use by the children.

EXAMPLE 12.2

Unit Plan Format: Resource Unit

A resource unit is a device to assist the teacher with long-term preparation in any subject area. The material included in a unit plan is outlined below. In general, the resource unit is assembled in the following order:

1. Cover Sheet
2. Overview
3. Objectives
4. Activity Suggestions
5. Evaluation
6. Appendix
7. References
    a. student reference materials
    b. teacher reference materials

The following information details what is found in each of the main sections of the unit plan.

1. *Cover Sheet*
    a. topic of the unit
    b. grade level for which the unit is prepared
    c. duration of the unit
2. *Overview*
    a. a list of the concepts, skills, and processes included in the unit
    b. a brief discussion of the importance of the area of science or mathematics to the children being taught
    c. a discussion of the prerequisite knowledge that the children should have before they begin the unit
3. *Objectives*
    a. List all of the general objectives for the unit.
    b. List the objectives in the order in which the suggested activities for the objectives appear.
4. *Suggested Activities*
    a. The activities should be separated into three categories: introductory activities, teaching activities, culminating activities.
    b. The individual activities should include a list of the materials needed to do the activity, de-

tailed directions for the activity, and suggestions as to whether the activity should be done as a discovery lesson, a demonstration lesson, or a field trip.
    c. Within each of the three categories, the activities should be ordered according to the sequence of the objectives.
    d. Also, include under activities suggestions for resource persons, field trips, games, films or other audiovisual aids, computer programs, and bulletin boards.
5. *Evaluation*
    a. Include with each activity, as a part of the activity, the means by which you will evaluate it.
    b. At the end of the unit, include a statement describing how you will evaluate the quality of the unit after it has been taught to the children in order to decide whether to revise the unit before teaching it again.
6. *Appendix*
    a. List all of the materials that you may need to effectively use the activities.
    b. Include a copy of any handouts, worksheets, evaluation forms, or other materials that you may need in using the activities effectively.
    c. Include a diagram of any bulletin boards that you may use for the unit.
7. *References*
    a. Include a list of all materials you used in preparing the unit plan.
    b. Include a list of any materials that would be helpful in teaching the unit, including trade books and other materials for use by the children and sources of information for use by the teacher.

LEARNING ACTIVITY 66

Developing a Unit Plan for Mathematics

Purpose: The purpose of this activity is to develop either a teaching unit or a resource unit for mathematics teaching.

Procedure:
1. Select a topic from either a third-grade-level textbook in mathematics or from the third-grade level of a state curriculum guide for mathematics.
2. Decide whether the unit plan will be a resource unit or a teaching unit.
3. Prepare the unit plan according to the outline for a unit given in this text. Be certain to include all of the following areas.
   a. Section One: Objectives
      1. general objectives for a resource unit
      2. specific objectives for a teaching unit

   b. Section Two: Prerequisites
      1. cognitive-developmental prerequisites
      2. content prerequisites
   c. Section Three: Body of the Plan
      1. introductory activities, teaching activities, and culminating activities for the resource unit
      2. specific lesson plans for the teaching unit
   d. Section Four: Evaluation
      1. techniques for evaluating the students
      2. techniques for evaluating the unit

LEARNING ACTIVITY 67

Developing a Unit Plan for Science

Purpose: The purpose of this activity is to develop either a teaching unit or a resource unit for science teaching.

Procedure:
1. Select a topic from either a third-grade-level textbook in science or from the third-grade level of a state curriculum guide for science.
2. Decide whether the unit plan will be a resource unit or a teaching unit.
3. Prepare the unit plan according to the outline for a unit given in this text. Be certain to include all of the following areas.
   a. Section One: Objectives
      1. general objectives for a resource unit
      2. specific objectives for a teaching unit

   b. Section Two: Prerequisites
      1. cognitive-developmental prerequisites
      2. content prerequisites
   c. Section Three: Body of the Plan
      1. introductory activities, teaching activities, and culminating activities for the resource unit
      2. specific lesson plans for the teaching unit
   d. Section Four: Evaluation
      1. techniques for evaluating the students
      2. techniques for evaluating the unit

stronger than other areas of a magnet. This would be an appropriate topic even though it is stated in thirteen words. A much briefer topic is The Universe. Although this easily is stated in two words, it is definitely too broad for any lesson and is also inappropriate for the third-grade curriculum.

Objectives

The objectives of a lesson detail exactly what is to be learned by the students as a result of the lesson. As was seen in the section on objectives of a unit plan, the specific objectives of the teaching unit are the objectives of the lesson plans. One additional point, however, needs to be made. The objectives of a lesson plan should include, for the science area, both content and process objectives. Consequently, a lesson plan for the science area might have two objectives:

1. After participating in the activity dealing with magnets, each student will be able to orally state that the poles of the magnet are stronger than the other areas of the magnet. (content objective)
2. While participating in the activity dealing with magnets, each child will be able to count the number of paper clips that each area of the magnet will hold and draw a conclusion on the basis of the data collected. (process objective, involving the process skills of using numbers and concluding).

Both of these examples fit the criteria for good objectives. First, the behavior expected of the students is observable: they will orally state, count, and draw a conclusion. Second, the objectives represent developmentally appropriate practice, since both are based on hands-on activities, using real materials and involving cause-and-effect concepts related to direct and immediate occurrences.

Materials

The materials section lists all of the materials that will be needed in order to teach the lesson. If small groups are to work at an activity, the materials generally list what each small group will need. If there are materials that will be used only by the teacher, these are listed separately. It is not necessary in this section to list those materials that are typically found in the classroom: books, pencils, paper, chalk, and so on.

Procedure

The procedure section details exactly what is to be taught in the lesson. In general, the procedure is divided into three sections.

The first section describes the introduction that will be used in the lesson. The introduction is designed to either alert the children about what to expect in the lesson or arouse curiosity through a demonstration, question, or quick activity.

The second part of the procedure describes the actual teaching activity. The focus here is on the procedure that is to be followed by the children as they accomplish the objective. The procedure directions should be given in a step-by-step fashion. If the directions are simple and easy to follow, they may be given orally. If the directions are complex, it is helpful to follow the oral directions with written directions. In this way, aural learners will hear the directions, visual learners will see them, and all the students will have twice as much exposure to them. Furthermore, students who have reading problems will be able to succeed because of the oral format.

The third and final part of the procedure is the discussion. In this section, the teacher details how the information obtained by the students during the activity will be collected for class consideration; the way in which the discussion of those results will be carried out, including the questions that will be asked; and the way in which the teacher will assist the class in drawing the activity conclusions. The summary is the part of the discussion that finalizes the lesson. The summary should review and repeat the conclusion of the activity, as well as any other information that is to be learned from the activity. Examples of the various types of lesson plans are included with each of the specific teaching strategies discussed here. The included lesson plans show how a single topic within each of the subject-matter areas—mathematics and science—can be taught using each of the methods.

Evaluation

The last section of any lesson plan should be the evaluation of the lesson. The evaluation should match the objectives so perfectly that it seems redundant. For example, if an objective states that "each child will be able to draw a picture of a plant and label the five main parts," then the evaluation should state, "Give each child a piece of paper and have each child draw a plant and label the five main parts." The evaluation should evaluate exactly what is stated in the objective. An inappropriate evaluation for the objective described above would be "On a written quiz, each child will name the five main parts of a plant and gives the function of each." This evaluation does not match the objective.

Using a Lesson Plan in the Classroom

A lesson plan is a highly organized and specific teaching plan, and, as such, it has the possibility of misuse in a classroom. It should always be remembered that a lesson plan is a guide rather than an absolute. If a lesson plan is a guide, then how should it be used in the classroom?

Lesson plans can always be modified if the teacher sees during a lesson that changes are needed. Modifications may be required in order to make the lesson more developmentally appropriate for the class. For example, a teacher who planned for children to work individually may see that because of the social nature of third graders, the lesson would be more appropriate if small groups were used instead. This is an easy modification to make as the lesson is being taught.

Modifications to a lesson may be made in order to incorporate student interests. For example, if a lesson is dealing with single pulleys and students show interest in how more than one pulley can be used at a time, the lesson which was to deal with single pulleys quickly can be modified to include investigations of multiple pulleys. Modifications also can be made to allow for digressions on the part of students. For example, a lesson in which students are asked to investigate the kinds of materials found in garden soil could be modified to also include investigation of earthworms or insect larvae.

Modifications may also be needed in a lesson in order to allow for the inclusion of prerequisites that are missing in the backgrounds of children. For example, in a lesson dealing with whether to classify invertebrates as insects or not insects, the teacher may discover that children are uncertain about the characteristics that make an invertebrate

an invertebrate. In this case, the lesson needs to be modified so the necessary information is taught before students are asked to classify.

And, finally, with classroom reality what it is, a lesson plan may need to be modified because of unexpected changes in schedule. A fire drill, severe storm warning, special assembly, or any number of other unexpected events may require changes in a lesson. In this case, time may allow for an introductory discussion, but not for the activity; or it may allow for the introduction and activity, but not for the follow-up discussion. In such cases, rather than rush through an entire lesson, it is better to modify the plan, perhaps breaking the lesson into two parts: one part at the time planned and another part at a future time.

TEACHING TECHNIQUES FOR THE DEFINED CURRICULUM

Once the topic for the lesson has been determined, it is necessary to decide on the teaching strategy that will be used. A variety of teaching strategies are available for the defined curriculum, and they will be discussed in the following pages. Remember, however, that the techniques used in both the unified and combined curriculum also have their places in the defined curriculum.

The Open-Discovery Teaching Strategy

Definition. The open-discovery strategy is a student-centered, problem-solving approach that allows the child to direct the activity and determine the problem to be investigated. In addition to emphasizing the child as investigator, the open-discovery method allows the integration of other subject areas into either the mathematics or science lesson.

Open Discovery in Science Teaching. In the science program, open discovery is used to engage students in active investigation of problems that they identify from a broad content topic selected by the teacher. In this teaching strategy, it is the teacher's task to initiate the topic, and then to aid the students in determining what they will focus on in the lesson. Within the physical sciences, the teacher may select a topic such as sound. An initiating activity for this topic would be to have students in small groups use tape recorders in various parts of the school building or school grounds to gather sounds during a ten- or fifteen-minute time period. After discussing and classifying the kinds of sounds that were heard, the teacher might ask students if they have any questions about the sounds they heard or about sound in general. The teacher also might ask the students what they would like to learn about sound. Students' questions or ideas are listed on a chalkboard or an experience chart. Students can then use the list to select topics for further investigation.

In the biological sciences, a similar sequence of events could take place. In a unit on plants, introduce children to the topic by taking a nature walk, using either drawings, a collection of a leaf from each of the various kinds of plants seen, or an instant camera to record what was seen. After returning to the classroom, the children discuss the kinds of plants that they saw on the nature walk. Once again, the teacher asks for any questions about plants that students might have or asks for a list of the kinds of things children might want to know about plants. From the questions and ideas, the teacher helps students to plan and carry out investigations.

Open Discovery in Mathematics Teaching. Open discovery in the mathematics area is used to promote conceptual development and demonstrate the problem-solving nature of mathematics. Open discovery can be used in working with computational skills in the following way. When exploring the concept of division, students can be given a bag of 504 dried lima beans and asked to find how many ways they can separate the beans into piles so that each pile has the same number. For example, there could be two piles of 252, four piles of 156, six piles of 84, seven piles of 72, eight piles of 63, twelve piles of 42, fourteen piles of 36, eighteen piles of 28, twenty-four piles of 21, twenty-eight piles of 18, and so on. By working with an activity like this, children can discover that division means equal groups and that one number can be divided into a variety of equally sized groups. In this strategy, the problem is given to the students and they have the opportunity to decide how they will solve the problem as well as to find a variety of possible

solutions. Additionally, the activity may lead children to try other quantities of beans and seeing how many groups they can make using other quantities. The use of other quantities often leads into the concept of a remainder in the division process. Open-discovery techniques can also be used with a noncomputational topic like geometry. In this case, students might be given straws, clay, and string and challenged to find how they can use the materials to make a variety of three-dimensional shapes that have eight corners, more than eight corners, or less than eight corners. After students have had a chance to solve the problem of making various figures, they can be classified into categories such as cubes, prisms, and pyramids, and then characterized according to their various traits. Example 3 shows a science lesson that uses open discovery as a teaching strategy. Example 4 shows an open-discovery plan for mathematics teaching.

The Role of the Teacher in Open Discovery

The role of the teacher in open discovery is different from the role of the teacher in a traditional teacher-directed lesson. First, the teacher selects a broad topic of inquiry and develops the starting point for students' investigation. Rather than telling students exactly what to do in order to carry out an investigation, the teacher develops a problem to be solved and allows the students to figure out how to solve it themselves. This does not, however, mean that the teacher abdicates all responsibility for the lesson. The second role of the teacher in open discovery is to help the students identify the problem and possible solutions. The teacher helps the students to identify some of the problems that could be investigated within the larger topic and provides guidance in how those problems may be investigated. Also, the teacher provides a broad problem and assists the students in developing their individual solutions. It is this assistance that makes up the third part of the role of the teacher. The teacher provides assistance in developing activities that can be used in investigating the problems selected by the students. The teacher cannot and does not simply step back and let the children work on their own. Since open discovery does have particular goals, it is the teacher's responsibility to see that those goals are reached.

EXAMPLE 12.3

Open-Discovery Lesson Plan: Science

Grade: Third

Subject Area: Science

Time Needed: 30–45 minutes

Topic: Sounds can be classified by pitch.

Materials: Clipboards, tape recorders, blank tapes, pencils, paper

Objectives:

1. As a result of the activity, each student will be able to identify some of the sounds heard in the classroom and in the school building.
2. During a follow-up discussion of the activity, each student will be able to contribute either a question dealing with sound or a method for investigating one of the contributed questions.

Procedure:

1. *Introduction*
   a. Ask the children to close their eyes and listen to the sounds in the classroom. After about a minute, have them open their eyes. Make a list on the chalkboard or overhead projector of the sounds they heard.
   b. Ask the children to predict some of the sounds that they might hear in other parts of the school building. Make another list of the predicted sounds.
2. *Body*
   a. Divide the class into groups of four. Provide each group with a pencil, paper, clipboard, and small tape recorder.
   b. Assign each of the groups to a different location within the school: hallway, near the principal's office, lunchroom, gym, playground, music room, and so on.

   c. Have each group report to the assigned area and, for ten minutes, record sounds using the tape recorder and the pencil and paper.
   d. Have each group read the list of sounds that they heard and play one or two minutes of their tape. Compare the sounds to the predictions.
3. *Discussion*
   a. Ask the students to think for a minute about the sounds that they heard and the topic of sound in general. Ask if they have any questions about sound that they would like to have answered.
   b. List their questions on the chalkboard or experience chart.
   c. Discuss how they could find the answers to the questions.
   d. Select one of the questions to investigate during the next lesson.
   e. Summarize the lesson.
      1. Review some of the kinds of sounds heard in the various locations. Place the tape recorders and tapes where children can listen and guess the sounds they are hearing.
      2. Remind the students of the question that they will investigate the next day.

Evaluation:

1. Use a checklist to note the names of the students who were able to identify some of the sounds heard in the building.
2. Use a checklist to note the names of the students who contributed either questions or methods for answering questions during the discussion.

EXAMPLE 12.4

Open-Discovery Lesson Plan: Mathematics

Grade: Third

Subject Area: Mathematics

Time Needed: 45–60 minutes

Topic: Three-dimensional figures include cubes, pyramids, prisms, and cylinders.

Materials: straws, clay, string, scissors, jar lids, chart with descriptions of the shapes listed below

Objectives:

1. Given straws, clay, plastic container lids, and string, each small group of children will be able to construct four of the six following shapes:
   a. a shape with eight corners and all sides squares
   b. a shape with eight corners and some of the sides longer than others
   c. a shape with five corners
   d. a shape with circles for the top and bottom
   e. a shape with four triangles for sides
   f. a shape with a triangle at each of the ends

Procedure:

1. *Introduction*
   a. Review the names of the plane shapes by having children go to the chalkboard and draw examples of squares, circles, triangles, and rectangles.
   b. Show the children a cube and ask them to describe it. Emphasize the shape of each of the sides and the number of corners. Record on the board that the object has eight corners and all sides are squares.

2. *Body*
   a. Show the following descriptions to the children and read them aloud:
      1. a shape with eight corners and all sides squares
      2. a shape with eight corners and some of the sides longer than others
      3. a shape with five corners
      4. a shape with circles for the top and bottom
      5. a shape with four triangles for sides
      6. a shape with eight corners and all sides squares
   b. Tell the class they will be working in small groups to see how many of the shapes they can make using the string, straws, clay, and jar lids.
   c. Distribute the materials and give time to work.

3. *Summary*
   a. Have the groups show and describe the shapes they constructed.
   b. Place the shapes in an area where they can be displayed and used for another lesson.

Evaluation:

1. Check to see if each group was able to construct shapes satisfying the conditions of four of the six descriptions.

However, it is not the teacher's responsibility to establish a narrow procedure to be followed by all students in precisely the same way. One of the strengths of open discovery is that it encourages flexibility in thinking and problem solving. Finally, the teacher's role is to provide the materials that are needed and make suggestions for substitutions when students request additional materials that are not available. For example, when students want to solve the "bean problem" by filling glasses with beans, the teacher might suggest plastic or styrofoam cups or even a different type of container.

Open discovery, then, focuses on the child and the development of flexible thinking skills through problem-solving activities. The next teaching strategy focuses more on the content to be taught and less on the problem-solving aspect.

LEARNING ACTIVITY 68

Developing an Open-Discovery Lesson Plan

Purpose: The purpose of this activity is to develop a lesson plan for either science or mathematics at the third-grade level that utilizes open-discovery teaching.

Procedure:

1. Select a topic from a third-grade mathematics textbook, a third-grade science textbook, or the state course of study for either of these two subject-matter areas.
2. Plan a lesson for the topic that illustrates the appropriate use of open-discovery teaching. Include in the lesson plan each of the following areas.
   a. Preliminary Information
      1. grade level
      2. subject-matter area
      3. approximate time for teaching
   b. Topic
   c. Objectives
   d. Materials List
   e. Procedure
      1. method for introducing the lesson
      2. procedure for the open-discovery teaching
      3. summary of the lesson
   f. Evaluation
3. Teach the lesson to a small group of children. Critique the lesson in terms of what went well and what changes would be needed to make the lesson more effective.

The Guided-Discovery Teaching Strategy

Definition. The second teaching strategy that is appropriate to the defined curriculum is guided discovery. Guided discovery is a content- and process-oriented approach that allows the development of specific concepts in either science or mathematics.

Guided Discovery in Science Teaching. In the science area, guided discovery is used to teach concepts that lend themselves to hands-on investigations through the use of process skills. Because physical-science topics, such as sound, matter, light, heat, simple machines, and magnets, lend themselves so easily to hands-on teaching with real materials, the guided-discovery approach is most appropriate in the physical sciences. This does not mean, however, that guided discovery cannot be used in working with biological sciences (investigating the factors that enhance the growth of plants) or earth-space sciences (investigating the components of soil). As a teaching strategy, guided discovery is highly structured so that the activity leads to a particular conclusion, but the structure is not always immediately self-evident. As an example of guided discovery in action, consider a lesson on levers.

The lesson on levers actually contains four parts. As an introduction, the teacher poses a problem for the class. The problem is a simple one with which many children are familiar:

> Two boys want to play on a seesaw. Consuelo gets on one end and the other end goes up in the air. As soon as Jimmy manages to get onto the other end, the seesaw moves so that Jimmy's feet touch the ground and Consuelo is up in the air. No matter what they do, Consuelo stays up in the air and Jimmy stays on the ground. What could be the problem? How could they solve this problem?

The problem is, of course, that Jimmy weighs far more than Consuelo and so the two boys cannot make the seesaw go up and down. The solution is to move Jimmy closer to the center. Many children will be able to figure out why the seesaw will not work just because they have been in that particular situation. The solution to the problem of two different weights, however, may not be so easy. Students in this lesson are encouraged to come up with as many possible ways of solving the problem as they can. The ideas for solutions are listed on the chalkboard or overhead projector for later reference. Once the seesaw problem has been posed, the children are introduced to an activity that will help them solve it. The materials are simple: a triangular block, a wooden yardstick, and a variety of materials presented in pairs so that one of the two objects in the pair is heavier than the other. Children are first told how to set up the materials by balancing the yardstick at the 18-inch mark on the triangular block. They then place the lighter of the two objects on one end of the lever and the heavier on the other end. Students are then told to move the objects on the lever until they can get it to balance once again. They are asked to record the answer to the following questions for each of the pairs of objects: Which object is closer to the triangular block? Which object is farther from the triangular block?

After the children have had a chance to try each pair of objects, the teacher collects the materials and then uses the chalkboard or overhead projector to organize the results of the activity. The data can be presented in the form of a simple chart of two columns with one column marked "closer" and the other marked "farther." Once the data are collected, the teacher asks students which object in each pair was heavier. Students quickly begin to see a pattern form in which the heavier object of the pair is always closer to the triangular block. Next, the teacher asks students to draw a conclusion from the data. The simple conclusion from this activity is that the heavier object is closer to the center.

After the students have worked with the materials and drawn a conclusion, the teacher can introduce the appropriate terminology. The yardstick is the bar of the lever, the triangular block is the fulcrum, and the objects are called the force and the load. Last, the students are asked to use the proper terms in their conclusions. The conclusion now is that the heavier object is closer to the fulcrum.

At this point, the teacher returns to the starting problem and asks, "What will Jimmy and Consuelo have to do in order to make the seesaw work?" The answer, that Jimmy will have to move closer to the middle, should now be easy. But, since there were a variety of ideas listed, the teacher should return to those ideas and discuss them in terms of what was found during the activity.

Guided Discovery in Mathematics Teaching. In mathematics, guided discovery can be used to help students understand computation through the development of rules that help solve problems easily and accurately. One of the most difficult types of subtraction problems for children to solve are those that require regrouping across a zero. This is a problem of the type $203 - 68 =$ _____. The strategy used for a problem of this type can be developed through the use of a guided-discovery lesson that involves students in the use of materials. In this case, bundles of popsicle sticks will be used as the manipulative material.

In the first step of this lesson, students solve problems involving a two-digit number subtracted from a three-digit number in which regrouping procedures are needed but no zeros are involved. For example, the teacher might give a problem such as $146 - 87 =$ _____. The children are asked to show the number 146 using their popsicle sticks. This involves one bundle of 100, four bundles of 10, and six separate sticks. The teacher then asks if it is possible to take away seven ones from the number students have displayed. Children should realize that it is possible, but only after one bundle of ten has been traded for ten ones. The seven ones, or seven single sticks, are then taken away. Again the teacher asks if it is possible to take away eight tens, or eighty, from what is shown. The students should again see the need to regroup. After the one hundred bundle is traded for ten tens, students should take away the eight tens. The popsicle sticks remaining represent the answer to the problem: 59. After practicing a few of these problems in order to review the regrouping process, students are given a problem that involves a zero. See Diagram 12.1 for an illustration of this procedure.

This new type of problem is introduced through teacher demonstration without student involvement. For example, the teacher indicates that the problem $305 - 79 =$ _____ will be solved. The teacher shows the 305 and explains that nine ones need to be taken away but only five are shown on the board. At this point, the teacher indicates that he or she needs to go to the tens place to exchange a ten for ten ones. On finding no tens in the tens place, the teacher asks the rhetorical

Showing 146 using popsicle sticks

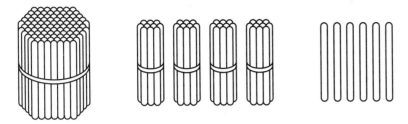

Regrouping from the tens place to the ones place

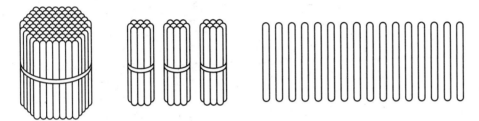

Subtraction of 87

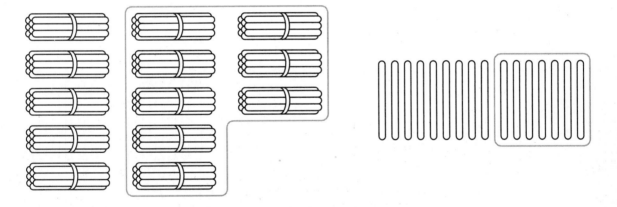

Final answer

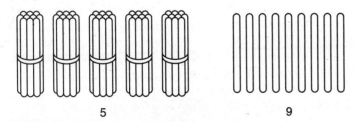

5   9

Diagram 12.1 Regrouping Without Involving Zero

Showing 305 using popsicle sticks

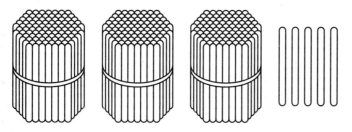

Regrouping from the hundreds to the tens place

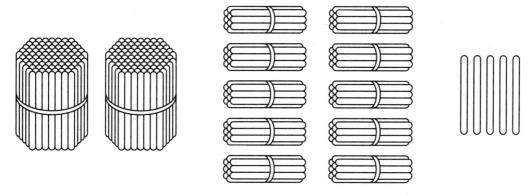

Regrouping from the tens to the ones place

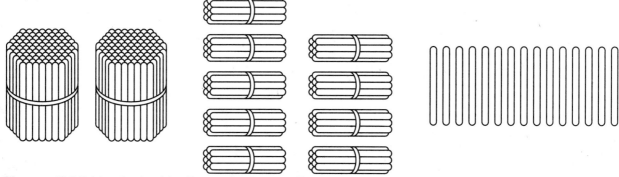

Diagram 12.2 Subtraction Involving Regrouping Across a Zero

question, "What do I do now?" The teacher then suggests trading one hundred for ten tens, demonstrating the process of regrouping for the students. Now, the teacher discovers that there are tens that can be traded in for ones. The teacher subtracts the nine ones and the seven tens. The teacher then demonstrates the procedure of inspecting the ones place to determine if regrouping is needed, going to the tens place for a ten to regroup as ones, and then finding that there are no tens so a hundred has to be

regrouped as ten tens. Finally, the teacher has the students direct the procedure as she or he demonstrates it. The students are then asked to solve some problems using their popsicle sticks and regrouping across the zero. See Diagram 12.2 for an illustration of this problem.

After students are familiar and at ease with the procedure that is used for regrouping across a zero, the teacher can pose a question along the lines of the following: "I want to tell other children how to

Diagram 12.2 Continued

Subtraction of 79

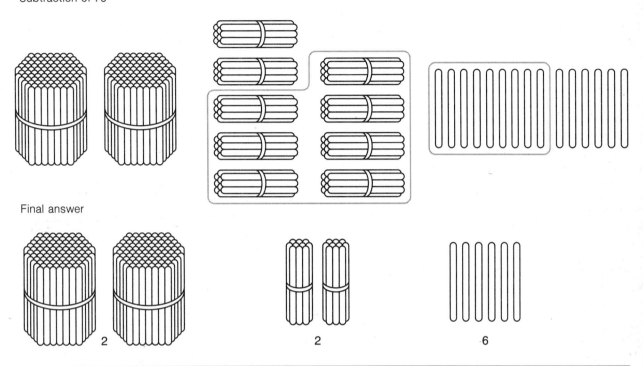

Final answer

2   2   6

---

solve a problem like the ones we have been doing. What could I tell them?" As an answer to this question, the students phrase a rule to be followed. The rule could be stated, "If you need to regroup to the ones place and there are no tens in the tens place, go to the hundreds place and regroup one hundred into tens. Then, regroup one of the tens for ten ones." Students can now be asked to apply this rule to additional problems. Example 5 shows a guided-discovery lesson plan for science and Example 6 shows one for mathematics.

The Role of the Teacher in Guided Discovery

The role of the teacher in guided discovery is different from the role of the teacher in the traditional classroom setting. The teacher in the traditional classroom is a purveyor of information. He or she tells students information or makes certain that students read information in textbooks or other sources. In guided discovery, the teacher is not a purveyor of information.

Instead, the role of the teacher in guided discovery is first to establish the parameters of the content to be developed. In terms of a lesson plan, the teacher delineates the objectives of the lesson or determines the exact content to be considered as the topic of the lesson. The teacher does not, however, tell this information to the students.

Instead, the teacher moves into the second role, that of developing the activity or activities that will allow the students to investigate the content information. The activity is selected after the topic and the objective of the lesson are chosen to insure that the activity will address the content desired. The teacher then presents the directions for the activity to the students and moves into the third role.

The third role of the teacher is that of a guide or assistant while the activity is being carried out. The teacher attempts to lend assistance in answering questions about the procedure or in gathering additional materials, but does not answer questions about why something is happening or if what is occurring is supposed to be occurring.

Finally, the teacher moves into the fourth and,

EXAMPLE 12.5

Guided-Discovery Lesson Plan: Science

Grade: Third

Subject Area: Science

Time Needed: 30–45 minutes

Topic: Pitch can be used as a way of classifying sounds.

Materials: tape recorder, tape of various musical instruments, different-sized boxes with one open side, rubber bands of different thicknesses and length

Objectives:

1. As a result of the activity, each child will be able to demonstrate how the pitch of a sound can be changed.
2. As a result of the lesson, each child will be able to classify sounds as having a high pitch or a low pitch.

Procedure:

1. *Introduction*
   a. Tell the children that you want them to listen very carefully to the sound that you are going to make. Blow across the top of an empty glass soda bottle so that it makes a whistling sound. Have the children describe the sound. Tell the children that you would like to change the way the bottle sounds. Ask them to suggest ways that you could change the sound. List their ideas on the board, but do not try them at this time.
   b. Tell the students that they are going to investigate how to change the way an object sounds by using rubber bands and boxes.

2. *Body*
   a. Divide the class into groups of three or four. Provide each group with different-sized boxes that have one open side and with rubber bands of differing lengths and thicknesses. Demonstrate how to make a "guitar" by stretching the rubber band over the box and plucking the rubber band. Tell the children to listen to the sound. Ask them to find some ways of changing the sounds made by the rubber bands. Have them keep a record of what they did to make the sound higher and what they did to make it lower.
   b. After the children have investigated, write on the chalkboard the methods they used to change the pitch. Use one column labeled "higher" and another labeled "lower."
   c. Use questions to help the children draw the conclusion that the more the rubber band is stretched, the higher the sound.
   d. Introduce the term *pitch* as a way of describing sounds.
   e. Play a tape of sounds made by musical instruments. Ask the children to decide whether each sound is high in pitch or low in pitch. Classify the various sounds on the chalkboard.
   f. Return to the original problem with the bottle. Ask the students which of the ideas on the list will work to change the sound. Try those ideas to see how they affect the pitch of the bottle. If no one suggests putting something in the bottle, put water in the bottle and test its effect on pitch.

3. *Summary*
   Have children describe how they can change the pitch of an object and have them name some high-pitched sounds and some low-pitched sounds.

Evaluation:

1. Have each child write a few sentences telling how to change the pitch of a rubber-band guitar.
2. Give each child a list of familiar sounds. Have the child classify the sound as high pitched or low pitched.

EXAMPLE 12.6

Guided-Discovery Lesson Plan: Mathematics

Grade: Third

Subject Area: Mathematics

Time Needed: Two class periods of approximately one hour each

Topic: Classifying solid geometric figures

Materials: Worksheets for each group, solid figures constructed previously during the open-inquiry lesson

Objectives:
1. Each child will be able to list the characteristics of a cube, rectangular prism, triangular prism, pyramid, and cylinder.
2. Each child will be able to classify solid geometric shapes as cubes, rectangular prisms, triangular prisms, pyramids, or cylinders.
3. Each child will be able to identify examples of the following shapes in the environment: cubes, rectangular prisms, triangular prisms, pyramids, and cylinders.

Procedure:
1. *Introduction*
   a. Have each group gather together the models of solid figures constructed previously during the open-discovery lesson.
   b. Have some of the children review the characteristics of their models by orally describing them.
2. *Body*
   a. Part I
      1. Ask one student to bring one of the models forward and put it on a table for the class to see. Have each group bring forward models of the same shape to classify with the first example.
      2. Continue this process until all models have been classified by shape.
      3. Locate the group of cubes and label the group with a name card with the word cube on it.
      4. Repeat step three for each of the following categories of shapes: rectangular prism, triangular prism, pyramid, and cylinder.

5. Remove, for the moment, any shapes that do not fit into all of the designated categories.
6. Discuss the characteristics of the classified shapes.
7. Return to the models that do not fit into any of the designated categories. Have the class decide on a name for that category of shapes.

   b. Part II
      1. Have the groups gather their models.
      2. On the chalkboard or overhead projector, place the following chart. Hand out copies of the chart to each of the groups.

Shape	Number of Sides	Shape of Sides	Number of Corners
Cube			
Rectangular Prism			
Triangular Prism			
Pyramid			
Cylinder			

3. Demonstrate how to fill in the chart by using the cube as an example. Count the sides and record the number on the chart. Describe the shape of the sides and record it. Count the number of corners and record it.
4. Have the children use their models to complete the group charts.
5. As a full class, complete the chart on the overhead projector or chalkboard.
6. Use questions to help children interpret the information on the chart.

   c. Part III
      1. Review the characteristics of the various solid shapes, using both the models and the chart.
      2. List on the chalkboard or overhead projector the names of the various solid shapes.
      3. Have the students find examples of the shapes listed among objects in the environment.

EXAMPLE 12.6 Continued

4. As students find examples, ask them to describe the characteristics of each object and why the object belongs in a particular category.

3. *Summary*

   a. Summarize the three parts of the lesson by naming each shape, reviewing its characteristics, and giving an example of it in the environment.

Evaluation:

1. Use a checklist to identify the students who have helped to classify the various shapes.

2. Collect the worksheets from each group and check that the chart is filled in correctly.

3. Have each child write down one example in the environment of each of the shapes.

4. Use a checklist to determine which groups constructed four of the six described shapes.

---

perhaps, most important role: questioner. As questioner, the teacher collects the data from the activity and asks questions that will allow the students to develop an understanding of the desired content. At no time does the teacher tell students what they were supposed to have seen or learned. When the activity does not come out as expected and students develop a conclusion that is in direct opposition to what scientists have found, the teacher's role is still that of questioner. In this case, the teacher describes what is typically determined as a result of the activity but asks students why their results could have differed from the typical. Collecting ideas as to why results differ is followed by trying out some of those possible reasons. The most important thing the teacher should not do is to tell students they got it "wrong" and to "learn the right answer." Not only is this poor teaching practice, but it also teaches children not to trust their own senses and is in conflict with the spirit of science and mathematics as problem-solving techniques. And, besides, in a science activity, students are more likely to believe and retain their own conclusion rather than the "right" answer that conflicts with their experiences.

The Role of the Child in Guided Discovery

The role of the child in guided discovery is different from the role of the child in the traditional classroom. In the traditional classroom, the child is a passive recipient of information, treated somewhat like an empty pitcher that must be filled by outsiders. In guided discovery, the child is treated not as a passive recipient, but as an active investigator. It is the child who participates in the activity, who uses the materials, who develops the concepts, and who

draws the conclusions. During the actual involvement with materials, the child utilizes problem-solving and thinking skills while developing content information or identifying computation rules. The child is not only physically active in guided discovery, but also is mentally active. That mental activity continues as the child actively organizes and interprets information. The active organization and interpretation of information occurs naturally as the child operates on materials during the activity and as the child answers questions and attempts to draw a conclusion from the activity.

The Role of the Materials in Guided Discovery

In guided discovery, the materials play a greater role than they do in the traditional classroom setting. Although materials are present in the traditional classroom, they frequently are more word-oriented than those used in guided discovery. Those materials that are concrete or hands-on in nature generally are used in the traditional classroom as illustrations or confirmations of information that has already been considered in written form. In guided discovery, such materials are used to actually teach the content information. The materials are the focal point of any lesson because it is through materials that the child investigates and develops content information. The materials in guided discovery, unlike those used in the traditional classroom, provide for a high level of interaction among children and between the individual child and the objects. Interaction, rather than passive learning by separated children, is of highest importance. Finally, printed material becomes less important than real objects within the guided-discovery approach. In the traditional classroom,

---

LEARNING ACTIVITY 69

Developing a Lesson Plan for Guided-Discovery Teaching

Purpose: The purpose of this activity is to develop a lesson plan for either science or mathematics at the third-grade level that utilizes guided-discovery teaching.

Procedure:

1. Select a topic from a third-grade-mathematics textbook, a third-grade-science textbook, or the state course of study for either of these two subject-matter areas.
2. Plan a lesson for the topic that illustrates the appropriate use of guided-discovery teaching. Include in the lesson plan each of the following areas:
   a. Preliminary Information
      1. grade level
      2. subject-matter area
      3. approximate time for teaching
   b. Topic
   c. Objectives
   d. Materials List
   e. Procedure
      1. Method for introducing the lesson
      2. Procedure for the guided-discovery teaching
      3. Summary of the lesson
   f. Evaluation
3. Teach the lesson to a small group of children. Critique the lesson in terms of what went well and what changes would be needed to make the lesson more effective.

---

printed materials are used more frequently than any other type of materials. This practice is not only developmentally inappropriate for children in the concrete operational stage but it also fails to convey the problem-solving nature of science and mathematics. In guided discovery, printed materials are used, but they are used after the child has interacted with materials and begun to develop an understanding of a concept. Printed materials are used to develop and extend what the child has already begun to grasp.

Demonstration Teaching as a Teaching Strategy

Teaching strategies in which the child is involved in the direct manipulation of materials and so is involved in the development of concepts are the most appropriate for the concrete operational child. However, the reality of the classroom, curriculum guide, and textbook is that all topics cannot be developed through discovery-oriented approaches in the classroom. There are times when the teacher must use directed teaching strategies. Such directed teaching strategies are used in demonstrating the standard algorithm for computation, showing how to use a meter stick or microscope, or

developing specific vocabulary. Additionally, demonstrations are used in the science area for activities that are dangerous for children to do themselves or spectacular and need not be conducted by all children in the class.

Demonstrations in Science Teaching

Definition. In the science program, demonstration teaching typically is defined as a demonstration that is geared to a particular point of content information. For example, the teacher may demonstrate the effect of heat on solids by showing the ball-and-ring apparatus. The ball fits through the ring when both are at room temperature but no longer fits through the ring after the ball has been heated in the flame of an alcohol lamp. In general, this is not something that the teacher wants third-grade children to do on their own. Not only is there the possibility of burns from heated metals and open flames, but the materials needed are relatively expensive and so usually not available in the quantities needed for all children to participate.

Reasons. When it comes to demonstrations, there are several reasons for demonstrating rather than doing a hands-on activity. First, the teacher should demonstrate when there is danger involved in an activity. The use of open flames, high-heat sources, glassware around high heat, or strong chemicals in an activity are good reasons for the teacher to demonstrate an activity. Second, the teacher should demonstrate when an activity has certain points that need to be seen by the students in order to make sense of what is going on. The teacher can stop the action at various points in order to discuss what is occurring. Third, the teacher can demonstrate when an activity involves something spectacular. The teacher may want to demonstrate setting off a model rocket or erupting a model volcano rather than having each child do these things. Finally, a good reason for demonstrating is a lack of materials. There are some activities that children should have an opportunity to see but that require materials unavailable for general use.

But, just as there are some good reasons for demonstrating, there are also some poor reasons for demonstrating. Keeping the room neat, keeping the children quiet, or saving time in the classroom are poor reasons for demonstrating. Not one of these reasons involves sound educational practice.

Conducting a Science Demonstration. A science demonstration is not a chance for the teacher to engage in show-and-tell. Instead, a science demonstration is an opportunity for the teacher to engage the children in the use of process skills and thinking skills while maintaining control over the actual activity. In conducting a demonstration, the teacher begins with an introduction. In general, the introduction to a science demonstration is both brief and direct. The introduction may be simply a case of telling students to watch carefully because they are going to try to figure out what happens. In other cases, the teacher may introduce the demonstration with a problem-solving situation.

Using the ball-and-ring demonstration previously mentioned, the teacher might introduce this activity with a question that poses a problem:

> Yesterday, I was driving over a long bridge. I noticed that my car bounced quite a bit, but the bounce was very regular—about every ten seconds. When I looked, I noticed that the metal plates that I was driving over had spaces between them. What do you think

could be the reason why that bridge had spaces between the metal plates?

After collecting the possible reasons, the teacher tells the students that he or she wants them to watch carefully because the demonstration they will be seeing will help to explain those spaces.

Now, the teacher brings out the alcohol burner, matches, ball-and-ring apparatus, and sand container. First, the teacher identifies each of the objects. The teacher asks the students to make observations of the ball and ring. Any observations the children make are listed on the chalkboard or overhead projector under the category "before." One of the specifics that should be observed is that the ball will fit through the ring. After all of the observations are made, the children are asked to watch while the teacher heats the ball in the flame of the burner. After the ball is hot, the teacher tries to put the ball through the ring. It will no longer fit. Once again, the teacher asks for observations of the ball and ring. These observations are listed under the category "after." Finally, the teacher asks the students what changes took place and then what could have been the cause of the changes. Through questions, the teacher helps the students to draw the conclusion that the heat caused the ball to get bigger, explaining why it could no longer fit through the ring. The term *expand* can be introduced after the conclusion is written.

Finally, the teacher returns to the introductory problem and asks if the children can determine why there are spaces between the metal plates that make up the bridge.

Roles Played in a Science Demonstration.   In considering this example of a science demonstration, it is easy to see that the role of the teacher is that of a demonstrator and a questioner, facilitating the students' use of problem-solving skills to develop the content of the demonstration. Additionally, it is easy to see that the role of the child is to use the science process skills and problem-solving skills to develop a conclusion that explains what occurred in the demonstration. In this demonstration, the process skills of observation, inference, conclusion, cause and effect reasoning, and communication were particularly prevalent. Example 7 shows a lesson plan for a demonstration in a science lesson.

EXAMPLE 12.7

Demonstration Lesson: Science

Grade: Third

Subject Area: Science

Time Needed: 30–45 minutes

Topic: Sound travels in all directions from a source.

Materials: tuning fork, rubber mallet, large tub of water, medicine dropper, small container of water, drawing paper

Objectives:
1. After participating in the demonstration, each child will be able to write one or more sentences to describe how sound travels.

Procedure:
1. *Introduction*
   a. Stand in front of the room. Strike a tuning fork with a rubber mallet or the rubber heel of a shoe. Ask the children to raise their hands if they could hear the sound. Strike the tuning fork several more times from different places in the classroom.
   b. Ask the students how they think the sound moves from the tuning fork to their ears. Record ideas on the chalkboard or overhead projector. Tell the students that they will find out how sounds travel to their ears.
2. *Body*
   a. Part I
      1. Seat the children in a circle on the floor. Tell them that they will be hearing a sound and that when they hear it they should raise their hands. Place a clock with a loud tick at the center of the circle.
      2. After the children raise their hands, ask if there was anyone who did not hear the sound.

   3. Ask the children whether the sound traveled in only one direction from the clock or whether it moved in all different directions. Ask how they know that it moved in all directions. Record the response on the chalkboard or overhead projector.
   b. Part II
      1. Place a large tub of water in the center of the circle of children. Make sure all the children can see the water. Wait until the water in the tub stops moving.
      2. Ask the children to close their eyes and listen carefully. Using a medicine dropper, drop some water into the center of the tub. Ask the children to describe the sound.
      3. Have the children open their eyes and watch how the sound was made. Ask them to describe what happens to the water in the tub after a drop of water falls into it.
      4. Have the children draw pictures of the waves caused by the dripping water.
      5. Discuss the pattern the children drew. Relate the pattern of waves in the water to the way in which sound travels through the air in all directions from the source. Record the conclusion on the chalkboard or overhead projector.
3. *Summary*
   a. Review the conclusions drawn for parts I and II of the demonstration.
   b. Return to the introduction and ask children to explain why everyone could hear the sound of the tuning fork no matter where the teacher was standing in the room.

Evaluation: Have each student write one or more sentences to describe how sounds travel.

EXAMPLE 12.8

Demonstration Lesson Plan: Mathematics

Grade: Third

Subject Area: Mathematics

Time Needed: 45 minutes

Topic: The surface area of a cube or a rectangular prism can be determined.

Materials: worksheets, rectangular prisms, cubes, square-inch pieces of paper

Objectives:

1. As a result of this lesson, each child will be able to determine the surface area of a rectangular prism or a cube through the use of square-inch materials.
2. As a result of this lesson, each child will be able to record the surface area of a rectangular prism or a cube through the use of square-inch materials.

Procedure:

1. *Introduction*
   a. Review with the children the meaning of the term *area* when it is applied to a square or a rectangle.
   b. Review with the children how to find the area of a square or a rectangle through the use of square units and objects.
   c. Demonstrate how to find the area of a square by using the square unit pieces of paper. Repeat the same procedure with the rectangle.
2. *Teacher Demonstration*
   a. Show a cube that is four inches by four inches by four inches. Tell students that they are going to learn how to find the area of two of the shapes they have been studying: cube and rectangular prism.
   b. Show the class what is meant by the surface area of a cube or rectangular prism.
   c. Demonstrate how to find the surface area of a cube by laying out the paper square inches to cover one side of the cube, counting the squares, and recording the number. Repeat until all six sides of the cube have been covered, counted, and recorded. Add the six numbers to find the total surface area.

   d. Repeat the same procedure with a cube that is six inches by six inches by six inches.
   e. Review the procedure used to find the surface area of a square using paper square inches.
   f. Show a rectangular prism that is four inches by five inches by six inches. Ask students what they would need to do to find the surface area of the rectangular prism.
   g. Follow the procedure given by the students, covering each side with square inches, counting, recording, and adding to find the total.
   h. Repeat the procedure with a second rectangular prism.
   i. Ask the students to tell the steps that are used to find the surface area of either a rectangular prism or a cube. Record the steps on the chalkboard.
3. *Student Practice*
   a. Have the students work in groups of three or four.
   b. Provide each group with four differently sized cubes, four differently sized rectangular prisms, and a packet of pieces of paper cut into square inches. The cubes and prisms should be numbered 1 through 8. Also provide a worksheet to record the results.
   c. Give the children time to work with the materials to determine the surface area of the various shapes.
   d. Collect the results on the chalkboard. Discuss any discrepancies in the areas found for each of the models.
   e. Ask students if they can think of easier ways to determine the surface areas of the objects. If the children realize that they can use multiplication skills to simplify the procedure, have them explain how to do it. Otherwise, do not consider the use of multiplication and continue to use the square-inch-paper technique.
4. *Summary*
   a. Review with the class the meaning of the term *surface area.*
   b. Review the technique that is used to determine the surface area of a cube or rectangular prism.

EXAMPLE 12.8 Continued

Evaluation:

1. Collect the worksheets that were completed by the small groups and check the accuracy of the determinations of surface area.

2. Provide each child with one cube, one rectangular prism, and sufficient paper square units to determine surface area. Have each child determine and record the surface areas of the models.

LEARNING ACTIVITY 70

Developing a Demonstration Lesson Plan

Purpose: The purpose of this activity is to develop a lesson plan for either science or mathematics at the third-grade level that utilizes demonstration teaching.

Procedure:

1. Select a topic from a third-grade-mathematics textbook, a third-grade-science textbook, or the state course of study for either of these two subject-matter areas.

2. Plan a lesson for the topic that illustrates the appropriate use of demonstration teaching. Include in the lesson plan each of the following areas:

   a. Preliminary Information
      1. grade level
      2. subject matter area
      3. approximate time for teaching
   b. Topic
   c. Objectives
   d. Materials List
   e. Procedure
      1. method for introducing the lesson
      2. procedure for the demonstration teaching
      3. summary of the lesson
   f. Evaluation

3. Teach the lesson to a small group of children. Critique the lesson in terms of what went well and what changes would be needed to make the lesson more effective.

Demonstrating in Mathematics Teaching

Definition. In the mathematics program, demonstrations are most frequently used to show a computation strategy after students have developed a conceptual basis. Demonstration teaching in mathematics is used at the third-grade level to establish a computational algorithm. In this case, it is usually the standard format that the teacher develops with the children.

Conducting Demonstration Teaching in Mathematics. The teacher can demonstrate in a mathematics lesson in order to establish the standard algorithm for solving a problem. For example, after the children have developed the rule of regrouping across a zero in subtraction through the use of popsicle sticks, the teacher can then demonstrate the standard numerical procedure through exam

ples that relate back to what students did with the concrete materials. In this case, the teacher is establishing the pattern for the standard algorithm. The role of the teacher in this type of mathematics teaching is to internalize the pattern and then apply the pattern to other problems of the same type. Example 8 shows a lesson plan for demonstration teaching in mathematics.

Resource Persons and Field Trips in Teaching

Just as there are some topic areas within the curriculum that do not easily lend themselves to discovery techniques, there are some topic areas that do not lend themselves to classroom investigation or instruction by the teacher. In cases like these, a field trip or resource person can be a highly effective teaching strategy.

Using a Resource Person. A resource person provides a depth of knowledge or expertise that the teacher may not have. Such a person also provides a link between the school and the real world, demonstrating for children that the information they learn in school is useful in life. In bringing a resource person into the classroom, certain steps make it easier.

First, select the person carefully so that the individual is not only knowledgeable, but also an appropriate role model for the children. Having a nurse come into the classroom to talk about nursing and the human body is a great idea, but be certain the nurse uses appropriate grammar and sentence structure. Having a nutritionist come into the classroom to talk about appropriate diet also is a great idea, provided that person does not advocate a macrobiotic diet of seaweed and lemonade.

Second, talk with the resource person well ahead of time. This will help you to determine whether the person is appropriate and also will assist the resource person in preparing an appropriate presentation. Talk to the resource person about the reason he or she is being asked to come to the classroom. Be certain that your goals in having the individual come to the class are clear. The previsit conversation should also establish the time frame so that the visitor realizes that only 30 minutes are available and you would like for the children to have time to ask questions. Be certain that the resource person knows the age and the background of the children. When bringing resource persons into the early-childhood classroom, make sure they can communicate effectively with young children. A scientist or mathematician who is used to communicating with graduate students needs some advance warning in order to be able to prepare to communicate effectively with young children. And, make certain that the resource person knows how the classroom is set up. The setting of the classroom can influence the individual's choice of visual aids or activities.

Third, prepare the children for the arrival of the resource person. This easily can be done with an activity or other experience that builds background information or acquaints the children with the resource person. The arrival of a stranger in the classroom should not be a complete surprise, especially if you want children to interact with the person through questions. The preparation can also prevent mistaken identities as in the case of the university professor who was introduced as "Doctor Smith" and was greeted by tears from three children and expressions of fear from most of the others. It turned out that the children had been inoculated against flu and associated the word *doctor* with someone who gave shots. Their immediate reaction was "more shots!"

Fourth, have a follow-up discussion of the information that was presented by the resource person. This will help to clear up any misconceptions that may have been generated by an individual unaccustomed to speaking to young children, as well as to further develop the ideas encountered. And, by all means, have the children write thank-you letters to the resource person. Example 9 shows a lesson plan for using a resource person in science. Example 10 shows a lesson plan for using a resource person in mathematics.

Using a Field Trip. A field trip can provide experiences that are not available within the classroom situation. The field trip can both expand the students' horizons and relate the work done in the classroom to the real world. Planning a field trip should include the following considerations.

First, visit the field trip location prior to the actual classroom visit. Do not rely on the recommendations of other teachers or of friends. Although such recommendations may give you possibilities, only you can determine whether the location is appropriate for your class. Visit the site in order to see what is actually there, talk with the person who will be the guide, and plan for exactly what will occur during the visit. If handicapped children have been mainstreamed into the class, be certain that the site is accessible to the orthopedically impaired child and that accommodations can be made for the visually or auditorially impaired child.

Second, if the site is outdoors, arrange time before the beginning of the formal presentation for the children to explore the site on their own. Children need to have a chance to run in a grassy meadow or "poke around" at the edge of a pond or stream. If they have a chance to move and explore freely before beginning the formal lesson, they are far more likely to give their attention to the guide. Additionally, the free exploration will provide information that children can use as they listen to

EXAMPLE 12.9

Resource-Person Lesson Plan: Science

Grade: Third

Subject Area: Science

Time Needed: approximately one hour

Topic: Hearing needs to be protected so that it is not lost.

Materials: poster paper, crayons, markers, paint

Objectives:
1. Prior to the arrival of the doctor, each child will write one or more questions to ask the doctor about hearing and protecting hearing.
2. After listening to the doctor, each student will be able to draw a poster to illustrate one way of helping to protect hearing.

Procedure:
1. *Prior to Arrival*
   a. Review with the class the name of the doctor and the reason for the visit to the classroom.
   b. Ask the children to make some predictions about what the doctor will talk about. Record their predictions on the chalkboard or overhead projector.
   c. Ask each child to write one or more questions to ask the doctor. Have some of the students read their questions to the class.
   d. Remind the class of the conduct rules to be followed.
      1. Listen carefully to the visitor in the classroom.
      2. Ask questions by raising hands.
2. *Arrival and Visit*
   a. Arrange to have two of the children meet the resource person and escort the person to the classroom.
   b. Introduce the resource person to the class and the class to the resource person.

c. Give the class some background information about the resource person: professional specialty, how long he or she has been a doctor, whether he or she has a private practice or is a part of a clinic, and so on.
   d. Turn the class over to the resource person.
3. *After the Visit*
   a. Discuss the visit with the class, making an experience chart of students' ideas and comments.
   b. Have each child create a poster that shows what can be done to protect a person's hearing.
   c. Have the children write thank-you notes to the resource person.

Evaluation:
1. Use a checklist to determine which children wrote questions to ask.
2. Collect the posters and evaluate them on their accuracy. Display the posters for other children in the school to see.

Checklist:
1. Date and arrival time confirmed with the resource person
2. Information to be included in the presentation discussed and confirmed with the resource person
3. Amount of time available confirmed with the resource person
4. Grade level of the students confirmed with the resource person
5. Procedure for meeting and escorting the resource person to the classroom reviewed with the children involved

EXAMPLE 12.10

Resource-Person Lesson Plan: Mathematics

Grade: Third

Subject Area: Mathematics

Time Needed: approximately one hour

Topic: An architect uses geometric ideas in designing buildings.

Materials: boxes, blocks, tape, glue, straws, construction paper, poster paper, scissors, cans, plastic lids, cardboard, etc.

Objectives:

1. Prior to the arrival of the architect, each child will write one or more questions to ask the architect about designing buildings.
2. After listening to the architect, each student will be able to describe in one or more sentences how an architect uses geometric ideas in designing buildings.
3. After listening to the architect, each small group of children will construct a building using the solid geometric shapes.

Procedure:

1. *Prior to Arrival*
   a. Review with the class the name of the architect and the reason for the visit to the classroom.
   b. Ask the children to make some predictions about what the architect will talk about. Record their predictions on the chalkboard or overhead projector.
   c. Ask each child to write one or more questions to ask the architect. Have some of the students read their questions to the class.
   d. Remind the class of the conduct rules to be followed.
      1. Listen carefully to the visitor in the classroom.
      2. Ask questions by raising hands.
2. *Arrival and Visit*
   a. Arrange to have two of the children meet the resource person and escort the person to the classroom.

   b. Introduce the resource person to the class and the class to the resource person.
   c. Give the class some background information about the resource person.
   d. Turn the class over to the resource person.
3. *After the Visit*
   a. Discuss the visit with the class, making an experience chart of students' ideas and comments.
   b. Divide the class into groups of four or five. Provide materials and ask each group to construct a building using the materials.
   c. After the buildings have been constructed, have each group describe the building using geometric terms. Place the buildings in an area where other classes can view them.

Evaluation:

1. Use a checklist to determine which children wrote questions to ask.
2. Evaluate the groups by looking at the building constructed and listening to the descriptions given.
3. Have the children write one or more sentences to describe the visit of the architect.

Checklist:

1. Date and arrival time confirmed with the resource person
2. Information to be included in the presentation discussed and confirmed with the resource person
3. Amount of time available confirmed with the resource person
4. Grade level of the students confirmed with the resource person
5. Procedure for meeting and escorting the resource person to the classroom reviewed with the children involved

LEARNING ACTIVITY 71

Developing a Lesson Plan for a Resource Person

Purpose: The purpose of this activity is to develop a lesson plan for either science or mathematics at the third-grade level that utilizes a resource person in the classroom.

Procedure:

1. Select a topic from a third-grade-mathematics textbook, a third-grade-science textbook, or the state course of study for either of these two subject-matter areas.
2. Plan a lesson for the topic that illustrates the appropriate use of a resource person in the classroom. Include in the lesson plan each of the following areas:
   a. Preliminary Information
      1. grade level
      2. subject-matter area
      3. approximate time needed for the resource person
      4. information to be included in the preliminary discussions with the resource person
   b. Topic
   c. Objectives
   d. Materials List
   e. Procedure
      1. method for introducing the lesson
         a. preparation of the children for the resource person
         b. information to be reviewed prior to the arrival of the resource person
         c. behavior rules to be established before the arrival of the resource person
      2. method for introduction of the resource person to the class
      3. concepts to be developed through use of the resource person in the classroom
      4. methods to be used for following up on the visit of the resource person
   f. Evaluation
3. Develop a list of resource persons in your community who would be appropriate to the science and mathematics curriculum of the third-grade level.

and try to understand the information given by the guide.

Third, arrange for transportation to the site and for return transportation to the school. Be certain to check on the transportation a day or two ahead of time just to confirm that all is ready.

Fourth, arrange for parents to accompany the students or, if possible, combine the field trip with a high-school-class trip to the same area. The young children will benefit by having their own guides and the older students will benefit by helping the younger students understand what they are seeing. It also solves the problem of having enough chaperons for the trip.

Fifth, prepare the students for the field trip with an activity or experience that will help them to build background for the trip. Students who are prepared will gain more from the trip than those who are simply going on a field trip. It is even helpful to have a set of questions for which students are to try to find answers.

Sixth and last, following the field trip, have a follow-up activity and discussion with the students to help them gain the most from the trip. Combining the science or mathematics of the field trip with language arts to have students write about their experiences shows the connections among the subject-matter areas. And, once again, if there was a specific guide for the field trip, be certain that the students write a thank-you note. Example 11 shows a lesson plan for a field trip in science; Example 12 shows one for a field trip in mathematics.

SUMMARY

The key to good teaching, whether in the defined curriculum or in other curricular models, is planning. Planning begins with the development of the unit plan and moves from there to specific lesson planning. Within the lesson, there are a variety of teaching strategies that can be used. The teaching strategy that is selected should be chosen for

EXAMPLE 12.11

Field-Trip Lesson Plan: Science

Grade: Third

Subject Area: Science

Time Needed: approximately three hours

Topic: An orchestra is made up of instruments that have a variety of different pitches.

Objectives:
1. As a result of the field trip to an orchestra rehearsal, each child will be able to write a paragraph telling about the various instruments in the orchestra and the pitch of those instruments.
2. Prior to the field trip to an orchestra rehearsal, each child will be able to write one or more questions to ask during the field trip.

Procedure:
1. *Before Trip*
   a. Remind the children of the destination and purpose of the trip. Ask them to predict the kinds of things they might see and hear at the orchestra rehearsal. Ask each child to write down one or more questions he or she would like to have answered. Have some of the children read their questions to the class.
   b. Review the rules for conduct on the trip.
      1. Talk quietly while on the bus.
      2. Walk with your buddy and with the class.
      3. Listen carefully to _____.
      4. Ask questions by raising your hand first.
      5. When you hear the teacher clap, get quiet and listen for directions.
2. *Field Trip*
   a. Go on the field trip to the orchestra rehearsal.
   b. If possible, leave with the orchestra members the questions children wrote that were not answered so that answers can be obtained.

3. *After Trip*
   a. Discuss the field trip with the class.
      1. Discuss the names of some of the instruments.
      2. Discuss the sounds made by the instruments in terms of the pitch of the instruments.
      3. Develop an experience chart with the class that details the field trip.
      4. Have the children read some of the questions that they wrote prior to the trip and determine the answers to them.
   b. Have the children write thank-you notes to the orchestra members and to the conductor.

Evaluation:
1. Have each student write a paragraph about the field trip to the orchestra rehearsal, including information about the instruments and the pitch of the instruments.
2. Use a checklist to determine whether children have written questions to ask during the field trip.

Checklist:
1. All parental permission slips are on file
2. Transportation reconfirmed
3. Chaperones reconfirmed
4. Arrival time and name of the contact person confirmed
5. Contact person apprised of the grade level of the children and the purpose of the field trip
6. Location of field trip and telephone number on file with the school office
7. Departure and return times on file with the school office

EXAMPLE 12.12

Field-Trip Lesson Plan: Mathematics

Grade: Third

Subject Area: Mathematics

Time Needed: approximately two hours

Topic: The various solid figures are found in the local environment.

Materials: instant cameras and film, poster board, markers, glue or paste

Objectives:

1. As a result of the field trip, each small group of children will be able to photograph examples of solid geometric figures in the local environment.
2. As a result of the field trip, each child will be able to identify two or more solid geometric figures found in the local environment.
3. Given a photograph of the local environment, each child will be able to identify two or more solid figures shown in the photograph.

Procedure:

1. *Before Trip*
   a. Review with the children the various solid geometric figures that they have studied to this point.
   b. Review with the children how to use an instant camera.
   c. Assign the children to groups of four and give each group member a particular task: one photographer, one keeper of the pictures, one keeper of the environment (makes sure no trash gets left behind), one recorder.
   d. Remind the children of the rules established for the field trip.
      1. Keep with the group and do your particular job.
      2. Talk quietly while inside the building.
      3. Visit only your assigned sites.
      4. Always stay with the chaperone.
      5. Return to the classroom in 45 minutes.

2. *Field Trip*
   a. Assign each group of children to one location in the school building and one location in the immediate community. Be certain the chaperone knows the locations.
   b. Have the children photograph the two locations in order to show the solid geometric figures in the environment. Children should use half the film in each location.

3. *After Trip*
   a. Have the students in each of the groups make a poster of their photographs. Beneath each photograph, have the group name the solid geometric figures that are shown.
   b. Have the groups share their posters with one another. Display the posters where they can be seen by other classes.
   c. Have the children write thank-you notes to the chaperones.

Evaluation:

1. Use a checklist to determine whether each group photographed and identified solid figures in the environment.
2. Check the completed poster to be certain that the solid geometric figures shown were correctly identified.

Checklist:

1. All cameras are loaded and ready to go.
2. All cameras have been tested and are working.
3. Chaperones have been contacted and locations for each chaperone's group have been reconfirmed.
4. The school office has been notified about the field trip and the purpose of the trip.

LEARNING ACTIVITY 72

Developing a Lesson Plan for a Field Trip

Purpose: The purpose of this activity is to develop a lesson plan for either science or mathematics at the third-grade level that utilizes a field trip as a teaching technique.

Procedure:

1. Select a topic from a third-grade-mathematics textbook, a third-grade-science textbook, or the state course of study for either of these two subject-matter areas.

2. Plan a lesson for the topic that illustrates the appropriate use of a field trip as a teaching strategy. Include in the lesson plan each of the following areas:

   a. Preliminary Information
      1. grade level
      2. subject-matter area
      3. approximate time needed for the field trip
      4. location of the field trip
   b. Topic
   c. Objectives
   d. Materials List
   e. Procedure
      1. preliminary planning for the trip
         a. obtaining permission from parents
         b. method of transportation
         c. provision for lunch or snacks
         d. method for including chaperones for the trip
      2. method for introducing the lesson
         a. preparation of the children for the trip
         b. information to be reviewed prior to the trip
         c. behavior rules to be established before the trip
      3. procedure for the actual field trip
      4. concepts to be developed through the field trip
      5. methods to be used for following up on the field trip
   f. Evaluation

3. Develop a list of possible field trips in the local community that would be appropriate to the third-grade level.

---

specific reasons. Open discovery is selected when problem-solving skills are to be enhanced through the lesson; guided discovery is selected when specific content information is to be developed through activity. The demonstration is used in the science class when there is content information to be developed but the teacher wants to have greater than usual control of the situation. In the mathematics class, the demonstration usually is used to show a standard computation procedure. Finally, the use of a resource person or the use of a field trip can help to extend the teaching situation beyond the classroom into the environment and into career opportunities.

Vocabulary Terms

Culminating Activity: an activity that comes at the conclusion of a unit of work and generally provides a summary for the unit.

Demonstration Teaching: (1) in science, a teaching strategy in which the teacher uses concrete materials and the students are involved through the use of process skills such as observation, inference, prediction, and conclusion; (2) in mathematics, a teaching strategy in which the teacher models a particular method or algorithm for the students.

Field Trip: a teaching strategy that takes children out of the classroom and into the community for a particular learning experience.

General Objective: an objective that indicates what is to be learned without specifying the behavior to be demonstrated by children or the level of competence to be achieved by children.

Guided Discovery: a teaching strategy that utilizes hands-on, process-oriented activities to develop content information.

Introductory Activity: an activity that is used at the start of a unit to arouse interest and curiosity on the part of students.

Lesson Plan: a short-range planning device for

organizing a particular lesson within the classroom.

Open Discovery: a teaching strategy based on the use of hands-on, process-centered activities in which children investigate questions and problems that they develop for themselves.

Prerequisite: a concept or skill that should be developed prior to the introduction and development of new information.

Resource Person: a person from the community who is brought into the classroom in order to present information to children.

Resource Unit: a long-range planning device that provides a list of possible activities, resources, and ideas for teaching a particular topic in the classroom.

Specific Objective: a statement that details exactly what is to be learned by the child in a lesson, the behavior that is to be demonstrated by the child, and the level of proficiency that is to be attained by the child.

Spiral Curriculum: a curricular pattern in which a topic is introduced at one grade level and developed in more detail at other grade levels.

Teaching Activity: an activity within a unit that is used to teach a specific skill or concept.

Teaching Unit: a device for long-range planning that details the precise learning outcomes, the activities to be used, and the sequence in which the activities will be presented.

Unit Plan: a long-term planning device that develops the content for a broad topic.

Study Questions

1. How does a unit plan differ from a lesson plan?
2. What are the similarities and differences between a teaching unit and a resource unit?
3. What relationships exist among the objectives, procedure, and evaluation sections of a lesson plan?
4. How does open-discovery teaching differ from guided-discovery teaching?
5. How do the roles of the teacher, materials, and children relate to one another in guided-discovery and open-inquiry teaching?
6. How does a demonstration differ from a discovery lesson?
7. When is it appropriate to use a demonstration in teaching science or mathematics?
8. A teacher at the third-grade level has tried using guided-discovery teaching in mathematics and science. The teacher has the children do the activity, fill out a worksheet, and then hand in the worksheet for a grade. The teacher has been disappointed by the results. What suggestions would you make to this teacher?
9. A teacher took a group of third graders to a meadow with a pond to observe the kinds of plants and animals there. The teacher gave students specific assignments to begin as soon as they arrived. The field trip was a disaster. Half of the children lost their assignment. One group began to play tag. Three children collected bouquets of wildflowers. Two children got lost. One fell into the pond. And three more got sunburned. What suggestions would you make to this teacher so the next field trip is a success rather than a disaster?
10. As a resource person for careers in mathematics, a teacher invited a mathematics professor from a local university. The professor talked about research in mathematics for nearly two hours while the class grew more and more restless. What could have caused this difficulty with the speaker? What suggestions would you make to the teacher?
11. Which teaching strategy would be best for each of the following topics? Why?

    a. The effect of heat on various solids
    b. The kinds of materials a magnet will pick up
    c. How to get a paper airplane to fly as far as possible
    d. Careers that use mathematics
    e. The characteristics of spheres, cubes, rectangular prisms, and cylinders
    f. How to solve a problem like 96 + 87 numerically
    g. Inventions based on discoveries in science and mathematics
    h. How to measure the classroom without a standard ruler

CHAPTER 13

Questioning and Questioning Strategies

Chapter Objectives

On completion of this chapter, you should be able to

1. list and discuss the uses of questions in the early-childhood program,

2. classify questions according to two different systems of classification,

3. write questions that reflect the various levels of Bloom's Taxonomy—Cognitive Domain,

4. discuss appropriate techniques for asking questions,

5. discuss the benefits of using wait time in the early-childhood classroom,

6. discuss the appropriate sequencing of questions,

7. write questions for a mathematics lesson and sequence those questions appropriately,

8. write questions for a science lesson and sequence those questions appropriately,

9. analyze the levels of questions found in the typical science textbook,

10. analyze the levels of questions found in the typical mathematics textbook,

11. define the term *operational question*,

12. differentiate between questions that are operational and questions that are not operational,

13. write and investigate an operational question, and

14. analyze a science textbook and a mathematics textbook to determine where operational questions could be effectively utilized in teaching.

Consider for a moment two third-grade class-rooms. Both of the classes do the same activity in which lima-bean seeds are planted in paper cups filled with soil gathered from the edge of the playground. The seeds are planted on Monday and by Friday there is no evidence of growth. The children return from the weekend to find that a few of the seeds have begun to grow. By Friday of the second week, many of the cups have bean plants that are two or three inches in height. Still, some of the cups *have no evidence of* growth. The children leave for the weekend. On Monday, the beginning of the third week, the children arrive to find that all but two of the cups have plants growing in them. In both classes, the children ask the teacher, "Why didn't all of the seeds grow?"

In Mr. Smith's classroom, the children are asked to take their seats. As soon as everyone is quiet, Mr. Smith begins to ask questions about the seeds:

1. Whose seeds didn't grow?
2. Tommy, did you follow all of the directions?
3. Do seeds need water to grow?
4. Tommy, did you water the seeds the way you were supposed to water them?
5. Do seeds need a warm place in order to grow?
6. Did you put your cup in a warm place?
7. Do plants need sunlight to grow?
8. Was your cup in the sunlight?

Mr. Smith concludes the "lesson" with the statement, "We all know that seeds need a warm place and water in order to grow and that plants need sunlight. Tommy's plants probably did not grow because he didn't give them one of the things plants need: sunlight, water, and warmth."

Considering that Tommy's cup of seeds is right between two of the cups that have the tallest plants and that the soil is still damp from having been carefully watered, the class can only be left wondering what the teacher is talking about. And, Tommy is left with the feeling that everything is his fault.

Across the hallway is Mr. Jones. Mr. Jones has the children in his class sit in a circle on the floor where he places the three cups with seeds that are

not growing. Next to him is a tablet of experience chart paper. Mr. Jones asks the following questions:

1. We seem to have some seeds that did not grow. What could be some of the reasons why these seeds might not have grown? (All of the responses are listed on the chart paper.)
2. We have a variety of possible reasons for the seeds not growing. What could we do to test some of these ideas?
3. Derrick said he thinks the seeds might have gotten rotten and that we should dig them up. What would the seeds look like if they have gotten rotten?
4. How do these seeds differ from the ones that we planted?
5. Katie said she thinks the seeds might be too deep and that we should see how deep they were planted. How deep did we say lima-bean seeds needed to be planted?
6. Do you think these seeds were too deep?
7. Julie said she thinks they were watered too much. How could we determine if they were watered too much?
8. What did we find out about the seeds that could tell us why they did not grow?

The children in this class were given the opportunity to solve the problem of the seeds that would not grow. They decided on a variety of possibilities and then checked out those possibilities to determine which were accurate. Since the children participated in trying to solve the problem, they have no difficulty with the idea that the seeds in the first cup were planted too deep and the seeds in the second got too much water. As for the third cup, they decided that the seeds were simply "duds."

It should be obvious that Mr. Jones had a better series of questions than Mr. Smith. The first set of questions focused on what a child did wrong, while the second focused on solving the problem of why the seeds did not grow. Good questioning skills enable children to learn. Poor questioning skills merely repeat information that may or may not be relevant to the lesson or the children.

THE ROLE OF QUESTIONS IN THE DEFINED CURRICULUM

There are three general uses of questions in the defined curriculum.

The first general reason for using questions in the defined curriculum is to help children organize and gain information from an activity or lesson. Questions can be used to help initiate an activity or an investigation. In the previous example of the seeds, the teacher used a question to initiate problem solving by having the students attempt to determine why the seeds did not grow. In a mathematics lesson, a question could be used to have students investigate the kinds of geometric figures that are found in the classroom. Questions from the teacher can help children to continue or redirect an investigation. In this case, children who have found five examples of geometric figures in the classroom can be challenged to find ten, or children who have decided on three reasons why the seeds did not grow can be challenged to find a fourth possibility. Questions from the teacher can help children to develop a concept from an investigation. Through skillful questioning, a teacher can help students to realize that the sides of a cube are squares and that at least two of the sides of a rectangular prism are rectangles. Questions can also help to initiate or develop problem solving and critical thinking. The seed description gives a good example of this use of questions. The teacher asked for possible reasons for the seeds not growing and then went a step further and asked students how they could find out if the reason was valid or not. And, finally, questions can help children to develop rules for computation or definitions for vocabulary. After developing the rule for regrouping across a zero through the use of concrete materials, students can be helped to state a rule that can be applied to all problems. The "helping" aspect of helping students to state a rule is the use of questions.

The second general use of questions in the defined curriculum is to reinforce concepts and skills. The teacher uses questions to review previously learned concepts or previously practiced skills. Prior to a lesson on addition of two two-digit numbers involving regrouping both from the units to the tens place and the tens to the hundreds place—a problem like $65 + 89 =$ _____—the teacher can use questions to review the previously learned skill of addition of two two-digit numbers with regrouping only from the units to the tens place. Questions can be asked to help students recall the procedures that are used in such problems. In the science area, the teacher can use questions to review information that is prerequisite to an understanding of the new lesson. For example, before beginning a lesson on the effect of heat on various solids, the teacher might want to review information on the properties of solids and liquids. Such a review is easily handled through the use of questions. Questions also can be used to reinforce previously learned concepts and skills. Each time questions are used to review prerequisite information, the concepts are reinforced in the child's mind.

The third general use of questions in the defined curriculum is to aid children in the development of concepts and skills. In this case, it is not the teacher who is using the questions, but the children. Questions can be used by the children in the class to initiate investigations. A question that begins with "What would happen if . . ." is often an invitation for the teacher to tell the child, "Try it and find out"—but only after considering the safety factor involved. A question such as "What would happen if I fed potato chips to the goldfish" is not an invitation to reply, "Try it and find out" unless one wants dead goldfish. Questions can also be used by the children to gain additional content information. Although it should not do so, this use of questions can cause the teacher some discomfort because children can easily ask questions to which the teacher does not know the answers. In this case, the teacher should be able to give the child a place to begin a search of an answer. Have students start with an encyclopedia and work their way through the library. If the question is one that would allow for hands-on investigation by the child, help the child to set up an investigation and determine the answer. Finally, questions can be used by children to review or clarify content information or skill use. Teachers should always invite children to ask questions about a lesson. Simply because it is an adult structuring information for a child, there is always going to be room for questions. The adult has background information that the child does not have. The adult has thinking skills that the child does not have. Expect questions and answer those questions the way you would want your own questions answered by a teacher. Just because a child asks a question, it does not mean that the child is suffering from a lack of listening skills. Perhaps it is the teacher who is suffering from a lack of communication skills.

The variety of uses for questions results in the need for a variety of types of questions and questioning techniques. The next section considers three methods for classifying questions.

CLASSIFYING QUESTIONS

The variety of uses of questions gives a good reason for the need for a variety of types of questions. Using methods for classifying questions helps teachers understand that different types of questions fulfill different functions and also helps assure that a wide variety of questions will be used in the classroom.

The Three-Category System

The three-category system for question classification represents the general types of questions that are asked in the typical classroom: (1) managerial questions, (2) convergent questions, and (3) divergent questions. All three types are necessary to the routine operation and instructional procedures of the classroom.

Managerial Questions. Managerial questions allow for the organization and smooth operation of the classroom. Questions that ask children to close the door, get out their books, or turn to a specific page in a textbook are all managerial questions. For the most part, managerial questions make up few of the questions asked in the classroom. There is, however, the possibility that managerial questions will become overused. Such overuse occurs when the teacher begins by asking a question such as "Will you please open your math books to page 35?" Fine. This is a typical managerial question. The problem occurs when the teacher then quizzes half the class on whether or not they have found page 35: Maxine, do you have page 35? Barry, do you have page 35? LaTonya, do you have page 35?

Manuel, do you have page 35? Not only does this waste a great deal of time, but it also trains children to wait until you ask them specifically rather than simply opening the textbook and getting into the next lesson.

Convergent Questions. Convergent questions call for a single correct answer or a set of correct answers and generally elicit the recall of knowledge. Convergent questions make up the bulk of questions used in the classroom and in a review. The following are all convergent questions:

1. What is the answer to $47 - 6 = $ _____?
2. How many sides does a cube have?
3. What does the term *right angle* mean?
4. What are the five main parts of a flowering plant?
5. What are the three categories of levers?
6. What does the term *predator* mean?

If you look at these questions, everyone of them asks the students to recall a specific bit of information. In questions 3 and 6, the child is asked to put the response into his or her own words, but there is still a right answer and a wrong answer.

Convergent questions are best used when information must be recalled so that it can be used as a basis for learning new information, or using problem-solving and critical-thinking skills.

Divergent Questions. Divergent questions have a variety of possible answers and call on children to use thinking skills rather than simply recall information. Divergent questions ask students to use information in a variety of kinds of situations. The following are examples of divergent questions:

1. How could we use the straws, clay, and string to construct different solid, geometric figures?
2. How many ways can you find to solve this problem? Miko went to the store and bought three pairs of shoes for $24.95 a pair. She gave the clerk a 100-dollar bill. How much change did she get?
3. We have four different possible answers to the division problem 256 divided by 17. How could we determine which of them is correct?
4. What are some of the ways we could classify the rocks we collected while we were on the field trip?

5. We have five reasons why the water in the fish tank always turns green. How could we find out which of these is the actual reason?
6. Each group planned a different menu to show a nutritious supper. How could we determine which of these meals is the most nutritious?

As can be seen from each of these questions, the students must have certain information as background, but must also use that information rather than simply recall it. Each of these questions has a variety of possible answers and so has a variety of possible correct answers. In questions 3 and 6, students are asked to decide how they could evaluate the appropriateness of answers that have been given to other questions. Divergent questions require children to think and use information.

Bloom's Taxonomy as a Method for Classifying Questions

The three-category system for classifying questions calls attention to the types of questions that can be asked in a classroom, but only considers general categories of questions. Bloom's taxonomy as a way of classifying questions goes beyond the general categories of managerial, convergent, and divergent and allows the teacher to look at the more specific kinds of questions that can be asked in a classroom.

Knowledge Level. Knowledge-level questions ask for the recall of information and so are convergent questions. In general, the kind of information asked for at the knowledge level can be memorized by the learner. The learner does not even need to understand the information that he or she gives back to the teacher. A good example of the knowledge level is the two and a half year old who has learned to repeat number names or letters in response to parental repetition. The words have no meaning, but the child repeats them because it makes Mommy and Daddy so happy. The following are examples of knowledge-level questions or requests that result in responses from students:

1. LaShaunda, say the nines table for multiplication.
2. What are the main characteristics of a square?
3. How many inches are in a foot?
4. Does the long hand on a clock point to the hour or the number of minutes?

5. What two characteristics of mammals did we mention in class yesterday?
6. What are the six categories of simple machines?
7. How many planets are in our solar system?
8. What are the four seasons?

As can be seen from each of these questions, the answers can be learned through memorization and easily can be given as responses whether or not there is any understanding of the words.

Comprehension Level. Comprehension-level questions ask not only for the recall of information, but for understanding of that information. Comprehension-level questions are convergent questions. At the comprehension level, students are asked to tell what information means or to give ideas in their own words rather than in the words of the teacher or textbook. The following are comprehension level questions:

1. In your own words, what is a *rectangle?*
2. What do we mean when we say addition is commutative?
3. What example could you give to show what is meant by division?
4. What are some examples of sets that you see in this classroom?
5. In your own words, what do we mean by the word *dissolve?*
6. What does a scientist mean when she uses the word *matter?*
7. What are some examples of friction that you see at home?
8. A friend of yours has never seen an insect. What would you tell your friend an insect is?

By comparing these questions with those at the knowledge level, it can be seen that the questions ask for a different kind of information. Rather than simply ask students to recall information, the questions require students to tell information in a way that is meaningful to them. Memorization is no longer enough to ask of students.

Application Level. Application-level questions require the students to use information in a particular situation. At this level, students must not only recall and understand the appropriate information; they must also show that they can use that informa-

LEARNING ACTIVITY 73

Convergent and Divergent Questions

Purpose: The purpose of this activity is to rewrite convergent questions in divergent form.

Procedure: All of the following questions are convergent. Rewrite each question so that it is a divergent question.

1. What three examples of solids were given on page 29 of the textbook?
2. What are the characteristics of a square?
3. What is the definition for a compound machine?
4. What is the answer to the problem 76 + 57?
5. What are the five main parts of a flowering plant?
6. How do the sides of a rectangle differ from those of a square?
7. In your own words, what is meant by the word "vibration?"
8. Measuring in feet and inches, how long is our classroom?
9. Which ball will bounce higher: a tennis ball or a basketball?
10. Is the answer to 5 × 17 the same as the answer to 17 × 5?
11. Classify the pictures of animals as mammals, birds, fish, reptiles, or amphibians.
12. What is the shape of a can of soup?
13. Which object will fall faster: a ten-pound rock or a one-pound book?
14. Does water evaporate better in sunlight or in shade?
15. If there are ten cows and six chickens in a farm yard, how many legs do the animals have altogether?

---

tion in a particular way. This is the first level in which students are asked to go beyond simply learning information to using it in a familiar or new situation. Application-level questions, depending on the amount of structure in the question, can be either divergent or convergent. The following are examples of application-level questions:

1. You have been sent to the grocery store to buy ground meat, hamburger buns, catsup, an onion, and a bag of potato chips. You would like to buy yourself a candy bar to eat as you walk home, but you are not certain you have enough money. How could you use rounding off or estimating to help decide whether you have enough money for the candy bar?
2. You are going to help plant a school garden. You can either plant a square garden that is 15 feet on a side or you can plant a rectangular garden that has one side 10 feet long and another side 17 feet long. How could you find out which will give you the larger garden?
3. Jamie says that chocolate ice cream is the favorite flavor in the class and Luis says the favorite is vanilla. Using graphing, how could you find out which is really the favorite flavor of ice cream?
4. Using what we have learned about the things a plant needs in order to grow well, where do you think we should plant our school garden?
5. Using what you know about simple machines, what could I do to move a heavy box from the floor of the classroom to the top of the cabinets?
6. Using what you know about how rocks and minerals are classified, what classification system could we develop for our classroom rock collection?

Each of the questions listed here goes beyond the recall of information and into the use of information. However, all six of the questions also require that information be recalled. For example, question 2 cannot be answered if students cannot recall the term *area* and do not understand what the word means. It is also possible that they will recall that the area of either of these figures can be calculated by multiplying the lengths of the sides. In question 6, students must recall the characteristics used to classify rocks and minerals, but they must also understand what is meant by terms such as *luster* and *hardness* so that these characteristics can be used in classification. Application-level questions build on both the knowledge and comprehension levels.

Analysis Level.   At the analysis level, the questions ask for reasoning and reflecting and often result in drawing a conclusion. This level extends the use of thinking skills that was begun at the application level. In the area of science, the analysis level is relatively easy to approach. Each time an activity does not work as expected, the analysis level can be used to have children try to determine why it did not work. Also, in the science area, the analysis level is used each time students are asked to draw a conclusion from the information collected during an activity or demonstration. This very often is referred to as analyzing data, reflecting the analysis level of thinking that is required. In mathematics, the use of the analysis level is more difficult. However, analysis-level questions can be used in developing rules or in looking back at problems to determine why answers were incorrect. Analysis-level questions promote critical-thinking skills and divergent-thought processes. The following are examples of analysis-level questions:

1. Look at the following division problems. As you can see, all of the answers are incorrect. Your task is to determine what the student is doing wrong in solving these problems.
2. You have now solved ten problems using the popsicle-stick method. What rule do you see for solving these kinds of problems?
3. Look at all of the examples of triangles that you have in front of you. What are some of the things that all triangles have in common? What are some of the things that differ from one triangle to another?
4. We have collected a lot of information about the way plants grow in different kinds of soil. What conclusion can we draw about the growth of plants?
5. Generally, using a pulley makes it easier to lift a heavy object. Our results show that a pulley makes it harder to lift a heavy object. What could be some of the reasons why our results differ from those of scientists?

6. Two groups that were investigating the kinds of materials that dissolve in water found that pepper will dissolve in water. Three groups found that pepper will not dissolve in water. What could be some reasons why the results from the two groups differ?

As can be seen from these questions, the analysis level asks students to go beyond simply applying information in a new setting. Instead of using information already acquired, the analysis level asks that students generate new information, organize information into a more understandable form, or solve a particular problem. In questions 3 and 4, students must generate new information by drawing a conclusion from their data. Questions 1, 5, and 6 involve problem solving. Question 2 requires the organization of information.

Synthesis Level.   At the synthesis level, questions require the students either to produce a plan or use information in a creative manner. The synthesis level often involves the use of imagination and easily allows students to combine science or mathematics with art or creative writing. Additionally, in the area of science, the synthesis level includes the development of an activity that will test a prediction or solve a problem. The synthesis level not only promotes creativity, but also develops problem-solving skills and divergent-thought processes. The following are examples of synthesis-level questions or requests:

1. All of the rulers in the world have suddenly disappeared. How many ways can you find to measure the length of our classroom without using a ruler?
2. Our school day has six hours. During that time, we have to have mathematics, science, reading, language arts, social studies, music, art, and physical education. You have decided that you do not like the schedule you follow everyday and want to plan a new schedule. Plan the school schedule you would like to follow. Remember to include all of the subject areas and don't forget lunch!
3. Using only square, circle, triangle, rectangle, and pentagon shapes, make a picture of something you might find outdoors.
4. One of the possible reasons our seeds did not grow was that they were given too much water.

What could we do to find out if this is the real reason that our seeds did not grow?

5. Write a story about a day in the life of a worm.
6. Create a mural that shows what it was like to live at the time of the dinosaurs.

In each of these questions, children are asked to think in ways that develop their creativity, as well as their problem-solving skills. With questions like number 5, the synthesis level can bring some fun into the classroom. The success of the synthesis level question depends on the creativity of the student and on the background information that she or he brings to the setting. It is impossible to use plane figures in a picture if those figures cannot be recognized. It is impossible to draw a mural about dinosaurs if information about dinosaurs is not known.

Evaluation Level.   Evaluation-level questions call for a judgment of quality. In general, evaluation-level questions are not asked in total separation from the rest of the lesson. Such questions ask students to evaluate ideas that they have already put forth. The evaluation level asks students to use information to evaluate and defend ideas. The following questions are on the evaluation level:

1. We have four different ways of solving the word problem that is on the chalkboard. Which of the ways we have listed do you think is the easiest way to solve the problem? What makes it the easiest way?
2. We have found out that there are a variety of ways to measure the length of the classroom: paces, body lengths, straws, string lengths, and books. Which of these ways would give the most accurate measurement? What makes it the most accurate?
3. We have a list of possible reasons why our pulley activity showed it was harder to pick up an object with a pulley than without a pulley. Which of these reasons do you think is the most likely? What makes that reason the most likely?
4. We have three designs for our gerbil cage. Which of these designs would be the best for our gerbils? What makes it the best design?

In each of these evaluation-level questions, children are asked to make a judgment. It should be noted that all of the questions are based on the experiences of the children. These experiences are necessary if children are to truly understand the purpose of evaluation and be able to effectively evaluate ideas.

Classification by Effect

The previous two classification systems have been based on the kinds of questions that are asked. In some cases, questions have been classified based on the number of responses expected; in other cases, questions have been classified based on the thinking skills involved. The third classification system involves a third aspect of questioning. In the third classification system, the effect of the question on the students is the criterion for classification.

Intrusive Questions.   Intrusive questions interfere with the child's activity by attempting to direct the activity along different lines or by asking for explanations or conclusions the child is not ready to provide. For example, a child is placing objects into a basin of water to determine which will sink and which will float. As the teacher observes the child at work, that teacher notices that some of the jar lids placed into the water float while others sink. The teacher then asks the child, "What is it that makes some of your jar lids float and some sink?" The child, who is busy with an entirely different problem, generally answers with an "I don't know" that causes the teacher to give an explanation of the phenomenon. In most cases, such an explanation is unwanted and ignored until the teacher goes away and the child can return to the investigation that was interrupted. Intrusive questions generally interrupt the child's meaningful investigation.

Neutral Questions.   Neutral questions comment on the child's investigation without asking for additional information. A neutral question neither attempts to guide the child into a new area of investigation nor to elicit from the child an explanation of what has been done to that point. Neutral questions could include the following:

1. You certainly have been trying a lot of different objects in the water, haven't you?
2. I wonder, what would happen if you put the lids into the water sideways rather than on the flat side?

LEARNING ACTIVITY 74

Identifying Questions According to Bloom's Taxonomy

Purpose: The purpose of this activity is to identify the level of Bloom's taxonomy on which a question should be placed.

Procedure: Read each of the following questions. Identify the level of Bloom's taxonomy on which each question should be placed. Give your rationale for placement on that level.

1. We want to make a collection of insects. One suggestion is to collect the insects and put them into cages so that we can watch them as they move and eat. Another suggestion is to make a collection of dead insects that we can look at under a magnifying glass. Which of these collections would be better? What makes it the better type of collection?

2. What is the name of the planet that is the closest to the Sun?

3. Plan an activity that would help us find out what kind of paper airplane will fly farthest.

4. What do scientists mean by the word *work*?

5. There is an elephant in the parking lot beside the school. I would like to be able to get that elephant into our third-grade classroom. What machine could you invent that would help move the elephant into the classroom?

6. Using what you know about the things a frog needs to survive, what should be put into a terrarium that will house a frog?

7. In your own words, what is meant by the term *habitat*?

8. What is the answer to the problem 45 − 18?

9. Look at all of the insects that are in our insect zoo. What are some of the things that all of the insects have in common? What are some of the ways the insects differ from one another?

10. How many legs does an insect have?

11. How many feet are there in six yards?

12. What do we mean when we say multiplication is commutative?

13. We have four different ways of measuring the length of our classroom without using a ruler. Which of the ways do you think is the most accurate? What makes it the most accurate?

14. Using what you know about leaves and plants, what classification system could you develop for our classroom plant-and-leaf collection?

15. You have solved five problems using the abacus and five problems using popsicle sticks. How is the method used on the abacus similar to the method used with the popsicle sticks?

16. There is only one pair of pandas left in the entire world. As the director of the zoo that will house those pandas, you are asked to design a cage for them. Draw a picture or build a model of the cage.

17. According to our graph, on what day did the bean seeds first start to grow?

18. The magnets that we used picked up many kinds of objects and did not pick up other kinds of objects. What conclusion can you draw about the kinds of objects magnets will or will not pick up?

19. Which of the following animals lay eggs: robin, frog, cow, alligator, penguin, polar bear?

20. Write a story about what it would be like to live in a place that has no way of adding numbers.

LEARNING ACTIVITY 75

Writing Questions in Science

Purpose: The purpose of this activity is to develop a series of questions showing all levels of Bloom's taxonomy for a chapter in a third-grade-science textbook.

Procedure:

1. Select a chapter from a science textbook for the third-grade level. Read the chapter carefully.

2. Using the chapter as a basis, write the following questions:
   a. three knowledge-level questions
   b. three comprehension-level questions
   c. three application-level questions
   d. four analysis-level questions
   e. four synthesis-level questions
   f. four evaluation-level questions

LEARNING ACTIVITY 76

Analysis of Science-Textbook Questions

Purpose: The purpose of this activity is to analyze the kinds of questions found in the teacher's edition of an elementary science textbook for the third-grade level.

Procedure:

1. Select a chapter from a third-grade, elementary-science textbook.

2. Carefully read both the teaching suggestions and the student text, keeping a record of any questions that you encounter.

3. Classify the questions that you recorded according to the levels of Bloom's taxonomy.

4. Tally the number of questions found at each level and draw any conclusions about the kinds of questions found in the textbook that are appropriate.

LEARNING ACTIVITY 77

Writing Questions in Mathematics

Purpose: The purpose of this activity is to develop a series of questions showing all levels of Bloom's taxonomy for a chapter in a third-grade-mathematics textbook.

Procedure:

1. Select a chapter from a mathematics textbook for third-grade level. Read the chapter carefully, including teaching suggestions and student textbook material.

2. Using the chapter as a basis, write the following questions:
   a. three knowledge-level questions
   b. three comprehension-level questions
   c. three application-level questions
   d. four analysis-level questions
   e. four synthesis-level questions
   f. four evaluation-level questions

LEARNING ACTIVITY 78

Analysis of Mathematics-Textbook Questions

Purpose: The purpose of this activity is to analyze the kinds of questions found in the teacher's edition of an elementary mathematics textbook.

Procedure:

1. Select a chapter from a mathematics textbook for the third-grade level.
2. Carefully read both the teaching suggestions and the student text, keeping a record of any questions you encounter.
3. Classify the questions that you recorded according to the levels of Bloom's taxonomy.
4. Tally the number of questions found at each level and draw any appropriate conclusions about the questions asked in the textbook from your records.

Although the second question appears to be intrusive, as if it is guiding the child to a new area of investigation, it is not. A suggestion is made in the question, but it is made in passing. In this case, the student may act on the question if he or she wishes.

Using Questions Appropriately

It is important for the teacher to know the kinds of questions that are available for use in the classroom. The use of a variety of questions allows the teacher to do more in the classroom than simply have children recall information. However, just asking a variety of questions is not enough. The teacher must also know how to ask those questions effectively. The following techniques help the teacher to become an effective user of questions.

Wait Time

Definition. Wait time is a period of time allowed for thinking after a question is asked and before an answer is expected or a comment is made by the teacher.

Types of Wait Time. In general, there are two periods of time that are known as wait time. Wait time one is a period of five seconds or more after a question is asked and before a response is expected. In this case, the teacher asks a question, waits for five seconds, and then calls on a student for an answer. Wait time two is a period of two or three seconds after a response is made by a student and

before the teacher comments or asks another question. In a schematic form, the questioning strategy looks like this:

QUESTION—PAUSE—RESPONSE—
PAUSE—COMMENT OR QUESTION

The actual classroom use of wait time is illustrated in the following example of classroom questions.

Teacher: Think about the following animals: dog, cat, tiger, bear, cow, guinea pig, and mouse. What are some of the ways in which all of them are alike?

(Pause of 5 seconds)

Joe: They have fur.

Sarah: They don't lay eggs.

Carmine: They feed milk to the babies.

(Pause of 2 seconds)

Teacher: There are still some other things. Picture the animals in your mind and try to decide on some other characteristics that make them alike.

(Pause of 5 seconds)

Kenny: They all have skin and bones and blood.

Margaret: They have different colors.

(Pause of 2 seconds)

Teacher: They do have different colors, but they are the same because they all do have color. What else can we find that makes these animals the same?

LaShanda: They feel warm when you touch them.

Felipe: They all have a backbone.

(Pause of 2 seconds)

Teacher: Good job! We've mentioned a lot of ways in which these animals are all the same. Today, we're going to find out the name of the group into which these animals are placed and then find out more about the animals in this group.

As can be seen from this brief example, the teacher asked a divergent question, paused, received answers from more than one of the children, commented after another pause, had more answers, and finally regarded all of the participants with a "good job!" Using wait time with this questioning strategy is particularly important because wait time, although it can be used with any type or level of question, is most appropriate with divergent questions and higher-level questions.

Benefits of Wait Time

The benefits of using wait time accrue to the children and to the teacher.

Benefits to the Children. For the children, the following are the main benefits of using wait time in the classroom.

1. Child-to-child interaction increases and teacher-to-child interaction decreases. Students talk more to one another in a productive manner and listen less to teacher clarifications and lectures.

2. Children begin to listen more effectively to one another. Because wait time allows children to comment on or expand the ideas of other children, they must listen more effectively to what is being said.

3. Children answer fewer questions with "I don't know." Often, children resort to "I don't know" when they have not been given enough time to actually recall or formulate an answer to a question. Given time to think about the answer and determine what to say, the children are more likely to answer correctly.

4. Students give longer and more complete responses to questions. Many rapid-fire questions require only a word or two as an answer. When children are given time to think about their answers, they also have time to formulate an entire sentence as a response. And, as they formulate entire sentences, they also begin to elaborate on those sentences and develop more effective communication skills.

5. Students begin to do more speculative thinking and give more speculative answers to questions. A part of this might result from the increased time to think and reflect on answers. A second reason for this increase in speculation may be the change in the kind of question that is asked. Wait time encourages the use of divergent questions, which encourage the use of thinking skills beyond the simple recall of information.

6. Students become more likely to give unsolicited but appropriate responses and so the lesson becomes more student oriented. Because the teacher does not immediately reply after each child's response, students begin to add many more responses to a single question. The students feel free to give other answers, comment on a response already made, or remark on the validity of someone else's ideas. The question-and-answer session becomes discussion.

7. Students become questioners. Rather than the teacher being in total control of the questions asked in a lesson, the students also begin to question. In many cases, the questions are asked of other students. In other cases, the questions are asked of the teacher. Either way, the students begin to use questions to solicit more information.

8. More students respond to the questions. In the typical question-and-answer session in the classroom, a few students answer most of the questions. The other students, knowing that Stella or Marco or Tonya or Woody will answer all of the questions, simply sit back and, perhaps, listen. Wait time encourages a wider variety of students to give answers to the original question, request clarification, or offer speculative ideas.

9. Students show greater confidence in expressing their answers. As students have the opportunity to think through their responses, reason out their answers, and see a variety of answers being accepted, they gain confidence in replying to questions. Fewer statements made by the children end with question marks.

10. Students become more frequent inquirers. As students engage in more speculative thinking, the opportunity for hands-on investigation increases. Students need the opportunity to see if their ideas are valid. And, the best way to determine if ideas are valid is to test them through activity.

Benefits to the Teacher.   Just as wait time benefits the students in the classroom, it also benefits the teacher. The list of benefits is shorter, but the benefits are no less important.

1. The teacher responds to the students with a more flexible attitude and manner. Because the pace of the questioning slows down with the use of wait time, the feeling of being rushed generally decreases. The teacher feels less pressure and so passes that feeling on to the students. Since a variety of responses to a question are offered, the teacher becomes more flexible.
2. The teacher begins to ask fewer questions, but the questions are of a higher level. In the typical classroom, the teacher asks mainly knowledge-level questions with a few comprehension-level questions and a periodic question above that level. Such questions encourage a rapid-fire approach to questioning. When wait time is used, the number of questions automatically decreases. Time is given for the students to think and discuss. Questions that encourage thinking and discussion are those at which the higher level, involving application, analysis, synthesis, and evaluation.
3. The teacher's expectations of the students begin to change. Teachers begin to find that the quiet or nonverbal students in the class are not so quiet. They simply needed more time to think and formulate their responses. Teachers who are certain their students are incapable of thinking discover that they are capable. Teachers who are certain that students can do little more than recall factual information have their expectations raised to include far more complex kinds of thought processes.

Using Wait Time Effectively

Using wait time and using wait time effectively are different concepts. Consider the following scenarios.

Scenario One

Teacher: The season is changing from winter to spring. What are some of the changes we can expect?

(Pause)

Gina: The weather will get warmer.

Todd: The trees start to get leaves and flowers come up.

Teacher: Very good, Todd! That's exactly what happens! Now, what are some other things that happen?

(Pause)

No one else answers.

Scenario Two

Teacher: The season is changing from winter to spring. What are some of the changes we can expect?

(Pause)

Kelsey: The days get longer.

Greg: You can go swimming.

Margaret: The plants start to grow and you get flowers.

(Pause)

Teacher: Keep going. There are lots of other things that happen.

(Pause)

Marissa: It gets warmer and warmer and then hot.

Erica: The birds start coming back.

Greg: Some birds stay here all the time.

Erica: Yeah, but you see more kinds in the spring than in the winter.

Felicia: The trees start to get leaves.

(Pause)

Teacher: We seem to have all of the ideas that we can get. All of you had good ideas, but today I want us to consider Margaret's and Felicia's ideas about plants.

In Scenario One, the teacher responded to Todd's answer with great enthusiasm. As soon as the teacher did that, the rest of the class stopped answering. In Scenario Two, the teacher kept collecting ideas until there were no more forthcoming. Only then did this teacher respond to the answers given. Everyone in the class received the reward of the teacher labeling the ideas as "good," but Felicia and Margaret received a double reward by also having their ideas mentioned a second time. In the first case, the reward stopped the discussion. In the second case, the reward was the punctuation to a completed discussion.

Rewards.   Rewards are statements or words that indicate the teacher's satisfaction or dissatisfaction with a response given by a student. Teachers use rewards frequently to let students know that what they have done is appropriate or inappropriate, good or bad.

Using Rewards with Wait Time.   When using wait time, too many rewards, especially those that excessively praise a response, cut down on the number of responses students will give to a divergent question. If the teacher says that Tommy's response was "wonderful!" then any other response to the question must be less than wonderful, if not simply awful. Rewards after each student's response are best used with knowledge-level questions when immediate feedback as to whether the answer was right or wrong is needed. When using wait time, rewards should be held until the end of the discussion. As answers are given, nod your head, smile, or say "OK" or "uh-huh." Another way of rewarding students that does not require teacher comments on quality after every response is to write the answers on the chalkboard. This shows that the answers being given are valuable enough to be recorded. Then, when the final response has been contributed, the teacher praises the entire group for its responses. If a question is a lead in to a lesson, even if the exact response the teacher wants is the

first one given, the teacher should continue to accept answers. The trick here is to remember who gave the desired response so that person can be rewarded by having the response recalled along with her or his name.

Handling Incorrect Responses.   In some cases, the answers received to a divergent question will be incorrect or silly. If answers are being recorded on the board, record these along with all of the others. If answers are being considered orally, accept them along with all of the others. Accepting all answers—right, wrong, or silly—maintains the flow of the discussion. To stop to correct wrong answers not only stops the flow, but also stops the discussion. When answers are immediately labeled wrong or silly, children are less likely to answer. How, then, are such answers handled? Consider the following answers to the divergent question "What are some examples of insects?"

grasshopper	sowbug	my brother
snail	slug	millipede
centipede	roach	moth
butterfly	bee	dragonfly
fly	black widow spider	ladybug
mosquito	frog	locust

If you look at this listing, some of the responses are indeed insects, while others are definitely not. Still, in order to keep the momentum of the discussion going, the teacher accepted all of the answers. The next step is to use classification to put these animals into categories. The easiest way of doing this would be as shown in the chart below.

Once the animals given as examples have been classified, the teacher uses questions to help students recall the major characteristics of insects: six legs, three body parts, hard outside skeleton, and no backbone. By applying these characteristics,

grasshopper	centipede	slug	black widow spider	frog	brother
butterfly	millipede	snail			
fly	sowbug				
mosquito					
roach					
bee					
moth					
dragonfly					
ladybug					
locust					

some of the animals on the list are immediately ruled out. The frog and brother are deleted from the list because both have backbones. The slug is deleted because it is soft on the outside rather than having a hard outer skeleton. The centipede, millipede, and sowbug have too many legs and the snail has too few. Students who are uncertain of the number of legs possessed by a spider can rule out the black widow spider on the basis of the number of body parts: two rather than three. By applying the characteristics of insects to the listing, the students finally conclude that only the animals listed in the first column are actually insects. This type of procedure allows students to apply thinking skills rather than simply being told the examples are right or wrong. The examples such as my brother usually are given to get attention or cause the class to laugh. Simply accepting such an idea and listing it among all of the others diffuses potential disruption.

Sequencing Questions Effectively

Simply asking a variety of questions is not enough. To be effective in the classroom, questions need to be sequenced so that students are given the greatest possible chance of responding correctly.

Simple to Complex.   The first idea included within the concept of sequencing questions is that of sequencing from simple to complex. For example, the teacher wants students to answer the following synthesis-level question: "What machine could you design that would allow you to move an elephant from the playground to our second-floor classroom?" The question requires a high level of thinking on the part of the students. In order to help students succeed, the teacher should begin with lower-level questions that ask the students to recall information and then check on their understanding of the information recalled. The following is a sequence of questions that could be used as preparation for the synthesis level:

1. What is a simple machine?
2. What are the six kinds of simple machines?
3. What are some examples of levers?
4. Draw a picture of a pulley.
5. Which two simple machines are used in a pencil sharpener?

6. What example of a wedge could be found in a tool box?
7. What is a complex machine?
8. What are some examples of complex machines we use everyday?
9. How does a complex machine differ from a simple machine?
10. What machine could you design that would allow you to move an elephant from the playground to our second-floor classroom?

Questions 1, 2, and 7 in this list are knowledge-level questions that check students' background information. Questions 3, 4, 5, 6, and 8 are comprehension-level questions used to determine whether the students understand the terms they have given in answer to the knowledge-level questions. Question 9 asks for analysis-level thinking. And, finally, question 10, the ultimate question, puts the focus of the lesson on the synthesis level. With the preparation offered by questions 1 through 9, the students will have a better chance of answering question 10 in an appropriate manner.

Appropriateness.   Sequencing questions also involves the concept of asking questions that are appropriate to all students in the class. Some students will not be ready to work with questions requiring higher-order thinking skills. Include lower-level questions for those students. But, for those students who will be challenged by the use of application, analysis, and synthesis questions, include those as well.

Multiple Sequences.   In the third method of sequencing, questions are ordered so that higher levels of thought are reached, followed by a drop back to simpler levels, then a progression to higher levels again. This is the idea of multiple sequencing. This seesawing within the progression allows all students to participate. Students who are not able to work with the thinking skills required by analysis, synthesis, or evaluation will still be able to participate in the discussion, while those who are able to handle the higher-order thinking skills also will be challenged. Sequencing can mean ordering from simple to complex, but it does not mean that the only questions asked toward the end of the sequence will be higher-order questions. Rather, student participation is continually emphasized by asking more than one sequence of questions. The following is an example of the use of multiple sequences.

In this example, students have been involved in a discussion of mammals. The questions that have been asked are shown here.

Teacher: What are some examples of mammals? (knowledge level)

Students: Dogs, cats, rabbits, horses, lions, tigers, whales, mice, guinea pigs, duck-billed platypus.

Teacher: Let's think about these animals. What are some ways in which they are alike? (comprehension level)

Students: They are warm, furry, have babies, feed the babies milk.

Teacher: What are some of the ways we could classify the animals that were named? (application level)

Students: By what they eat, where they live, whether they are wild or pets.

Teacher: Let's classify them. (At this point, the students try out each of the three methods mentioned.) Which of the methods worked best? (evaluation level)

Students: What the animals eat worked best because it was easy to use.

Teacher: Let's go back for a minute to our list of mammals. One of the animals doesn't seem to fit all of our characteristics for mammals. Which one is it? (comprehension level)

Students: Whales.

Teacher: What is it about whales that make them seem not to fit the characteristics of mammals? (knowledge level)

Students: They don't have fur.

Teacher: Why do you think whales are included as mammals? (analysis level)

In this sequence, the students move from knowledge level to evaluation level. After the evaluation level is used to determine which classification system was best, the teacher dropped back to the comprehension level and the knowledge level, and

then moved back to the analysis level. There are two sequences of questions within a single questioning strategy.

General Principles for Using Questions in the Classroom

Using questions includes the way in which teachers ask questions, the way in which teachers listen to responses from students, and the way in which teachers respond to students' questions.

Asking Questions

1. Ask questions that students can be expected to answer. When beginning a unit on vertebrates, a topic that students have not previously studied, a question such as, "What are the characteristics of vertebrates?" is inappropriate. An appropriate question might be, "What are some of your favorite kinds of animals?"

2. Ask only one question at a time. When a question is asked and students do not answer immediately, use wait time. If answers still do not come then rephrase the question. If answers are still not forthcoming, try a different question entirely. Try to avoid asking one slightly different question after another without using wait time between the questions.

3. Always ask a question before designating who is to answer the question. If the teacher indicates that the question is directed toward John, then the likelihood is that many children will simply leave it to John to answer and give no attention to the question.

4. Ask questions suited to all students in the class. This idea has already been considered under sequencing, but bears repeating.

5. Phrase a question as a question rather than beginning it as a statement and turning it into a question at the last moment. Students listen differently to questions and statements. By beginning as a statement and ending as a question, a teacher confuses the kind of thinking skills needed and so can cause the question to be left unanswered.

6. Ask questions that elicit a variety of responses. Use convergent question to elicit information

and divergent questions to further develop information or obtain a multiplicity of ideas based on a single question.

7. Ask questions that are carefully planned. The easiest way to be certain that a teacher is asking a variety of kinds and levels of questions is to plan those questions ahead of time. This systematizes the questions asked. It also is reassuring for the new teacher to have a list of good questions rather than having to think of a variety of questions instantaneously during a lesson.

Listening to Responses

1. Really listen to the responses that the children give. Try to avoid looking at what comes next in the lesson plan or text or trying to take care of disturbances while a child is responding. If a disturbance occurs, ask the child who is responding to wait for a moment, take care of the disturbance, then return to the child and listen to the response. Demonstrate to the child that you value the response by giving it your full attention.

2. If the answer a child gives to a question is unclear, ask the child to clarify the answer. Having the child clarify is a better strategy than telling the child what you think he or she meant. The teacher may not have heard what the child was actually trying to communicate, but most children will not contradict the teacher by saying he or she is incorrect.

3. Provide materials for the child to use to illustrate what is being said. Remember that these children are preoperational or early concrete operational in their thinking skills. This means that they think more easily when concrete materials are available. The children may be able to respond more fully and more appropriately when they are able to use illustrative materials.

4. Try to determine the cause of an incorrect answer. If a child answers that a frog is a reptile, ask why the child has classified the frog among reptiles rather than simply telling the child, "No, a frog is not a reptile." The child's explanation may give the teacher insight into

her or his misconceptions, as well as other children's misconceptions.

5. Try to avoid rejecting an answer entirely. When collecting answers to a divergent question, accept all responses, whether right, wrong, or absurd. Have students use thinking skills to differentiate among the categories. When a child gives a response that seems "off the wall," ask the child what he or she was thinking when the response was given. A child's thought processes are so different from those of an adult that the child may have a perfectly legitimate reason for the answer—one the teacher never even considered.

6. Reward answers with discretion. When using wait time, follow the previously discussed techniques for rewarding. In other cases, reward in such a way that the student knows the reason for the reward. "Good" can mean "good answer," "good try," or "good use of English." If the "good" means that the response was good, say so. If the student gave an incorrect answer but at least gave it a try, say so. Let the child know exactly what behavior is being rewarded.

Responding to Student Questions

1. Whenever possible, turn the question back to the students and ask if they have any ideas about possible answers. This helps the teacher to understand the kinds of ideas children consider on hearing a question and, therefore, may bring out misconceptions. It also fosters discussion.

2. Try to avoid a quick, content-oriented answer for which children may not be ready. Teachers always want to communicate information to others. In this case, instead of giving information, help students decide where they can go to find an answer for themselves.

3. When students ask a question for which you do not have an answer, tell them that you do not know the answer. Then, follow up by helping students decide where the information could be found.

4. When a question lends itself to investigation using concrete materials, investigate. Students learn more through hands-on experience than

through listening or reading. Developing a way of investigating a question uses problemsolving skills and involves students at the synthesis level. Drawing a conclusion involves critical thinking and working at the analysis level. One way of investigating a question is through a technique known as operational questioning.

Using Operational Questions

When questions asked by students lend themselves to investigation, use the strategy of operational questions to facilitate the investigation.

Definition

An operational question can be investigated through the use of simple materials.

Characteristics of Operational Questions

The following list shows the characteristics of operational questions:

1. Operational questions do not begin with the word *why*.
2. Operational questions cannot be answered with a simple "yes" or "no" answer.
3. Operational questions allow for hands-on investigation using simple materials.
4. Operational questions generally allow for many changes in some factor being investigated.
5. Operational questions are asked by the students rather than by the teacher.

Examples of Operational Questions

The following are examples of operational questions:

1. What would happen if seeds were grown in different kinds of soils?
2. How does stirring affect how quickly different kinds of materials dissolve in water?
3. What things affect how quickly an ice cube will melt?
4. In what kinds of problems does the rule "push the sets together and regroup" apply?
5. What would have to be done to change a square into a rectangle?
6. How many ways are there to use the materials to show one ounce?

Uses of Operational Questions

Operational questions in the science area can help children develop content information, process skills, and the ability to carry out an independent investigation. They also increase the child's self-confidence in investigating the world and determining answers for himself or herself. Operational questions in mathematics can help children determine the validity of computation rules or develop mathematical concepts.

Whether used in mathematics or in science, operational questions are investigated by students in such a way that they are the ones answering the questions and generating the ideas and concepts. The teacher's role is to model using operational questions in the classroom and aid students in developing their investigations.

SUMMARY

The questions that are asked in a classroom can either enhance or stifle the thinking skills of children. In order to aid the teacher in developing good questioning skills, the kinds of questions asked should be considered first. Questions can be classified in a variety of possible ways: according to the number of answers given, according to the level of thought processes used, or according to the effect on the child. A variety of questions that are appropriately sequenced and appropriately asked is essential to any good classroom situation. The teacher should plan the questions that will be asked in order to check for variety and sequencing.

One particularly effective technique for asking questions involves the use of wait time—that few seconds that give children an opportunity to think and formulate their answers. Asking questions also involves a variety of other techniques in addition to wait time.

Finally, the use of operational questions involves the child in investigations that generate new information through the use of hands-on materials and higher-order thinking skills.

LEARNING ACTIVITY 79

Analyzing Classroom Questions

Purpose: The purpose of this activity is to analyze the kinds of questions asked in the third-grade classroom.

Procedure:

1. Observe at least three third-grade science lessons and at least three third-grade mathematics lessons, giving particular attention to the questions asked and the questioning strategies used.

2. Analyze the questions asked according to whether those questions were convergent or divergent. Draw any conclusions that are appropriate to the data collected about the kinds of questions asked during the lessons.

3. Describe the questioning strategies used by the teacher, including the effect of those questioning strategies on the children in the class.

Vocabulary Terms

Application-Level Question: a type of question that asks children to use information in a new situation.

Analysis-Level Question: a type of question that asks children to draw a conclusion from a set of information or to utilize problem-solving techniques in determining the cause of a particular outcome.

Comprehension-Level Question: a type of question that determines whether children understand information.

Convergent Question: a question that has only a single correct answer.

Divergent Question: a question that has a variety of correct answers; divergent questions often encourage speculative thinking.

Evaluation-Level Question: a question that asks students to (1) make a judgment of quality based on specified criteria or (2) give and support an opinion.

Intrusive Question: a question that interferes with a child's activity by attempting to direct the activity along new lines or by asking for a causal explanation or conclusion that the child is not yet ready to supply.

Knowledge-Level Question: a question that asks for the recall of a specific bit of information.

Managerial Question: a question that is used to organize a classroom rather than to consider subject-matter information.

Neutral Question: a question that comments on a child's investigation without asking for additional information or attempting to guide the child into a different investigation.

Operational Question: a question asked by a child and answered through hands-on investigation by the child.

Synthesis-Level Question: a question that (1) asks the child to develop an activity or (2) asks the child to use information creatively: drawing, making a diagram, writing a story, and so on.

Wait Time: a questioning technique that gives children time to think before giving an answer by allowing approximately five seconds between the conclusion of a question and the expectation of an answer and two or three seconds between the conclusion of an answer and a comment by the teacher.

Study Questions

1. What are the main uses of questions in the early-childhood-education program?
2. How do convergent questions differ from divergent questions?
3. You want to ask children to develop the rule for subtracting across zero in a problem such as 205 − 79. What questions and in what sequence would you ask the students?
4. Your final question for a science lesson asks students to develop an activity to see what

kinds of seeds sprout most quickly. What questions might you ask and in what order would you ask them?

5. Compare and contrast the levels of Bloom's taxonomy as they apply to questioning.

6. How does the use of wait time affect the children in a classroom?

7. Your class has been studying simple machines. One of the children asks whether two pulleys work better than one. How could you use operational questions to help students investigate this question?

8. A teacher complains that when she asks questions only three or four of the children ever answer. You observe the teacher and discover that she asks only knowledge-level questions and expects immediate responses. What suggestions might you make to this teacher?

CHAPTER 14

Teaching in the Quantitative Curriculum

Chapter Objectives

On completion of this chapter, you should be able to

1. define the term *quantitative curriculum*,

2. discuss the relationship of mathematics and arithmetic to the quantitative curriculum,

3. discuss the components of the quantitative curriculum as recommended by the National Council of Teachers of Mathematics,

4. discuss the general teaching sequence that allows the development of the total quantitative curriculum,

5. discuss the use of manipulative materials in developing counting, place-value, computation, and problem-solving skills,

6. plan a sequence of lessons to demonstrate appropriate teaching in the quantitative curriculum, and

7. discuss the appropriate use of calculators and computers in the classroom.

Consider for a moment the following third-grade mathematics lesson. The teacher asks the students to open their textbooks to page 125. "Look at the box at the top of the page. Josh, read the box, please." Josh reads the box that gives definitions for the two numerals in a common fraction: "The numeral above the line is the numerator. It tells the number of parts being named by the fraction. The numeral below the line is the denominator. It tells the number of parts into which something has been divided." After having these definitions read, the teacher takes a piece of paper and folds it so there are four parts. She takes a crayon and colors one of the four parts red. "This is one fourth," the teacher says, writing the appropriate fraction on the chalkboard. She colors a second section red. "Now we have two fourths." Again, she writes the fraction. Finally, she colors a third section and writes the fraction for three-fourths. With that as background, the children are told to complete the problems on page 125. A worksheet is handed out to further reinforce the "concept" taught that day. As soon as the children begin to try to do the problems on page 125, hands go up. The teacher spends the remainder of the time allotted to mathematics moving rapidly from one student to another trying to help each one individually to understand what is to be done. By the end of the class time, both the teacher and the children are frustrated by the entire lesson.

The lesson did not work the way it was expected to work. The teacher saw this beginning lesson on fractions as something easy that the children should grasp with little difficulty. The children saw it as something difficult, something too hard to be understood. And, together they discovered the lesson was not effectively communicated. Even though mathematics lessons are frequently not communicated well, the typical method for teaching a mathematics lesson to children is this type of demonstration lesson described. Children do not develop the "concept" because the concept is not presented. They do not develop the ability to work with fractions or other skills because they have been introduced to numerals before understanding has been developed.

In this chapter, we will consider techniques that will help children to develop both concepts and skills in a way that allows them to succeed and frees the teacher from having to teach every child on an individual basis. There is nothing wrong with individual instruction unless it happens solely because a child has not understood teacher instruction and therefore requires special attention.

THE QUANTITATIVE CURRICULUM

Conceptualization of fully unified concepts from both the mathematics and science areas are emphasized at the preschool and kindergarten levels so that children construct a rich background of information. As the child progresses into the second- and third-grade levels, the focus turns to mathematics concepts and science process skills, with overlap occurring between the two areas. As the child progresses into the defined curriculum of the third-grade level, the mathematics of the previous years and the skills necessary for computation are both a part of the program. Now, with mathematics and arithmetic integrated, the child begins to experience a quantitative curriculum.

The quantitative curriculum is formed when mathematics and arithmetic are interrelated so that the child is able to conceptualize the computation skill and, therefore, compute with understanding rather than through rote memorization of a sequence of events. Additionally, the quantitative curriculum focuses on the development of problem-solving skills and critical-thinking skills.

The National Council of Teachers of Mathematics

The quantitative curriculum is based on the integration of mathematics with arithmetic. However, the topics found within the quantitative curriculum can be more specifically defined and have been listed by the National Council of Teachers of Mathematics (NCTM) in their 1989 publication *Curriculum and Evaluation Standards for School Mathematics.*

Goals for Students. According to the National Council of Teachers of Mathematics, the educational goals of the quantitative curriculum should demonstrate the importance of mathematical literacy. In order to promote mathematical literacy, the program should reflect five goals:

1. *Students should learn to value mathematics,* including experiences related to the cultural, historical, and scientific changes that have occurred in mathematics and that have helped to shape society. Additionally, students should explore the relationship of mathematics to the life, physical, and earth-space sciences; the social sciences; and the humanities.

2. *Students should become confident in their ability to do mathematics* by developing quantitative skills to use in solving everyday problems. Students should be helped to perceive themselves as competent in all areas of the quantitative curriculum.

3. *Students should become mathematical problem solvers* so that problem solving becomes the focus of the quantitative curriculum. The definition of problem solving is expanded from the simple solving of computation problems to the use of mathematics and arithmetic in new situations where the solution to a problem may not be readily seen.

4. *Students should learn to communicate mathematically* by using signs, symbols, and terms appropriately. Additionally, students should have the opportunity to read about mathematics and to write within the quantitative curriculum.

5. *Students should learn to reason mathematically* through opportunities to make conjectures, gather evidence, support their ideas, and generally demonstrate their growing abilities to reason well in quantitative situations.

These goals indicate that students should have numerous and varied experiences in mathematics, including opportunities to explore concepts, to guess at possible solutions, to make and correct errors, and to find and demonstrate alternative methods for solving problems both computational and general.

Curriculum Assumptions. In addition to the program goals, NCTM has stated that certain assumptions should shape the quantitative curriculum for the young child.

First, the quantitative curriculum should be conceptually oriented so that mathematical understandings and relationships are reflected in the content and emphasized in the classroom. A strong conceptualization allows children to develop skills meaningfully and supports their development of problem-solving skills.

Second, the quantitative curriculum should involve children in actively doing mathematics. This means that teachers need to create an environment that encourages children to explore, develop, test, discuss, and apply ideas. The teacher needs to listen to the discussions of children and encourage them in their efforts, including allowing children to make mistakes and find how to correct those mistakes by themselves. And, the classroom should contain a variety of manipulative materials that children can use as they explore and conceptualize within the quantitative curriculum.

Third, the quantitative curriculum should emphasize the development of children's mathematical thinking and reasoning abilities. Reasoning and problem-solving experiences should be an integral part of the curriculum rather than additions to the curriculum, divorced from the flow of the content and practiced as discrete exercises.

Fourth, the quantitative curriculum should emphasize the applications of mathematics. This assumption about the quantitative curriculum emphasizes the usefulness of mathematics to daily living and to the child as a problem solver. Children, therefore, learn to compute because computation is useful in a variety of situations, not simply to learn to compute accurately.

Fifth, the quantitative curriculum should have a broad range of content. In order to be mathematically literate, children need to know more than arithmetic. Instead, they need to know how to work with and use concepts and skills from measurement, geometry, statistics, and probability. In particular, children should be engaged in the active use of these concepts in problem-solving situations.

And, sixth, the quantitative curriculum should make appropriate and ongoing use of calculators and computers. Calculators should be used as an integral part of the quantitative curriculum and not as enrichment or supplemental work. Computers also have a vital role to play in conceptual development, drill and practice, and also in presenting problem-solving situations to children.

Areas of Increased and Decreased Content Emphasis in the Quantitative Curriculum. NCTM has listed six content areas that should receive increased emphasis in the curriculum:

1. *Number:* Increased emphasis should be given to place-value concepts, estimation, and the meaning of fractions and decimals.
2. *Operations and Computation:* Increased emphasis should be given to the meaning of operations, mental computation, estimation and consideration of the reasonableness of answers, selection of appropriate computational methods, the use of calculators for more complex calculations, and thinking strategies for basic facts.
3. *Geometry and Measurement:* Increased emphasis should be given to properties of geometric figures, geometric relationships, process of measuring, spatial sense, actual measuring, estimation of measurements, and the use of measurement and geometry ideas throughout the curriculum.
4. *Probability and Statistics:* Increased emphasis should be given to the collection and organization of data and to the exploration of concepts of chance.
5. *Patterns and Relationships:* Increased emphasis should be given to the recognition and description of patterns and the use of variables to express relationships.
6. *Problem Solving:* Increased emphasis should be given to word problems, use of everyday problems, applications of mathematics, study of patterns and relationships, and problem-solving strategies.

In addition, NCTM has stated that four areas of the quantitative curriculum should receive decreased emphasis. These areas are as follows:

1. *Number:* Decreased emphasis should be placed on early attention to reading, writing, and ordering numbers symbolically.
2. *Operations and Computations:* Decreased emphasis should be given to complex paper-and-pencil computations, isolated treatment of paper-and-pencil computations, addition and subtraction without regrouping, isolated treatment of division facts, long division with and without remainders, paper-and-pencil fraction computation, and use of rounding in estimation.
3. *Geometry and Measurement:* Decreased emphasis should be given to naming geometric

figures and memorizing equivalences between units of measurement.
4. *Problem Solving:* Decreased emphasis should be given to use of clue words to determine which operation to use.

Areas of Increased and Decreased Attention in Instructional Practices. NCTM has suggested that certain instructional practices be emphasized in the classroom. These include (1) using manipulative materials, (2) working cooperatively, (3) discussing mathematics, (4) using questioning strategies, (5) asking children to justify their thinking, (6) writing about mathematics, (7) using a problem-solving approach to instruction, (8) integrating mathematics into other content areas, and (9) using calculators and computers as parts of the instructional procedure. NCTM has recommended that the following areas receive decreased emphasis in teaching: (1) rote practice of computation, (2) rote memorization of rules, (3) techniques that emphasize the use of only one method for calculation of one answer, (4) use of worksheets and written practice, and (5) teaching by telling.

A TEACHING STRATEGY FOR THE QUANTITATIVE CURRICULUM

The teaching strategy that will be discussed here is a general teaching sequence that allows the development of mathematical concepts or arithmetical skills in an order from highly concrete to highly abstract. It emphasizes the use of concrete materials along with problem-solving skills so that students not only develop the ability to compute accurately, but also develop the ability to think and to apply their new skills in a variety of situations. The strategy is based on four sequential stages.

Stage One

Stage one of the teaching strategy is specifically designed to enhance conceptual development. In stage one, the concept or skill is presented through the use of concrete materials. Only materials are used at this time. No symbols are written. Since no symbols are used, instruction is conducted orally. The children are involved in the lesson through materials, discussion, and problem solving.

A stage-one lesson on multiplication of a two-digit number by a single-digit number through use of repeated addition might progress in the following manner:

1. The teacher demonstrates how to solve a problem such as 5×23 through the use of popsicle sticks. The teacher displays a set of twenty-three popsicle sticks using three singles and two bundles of ten. He names the number shown 23.
2. The teacher sets up a second set of twenty-three using three singles and two bundles of ten.
3. The teacher sets up a third set of twenty-three using the same format.
4. The teacher demonstrates that to find the total number, the units are first pushed together and counted. There are nine. Then, the tens are pushed together and counted. There are six tens, or sixty.
5. The teacher "reads" the final answer to the problem as six tens and nine ones, or 69.
6. The teacher demonstrates two or three additional problems while the students watch but do not work along.
7. After the procedure is well established, the teacher asks the students to help in solving the next two or three problems by directing the teacher through oral statements.
8. After the students have demonstrated that they are fully able to use the strategy, they are given popsicle sticks and asked to solve approximately five problems using the idea of repeated addition as a means of solving a multiplication problem. The problems are given orally, one at a time. The students solve the problems concretely, and then the answers are given orally.
9. Finally, students are asked to describe in their own words the sequence of events used in solving a problem.

Stage-one teaching is designed to allow the students to develop the concept that multiplication is a form of addition. The popsicle sticks, as a type of concrete material, play on the idea of addition as the union of sets and of multiplication as the union of more than one equivalent set.

Stage Two

Stage-two teaching is designed to develop the concept or skill begun in the first stage of teaching through the use of concrete materials. At stage two, the students are introduced to recording problems through the use of diagrams or drawings. This is the first step in teaching a meaningful recording of problems or other information. In stage two, a drawing or diagram is used to represent a real object or to record the results of a mathematical activity. If the drawings or diagrams are used to represent a real object as part of a mathematics activity, then the students should be involved in their use. If the drawings or diagrams are used to represent a computational skill in an arithmetic lesson, then the teacher should be the only person recording. The reason for having the teacher as the only person recording during a computation skill is to allow children to concentrate on connecting the method with the recorded format without immediately having to produce both a solution and recorded format. An example should help to differentiate between these two situations.

Students have been involved with the use of pattern blocks in developing a concept of fractions. The yellow hexagon is used as the "whole" in the exploration. Students discover that two red trapezoids will completely cover the yellow block. They discover that three blue "diamonds" will cover the block, as will six small green triangles. The students record their discoveries by drawing pictures of the blocks that are the same size and that use the same colors. In this case, a concept is being developed and the students are recording exactly what they see (see Diagram 14.1).

In another lesson, students are involved in learning to add two three-digit numerals without any necessity for regrouping. This would be a problem of the type $324 + 561 =$ _____. In order to solve this type of problem, the students have been using bundles of popsicle sticks. Rather than having the students diagram this type of problem, the teacher diagrams the problem by recording proportionately sized rectangles that are not exact representations of the popsicle sticks. Having the teacher diagram enables students to concentrate more on the method for determining a solution and less on the means to record (see Diagram 14.2).

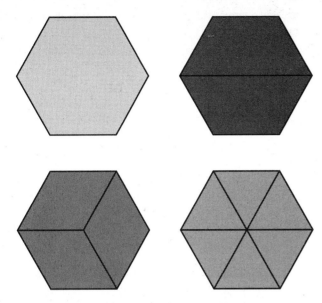

Diagram 14.1 Recording by Children in Stage Two: Using Pattern Blocks

In working with a stage-two lesson, the procedure is essentially the same as that for a stage-one lesson. Returning to the repeated addition problem, the steps in teaching are as follows:

1. The teacher demonstrates how to solve a problem such as 4 × 22 through the use of popsicle sticks. The teacher sets up a set of twenty-two popsicle sticks using two singles and two bundles of ten, and then records on the chalkboard the number shown by drawing two single sticks and two large blocks to represent the two tens. She names the number shown 22. The teacher sets up a second set of twenty-two using two singles and two bundles of ten, and then records the second set below the first set.
2. The teacher sets up the third and fourth sets of twenty-two using the same format, including recording through a diagram.
3. The teacher demonstrates finding the total number by first pushing the units together and then counting them. There are eight units. Then, the tens are pushed together and counted. There are eight tens, or eighty. The answer is also diagramed (see Diagram 14.3).
4. The teacher "reads" from the diagram the final

answer to the problem as eight tens and eight ones, or 88.

5. The teacher demonstrates two or three additional problems while the students watch but do not work along.
7. After the procedure is well established, the teacher asks the students to help in solving the next two or three problems by directing the teacher through oral statements.
8. After the students have demonstrated that they are fully able to use the strategy, they are given popsicle sticks and asked to solve approximately five multiplication problems using repeated addition. The problems are given orally, one at a time. The students solve the problems concretely and tell the teacher how to record the answers on the chalkboard or overhead using diagrams. Finally, the students give the answers orally.

Stage two of the teaching strategy develops the concept of recording problems. The record is seen as a way of showing the outcome of a problem but numerals are not yet used. The students are given the opportunity to make the connection between the written format and the problems that they are solving.

Stage Three

In stage three, the concept or skill is further developed but the numeral symbols are now introduced. In mathematics, the symbols may be numerals, sentences, or tally marks, depending on the activity. In arithmetic, the symbols used are generally numerals as well as the accompanying symbols, such as the plus sign, equals sign, division radical, multiplication sign, or subtraction sign used in the standard algorithms. Even though the standard symbols are used, the students are still solving the problems through the use of concrete materials.

A stage-three lesson is generally conducted in the same manner as lessons in other stages. The major difference between stage two and stage three is that numerals are used rather than diagrams.

1. The teacher demonstrates how to solve a problem such as 4 × 22 through the use of popsicle sticks. The teacher displays a set of twenty-two popsicle sticks using two singles and two

First Quantity:

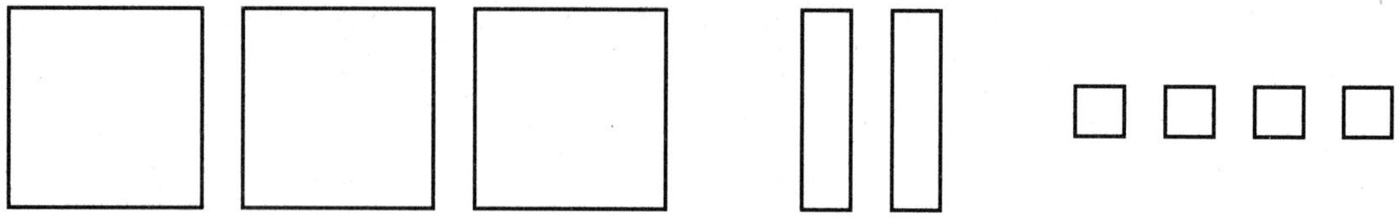

Second Quantity:

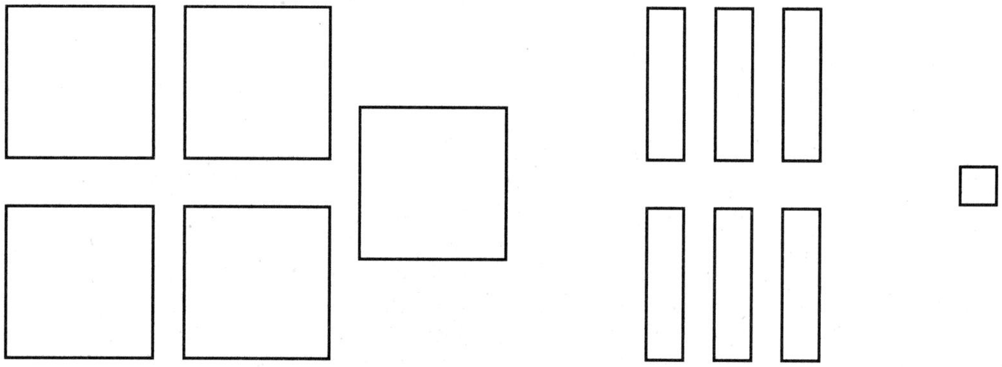

Total Quantity:

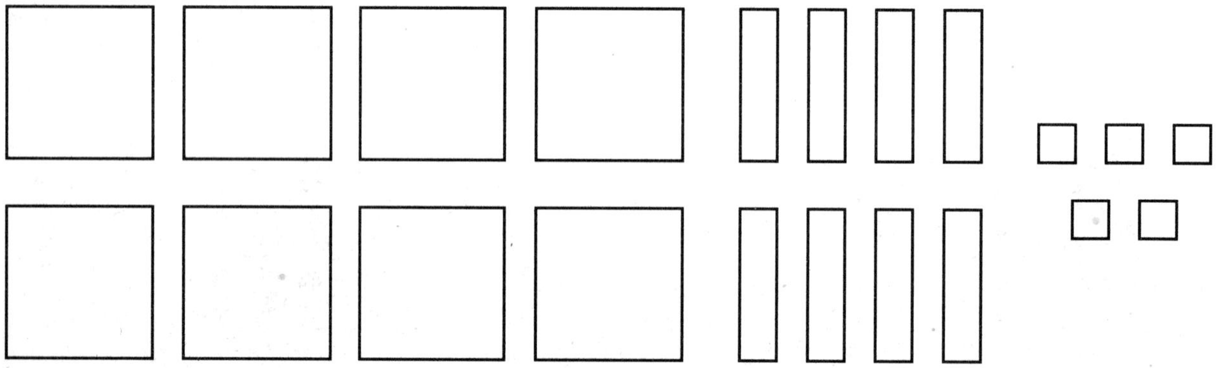

Diagram 14.2 Recording by the Teacher in Stage Two: Diagrams

Step One:

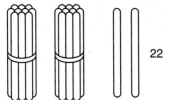

22

Step Two:

22

Step Three:

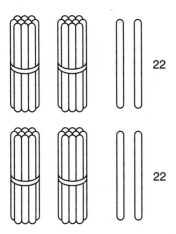

22

22

Step Four:

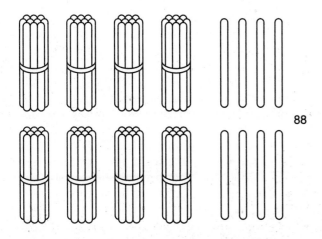

88

Diagram 14.3 Recording by the Teacher in Stage Two: Diagrams and Numerals

bundles of ten, then records on the chalkboard the numeral 22. She names the number shown 22. The teacher sets up a second set of twenty-two using two singles and two bundles of ten and records the second set below the first set.

2. The teacher sets up the third and fourth sets of twenty-two using the same format, including the numerals.
3. The teacher demonstrates finding the total number by pushing the units together and then counting them. There are eight units. Then, the tens are pushed together and counted. There are eight tens, or eighty. The answer is then recorded in numerical form.
4. The teacher states that the final answer to the problem is eight tens and eight ones, or 88.
5. The teacher demonstrates two or three additional problems while the students watch but do not work along.
6. After the procedure is well established, the teacher asks the students to help in solving the next two or three problems by directing the teacher through oral statements.
7. After the students have demonstrated that they are fully able to use the strategy, they are given popsicle sticks and asked to solve approximately five multiplication problems using repeated addition. The problems are given orally, one at a time. The students solve the problems concretely, recording the problems and answers as they solve them. They then give the answers orally.
8. As students become more and more familiar with the problem format, write the problems on the chalkboard and ask the students to solve approximately five problems on their own before engaging in a discussion to determine the correctness of their answers.

Stage three is designed to enhance the understanding of both the algorithm and computation skill. Since students solve the problem first through the use of the materials and then record the final answer, it is difficult for students to make errors. Because of the high success rate in working with the materials, students gain confidence in their ability to solve the problems. Additionally, some students will begin to see for themselves that the problems easily can be done with numerals and, therefore,

will begin to use a purely numerical format without any prompting.

Stage Four

In stage four, the concept or skill is extended into the use of symbols. At this point in the teaching strategy, the standard algorithm for a computational skill is developed or the form for recording a mathematical activity is developed.

In general, the sequence of events for this level is as follows:

1. Review the computation skill or mathematical skill through the use of concrete materials and written format.
2. Demonstrate the standard algorithm format for the students and then check the answers using the materials.
3. Demonstrate the use of the standard format with the children, but also include a discussion of other ways that could be used to solve problems. As children describe and discuss their techniques, they often help children who are uncertain of a procedure understand or find a technique that will be useful to them as well as accurate to them.

At this point, the students should be expected only to use a numerical format to solve problems or to record mathematical skills. However, children should be encouraged to use and find alternative methods for problem solution and not simply be told they must use a standard format. Also, children who still need to use concrete materials in order to support their understanding should have those materials available to them. Children should not be introduced to the purely symbolic level until they are ready for that level. Children who rely heavily on the manipulation of materials for understanding and solving problems are not yet ready for the symbolic level. Those children who can accurately solve computation problems only when they use concrete materials should be allowed to use those materials until they begin to show an abstract understanding of the skill. For the most part, those children who are ready for complete symbolization will demonstrate that readiness by giving up concrete materials on their own. They will naturally make the transition from stage three to stage four in the teaching strategy.

The use of symbolization does not mean that children should be limited to a single technique for solving a problem. Rather, they should be encouraged to find alternative methods for solving problems and should be encouraged to discuss how they solved those problems. Although arithmetic computations do have a correct answer, there are frequently many methods that can be used to obtain that answer. Children should be encouraged to find a variety of possibilities for solving problems and to share those possibilities with one another. Examples 14.1 through 14.4 show the four stages of the teaching strategy in lesson-plan format and demonstrate how a single type of problem is taught through each of the stages.

USING MANIPULATIVES IN THE QUANTITATIVE CURRICULUM

Manipulatives in Teaching Place-Value Concepts

The key to teaching concepts of place value is to use manipulatives that allow children to construct the quantities represented by the various places within the place-value system and that visually demonstrate the difference in quantity represented by each place. This means that both the abacus and the traditional place-value chart labeled with the units, tens, and hundreds places are ineffective as initial teaching materials.

Two materials are particularly effective in helping children to conceptualize place-value concepts: Unifix Cubes and popsicle sticks. Unifix Cubes are plastic cubes that come in a variety of different colors and are constructed so that they may be attached to form stacks of any length. Although the individual cubes can be given any value, each cube generally is considered to represent the quantity one. Popsicle sticks are often sold in craft stores as craft sticks. In order to use them effectively, rubber bands are needed so that the sticks can be bundled into groups of ten, one hundred, or one thousand. In addition to the Unifix Cubes or popsicle sticks, a board showing two or more sections in differing colors is needed (see Diagram 14.4).

In working with place value as a concept, quantities other than ten can and should be used in a game format. The game involves the use of a "magic number" that children are not permitted to say as a part of the counting sequence. The game is played in the following manner:

1. The teacher selects a number, generally less than ten, and writes it on a piece of paper that is folded so the number cannot be seen. The teacher then tells the class that there is a magic number on the paper and has the class guess the number. After the children have had an opportunity to guess the number, the teacher shows it to the students and tells them that the number on the paper can no longer be said in the classroom.

2. The teacher asks for words that could be used instead of the magic number and gets a variety of possibilities. The teacher lists the possibilities on the board and the class selects one to use. The word used can be as silly as the children want it to be. Some words that have been used include pizza, frog, popcorn, boing, crinkle, and worm.

3. The teacher practices counting using the substitute numeral (word) always beginning with zero. For example: "zero, one, two, three, four, five, pizza." After the substituted word is reached, the teacher returns to zero once again and counts forward. Then, the teacher has students practice counting backward. The children should be able to count easily in both a forward and a backward direction, substituting the term for the magic number.

4. The teacher counts using the board along with Unifix Cubes or popsicle sticks. The teacher demonstrates so that the children see the individual cubes counted on the right side of the board. When the magic number is reached, the teacher demonstrates stacking the cubes or bundling the sticks and moving them to the left side of the board. For example, the teacher counts zero, places one cube and says "one," places a second cube and says "two," and so on until five cubes are on the board. The next numeral is "pizza," so the teacher stacks the cubes or bundles the sticks and delivers the "pizza" to the other place on the board (see Diagram 14.5).

EXAMPLE 14.1

Stage-One Lesson Plan

Grade: Third

Subject Area: Mathematics

Time Needed: approximately 45 minutes

Topic: basic division facts

Materials: approximately 100 popsicle sticks per student

Objectives:
1. Given popsicle sticks and rubber bands, each child will be able to solve and orally state the solutions to seven problems of the type $6\overline{)36}$.

Procedure:
1. *Introduction*
   a. Orally present the children with the following problems one at a time. Ask them how they could solve the problems. Record their responses on the chalkboard or overhead projector.
      1. There were twenty-one cupcakes in a box. Each person can have three cupcakes. How many people can eat cupcakes?
      2. There are fifteen beads that have been made into necklaces. Each necklace has five beads. How many necklaces are there?
      3. Eighty-one children came to the park to play baseball. If each team has nine players, how many teams will there be?
2. *Teacher Demonstration*
   a. Tell the children that you have twenty-five popsicle sticks. Show the sticks. Tell them that you want to find out how many bundles of five sticks you can make. Count out five sticks and bundle them together using a rubber band. Continue counting and bundling until no single sticks remain. Count the number of bundles. State the answer to the problem: "There are five bundles of five sticks in twenty-five."

   b. Repeat the demonstration with the following problems.
      1. How many bundles of eight sticks are there in fifty-six sticks?
      2. How many bundles of six sticks are there in twenty-four sticks?
   c. Do one more problem, but this time have the class tell you how to solve the problem step by step.
3. *Student Practice*
   a. Distribute the popsicle sticks to the class.
   b. Have the children solve the following problems one at a time with the sticks and then orally state the answers.
      1. How many bundles of nine sticks are there in seventy-two sticks?
      2. How many bundles of six sticks are there in thirty-six sticks?
      3. How many bundles of seven sticks are there in twenty-eight sticks?
      4. How many bundles of four sticks are there in thirty-six sticks?
      5. How many bundles of five sticks are there in forty-five sticks?
      6. How many bundles of eight sticks are there in forty-eight sticks?
      7. How many bundles of three sticks are there in twenty-seven sticks?
4. *Summary*
   a. Review the steps used in solving the problems by having students state the steps. Record them on the chalkboard or overhead projector.
   b. Return to the introductory problems and solve each of them.

Evaluation: During the student practice, observe the children at work to determine whether they can solve the problems using the sticks and then orally give the answers.

EXAMPLE 14.2

Stage-Two Lesson Plan

Grade: Third

Subject Area: Mathematics

Time Needed: approximately 45 minutes

Topic: basic division facts using repeated subtraction

Materials: approximately one hundred popsicle sticks per student

Objective:

1. Given popsicle sticks, each child will be able to solve and assist the teacher in recording, through repeated subtraction, seven problems of the type $7\overline{)42}$.

Procedure:

1. *Introduction*
  a. Review basic subtraction facts using a game format.
  b. Review the technique used for solving problems of the type "How many bundles of six sticks are there in forty-two sticks?"
    1. Count out the total number of sticks.
    2. Count the number of sticks in each bundle and put a rubber band around them.
    3. Continue counting and bundling until no sticks remain.
    4. Count the number of bundles to find the answer to the problem.

2. *Teacher Demonstration*
  a. Tell the children to watch carefully as you write and solve the following problem on the board: "How many bundles of six sticks are there in twenty-four sticks?"
    1. Write $6\overline{)24}$ on the board in standard notation as you state the problem.
    2. Count and bundle six sticks. Orally state that there were twenty-four sticks, six were bundled, and, therefore, there are eighteen single sticks left. Record the following problem:

$$\begin{array}{r} 24 \\ -\ 6 \\ \hline 18 \end{array}$$

3. Count and bundle six sticks. State that there were eighteen sticks left, six were bundled, and, therefore, there are twelve single sticks left. Record the following problem:

$$\begin{array}{r} 18 \\ -\ 6 \\ \hline 12 \end{array}$$

4. Count and bundle six sticks. State that there were twelve single sticks left, six were bundled, and, therefore, there are six single sticks left. Record the following problem:

$$\begin{array}{r} 12 \\ -\ 6 \\ \hline 6 \end{array}$$

5. Count and bundle six sticks. State that there were six single sticks left, all six were bundled, and, therefore, there are zero single sticks left. Record the following problem:

$$\begin{array}{r} 6 \\ -\ 6 \\ \hline 0 \end{array}$$

EXAMPLE 14.2 Continued

6. Demonstrate that the answer to the problem can be found by counting the number of bundles or by counting the number of sixes that were subtracted. Record the quotient in the proper location.

```
          24
         -⑥
          18
    4    -⑥
 6⎯24     12
         -⑥
          6
         -⑥
          0
```

4 bundles

b. Repeat steps 1 through 6 with the following problems:
   1. 9⎯72
   2. 5⎯30
c. Do two additional problems, but have the students direct you through the steps of the repeated-subtraction format.
   1. 4⎯16
   2. 7⎯63

3. *Student Practice*
   a. Present the following problems one at a time to the students. Have the students direct you in the recording of each problem.

   1. 8⎯56
   2. 3⎯18
   3. 5⎯40
   4. 4⎯28
   5. 6⎯42
   6. 7⎯35
   7. 9⎯36

4. *Summary*
   a. Summarize the steps used in solving and recording problems.
      1. Count out and record the total number of sticks. Show the number of sticks in each bundle and complete the written problem.
      2. Count and bundle the sticks. Subtract the number in each bundle and record how many sticks are left.
      3. Repeat step 2 until no single sticks remain.
      4. Count the number of bundles or the number of subtractions and record the answer.

Evaluation: During the student practice, observe the students to determine if they can assist in solving and recording the problems through a repeated-subtraction format.

EXAMPLE 14.3

Stage-Three Lesson Plan

Grade: Third

Subject Area: Mathematics

Time Needed: approximately 45 minutes

Topic: solving basic division facts through repeated subtraction

Materials: pencils, paper, approximately one hundred popsicle sticks per student

Objective:
1. Given popsicle sticks, each child will be able to solve and record in repeated-subtraction format ten problems of the type 6⎯42.

Procedure:
1. *Introduction*
   a. Review basic subtraction facts using a game format.
2. *Teacher Demonstration*
   a. Review the repeated-subtraction format presented in the previous lesson using the problems 7⎯42 and 9⎯36.
   b. Demonstrate one more problem, but begin by writing the problem on the board and then counting out the total number of sticks needed. Continue to count, bundle, and subtract until the problem is solved. Emphasize reading and interpreting the written problem.

EXAMPLE 14.3 Continued

3. *Student Practice*
   a. Write the following problems on the chalk-board. Have the students copy each problem, solve it, and record it in repeated-subtraction format.
   b. Problems:
      1. $3\overline{)15}$
      2. $4\overline{)24}$
      3. $5\overline{)45}$
      4. $6\overline{)48}$
      5. $7\overline{)63}$
      6. $8\overline{)40}$
      7. $9\overline{)72}$
      8. $6\overline{)54}$
      9. $7\overline{)49}$
      10. $8\overline{)56}$

   c. After the problems have been solved, have students demonstrate their solutions.
4. *Summary*
   a. Review with the students how to read a problem written in the standard-division format.
   b. Review with the students the steps used in solving a problem through repeated subtraction.

Evaluation: Collect and evaluate the written records of each student to determine if all ten problems were correctly solved and recorded.

EXAMPLE 14.4

Stage-Four Lesson Plan

Grade: Third

Subject Area: Mathematics

Time Needed: approximately 45 minutes

Topic: solving basic division facts through repeated subtraction

Materials: pencils, paper, popsicle sticks for students who still need to use materials to solve the problems

Objective:
1. As a result of this lesson, each student will be able to solve ten problems of the type $9\overline{)36}$ using repeated subtraction.

Procedure:
1. *Introduction*
   a. Review basic subtraction facts using a game format.
2. *Teacher Demonstration*
   a. Tell the class that they will be learning how to solve division problems without using the popsicle sticks.

   b. Demonstrate the use of repeated subtraction with each of the following problems. Emphasize the use of basic subtraction facts in solving the problems.
      1. $5\overline{)20}$
      2. $6\overline{)36}$
      3. $7\overline{)42}$
   c. Solve two additional problems having the children direct you in the procedure.
      1. $8\overline{)32}$
      2. $9\overline{)36}$
3. *Student Practice*
   a. Put the following problems on the chalkboard:
      1. $8\overline{)56}$
      2. $5\overline{)45}$
      3. $2\overline{)14}$
      4. $3\overline{)12}$
      5. $9\overline{)72}$
      6. $7\overline{)49}$
      7. $4\overline{)20}$
      8. $6\overline{)48}$
      9. $8\overline{)40}$
      10. $7\overline{)56}$

EXAMPLE 14.4 Continued

b. Have the students copy, solve, and record the problems using repeated subtraction.

c. After the problems have been solved, have the students demonstrate how they solved them.

4. *Summary*

Review the steps used in solving the problems through repeated subtraction.

Evaluation: Collect and evaluate the written problems accomplished during the student-practice phase of the lesson.

Units and Tens Place-Value Board:

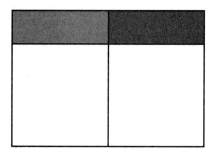

Units, Tens, and Hundreds Place-Value Board:

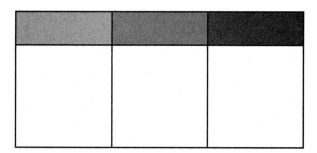

Units, Tens, Hundreds, and Thousands Place-Value Board:

Diagram 14.4 Place-Value Boards

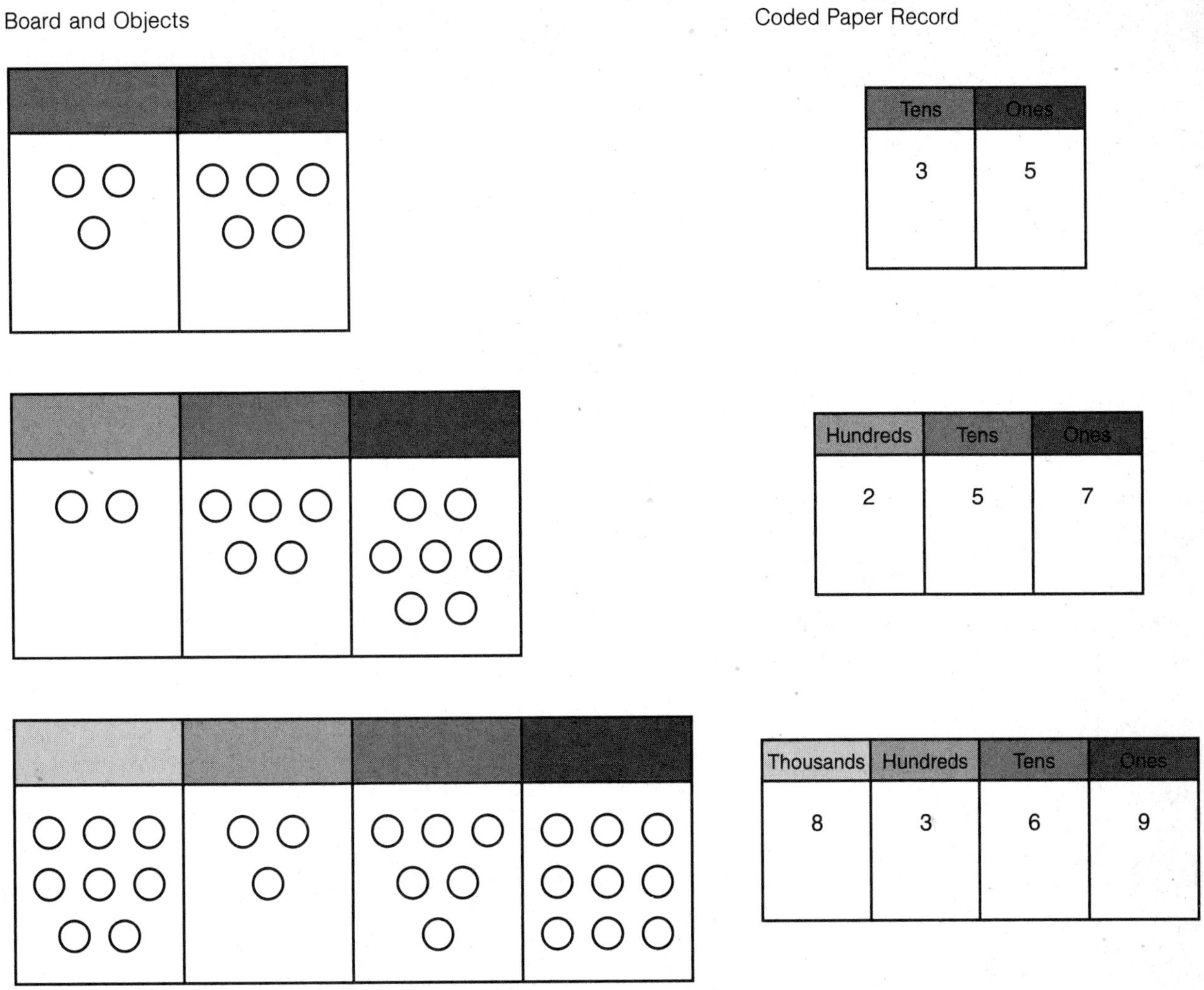

Board and Objects

Coded Paper Record

Tens	Ones
3	5

Hundreds	Tens	Ones
2	5	7

Thousands	Hundreds	Tens	Ones
8	3	6	9

Diagram 14.5 Recording Place Value with Coded Paper

5. The teacher has the children count along until they are comfortable with making "pizza" and moving them to the other place on the board. Then, the teacher has students count beyond a single pizza: "one pizza, zero; one pizza, one; one pizza, two," and so on.

6. After practicing along with the teacher, the children should be given the opportunity to count on their own. The teacher claps or rings a bell and the children begin to count their cubes or sticks in terms of "pizzas" and ones. When the teacher claps or rings the bell a second time, the children stop counting and are asked how many cubes they have on their boards.

7. In the next step, children are asked to show various quantities with their cubes or sticks. For example, children can show five pizzas, three or two pizzas, one.

8. Finally, children are asked to show a certain quantity and then count backwards from that quantity, regrouping a "pizza" into ones whenever necessary.

The purpose of the game is to develop a concept of place and of each place on the board representing a particular quantity. While children are playing this game, they are not only exploring concepts of place and place value; they are also developing concepts involved in regrouping. Before going to ones, tens, and hundreds—our base-ten system—children should play the magic-number game with a variety of other quantities.

In order to add the appropriate terms to the place-value concepts, children should work with the magic-number ten. After they are able to count forwards and backwards easily, the teacher can take the following steps:

1. Ask children how many cubes or sticks are placed on the board at one time in the right-hand place. The cubes or sticks are placed one at a time and so this is designated the ones place.
2. Ask the children how many cubes or sticks are placed at one time in the next place. The cubes or sticks are placed in a stack or bundle of ten all at one time. This is then designated the tens place.
3. Repeat the same procedure for the hundreds place and the thousands place if these are used.

Introduce children to recording quantities by having them first show quantities on the place-value boards and then record the same quantities using numerals on coded paper to indicate the various places (see Diagram 14.5).

In playing the magic-number game with children, be certain that children always begin to count in the ones place and move to the tens place (or whatever quantities are used). Also, as children record the numerals they are showing, be certain that they begin the recording with the ones place and move to the tens place. Establishing the progression from ones to tens to hundreds at this point makes it easier to prevent children from computing from left to right rather than from right to left.

Manipulatives in Whole-Number Computation

Whole-number computation using manipulative materials is based on the concept of place value and the magic-number game considered previously. In keeping with the natural development of quantitative concepts in children, addition and multiplication will be considered together, followed by subtraction and division. In this way, multiplication can be considered as repeated addition, and division as repeated subtraction.

Addition and Multiplication. Addition and multiplication easily can be handled using Unifix Cubes or popsicle sticks. Addition involving no regrouping is extremely easy and, unless there is a counting error, it is virtually impossible for children to make errors. The cubes or sticks and the place-value board are needed in working with addition. The following steps make the procedure easy. The problem being shown is 35 + 42 = _____.

1. Practice counting and regrouping with the class so that the children are comfortable with the concept of stacking or bundling ten items and moving them from the units to the tens place.
2. Have the children show the numeral 35, beginning with five cubes or sticks in the ones place and then showing the three tens in the tens place on the board.
3. Show the numeral 42 again, beginning with the ones place and moving to the tens place. Keep the two sets of materials separated so that both the quantity 35 and the quantity 42 can be seen easily.
4. Push together all of the objects in the ones place and count. The total in the ones place is seven.
5. Push together all of the bundles or stacks in the tens place and count. The total is seven tens, or seventy.
6. Read the total quantity as seven tens, five ones, or 75 (see Example 14.5).

As a caution to the teacher in working with this type of problem, be certain that both the teacher and the children are counting as the tens are placed: "ten, twenty, thirty . . ." or "one ten, two tens, three tens . . ." and not simply "one, two, three . . ." The teacher and the children should continually emphasize the correct terminology for the places on the board.

Although solving a problem that requires regrouping is more difficult than solving one that doesn't, the problem is not that much more difficult. Successful accomplishment of this type of problem requires that children be able to use easily the concepts of place value considered in the magic-number game. The procedure for a regrouping problem is shown using the problem 58 + 69 = _____.

EXAMPLE 14.5

Solving 35 + 42 = _____ with Manipulatives

Step One: Show 35

Step Four: Combine tens and count

7 tens   7 ones

Step Two: Show 42

Step Five: Read the final answer from the board

7   7

Step Three: Combine ones and count

7 ones

1. Play the magic-number game with the children, emphasizing the regrouping procedure each time ten sticks or ten bundles are found in a particular place on the board. Since the problem to be solved requires regrouping into the hundreds place, children should practice counting involving hundreds.
2. Have the class show the quantity 58, beginning with the eight ones and then showing the five stacks or bundles of ten.
3. Keeping the quantity separated from the first addend, have the class show the quantity 69, beginning with the nine ones and moving to the six bundles or stacks of ten.
4. Push together the ones. Count and regroup as necessary. Place the bundle or stack of tens in the tens place on the place-value board. Ask the children how many ones are left. There should be seven ones remaining in the ones place.
5. Push together and count the stacks or bundles of ten. Regroup ten bundles of ten into one hundred and place the hundred into the hundreds place on the board. Ask the children how many tens are left in the tens place. The answer should be two tens, or twenty.
6. Read the answer from the board as one hundred, two tens, seven ones, or 127 (see Example 14.6).

Once again, be certain to emphasize movement across the place-value board from units to tens to hundreds, as well as the proper terminology for each of the places. The bundle of sticks or cubes in the hundreds place is not simply "one," but is "one hundred."

Multiplication is based on the concept of repeated addition, so a problem such as $3 \times 21 = $ _____ can be written as $21 + 21 + 21 = $ _____. A multiplication problem being considered as a repeated-addition problem can be read as "How many cubes (sticks) are there in three groups of twenty-one?" The following numbered list is the sequence that would be used in solving a multiplication problem of the type $4 \times 36 = $ _____. The problem can be read as "How many sticks (cubes) are there in four groups of thirty-six?"

1. Practice showing and regrouping using the place-value board and Unifix Cubes or popsicle sticks. In this case, children should practice showing quantities such as thirty-two by placing two ones and three tens without having to count and bundle beginning at one.
2. Have the children show four groups of thirty-six by showing six ones and then three tens and repeating this procedure until all four sets of thirty-six are displayed separately on the place-value board.
3. Push together all of the ones. Count and regroup as necessary. Ask the class how many ones remain in the ones place. There should be four ones remaining and two tens should have been regrouped.
4. Push together all of the stacks or bundles of ten and regroup as necessary. Ask the class how many tens remain in the tens place. There should be four tens. Ten tens should have been regrouped into one hundred and placed in the hundreds place.
5. Read the solution to the problem as one hundred, four tens, four ones, or 144 (see Example 14.7).

In working with a problem of this type, be certain that students are showing four sets of thirty-six objects and not showing four sets of six and then four sets of thirty. The integrity of the number needs to be maintained throughout the problem. Also, be certain always to refer to the quantities shown by their appropriate place-value terms.

Subtraction and Division. It is easy to see that working with manipulatives to solve addition and multiplication problems makes those problems particularly easy to solve. The same is true for subtraction and division problems. When working with manipulatives, subtraction problems are treated as "take-away" problems and division as repeated subtraction. These models of subtraction and division are especially appropriate for children because they do not require the reversibility of thought that is necessary if subtraction is considered as the inverse of addition and division as the inverse of multiplication.

In working with subtraction problems, there is nothing that could be easier than solving a subtraction problem without regrouping. The following steps are used with a problem of the type $58 - 26 = $ _____.

EXAMPLE 14.6

Solving 58 + 69 = _____ with Manipulatives

Step One: Show 58

Step Two: Show 69

Step Three: Combine ones

Step Four: Regroup ones

Step Five: Combine tens

Step Six: Regroup tens

Step Seven: Read the final answer

1	2	7

EXAMPLE 14.7

Solving 4 × 36 = _____ with Manipulatives

Step One: Show one set of 36

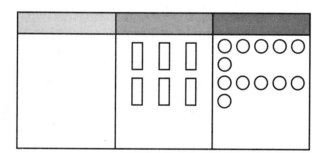

Step Two: Show a second set of 36

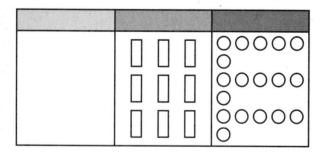

Step Three: Show a third set of 36

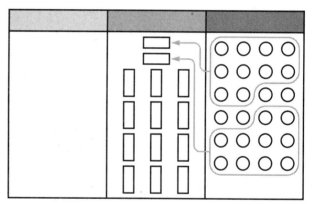

Step Four: Show a fourth set of 36

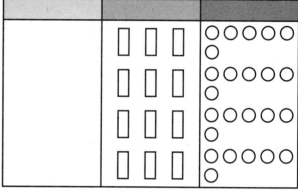

Step Five: Combine ones

EXAMPLE 14.7 Continued

Step Six: Regroup ones

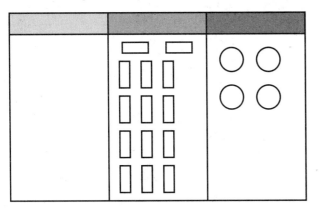

Step Seven: Combine tens

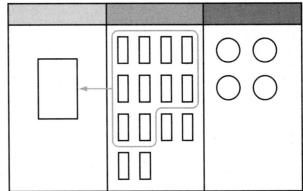

Step Eight: Regroup tens

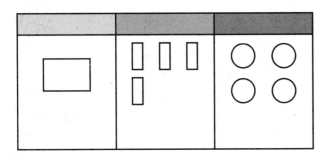

Step Nine: Read the final answer

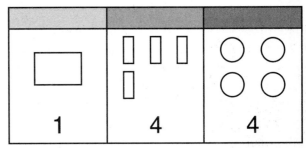

1. Have the children practice showing quantities on the place-value board, being certain to emphasize the importance of showing the units place and then the tens place or hundreds place.
2. Have the children show the larger of the two quantities in the problem—in this case 58—beginning with the units place and then showing the tens place.
3. Inspect the numeral 26 to determine how many ones are to be taken away from the total quantity of fifty-eight. Ask students if there are enough ones to be able to take away six ones.
4. Remove the six ones from the place-value board. Ask how many ones are left on the board. There should be two left.
5. Inspect the quantity 26 to determine how many tens are to be taken away from the quantity represented on the place-value board. Ask the students if there are enough tens on the board that they can take away two tens, or twenty.
6. Remove the two tens from the board. Ask the students how many tens remain on the board. In this case, there should be three tens remaining.
7. Read the answer from the place-value board as three tens, two ones, or 32 (see Example 14.8).

In working with this procedure, it is important to be certain the students begin with the correct number on the board. It is very difficult to solve a problem of this type incorrectly unless students begin with the wrong quantity. The questions dealing with whether there are enough ones or tens to be able to take away a particular quantity that

LEARNING ACTIVITY 80

Manipulatives with Addition or Multiplication

Purpose: The purpose of this activity is to develop a teaching strategy using manipulative materials with addition or multiplication.

Procedure:

1. Select a chapter on addition or multiplication from a third-grade mathematics textbook. Select one type of problem from that chapter: for example, an addition problem involving a two-digit number plus a two-digit number with regrouping (36 + 85 = _____) or a multiplication problem involving a one-digit number times a two-digit number without regrouping (4 × 21 = _____).

2. Plan a strategy for teaching the selected topic that shows only the first stage of the four-stage teaching strategy.

3. Present your teaching strategy as a lesson plan and include a topic, objectives, materials, a procedure, and an evaluation.

4. Try your strategy with a group of five or six third-grade children.
   a. How did the children respond to the strategy?
   b. How would you rate the success of your strategy?
   c. What changes would you suggest to make your teaching strategy more effective?

---

appears in steps three and five may seem unnecessary, but they are establishing a procedure. In this case, the procedure is to inspect the quantities shown in order to determine whether it is necessary to regroup or not. This will be especially important when students are asked to perform subtraction problems where regrouping from hundreds to tens or tens to ones is necessary.

Problems requiring regrouping in subtraction are more difficult than those that do not require regrouping. Problems of regrouping across a zero are particularly difficult. The following example shows the procedure used for regrouping problems, including the difficulty of regrouping across a zero. The problem demonstrated is 204 − 58 = _____.

1. Have children practice showing various numbers on the place-value board and then counting backwards from the numbers shown to lower values. In particular, children should have to regroup as they are counting backward. Emphasize the regrouping procedure in which one hundred is regrouped as ten tens and one ten is regrouped as ten ones.

2. Have the children show the number 204 on the place-value board.

3. Inspect the quantity 58 to determine how many ones are to be taken away. Ask children if there are enough ones in the ones place on the board

that eight can be taken away. The answer should be "No." Ask children to recall what they did when they were counting and "ran out" of ones. They should recall that they regrouped one ten as ten ones.

4. Have the children look at the tens place on the place-value board. Ask if there are any tens to regroup as ones. Since there are not, ask what they could do to "get some tens." They need to go to the hundreds place and regroup one of the hundreds as ten tens. Ask children if they have enough ones that they can take away eight ones. They still need to regroup one of the tens for ten ones.

5. Now have the children take away the eight ones. Ask how many ones are left in the ones place. They should find that they have six ones left in the ones place.

6. Have the children inspect the numeral 58 to see how many tens are to be taken away. Ask if there are enough tens in the tens place that they can take away five tens. There are enough tens.

7. The children should take away the five tens. Ask how many tens remain. There should be four tens.

8. Have the children inspect the numeral 58. Ask if there are any hundreds to be taken away. Since there are not, the children should look at the place-value board to read the answer to the problem.

EXAMPLE 14.8

Solving 58 − 26 = _____ with Manipulatives

Step One: Show 58

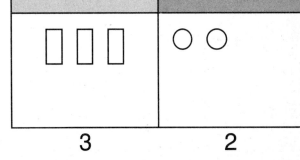

Step Two: Subtract six ones

Step Three: Subtract two tens

Step Four: Read the final answer

3   2

---

9. The answer is one hundred, four tens, six ones, or 146 (see Example 14.9).

In working with subtraction problems that require regrouping, be certain that children inspect each place to determine whether or not regrouping is necessary. Children should then do the regrouping procedure and complete the subtraction for that particular place. Only after necessary regrouping and subtraction have been completed for a particular place value should the child move to the next place value in the problem. This sequence of inspection, regrouping, subtraction for each place helps to eliminate problems of unnecessary regrouping in problems where some place values require regrouping procedures and some do not.

Division is treated as a repeated-subtraction procedure. In this interpretation of division, a problem such as 6⟌36 is read as follows: "How many groups of six can be subtracted from a group of 36?" Problems involving remainders can be shown using repeated subtraction just as easily as

EXAMPLE 14.9

Solving 204 − 58 = _____ with Manipulatives

Step One: Show 204

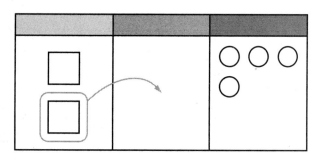

Step Four: Subtract eight ones

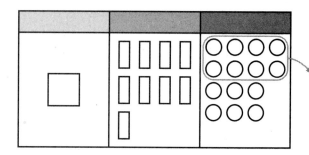

Step Two: Regroup one hundred as ten tens

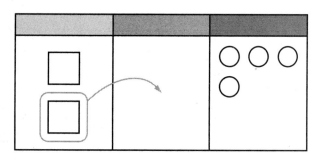

Step Five: Subtract five tens

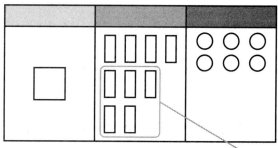

Step Three: Regroup one ten as ten ones

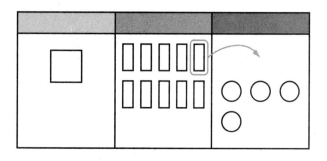

Step Six: Read the final answer

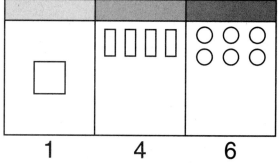

1   4   6

can problems without remainders. In fact, the repeated subtraction technique helps children to understand what is meant by a remainder in a division problem. Two problems are shown here. The first does not involve a remainder, while the second does involve a remainder. The first problem is $9\overline{)45}$.

1. Practice with the class showing numbers on the place-value board and counting backwards to a lower number. Emphasize the regrouping procedure that is used when counting backwards.
2. Show the number 45 on the place-value board, beginning in the ones place and moving to the tens place.
3. Read the following problems: "How many groups of nine cubes (sticks) are there in a total group of 45 cubes (sticks)? How many cubes (sticks) are going to be in each of the groups that are taken away?"
4. Have the children inspect the number of cubes (sticks) shown in the ones place on the place-value board. Ask if there are enough to be able to take away a group of nine.
5. Regroup one ten as ten ones. Ask if there are now enough cubes (sticks) to be able to take away a group of nine.
6. Take away a group of nine cubes or sticks and pile them where they can be easily located.
7. Continue to inspect, regroup, and subtract groups of nine until there is nothing left on the board.
8. To determine the answer to the problem, count the number of groups of nine that were subtracted. There should be five groups of nine (see Example 14.10).

In working with this procedure, children should regroup only when it is necessary so that a group of nine can be subtracted. They should not simply show forty-five ones and then subtract groups of nine from the pile. If forty-five ones are shown, concepts of place value are no longer being used. Probably the most difficult aspect of the repeated-subtraction procedure is to keep track of the piles of sticks or cubes that have been subtracted. Encourage children to designate a particular location where they will put their subtracted cubes or sticks.

The second type of problem involves a remainder. In this case, the problem is handled in exactly the same manner as a problem without a remainder, but the meaning of those objects that are left after all of the subtractions have been completed is considered. The problem shown here is $7\overline{)61}$.

1. Practice with the class showing numbers on the place-value board and counting backwards from each number to a lower number. Emphasize the regrouping procedure that is used when counting backwards.
2. Show the number 60 on the place-value board, beginning in the ones place and moving to the tens place.
3. Read the following problems: "How many groups of seven cubes (sticks) are there in a total group of sixty-one cubes (sticks)? How many cubes (sticks) are going to be in each of the groups that are taken away?"
4. Have the children inspect the number of cubes (sticks) shown in the ones place on the place-value board. Ask if there are enough to be able to take away a group of seven.
5. Regroup one ten as ten ones. Ask if there are now enough cubes (sticks) to be able to take away a group of seven.
6. Take away a group of seven cubes (sticks) and pile them where they can be easily located.
7. Continue to inspect, regroup, and subtract groups of seven until it is impossible to subtract another group of seven. At this point, children should see that there are five cubes left. Ask children if it is possible to subtract a group of seven. Discuss with them the idea that the number remaining is less than seven and so its units will remain there on the board as only part of a group of seven.
8. To determine the answer to the problem, count the number of groups of seven that were subtracted. There should be eight groups of seven with five left over, or eight groups with a remainder of five (see Example 14.11).

In working with division problems, remind children to continually look to see if it is necessary to regroup or whether they can subtract more than one group before they must regroup one ten for ten ones or one hundred for ten tens.

EXAMPLE 14.10

Solving 9)45 with Manipulatives

Step One: Show 45

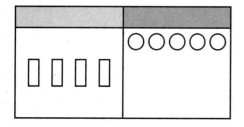

Step Two: Regroup one ten as ten ones

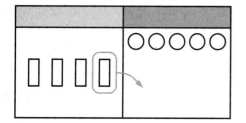

Step Three: Subtract one set of nine

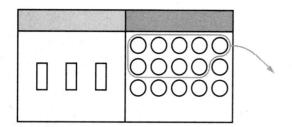

Step Four: Regroup one ten as ten ones

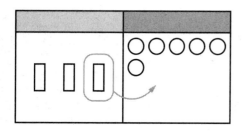

Step Five: Subtract a second set of nine

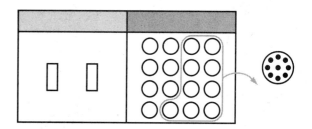

Step Six: Regroup one ten as ten ones

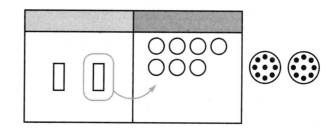

Step Seven: Subtract a third set of nine

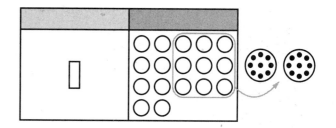

Step Eight: Regroup one ten as ten ones

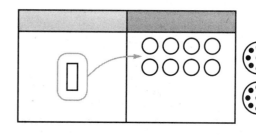

EXAMPLE 14.10 Continued

Step Nine: Subtract a fourth set of nine

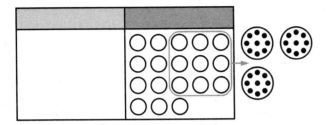

Step Eleven: Count the number of groups subtracted to obtain the answer

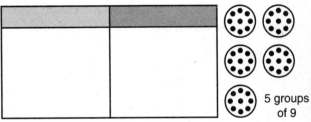

5 groups of 9

Step Ten: Subtract a Fifth set of nine

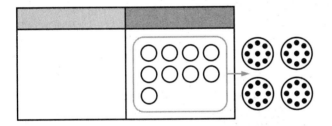

EXAMPLE 14.11

Solving 7√61 with Manipulatives

Step One: Show 61

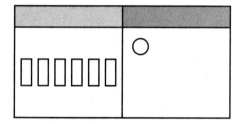

Step Four: Regroup one ten as ten ones

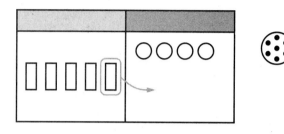

Step Two: Regroup one ten as ten ones

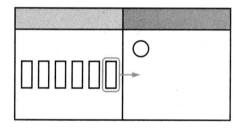

Step Five: Subtract a second set of seven

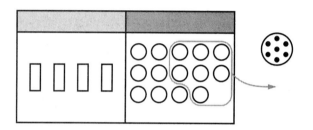

Step Three: Subtract one set of seven

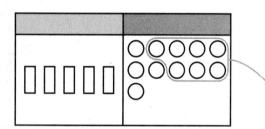

Step Six: Subtract a third set of seven

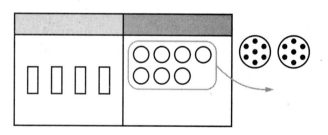

Step Seven: Regroup one ten as ten ones

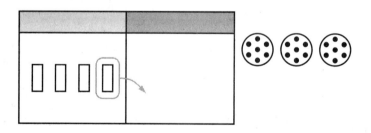

EXAMPLE 14.11 Continued

Step Eight: Subtract a fourth set of seven

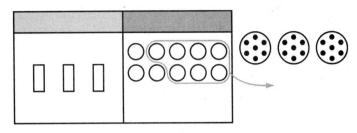

Step Nine: Regroup one ten as ten ones

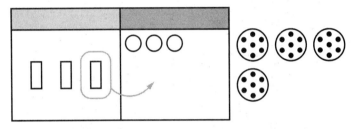

Step Ten: Subtract a fifth set of seven

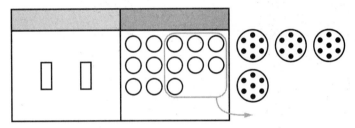

Step Eleven: Regroup one ten as ten ones

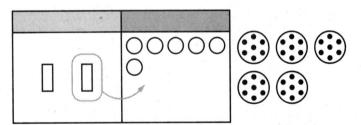

Step Twelve: Subtract a sixth set of seven

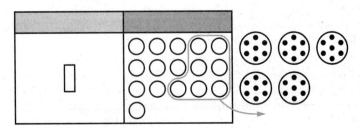

EXAMPLE 14.11 Continued

Step Thirteen: Subtract a seventh set of seven

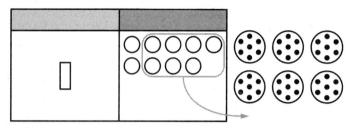

Step Fourteen: Regroup one ten as ten ones

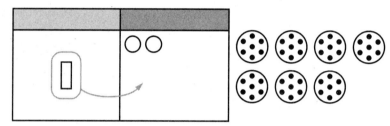

Step Fifteen: Subtract an eighth set of seven

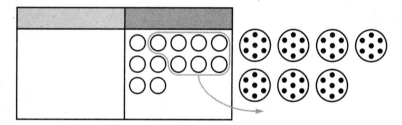

Step Sixteen: Determine the final answer

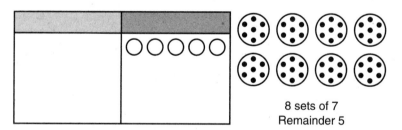

8 sets of 7
Remainder 5

Both of the division problems considered had only a single-digit divisor. If double-digit divisors are used, as in a problem such as $21\overline{)63}$, children should be reminded that they do not need to subtract 21 ones, but can much more easily subtract one from the ones place and then go to the tens place and subtract two tens.

Manipulatives for Developing Concepts of Fractions

Manipulative materials can be used effectively in developing concepts of fractions such as what a fraction represents, comparative sizes of fractions, and equivalent fractions. Pattern blocks, among

LEARNING ACTIVITY 81

Manipulatives with Subtraction or Division

Purpose: The purpose of this activity is to develop a teaching strategy using manipulative materials with subtraction or division.

Procedure:

1. Select a chapter on subtraction or division from a third-grade-mathematics textbook. Select one type of problem from the chapter: for example, a subtraction problem involving a three-digit number minus a two-digit number without regrouping (146 − 32 = _____) or a basic-division fact such as 5⌐45.
2. Plan a strategy for teaching the selected topic that shows only the first stage of the four-stage teaching strategy.
3. Present your teaching strategy as a lesson plan that includes a topic, objectives, materials, a procedure, and an evaluation.
4. Try your strategy with a group of five or six third-grade children.
   a. How did the children respond to the strategy?
   b. How would you rate the success of your strategy?
   c. What changes would you suggest to make your teaching strategy more effective?

---

other materials, are especially helpful in teaching fractional concepts. Pattern blocks consist of five different geometric shapes in five colors. Use pattern blocks in developing a concept of fractions, written notation for fractions, and equivalent fractions.

Using Pattern Blocks to Develop Fractional Concepts and Notation. Pattern blocks consist of yellow hexagons, blue rhomboids (diamonds), green triangles, red trapezoids, orange squares, and white rhomboids that are narrower and more elongated than the blue. The yellow, blue, green, and red shapes are fractional parts of one another and so can be used to explore the concept of fractional parts. The yellow hexagon can be covered by a variety of other shapes (see Example 14.12).

Once children have had the opportunity to find as many ways as possible to cover the hexagon, focus on those possibilities that use only one color of pattern block to cover the hexagon: for example, two red trapezoids, three blue rhomboids, six green triangles. Discuss with the children that these blocks are not only the same in color but in all possible ways. For example, the trapezoids are red, wood, and have the same size, thickness, shape, odor, weight, and texture. The purpose of this discussion is to establish that all fractional parts

must be identical if they are to be considered fractions. After demonstrating how all of the parts are the same, develop the notation for writing fractions. For example, a red trapezoid is "one out of two parts," which can be written as ½ (read at first as one out of two parts.) See Example 14.13 for the development of written notation.

Using Pattern Blocks to Develop Concepts of Equivalent Fractions. Equivalent fractions can be developed using pattern blocks by beginning with the yellow hexagon and finding its fractional parts. For example, trapezoids represent one-half, blue rhomboids represent one-third, and green triangles represent one-sixth. Once these fractional parts have been established, students should be encouraged to explore further, finding that one red trapezoid can be covered by three green triangles. One-half can be shown as equivalent to three-sixths: the blue rhomboid that represents one-third can be covered by two green triangles representing two-sixths. The equivalence of the fractions one-third and two-sixths is therefore developed. See Example 14.13 for illustrations of this and other examples.

Using Pattern Blocks in Ordering Fractions. Ordering fractions can be difficult for children because the order of fractions is contrary to what they

EXAMPLE 14.12

Using Pattern Blocks to Show Fractional Parts

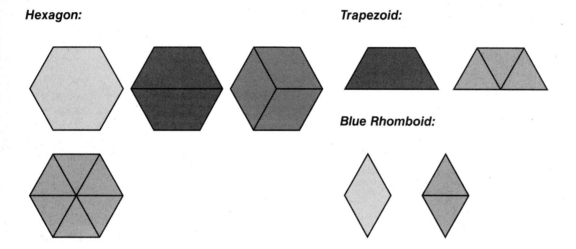

Hexagon:

Trapezoid:

Blue Rhomboid:

know about whole numbers. When considering whole numbers, five is larger than four, six is larger than nine, and seven is smaller than ten. In working with fractions, however, the larger the denominator of the fraction, the smaller the quantity represented by the fraction. Therefore, one-fifth is smaller than one-fourth, one-sixth is smaller than one-ninth, and one-seventh is larger than one-tenth.

By using the pattern block, children easily can see the order of fractions through the size of the blocks involved and, therefore, can quickly order fractions by size. The blocks make it easy to order both unitary fractions—those with one in the numerator—or nonunitary fractions such as two-thirds (see Example 14.14).

Begin by establishing the fractional quantities on the basis of the yellow hexagon. Once the fractional names of each of the blocks are established, have children determine which is larger: one-half or one-third. Repeat the same procedure using pairs of fractions and then using fractions

grouped by threes. For example: "Order from largest to smallest the fractions one-third, one-half, and one-sixth." Once children are able to order unitary fractions easily, then they can be asked problems such as the following: "Place in order from largest to smallest the fractions two-thirds, five-sixths, and one-half (see Example 14.15).

Pattern blocks make it easy to develop a concept of fractions, to develop a concept of equivalent fractions, and to order fractions. There are a few cautions in developing ideas of fractions with children. First, be certain children develop the concept that all of the parts must be identical for the parts to be considered fractional parts. Second, introduce terminology after students have developed the concept rather than before. Once children understand that one-half means one of two identical parts, the terms *numerator* and *denominator* can be developed. Finally, allow students to discover ideas for themselves, rather than giving rules that are to be followed.

EXAMPLE 14.13

Developing Equivalent Fractions with Pattern Blocks

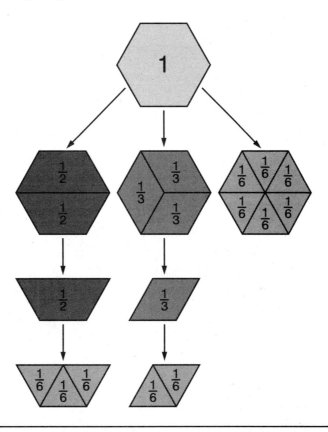

EXAMPLE 14.14

Ordering Unitary Fractions with Pattern Blocks

Not Ordered:

Note: All fractional parts are based on relationship to the yellow hexagon

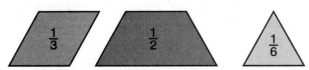

Ordered Largest to Smallest:

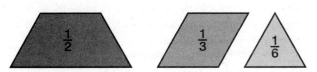

EXAMPLE 14.15

Ordering Nonunitary Fractions with Pattern Blocks

Not Ordered:

Note: All fractional parts are based on relationship to the yellow hexagon

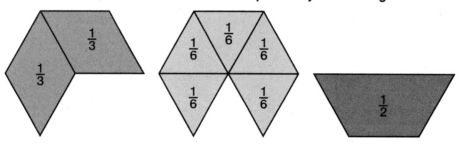

Ordered from Largest to Smallest:

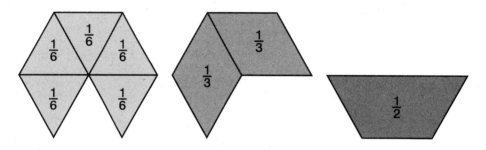

USING CALCULATORS AND COMPUTERS IN THE CLASSROOM

Calculators and computers provide additional means for children to explore number and number concepts and to practice skills that have been developed. The computer and the calculator should not become a substitute for hands-on experiences, but should enhance those experiences.

Using Calculators in the Classroom

Davies University Arithmetic, published in 1864, contains the following problem for students to solve:

Divide 4715714937149387 by 17493.

In 1864, when all computation was done by hand, the ability to solve this type of problem was probably an important skill. Fortunately, today's textbooks do not contain problems in which a sixteen-digit number is divided by a five-digit number. Those textbooks do, however, contain long division problems of the type 44651 divided by 312. Any adult faced with either of these problems is far more likely to reach for a calculator or a computer than for a pencil and paper. Calculators are a part of daily reality and children need to learn to use calculators in appropriate situations.

The use of calculators in the classroom often raises fears that children will not learn to compute mentally or with pencil and paper and, therefore, will be at a complete loss if left without a calculator. This kind of fear can be quickly allayed if calculators are made an integral part of a total program rather than an addition to a program or the total program in themselves.

Within the total quantitative program for children, three types of computation should be consid-

LEARNING ACTIVITY 82

Manipulatives with Fractions

Purpose: The purpose of this activity is to develop a teaching strategy using manipulative materials with fractions.

Procedure:
1. Select one of the following topics dealing with fractions:
   a. Concept of a fraction
   b. Recording fractions numerically
   c. Equivalent fractions
   d. Ordering fractions
2. Plan a strategy for teaching the selected topic to third-grade children. The topics of concept of a fraction, equivalent fractions, and ordering fractions will show only the first stage of the four-stage strategy. Recording fractions numerically will

show the first two stages of the four-stage strategy.
3. Present your teaching strategy as a lesson plan including a topic, objectives, materials, a procedure, and an evaluation.
4. Try your strategy with a group of five or six third-grade children.
   a. How did the children respond to the strategy?
   b. How would you rate the success of your strategy?
   c. What changes would you suggest to make your teaching strategy more effective?

LEARNING ACTIVITY 83

Developing a Four-Stage Strategy for Mathematics Teaching

Purpose: The purpose of this activity is to develop a teaching strategy for one week of mathematics teaching that includes all four stages of teaching.

Procedure:
1. Select a topic from a third-grade mathematics textbook or from a course of study for the third-grade level. The topic should be very limited. Addition of two two-digit numbers with regrouping is an appropriate topic. Addition itself is too broad for a one-week time period.

2. Plan a strategy for teaching the topic that shows all four stages in teaching and that uses five class periods. One of the stages will last for two days of teaching time.
3. For each day of teaching, include the stage that is being used, as well as all of the necessary information included in a typical lesson plan: a topic, objectives, materials, a procedure, and an evaluation.

---

ered. First, children should be helped to understand that there are some situations in which mental computation will be the quickest and easiest way of doing a problem. No one should have to pull out a calculator or a piece of paper to decide how many cookies each of three people will receive if there are nine cookies in all. Second, children should be helped to determine when a pencil and paper will be effective and efficient in solving a

problem. For children, a problem such as $42 - 9$ can be solved easily with a pencil and paper. And, third, children should know when a calculator is going to be helpful. When adding columns of numbers or solving long-division problems, the calculator is an appropriate tool.

Calculators can be appropriately used in the classroom in a variety of ways. Some of the uses of calculators are as follows:

1. solving computation problems in which the calculator is the most effective and efficient means of solving the problem;
2. solving practical problems in which the numbers are too large for children to easily handle —for example, consumer problems such as trying to determine the actual cost for having a Halloween party;
3. providing estimates of answers prior to actual computation;
4. checking answers to classwork and homework problems to get immediate feedback on accuracy;
5. solving a variety of problems of the same type and looking for patterns within the numbers— for example, investigating palindromes in which numbers read the same from right to left and left to right;
6. determining correct answers in board games involving computation skills;
7. checking the accuracy of predictions made during activities;
8. providing immediate feedback as basic facts are learned—children can state the solution to a basic-fact problem and then use the calculator to determine immediately whether the answer is correct or incorrect;
9. providing motivation for young children since calculators are fun to use and can allow any child to be successful; and
10. allowing children to create and solve their own problems without constraints on the size of the quantities involved.

Using Computers in the Classroom

Although the computer can be used as a calculator, the computer goes far beyond the calculator in its potential uses. In particular, computers can function in five ways in which calculators cannot. First, computers can help the teacher to present difficult concepts through the use of pictures and graphics. Concepts from geometry, in particular, easily can be shown and investigated through computer graphics. Second, computers can store and allow the manipulation of large amounts of data. As children engage in practical problem solving, the computer can assist in the collection and display of information. Third, computers can provide unlimited numbers of individualized lessons so that the children can be presented with review, practice, and enrichment lessons as they are needed. Fourth, the computer can put students in touch with both people and information quickly through data banks and electronic mail systems. And, fifth, the computer can present children with complex problem-solving activities through the use of simulations and games.

In using computers in the classroom, it is important to first decide on the objectives for the lesson and then to look for the software that will allow the objectives to be reached. Computer software can be classified into four categories: drill and practice, tutorial, simulation, and educational game.

Drill-and-Practice Programs. Drill-and-practice programs give extensive repetitive work that reinforces previously learned concepts. Good programs of this type are not merely workbook pages transferred to a computer monitor. Instead, a good drill-and-practice program imitates one-to-one work between the student and the teacher. A good drill-and-practice program should

1. focus clearly on appropriate instructional objectives,
2. state the problem or question so that the student knows exactly what to do,
3. refrain from giving irrelevant cues to the student,
4. provide the student with appropriate advice, tools, or prerequisite information so that a response can be given,
5. give immediate feedback for the learner's response,
6. provide remedial information as needed,
7. move to easier or more difficult levels of questions as the learner's responses indicate, and
8. provide continued practice until the learner demonstrates mastery of the objective under consideration.

Tutorials. Tutorials are programs that function in a role similar to that of a teacher or textbook. The tutorial program explains information or concepts to the learner. In essence, the tutorial is a more sophisticated version of a drill-and-practice program. However, the tutorial differs from the drill-and-practice program in that it presents new information rather than practices what is already known by the student. Many tutorial programs engage in a dialogue with the student as the information is presented so the student is actively involved in the learning process. The advantage of the tutorial program over the traditional textbook is that the tutorial provides immediate, interactive feedback for the student. Additionally, the tutorial can focus attention more precisely on a single concept than can the traditional textbook. And, finally, the tutorial can present the new information through the use of animated graphics or an interactive video format.

Simulations. Simulations are sophisticated programs that provide opportunities to apply mathematical skills in interesting and practical situations. The simulation attempts to put the student into a real-life situation in which choices are presented and the student makes decisions. The student must also face the consequences of those decisions. Simulations, however, do have the problem of requiring a great deal of reading and a long attention span. Additionally, simulations may not provide the amount of practice the teacher desires —either of mathematics skills or of problem-solving skills.

Educational Games. Educational games are programs that provide specific types of drills or test cognitive skills in a gamelike atmosphere that often resembles arcade games. The educational game generally provides a painless learning format in an enjoyable atmosphere. Because of the format and the enjoyment, educational games can be highly motivating for children. One problem with educational games is that they often require quick reaction times and good hand-eye coordination. Children who do not possess these skills may feel frustration in playing such games.

Calculators and computers have a definite role to play in the quantitative curriculum. The calculator can be particularly useful in enhancing the computational aspect of the curriculum. The computer not only reviews and teaches, but also presents problem-solving situations that encourage thinking in students. Computers can also provide enjoyable learning experiences through games.

SUMMARY

The National Council of Teachers of Mathematics has made a number of suggestions for the quantitative curriculum of the early childhood program. In particular, NCTM has suggested that students learn concepts as well as skills, that children become actively involved in the learning of mathematics, that application of mathematics concepts and skills be emphasized, that the program include the appropriate use of calculators, and especially that the quantitative curriculum focus on problem solving. These new areas of emphasis also mean that students engage in less drill, practice, and rote memorization of procedures and more learning for understanding.

Active involvement in learning means the use of manipulative materials in the classroom. In particular, computation skills such as addition, subtraction, multiplication, and division, as well as concepts of fractions, can be approached through the use of manipulatives such as Unifix Cubes, popsicle sticks, and pattern blocks.

The use of technology in the classroom means that children must be taught not only to use calculators, but also when calculators are more effective and efficient than mental computation or pencil and paper computation. Technology use also extends to the use of computers in the classroom. Computers can be used for drill and practice in order to help children master certain computation skills; but they can also be used for tutorials, simulations, and games.

Vocabulary Terms

Calculator: hand-held electronic device used in computation.
Computer: an electronic device that has computational possibilities and also allows for developing and running programs designed for practice, tutorial, simulation, or games.
Drill-and-Practice Program: a computer program that provides children with individual practice of a computation skill.
Educational Game: a computer program that allows children to use previously learned skills and concepts in a game format.

LEARNING ACTIVITY 84

Evaluating a Mathematics Textbook

Purpose: The purpose of this activity is to evaluate a third-grade-mathematics textbook for the type of teaching strategies in use.

Procedure:

1. Select a single chapter from a mathematics textbook for the third-grade level.
2. Carefully read through the chapter, giving special attention to the following areas:
   a. suggested teaching techniques,
   b. suggested uses of calculators and computers, and
   c. the development of problem-solving skills.

3. Discuss the levels of the teaching strategy that are represented by the teaching suggestions given in the textbook. Which levels are represented? Which levels are not represented?
4. Discuss the suggested uses of computers and calculators in the textbook.
5. Discuss the use of problem-solving skills in the textbook.
6. Discuss what could be done to more effectively implement the four-stage teaching strategy, problem solving, and the use of computers and calculators with the textbook.

LEARNING ACTIVITY 85

Mathematics Activity File

Purpose: The purpose of this activity is to develop a file of activities that could be used in the teaching of third-grade mathematics.

Procedure:

1. Research the kinds of topics that are generally included at the third-grade level in textbooks and in the course of study for mathematics.
2. Develop an activity file of ideas for teaching those topics. Include in the file the following kinds of ideas:
   a. activities using concrete materials for concept development,
   b. activities using concrete materials for skill development,
   c. ideas for learning centers,
   d. ideas for mathematics-fair projects,
   e. ideas for bulletin boards,
   f. ideas for helping students connect mathematics in school to mathematics in daily living,
   g. ideas for using problem-solving skills in mathematics,
   h. ideas for showing the role of men, women, and various cultures in mathematics,
   i. ideas for games—board games, small-group games, whole-class games,
   j. reviews of computer programs appropriate to the curriculum,
   k. activities for using calculators in the classroom, and
   l. ideas for developing career possibilities in mathematics.

Equivalent Fractions: two or more fractions that represent the same quantities: ½, ²/₄, ⁴/₈, and so on.
Manipulative: concrete and generally three-dimensional object that can be used to represent numerical quantities.
Number: the quantity represented by a particular numeral.
Numeral: the symbol used to represent a particular quantity.

Ordering Fractions: placing fractional quantities into sequence from largest to smallest or smallest to largest.
Pattern Blocks: concrete objects in a variety of geometric shapes that are used in working with patterning and with fractions.
Place Value: the underlying pattern of a system of numeration that allows the location of a numeral to determine its total value.

Place-Value Board: a device used with Unifix Cubes or popsicle sticks that visually demonstrates the place-value location of the objects in use.

Quantitative Curriculum: a term used to denote the curriculum that includes both mathematics and arithmetic.

Regrouping: the process of exchanging ten tens for one hundred or ten ones for one ten, and so on, as a part of computation.

Simulation Program: a computer program that presents children with real-life situations and enhances children's problem-solving skills.

Stage-One Lesson: the first stage in the four-stage teaching strategy in which only concrete materials are used so that children develop a concept of the computational skill taught.

Stage-Two Lesson: the second stage in the four-stage teaching strategy in which children are introduced to the recording of problems by using drawings and diagrams.

Stage-Three Lesson: the third stage in the four-stage teaching strategy in which children are introduced to recording using numerals.

Stage-Four Lesson: the final stage in the four-stage teaching strategy in which children solve problems numerically.

Tutorial Program: a computer program that teaches new material to children and so functions as a teacher.

Unifix Cubes: interlocking plastic cubes in a variety of colors that are used for teaching concepts of quantity, as well as place value and computation.

Study Questions

1. What changes has the National Council of Teachers of Mathematics suggested for the quantitative program in the elementary school?

2. How does the four-stage teaching strategy discussed here differ from traditional teaching of arithmetic?

3. How does the concept of the quantitative curriculum differ from that of teaching arithmetic?

4. How do the four stages of the teaching strategy differ from one another?

5. A third-grade mathematics text suggests that the teacher demonstrate using popsicle sticks how to solve a problem such as $7 \times 5 =$ _____ then go immediately to the written format. Which stages of the strategy are not represented? What would you do to include them?

6. A teacher complains that the children in her class cannot solve a problem such as $196 + 85$ = _____ accurately even though he has done at least ten problems of that type on the chalkboard to show how to solve them. What suggestions would you make to this teacher?

7. How can manipulatives like Unifix Cubes, popsicle sticks, and pattern blocks be used to help children develop the concepts that underlie the various computation skills?

8. How can the calculator be used to enhance the program of the quantitative curriculum?

9. What are the four major categories of programs available for the computer? How do these programs differ from one another?

10. What factors should be taken into account when selecting a drill-and-practice program for the third-grade classroom?

CHAPTER 15

Strategies for Teaching Science

Chapter Objectives

On completion of this chapter, you should be able to

1. discuss the three areas of science that should be parts of the defined curriculum,

2. discuss the kind of content that is appropriate for the defined curriculum at the third-grade level,

3. identify and discuss traditional topics that are inappropriate to the third-grade-level child,

4. identify and discuss those topics that are motivational in the defined curriculum,

5. identify the process skills that are most appropriate to the defined curriculum,

6. discuss and develop activities that can be used to develop science process skills,

7. discuss the use of science process skills in the development of science-content information,

8. discuss content areas that are appropriate for the defined curriculum at the third-grade level,

9. discuss the use of a semantic map for introducing a science-textbook chapter or unit,

10. discuss the use of a semantic map for reviewing a science-textbook chapter or unit,

11. plan an appropriate science lesson for the third-grade level using a hands-on activity, and

12. plan for the use of a science textbook at the third-grade level.

Why is grass green? Why is the sky blue? How does a car work? What causes a boat to float? Where did all the dinosaurs go? What is it like on the Moon? Do sharks eat all the time? How do birds fly? Why do teeth fall out, then new ones grow? How does spaghetti turn into bones and blood? How come a magnet picks up paper clips? What makes dirt? Where do rocks come from? Where do birds go when they fly south? What happens to butterflies in the winter? Where does the salt go when it dissolves in water? Why is the ocean salty?

The list of questions that children ask is endless. If those questions are really considered, they have one thing in common. Everyone of the questions listed here and most of those that are typical of children are science-oriented questions. Children want to know about their world. They are interested in those topics that adults classify as science. Consequently, it is not the teacher's problem to interest children in science, but to maintain that interest.

Unfortunately, much of what passes under the guise of science for children seems to have been designed to destroy the natural interest that children have. Facts are emphasized. Terms are defined in isolation. Children read about science rather than practice science as a way of thinking. In order for school science to maintain the curiosity that is natural to the young child, the nature of science must be considered. And, the nature of science must form the basis for the teaching of science.

THE NATURE OF SCIENCE

Most high-school students once memorized a definition of science. In that definition, science was considered to be an organized body of knowledge. That definition focused on the content of science, the stuff that has been learned over the centuries as the scientist sought to explain and describe the workings of the world. It is, however, only a partial definition. Science is definitely the content information that has been developed over the centuries. But science is also the means by which that content information is learned. Science includes the techniques that are used to gain information. These techniques are known as the scientific processes. Content and process are two-thirds of the totality

of science. The other third of science, which completes the picture, is the scientific attitudes. These are the characteristic attitudes of the scientist. Science at the third-grade level can and should develop all three areas of science. In *Project 2061: Science for All Americans,* the American Association for the Advancement of Science called this combination of content, process, and attitudes *scientific literacy.* So that scientific literacy can be developed in children, the defined curriculum should include all three of these areas.

Content

Science content is the body of knowledge that has been developed over the centuries by the scientific community. The body of knowledge is so broad that the areas chosen must be selected with great care. The basis for the selection of that content is not the inclinations of the teacher or the dictates of the scientific community, but the characteristics of the child. The body of content includes both appropriate and inappropriate topics. Consequently, the content must be carefully selected so that it is appropriate to the cognitive development of the third-grade child. In general, appropriate content is content that the child can develop through the use of concrete materials. Science content that is inappropriate is generally learned only through reading, listening to the teacher, or watching films and filmstrips.

Process

Science process skills are the techniques used by the scientist in gaining information. In essence, these are the skills and techniques that the scientist in the laboratory or field uses as he or she gains new information about the world. Translated into the classroom, the science process skills are the techniques that children use in gaining information on a first-hand basis from their activities. There is a wide variety of process skills, from the observation to the true experiment in which variables are controlled and hypotheses are tested. Because of the wide variety of process skills available, care must be taken to select those skills that are most appropriate to the child's developmental level. Two sets of process skills are appropriate. The first of these sets has already been considered as a part of the combined curriculum. The basic processes are as appropriate at the third-grade level as they are at the first- and second-grade levels. The second set of process skills contains the causal processes. The causal processes include predicting, concluding, inferring, cause-and-effect, and interaction and systems. These are most effectively used by children who have developed or are making the transition to an understanding of true causality. All of the causal processes should be introduced at the third-grade level. The type of causal relationships considered first should involve cause-and-effect relationships that are immediate in space and time. After those causal relationships have been developed, students should be introduced to those cause-and-effect relationships in which the cause and effect are separated in time or in which a part of the system is not readily observable.

Attitudes

The scientific attitudes should also be developed at the third-grade level. Scientific attitudes include qualities such as objectivity, willingness to suspend judgment, skepticism, respect for the environment, and a positive approach to failure. These attitudes are the modes of thought that are said to characterize the scientifically literate individual.

Objectivity is the attitude of looking at the many sides of a controversial issue before making a decision. This is probably the most difficult scientific attitude to teach or learn. It is difficult for two reasons. First, adults tend to have developed opinions on most topics and consider their opinions to be correct. Consequently, it is difficult for many adults to listen to or present information about the other side of an issue. Second, although children at the third-grade level are declining in egocentricity, they are still egocentric to some degree. This characteristic makes it difficult for them to listen to and compare the various sides of an issue. However, the child at the concrete operational period is decreasing in egocentricity and the child of eight or nine is beginning to listen to other points of view. Therefore, it is an appropriate time for the teacher to model objectivity as a scientific attitude.

Willingness to suspend judgment might be considered an outgrowth of objectivity. In essence, willingness to suspend judgment means waiting until all of the evidence is in before making a decision. This attitude can easily be modeled when

small groups working in a guided-discovery setting arrive at differing conclusions. The results can be collected, the data considered, and the textbook consulted before the teacher aids the students in developing a final conclusion.

The next scientific attitude is skepticism. A skeptic is an individual who questions all things. Children should be helped to develop a skeptical attitude about many things in their environment. Skepticism can be developed by the teacher asking students where information could be found, whether certain ideas are correct or incorrect, whether they could check on the information that they are giving. At the third-grade level, peer pressure is beginning to enter the picture and a skeptical attitude can help children question some of the kinds of acts advocated by the peer group.

Respect for the environment is also a scientific attitude. In practice, this can mean going on a nature walk and selecting one or two leaves from a plant for a leaf collection rather than stripping an entire tree, putting insects in a living insect zoo rather than in a killing jar, or raising tadpoles and then returning the adult frogs to the natural habitat.

The final scientific attitude considered here is a positive approach to failure. Although this sounds as if students are to be happy if they fail on a test or project, it actually refers back to making predictions as part of an activity. The concept behind a positive approach to failure is that, even if the prediction is incorrect, the student has still learned from the activity. Not only has the student learned from the activity, but he or she also has been exposed to the idea that scientists often do not know what will happen when they conduct an experiment or go into the field to observe.

Scientific attitudes are not taught directly to the students, but are modeled by the teacher during the science lesson and throughout the school day. The scientific attitudes are modeled at grade levels earlier than the third grade but, with the exceptions of curiosity and respect for the environment, should not be expected of younger children. The reason for this is that the attitudes require the ability to look at ideas from a variety of viewpoints. Children cannot be expected to exhibit objectivity, skepticism, and other scientific attitudes until they experience the decrease in egocentricity that occurs as concrete operational thought develops.

CONTENT FOR THE DEFINED CURRICULUM

A balance of content, process, and attitude should be present in the defined curriculum. This balance means the inclusion of content appropriate to the child at the third-grade level. Before the necessary cognitive structures are present, the teaching of science content results in rote memorization of quickly forgotten material. In order to assist in the selection of appropriate content, the following list of criteria can be applied.

1. The topic should allow the students to use concrete materials in investigating.
2. The topic should allow interaction with real materials rather than with models or similar items.
3. The topic should allow students to use a variety of science process skills.
4. The topic should be directly experienced by the child or based on past direct experience.
5. The topic should allow for direct observation of all phenomena associated with the content to be learned.
6. The topic should allow for the use of mathematical skills in a way that is appropriate rather than contrived.
7. The topic should allow investigations that will aid children in understanding the environment that they are experiencing.

If these criteria are used in the selection of content, it quickly becomes evident that they are most consistent with the physical sciences. Magnets, simple machines, sound, bulbs and batteries, pendulums, matter, physical changes, mixtures, solutions, and the effects of heat on matter are all fully consistent with the criteria.

A second category of science topics that are appropriate come from the biological sciences. The biological sciences are sometimes difficult because of the length of time between cause-and-effect relationships or because of the invisibility of phenomena such as the effect of fertilizers on growth. Additionally, the biological sciences have the tendency to deteriorate into "show-and-tell" lessons in which kinds of animals are named or parts of plants are identified. The biological sciences also pose problems because of experimentation with plants and animals. Children should not be involved in activities that cause harm to living creatures. Insects can be studied far more effectively as living creatures in terraria or insect zoos than they can if pinned to a board and observed in preserved form. Plants are far more interesting when growing than when being pushed toward death by lack of water or sunlight. However, despite the difficulties of teaching the biological sciences, there are many biology topics that are appropriate for the defined curriculum.

The final category of sciences is the earth-space sciences. This category has some topics that fit the criteria listed above, but has many more that do not fit the criteria. For example, investigations of soil and water or of rocks and minerals do fit the criteria.

Some topics that are traditionally included in the science curriculum for the young child are not appropriate for children and should be eliminated from the third-grade science curriculum. The first of these topics is the cause of the four seasons. Such a topic appears to be within the abilities of children because it is experienced, but one needs to consider the topic from a slightly different viewpoint. In order to comprehend this topic, the child must first comprehend that the Earth is a planet that is spinning on an axis while moving through space in an elliptical orbit around the Sun. Not one of these ideas is a concept that can be developed concretely through the manipulation of materials. Indeed, the only ways to consider such concepts are by using models in which size and distance relationships cannot generally be shown, or through reading and listening. Materials cannot be manipulated. Factors cannot be changed to determine their effects.

A second category of inappropriate concepts is causes of weather. This is not to say that the third grader cannot set up a weather station with a thermometer and child-constructed anemometer, barometer, wind vane, and rain gauge. Taking measurements, recording observations, and determining a weather forecast that can be checked against what actually occurs is appropriate. Weather is an appropriate topic as long as it involves observing weather conditions, which allows students to use the processes of observing, communicating, using numbers, and predicting. The relationship of wind to uneven heating of the Earth's surface, the causes of fronts, and the causes of changes in barometric pressure all are inappropriate topics because they rely on invisible factors and on cause and effect, which cannot be manipulated by the child. Determining the cause of weather and attempting to relate conditions on the Earth to the development and passage of weather fronts is inappropriate.

A third area of inappropriate content is the structure of the Earth and the processes that cause changes in the surface of the Earth. Such processes occur over extended periods of time—geological time—and so are not directly observable. The structure of the Earth is not directly observable. In fact, it has never been directly observed, only inferred from indirect evidence. Such content cannot be comprehended by the child, only memorized.

Gases, including air, are a fourth inappropriate topic. The child at early concrete operations is tied to concrete objects and direct sensory input if content is to be comprehended. Consider air for a moment. To us, it is odorless, colorless, tasteless, soundless, and silent. The five senses cannot give direct experience with air. Other gases have similar characteristics and so cause similar problems of observability. Within the study of matter, solids and liquids are excellent topics, while gases are inappropriate.

Other inappropriate topics are chemical changes and the concept of the atom. The results of a chemical change such as rusting or burning easily can be seen. The problem arises when explanations for such changes are attempted. The explanation involves the idea of invisible particles interacting with other invisible particles. As with the topic of gases, such interactions are "unseeable" and require the use of abstract thought for understanding.

Finally, climates of the Earth are an inappropriate topic. Children can become familiar with the characteristics of their own environment through direct experience, but the concept of the Arctic or Antarctic is impossible for a child who has never seen snow. Similarly, a child who lives in an area of distinct seasons may have difficulty with the concept of a tropical area in which seasons do not occur.

There are two additional topics that should be considered as problematic. These topics are inappropriate according to the listed criteria but should probably never be removed from the curriculum

for the young child because of their motivational qualities. The two topics are dinosaurs and space.

From the viewpoint of the cognitive level of the child in third grade, dinosaurs is an inappropriate topic. The real object no longer exists on the Earth. The student cannot manipulate materials to investigate the effect of changes on those materials. Direct observation of dinosaurs and other extinct creatures is impossible, and the study of dinosaurs does not directly contribute to the child's understanding of the environment that is being experienced. However, children love the names, the sizes, and the appearances of dinosaurs. Children who can barely pronounce their own names have words such as tyrannosaurus and apatasaurus on the tips of their tongues. Dinosaurs are inherently fascinating to children and, therefore, provide a definite motivational quality. It is this motivational quality that justifies the inclusion of dinosaurs in the curriculum even though the topic is not strictly appropriate. Some things, however, should not be considered in studying dinosaurs with young children. First, the time period involved is meaningless to children. Older teachers often report having students ask if there were any dinosaurs around when they were young. Obviously, the concept of millions of years is inconceivable to the young child. The idea of a fossil is appropriate for children, especially if fossils are available for handling. The formation of a fossil, because of the time period involved and the invisibility of the process, is not appropriate. Also inappropriate is the development of the concept that dinosaurs were horrible creatures ready to attack and kill anything on sight. There were predatory dinosaurs just as there were grazing dinosaurs. A better approach would be to foster an ecological perspective by having students compare dinosaur habits and habitats to those of currently existing animals. And, finally, the concept of extinction is inappropriate for children unless it is related to what is occurring with animals in today's world.

The second topic that is inappropriate developmentally but motivational in nature is space. A fascination with space seems to stem from films and from launches of the space shuttle. Children are excited by the adventures shown in films and the idea of traveling in space. As a developmentally appropriate topic, however, space does not fit the criteria listed previously. Still, there are some ideas from the topic that are appropriate for children. Children can be exposed to the names of the planets and the conditions on each of the planets, especially if they are compared to the Earth and the local area. Space can also be approached from a problem-solving viewpoint. Planning a trip to another planet is a problem-solving activity. Children enjoy planning a trip to Mars or Jupiter and can relate the items they would need to take with them to what they need in order to survive on Earth. In this way, the criterion of past experience is met. Also, the topic of space can be handled in a way that develops critical-thinking skills by comparing what is really known about space to films or stories.

TEACHING SCIENCE CONTENT THROUGH PROCESS SKILLS

Certain science process skills were considered as parts of the combined curriculum. Children learn to use observation, classification, numbers, space relations, communication, cause-and-effect, inference, conclusion, and prediction. These same process skills are used at the third-grade level as parts of the defined curriculum. At this point, however, the process skills are used more systematically in the collection and interpretation of data from activities.

The Basic Processes

The basic processes, including observation, using numbers, using space relations, communication, and classification, are used to gather information from activities. All third-grade students can learn to use these process skills: Average, gifted, or handicapped children use these processes easily. Children do, however, need to be instructed in how to use observation, how to record their information or communicate it to others in some form, how to measure or describe location, how to use their arithmetic skills, or how to classify. Consequently, activities in which children are asked to classify items on the basis of certain characteristics; measure length, width, weight, or temperature; or use their developing arithmetic skills to solve a particular problem should follow direct instruction. The teacher needs to use specific activities to develop

these skills rather than assume that children will naturally be able to work well with these basic processes in obtaining information.

The Causal Processes

The second category of process skills that will be used by the third-grade children in science are the causal processes. The causal processes are based on cause and effect and include inferences, predictions, conclusions, cause and effect, and interaction and systems. Since cause and effect is the basis for each of these process skills, some children at the third-grade level will experience difficulty in using the skills unless the cause and the effect are immediate in space and time. However, the child of third-grade level is moving toward an understanding of true cause and effect and so activities can begin to move the child from immediacy to greater distance or time between cause and effect. A new process skill introduced at this level, interaction and systems, helps the child to develop a greater understanding of cause and effect and a greater ability to use the causal processes.

Interaction and systems as a process consists of two aspects. The first aspect is the idea of a system. Simply defined, a system is all of the material objects necessary to cause something to happen or to construct something. For example, if a child is constructing a paper airplane, the parts of the system are the paper, the child's hands and fingers, and the table on which the child works. If the plane is flown, air, arm and shoulder, and the floor on which the plane lands are added to the system. The second aspect of interaction and systems is the idea of an interaction. Interactions occur when two parts of the system work together to cause something to happen. In the paper airplane example, the fingers and hand interact with the paper, the paper interacts with the air, the paper interacts with the floor, and the hands interact with the arm and shoulder. Together, interaction and systems begins to help develop a concept of cause and effect by asking the child to look carefully at an activity and to list the items that were needed and the items that interacted in some way. The child is helped to rule out extraneous factors and look logically at an activity.

Once the process skills have been fully developed, the child has all of the skills needed for

LEARNING ACTIVITY 86

Analysis of Science-Textbook Content

Purpose: The purpose of this activity is to analyze the appropriateness of content found in a science textbook for the third-grade level.

Procedure:

1. Select three chapters from the third-grade-level teacher edition of a science textbook. One chapter should deal with the physical sciences, one with the biological sciences, and one with the earth-space sciences.
2. List the concepts for each of the three chapters. These concepts are generally found at the begin-ning of the chapter but may also appear at the beginning of each separate lesson.
3. Using the criteria listed in this chapter for appropriate science content, determine whether the listed concepts are appropriate to the third-grade-level child's cognitive ability.
4. Discuss any changes that could be made to make the listed concepts more appropriate to the third-grade child.

---

conducting and interpreting a science activity. Activities in the science curriculum can be used both to enhance the process skills and to develop content information. Content-oriented activities such as an activity designed to determine what kinds of objects a magnet will pick up, can be analyzed to determine the kinds of process skills that were used in the activity. Even those activities that focus on content that is developmentally inappropriate for the child can be used to work with process skills. Children may not be able to comprehend the mechanism that allows a chemical change to occur, but they can observe, make inferences, predict, communicate their observations, develop a list of the parts of the system and the interactions that occurred, and use numbers to measure things such as time or temperature. Activities that are narrowly focused on a particular piece of content can be made more open ended through the use of process skills. Observations can be made, interaction and systems used, predictions developed, and results communicated during and after the activity.

After process skills can be used with some ease, they should be used to help in the development of science-content information.

Using Science Activities to Teach Content

The content-oriented activities that are selected should be geared to the developmental level of the students so that the content outcomes will be understood. Activities in which children use real objects, change factors to determine what will happen, collect observations or measurements, and draw a conclusion from collected results are fully appropriate. Once the activity has been conducted, it becomes the teacher's role to help the students to develop that content. A sequence of events that aids in developing the content from a science activity is as follows.

1. The students complete the activity, including the collection of any observations.
2. The teacher has the students briefly review what was done in the course of the activity and what they were trying to find out from the activity.
3. On the chalkboard or overhead projector, the teacher collects the observations or other kinds of data from the students. If a number of small groups were working on the same activity, the observations of each group are collected or tallied.
4. The teacher then asks the children to name the parts of the system and the interactions that occurred. After collecting the interactions, the children are asked to identify those interactions that are the "most important" to the activity.
5. Using questions, the teacher focuses the attention of the students on the interaction that was identified as most important and on the observations or data collected. The purpose of the

LEARNING ACTIVITY 87

Analysis of Science Process Skills in Textbook Activities

Purpose: The purpose of this activity is to determine the appropriateness of the science process skills used in activities found in a third-grade science textbook.

Procedure:
1. Select three activities from either a teacher edition or a student edition of a third-grade textbook. One activity should come from a chapter dealing with biological science, one from a chapter dealing with physical science, and one from a chapter dealing with earth-space science.

2. Carry out the three activities yourself.
3. After carrying out the activities, analyze them for the kinds of process skills that were used in the activity.
4. Would you consider each activity appropriate for the third grade in terms of the process skills used? Why or why not?
5. If the activity is inappropriate, what would you suggest be done to make the activity more appropriate?

---

questions is to discuss what occurred in the activity.
6. Using questions, the teacher helps the students to draw a conclusion from the activity. The conclusion is recorded on the chalkboard or overhead projector.
7. The validity of the conclusion is checked against the observations or other data and then against the textbook or other source of written information.
8. If the conclusion drawn from the activity is contrary to what is generally found, the teacher engages the students in a discussion of some of the reasons why their conclusion differs from that given by others. As often as possible, the reasons given are tested.

Selecting Appropriate Science-Content Activities

All content-oriented activities are not created equal. Some activities simply ask children to follow a set of directions in order to construct a particular model. Such activities are written as if the child were learning to cook rather than to work with science. By following a certain narrowly focused set of directions, the child simply confirms something that has already been read or discussed. Although activities in which models are constructed or in which a cookbook approach is used can be fun for children, the amount of learning is limited. A good science activity will meet the following criteria:

1. The activity is done prior to reading the content information.
2. The activity allows the child to make changes in some factor or factors as part of the investigation.
3. The activity allows for a discussion of results and the development of a conclusion.
4. The activity uses process skills that are developmentally appropriate to the children.
5. The activity has a content outcome that is developmentally appropriate to the children.
6. The activity encourages children to try to solve questions that arise during the course of the activity.

In applying these criteria, consider each of the following activities.

Activity One
In the following activity, you will find out that a magnet picks up some kinds of materials but not all kinds. The materials that a magnet picks up are made from iron or steel. So, a magnet will pick up a steel paper clip but will not pick up a plastic paper clip.

Materials: bar magnet, steel paper clip, plastic paper clip, penny, chalk, paper, iron nail, marble, styrofoam cup, scissors, rubber band

Procedure: Touch the end of the magnet to each of the objects. Decide whether the magnet picks up the object. Write in one column the names of the objects that are picked up. Write in another column the names of the objects that are not picked up.

Answer the following question: What kinds of objects will a magnet pick up?

At first glance, this seems to be a good activity. Children are using real materials and are investigating in a hands-on manner. A careful consideration of the activity, however, points out certain problems. First, the paragraph at the start of the activity tells students not only what they will be learning, but specifically details how two of the objects to be tested will react. Second, the number of objects used is both delineated and limited. The children have no option to try other materials or to see how the objects will react if touched by the center of the magnet or the edge. Finally, the students are asked a question that could be answered simply by rewriting the paragraph at the start of the activity. There is not a need for thought or even for doing the activity. This particular activity is an example of the standard "cookbook science activity."

Activity Two

Magnets will pick up some kinds of materials but not all kinds of materials. In this activity, you will be finding out what kinds of things a magnet will pick up and what kinds of things it will not pick up.

Materials: magnet, piece of paper, pencil

Procedure: Touch your magnet to as many different kinds of objects as you can. Make a list of the objects your magnet will pick up or move. Make a second list of the objects your magnet will not pick up or move.

Answer the following questions:

1. Look at the list of things your magnet will pick up or move. How are all of the things alike?
2. Look at the list of things your magnet will not pick up or move. How do they differ from the things in your list of objects that would be picked up?
3. Look at the following list. Which do you think the magnet might pick up or move?

   a piece of glass

   a paper clip

   a plastic spoon

   a tack

   a screw

   a piece of chalk

   a piece of paper

4. A friend from another class has never used a magnet. Your friend wants to know what kinds of things a magnet will pick up or move. What would you tell your friend?

This second activity is accomplishing the same purpose as the first activity, but it is a far better experience for children. Like the first activity, it does involve students in a hands-on activity that uses real materials. After that similarity, however, the differences are quite clear. First, the introductory sentences do not tell the students what the results of the activity will be. The student is told that he or she will learn what a magnet will pick up, but no indication is given as to what will actually be found. Second, the child is given a choice of the kinds of objects that will be tested and how they will be tested. A wider variety of objects can be considered. Finally, the questions ask the children to think about what was done in the activity, try to find similarities and differences, make predictions, and draw a conclusion. In other words, the child is asked to think about what was done rather than simply repeat what was stated in the introduction.

Activities from the physical sciences tend to match the listed criteria more fully than do those from the earth-space or biological sciences. However, activities from all of these science-content areas can be taught through the use of hands-on activities. From the physical-sciences, activities dealing with energy and matter can be included. From the earth-space sciences, activities dealing with rocks, minerals, soil, weather conditions, and water can be used. From the biological sciences, activities dealing with plant growth and observations of animals can be included. Additionally, the curriculum should include activities that show the interrelationships among the earth, physical, and biological sciences.

Once the activity has been carried out, it is the teacher's responsibility to help the children to understand the content information. For example, in the second activity dealing with magnets, the teacher would list on the chalkboard or overhead projector examples of objects the magnet will pick up or move and examples of objects it will not pick up or move. Through questions, children are helped to see that the first list contains objects made of metals, while the second list contains some metals, plastic, wood, fabric, leather, or anything else. The teacher then helps the children to come to a conclusion. The appropriate conclusion to this activity would be that a magnet will pick up or move objects made from some kinds of metals. Finally, the textbook could be used to find out what kinds of metals will be picked up; in other words, to refine the conclusion and make it more specific.

The purpose of the science activities included within the defined curriculum is to enable children to use thinking and problem-solving skills to develop science-concept skills for themselves. The role of the teacher in this type of teaching situation is to use skillful questioning to aid the children in the development of this content.

USING A SCIENCE TEXTBOOK APPROPRIATELY

The textbook in science teaching is only one part of the total curriculum. At the third-grade level, the textbook is a supplement to the hands-on activities of the science program. It is a way of checking the accuracy of an activity and of extending the information gained through the activity. Very often, however, textbooks in science are sources of problems in the curriculum.

The textbook as a source of problems often begins with the reading level. Reading in the content area is far more difficult than reading from a basal reader or from a carefully selected selection of prose. The major reason for this difficulty is in the vocabulary presented by the text. Terms such as photosynthesis, molecule, or lever are not generally met outside of the science textbook. Thus, textbook vocabulary often is unfamiliar. Second, science vocabulary is both specific and general. It is specific in that photosynthesis refers to a specific process in plants. It is general in that the process of photosynthesis involves a sequence of events and reactions. These characteristics of science terminology mean that each term reflects a concept. If the concept has not been developed, then the term is not understood. The concept of inertia is easy to understand if one has been in a car when the brakes have been suddenly slammed on to stop. The car stops, but the passenger continues to move until stopped by the seatbelt or the dashboard.

If the reading level is the first of the problems with textbooks, then the backgrounds of the students is the second problem. Students may have little background on which to draw. As a result, topics may be difficult to comprehend. A student who has never experienced the dry climate of a desert or the permafrost of the tundra will have difficulty with these concepts unless there is appropriate background information on which to draw. Also, students may have erroneous concepts that cause them to dismiss the content of the textbook as incomprehensible. A student who has the concept that the northern states are always cold and covered with snow has difficulty comprehending the succession of the seasons. A student who considers only animals to be living organisms has difficulty comprehending a discussion of the needs of plants as living things.

These difficulties with textbooks point out two needs in the use of textbooks. First, teachers need to have strategies for working effectively with textbooks. The use of semantic mapping strategies for introducing a textbook chapter, identifying student background information, and reviewing a textbook chapter is a highly effective way of assisting students in using a textbook.

Semantic Mapping Strategies

Introducing a New Chapter.   A semantic map can be used to introduce a new chapter in the textbook to students. The following steps are used in this technique.

1. Identify the main topic of the textbook chapter or section to be considered if the chapter or section is lengthy. Write the topic, using only one or two words, in the center of the chalkboard or overhead projector. Draw a box around it.
2. Have the students try to predict some of the topics that will be considered in the chapter. List these on the board.
3. Skim the chapter, looking at the section titles to locate the topics that are actually in the textbook. Add to the list of predicted topics any that were not predicted. Delete those that were predicted but not included.
4. Show how these topics are related to the major topics by drawing a diagram using the primary topic as the central point in the diagram.

LEARNING ACTIVITY 88

Increasing the Appropriateness of Textbook Activities

Purpose: The purpose of this activity is to rewrite science-textbook activities to make them more appropriate for third-grade-level students.

Procedure:

1. Select three activities from either a teacher edition or a student edition of a third-grade science textbook. One activity should come from a chapter dealing with biological science, one from a chapter dealing with physical science, and one from a chapter dealing with earth-space science.

2. Carry out the three activities yourself.
3. Consider the list of characteristics of a good science activity given in this text. How well do the activities that you have selected match the given criteria? What could be done to make the activity more appropriate for the third-grade level?
4. Rewrite each of the activities to bring them into line with the criteria given for good science activities.

---

5. Use the diagram to help students see the relationship of one topic to another.

Determining Background Knowledge.   A semantic map can also be used to determine the background knowledge that students have about a topic. This can help the teacher to determine students' knowledge level and misconceptions so that concepts can be emphasized or deemphasized. The following steps are used in developing a semantic map to assess student background:

1. Choose a word or two that identifies the topic under consideration. Write the word in the center of the chalkboard or overhead projector. Draw a box around it.
2. Have the students think of as many words as they can that are related to the selected word or words. Accept all of the possibilities given by the students and list them on the chalkboard or overhead projector. Do not make judgments as to the correctness or appropriateness of the terms.
3. Have the students categorize the words using general topics. Add these topics to the beginning word using lines to show relationships.
4. Categorize all of the terms given by the students by adding them to the map under the appropriate categories.
5. Words that cannot be classified are often those that are unrelated to the topic or that indicate erroneous ideas. These can be deleted.

6. Areas in which students have shown an understanding of the topic can be deemphasized in the classroom, while those for which there is little understanding or many incorrect ideas can be emphasized.

Reviewing a Chapter.   Semantic mapping can also be used to review a textbook section that has already been studied. The result of this type of mapping is a thorough review of the topic with the development of a study guide. If a test is to be given on multiple textbook chapters, small groups of students can be assigned to develop maps for separate chapters and the final review can be pooled. The steps for using this technique are given here.

1. Write the topic to be reviewed in the center of the chalkboard or overhead projector. Have students write the topic in the center of a sheet of paper.
2. Have the students skim the chapter to find the secondary topics and show the relationship of those secondary topics to the original topic using lines.
3. Have the students close their books.
   a. Have each student work independently to add details to his or her own chart.
   b. Once the students have added all the details they can independently, have them work in small groups to develop group charts.

Term: Animals

Predictions: lions, tigers, dogs, cats, furry, cold, warm, big, little, birds, feathers, pets, mammals, insects, amphibians, grow, change, food

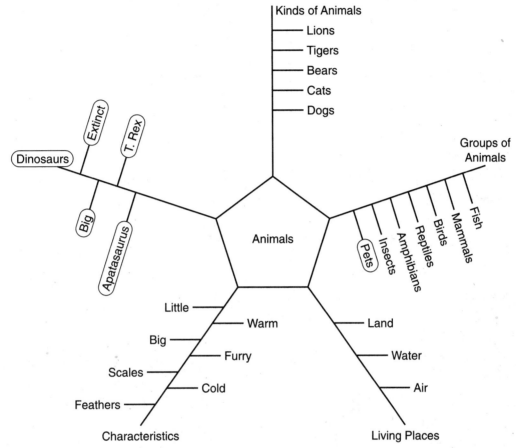

Note: The circled items are not included in the text but were predicted by students during the development of the semantic map.

DIAGRAM 15.1 Introductory Semantic Map

4. As a class, pool all of the information to develop a semantic map for the chapter. Use the chalkboard or overhead projector while the students work with their paper maps.
5. Have the students reread their textbooks in order to add any additional information to their maps.
6. Once the final map is complete, lead a discussion, emphasizing the concepts of the material and the vocabulary terms.

7. The map then can be used by the students as they study the information for the test.

Diagram 15.2 shows a semantic map that was developed as a review for a chapter in a third-grade science textbook.

The use of semantic mapping in working with a textbook has advantages for both the students and teacher. The students gain because teaching is based on their experiences and perceptions. The

Chapter: Weather

Completed map is shown here

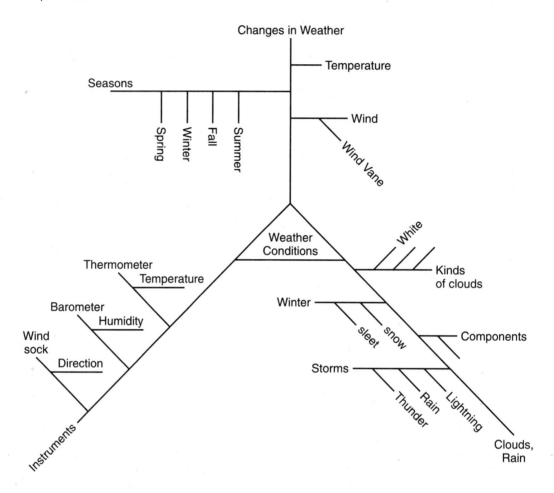

DIAGRAM 15.2 Review Semantic Map

content presented in the unit is geared to the students. The students also benefit by the thorough review that is afforded through the use of the map. The teacher benefits by knowing the strengths and weakness of the students prior to beginning to teach. Knowing the concepts already held by the children is an aid to the teacher who is planning for teaching. Additionally, the teacher benefits by knowing the erroneous concepts held by students that may interfere with learning. Those concepts can be directly addressed so that learning can be made more effective.

SUMMARY

The science curriculum for the defined curriculum should include content information, process skills, and scientific attitudes. The content information developed in the curriculum should come from the activities. The activities rely on the use of process skills. Therefore, both the content and process aspects of the curriculum are based on the active involvement of the students in the curriculum. The

LEARNING ACTIVITY 89

Developing a Semantic Map

Purpose: The purpose of this activity is to develop a semantic map that could be used to review a chapter in a third-grade science textbook.

Procedure:

1. Select a chapter from a third-grade science textbook.
2. Read the chapter carefully, making notes on the major topics, main points within the topics, and vocabulary terms developed in the chapter.

3. Develop a semantic map that could be used to review the chapter.
   a. Place the chapter topic in the central "box" that begins the map.
   b. Draw lines from the "box" to represent the main topics considered in the chapter.
   c. Add to the map the chapter details about each main topic and the vocabulary terms developed in the chapter.

LEARNING ACTIVITY 90

Science Activity File

Purpose: The purpose of this activity is to develop a file of activities that could be used in the teaching of third-grade science.

Procedure:

1. Research the kinds of topics that are generally included at the third-grade level in textbooks and in the course of study for science.
2. Develop an activity file of ideas for teaching those topics. Include in the file the following kinds of ideas:
   a. activities using concrete materials for concept development;
   b. activities using concrete materials for process-skill development;
   c. ideas for learning centers;
   d. ideas for science-fair projects;
   e. ideas for bulletin boards;
   f. ideas for helping students connect science in school to science in daily living;
   g. ideas for using problem-solving skills in science;
   h. ideas for showing the role of men, women, and various cultures in science;
   i. ideas for games—board games, small-group games, and whole-class games;
   j. reviews of computer programs appropriate for use in science education; and
   k. ideas for developing career possibilities in science.

inclusion of scientific attitudes comes as the teacher models the appropriate attitudes for the children.

The sheer volume of scientific content requires that decisions be made about what should or should not be included in the science area of the defined curriculum. In selecting content, the characteristics of the concrete operational child should be taken into account. The major characteristic of appropriate science content is that such content be taught through hands-on activities utilizing the real objects.

Once the content area has been selected, the teacher should give attention to the activities that are selected and the presentation of those activities. Activities should involve the children in situations in which the outcome is unknown, factors can be changed, and the students can draw the content conclusion for themselves. Following the activity, it is up to the teacher to help the students to draw appropriate conclusions.

Finally, the textbook does have a place in the defined curriculum. The textbook is used as a means for assessing the validity of the content learned through activities and is a way of extending ideas beyond the content found in a hands-on activity. Learning from the textbook is enhanced through the use of hands-on activities prior to reading, as well as through the use of semantic mapping strategies.

Vocabulary Terms

Attitudes: habits of mind that guide scientific thought processes.

Content: the facts, laws, principles, or theories that make up the body of knowledge in science.

Interaction and Systems: one of the causal processes; asks for the determination of what objects are necessary for a phenomenon to occur and then asks how those objects work together to cause the phenomenon.

Objectivity: a scientific attitude; asks that an individual look at all sides of an issue prior to making a decision.

Positive Approach to Failure: a scientific attitude; indicates that even if a prediction is shown to be incorrect, information has been gained.

Process Skill: skill used in obtaining information during a science activity.

Respect for the Environment: a scientific attitude; indicates an understanding of the interconnectedness of all aspects of the environment.

Semantic Map: a visual means for demonstrating student knowledge of a particular science-content area.

Skepticism: a scientific attitude; asks that information be questioned prior to acceptance.

Willingness to Suspend Judgment: a scientific attitude; asks that a person wait until all of the evidence is in before making a decision.

Study Questions

1. What are the three areas that should be included in the science curriculum? How do these areas relate to one another?
2. Which of the following content areas are inappropriate to the third-grade science program? Why are they inappropriate?
    a. A flowering plant has roots, stem, leaves, flower, and fruit.
    b. The molecules of a liquid are closer together than those of a solid.
    c. In winter, the Earth is closer to the Sun than it is in the summer.
    d. Clam, oyster, and mussel shells are both similar to and different from one another.
    e. A gerbil is a nocturnal animal.
    f. Life below the surface of the ocean is very different from life on land.
    g. A fruit is the seed containing part of a plant. Consequently, oranges, cucumbers, green peppers, and bananas are all fruits.
3. How are the science process skills used to develop science-content information?
4. Discuss the similarities and differences among semantic maps for introducing a unit and for reviewing a unit.
5. Children have just completed an activity in which they investigated the kinds of materials a magnet will or will not attract. It is now time to help the children understand the results of the activity, particularly the concept that "magnets pick up some kinds of metals." What would you do, as the teacher, to help children develop this content information from their activity?

PART FOUR

Evaluation

INTRODUCTION

For most teachers, evaluation means tests, worksheets, and homework assignments. For most parents, evaluation means grades and report cards. From both of these viewpoints, evaluation focuses on content information and on the success of the child in acquiring those predetermined bits of content information. Rarely does the general concept of evaluation include evaluation of the teaching process. However, evaluation is an inclusive term that includes both the evaluation of teaching and the evaluation of learning. The purpose of evaluation is actually threefold.

First, evaluation should form the basis for decisions about teaching procedures. Each lesson and each activity should be considered from the viewpoint of how well it conveyed the information to the children. Lessons or activities that did not work as expected, resulted in more questions than answers, and caused frustration or failure need to be evaluated to determine what it was that caused the problems. Lessons that can be revamped to allow for success should be changed while others should be eliminated. Only by evaluating each lesson can the teacher know what works and what does not work.

Second, evaluation should help the teacher to determine whether the educational program is based on the developmental level of the children being taught. Evaluation, therefore, should be based on determining strengths and weaknesses in relation to the child's developmental level. Evaluation should help the teacher to determine whether a lesson or unit of work was unsuccessful because of the teaching strategies and activities used or because the content was developmentally inappropriate to the children being taught. A unit on how energy changes from one form to another may involve children in a variety of hands-on activities and still be unsuccessful because it asks students to use concepts and cognitive skills that are not yet accessible.

Third, evaluation should assist the teacher in determining the most appropriate educational experiences for the child. In this case, the teacher is evaluating the child's developmental level and background experiences. The preoperational thinker needs different kinds of experiences than the concrete operational thinker. The child who has never before ventured beyond his or her front yard needs different kinds of experiences than the child four or five who is a world traveler. Assessing the child's background and developmental level can help the teacher to make informed decisions about the experiences that the child should have. Finally, at the early childhood level, evaluation should be used to place the child in a position of success rather than in a position of failure. Evaluation should be based on the abilities of the child rather than on how well the child meets a predetermined set of adult expectations.

The type of evaluation that is done should match the curricular pattern in which the child and the teacher are participating. The goals of each of the three curricular patterns differ and, therefore, the emphasis of the evaluation should differ. The child who is experiencing the unified curriculum is developing background knowledge through open-ended and nondirective experiences. The knowledge that is gained is idiosyncratic to the child and so cannot be assessed according to a listing of definite criteria. The child in the combined curriculum is meeting certain expectations, but these are expectations that involve the development of thinking and problem-solving skills in mathematics and in science. And, the child in the defined curriculum is involved in specific content expectations and should be evaluated on those content expectations. Each of the curricular patterns has different expectations that should be reflected in the evaluation forms.

The type of evaluation should also match the kinds of teaching techniques that are being used. Children who are experiencing an open-inquiry approach are evaluated differently from those who are working in centers or participating in guided-discovery activities.

Finally, the type of evaluation should match the developmental level of the children in each of the curricular patterns. Preoperational children need to be evaluated in ways different from the techniques used with children who are in the concrete operational stage of development. Pencil-and-paper techniques are inappropriate for the preoperational child but are becoming appropriate for the concrete operational child.

Evaluation is a means for the teacher to determine how effective her or his teaching has been. Evaluation is a way of determining whether the curriculum is appropriate for the child. Evaluation is a way of determining whether activities or content are appropriate to the children being taught. Evaluation is not a way of labeling young children as failures.

CHAPTER 16

Evaluation in the Early-Childhood Science and Mathematics Program

Chapter Objectives

On completion of this chapter, you should be able to

1. list the characteristics of evaluation that are appropriate to the unified curriculum,

2. discuss evaluation that is appropriate to the unified curriculum,

3. list the characteristics of evaluation that are appropriate to the combined curriculum,

4. discuss evaluation that is appropriate to the combined curriculum,

5. list the characteristics of evaluation that are appropriate to the defined curriculum, and

6. discuss evaluation that is appropriate to the defined curriculum.

In school today, Mary painted three pictures, pretended to be a princess and a doctor, made four bead necklaces, discovered that turtles pull their heads inside their shells when they become frightened and that beetles look funny when they get turned on their backs, told a friend the entire story of the three bears, and learned that when blocks are piled too high they fall over with a loud crash. She went home with sand in her shoes, paint on her hands, and grass stains on her knees. Mary had a wonderful time in school. Too bad she is a slow learner and will fail the year. Mary is three and a half. The curriculum guide for her academic preschool states that she should be able to count to 20; say the entire alphabet; recognize her name when it is written; identify the colors red, blue, yellow, green, orange, purple, black, brown, and white; and identify the shapes of circles, squares, triangles, and rectangles. Mary is not quite able to accomplish the kinds of things the teachers expect. When she is evaluated, she is evaluated on the basis of what adults think she should be able to accomplish rather than on her accomplishments. When children at the early-childhood level are evaluated, it is their accomplishments that should be documented rather than their failures. The kinds of evaluation used to document these accomplishments should change with the kind of curriculum in which the child is involved.

EVALUATION IN THE UNIFIED CURRICULUM

Evaluation of the Children

Within the unified curriculum pattern, evaluation of the children should first consider the concept that general knowledge rather than specific predetermined bits of knowledge is being developed. Consequently, children should be evaluated on the basis of what they have discovered rather than on the basis of what the teacher thinks should have been learned through an activity. Additionally, children should be evaluated individually since what one child learns from an activity will not necessarily be what another child learns.

Children should also be evaluated in terms of the contribution that the activity made to their general understanding of the environment in which they are living rather than on the basis of specific mathematical or scientific content. Children are learning about plants and animals, energy and matter, rocks and soil, space and time, but they are not learning specific facts about those areas. Evaluation should show the development of the child rather than the development of the subject matter.

Evaluation of the Activities

Evaluation of the activities should first look at the contribution made by the activity to the total development of the child. In particular, the activities of the unified curriculum should be evaluated on the basis of the degree of autonomy afforded to the child and the level of investigative behavior that is possible. Children should be making their own decisions, developing their own ideas, and identifying their own problems to be solved.

Activities should also be evaluated on the basis of their developmental appropriateness. In particular, the activity should be considered from the viewpoint of the thinking abilities available to the preoperational child and the way in which the preoperational child develops new information. Activities should allow the child to participate as fully as possible in the activity without having to use thinking or investigative skills that are not yet developed.

Evaluation of the Teaching Strategies

Teaching strategies should be evaluated on their appropriateness to the child and to the curricular pattern. In looking at the strategies, the kinds of materials used should first be considered. The evaluation should ask whether the materials are appropriate and, if they are not appropriate, what changes should be made. The degree of flexibility afforded by the teaching strategy should also be considered. Teaching strategies for the unified curriculum should allow for the highest possible level of flexibility, both for the teacher and for the students. Children should have the opportunity to pursue investigations of interest to them and the teacher should have the flexibility to modify the activities and procedures as needed to suit them more effectively to the children.

Evaluation Techniques

Three types of evaluation techniques are particularly suited to the unified curriculum pattern. The first of these is highly informal and consists simply of teacher observation of the children at work. Any written records from this type of evaluation consist of the effect of an activity on the total group or on small groups as students participate in the activity. It is not the purpose of this type of evaluation to focus on particular children. Rather, the focus is on the activity and its effect on the children. The second type of evaluation is also based on teacher observation, but the result of this type of observation is an anecdotal record. The anecdotal record focuses on the behaviors of specific children within the activity. Anecdotal records provide a continuous record of child activity through which the teacher can see evidence of changes in investigative behavior and understanding. The third type of evaluation also involves teacher observation but is more formalized in that it involves a checklist. The checklist is a tool that allows the teacher to make systematic observations of certain skills and investigative behaviors as they are used or developed in children. The checklist is useful if standardized records are needed by a school program but needs to be carefully constructed to reflect the investigative behaviors and the developing thinking skills of children rather than on a list of predetermined content or behaviors.

Inappropriate forms of evaluation for the unified curriculum consist of written materials that are required by all children: worksheets are a particularly prevalent form of inappropriate evaluation for the unified curriculum. Additionally, standardized tests are especially inappropriate for the child in the unified curriculum. Such tests not only assume that all children within a particular class should learn the same things at the same time but also that all children everywhere should be learning those same things. Additionally, the verbal format of standardized tests is inappropriate to the young child's thinking abilities. The preoperational child thinks through the use of concrete materials and uses language ineffectively. Consequently, the preoperational child is at a disadvantage when evaluated verbally. Examples 16.1, 16.2, and 16.3 show an anecdotal record, an activity checklist, and an activity evaluation form, respectively.

EVALUATION IN THE COMBINED CURRICULUM

Evaluation of the Children

As with the unified curriculum pattern, evaluation in the combined curriculum should continue to evaluate the child as a child. Because subject matter, in the form of both conceptual knowledge and process skills, is a part of the curriculum, there are certain ideas and skills that are expected. However, these skills and ideas should be evaluated in terms of the child's progress rather than in terms of acquiring certain concepts or skills by a certain point in time.

At the first- and second-grade levels, some children will remain in the preoperational level, while others will be moving into concrete operational thought processes. In evaluating the children, the differences in thinking abilities of these two levels should be taken into account. For example, the preoperational child will not yet have a stable concept of number, while the concrete operational child will have attained conservation of number. To evaluate the preoperational child on an understanding of number is inappropriate. But both the preoperational and the concrete operational child can work with the science process skills of observation and classification and, therefore, can be evaluated in the same manner.

The child's developing problem-solving skills also need to be evaluated as a part of the combined curriculum. Children are continuously engaged in problem solving as they plan and carry out activities within an open-ended framework. The ability of children to plan, to implement, and to discuss their investigations should be evaluated. In particular, evaluation should be geared to determining whether the child's ability to use problem solving is developing and being extended during investigations.

Problem solving is a part of investigative behavior; therefore, evaluation within the combined curriculum should continue to emphasize the investigative behaviors of the child. At this point, however, because the centers and other activities in which the children participate have specific outcomes, the children can also be evaluated in terms of the product or outcome of the activities.

EXAMPLE 16.1

Unified Curriculum: Anecdotal Record

Activity: Investigating Towers and Constructions
Antonio began by trying to build a "house" using the boxes and blocks. The boxes made a shaky base so the "house" kept collapsing. After the third time it collapsed, he knocked over the remaining blocks and left the area. After ten minutes away, he returned and tried putting the blocks on the bottom and the boxes on top. It made a more stable building.

Activity: Investigating Splashes
Jenny began by carefully placing objects on the top of the water so as not to make any kind of a splash. When Pilar caused water to splash onto the table Jenny immediately went to get paper towels to clean up. But, after a few minutes of watching Pilar splash water, Jenny joined into the splashes and announced that "big things make a big mess."

Activity: Sinking and Floating
Marcus noticed that jar lids would float if they were put gently into the water but would sink if they were pushed. He began to see if there were other objects that would both sink and float. Beside Marcus, LaToya discovered that she could put a washer on top of a jar lid and the washer would float. Marcus saw what she was doing and they began to compete to see who could put the most weight on the top of the jar lids and still have them float.

Activity: Balancing
George and Eric discovered that all of the styrofoam packing pieces would not balance even one of the rocks.

Carol discovered that two of the blocks would make the scale balance, but if a bead was placed with the block it would no longer balance.

Lisa and Jeannie found that a cup of water was heavier than a rock and heavier than a bag of crayons.

EXAMPLE 16.2

Unified Curriculum: Activity Checklist

Activity:

Child's Name:

1. Length of time participated
   a. less than 10 minutes
   b. more than 10 minutes
   c. left and returned to the activity
2. Used a variety of materials in the investigations
   a. yes
   b. no
   c. used additional materials after observing activities of other children
3. Pursued a variety of investigations
   a. yes
   b. no
   c. pursued a variety only after seeing others involved
   d. intensely pursued a single investigation

4. Worked with other children on investigations
   a. yes
   b. no
   c. worked in parallel
   d. watched others work but returned to own investigations
5. Was able to describe what was happening in the investigation
   a. yes, to other children
   b. yes, to the teacher
   c. no, but could demonstrate using materials
   d. no, could neither describe nor demonstrate
6. Demonstrated interest and enthusiasm for investigations
   a. yes
   b. no

EXAMPLE 16.2 Continued

7. Spontaneously described or demonstrated findings for others
  a. yes
  b. no

8. Pursued unusual lines of investigation
  a. yes
  b. no
  c. kinds of investigations pursued:

EXAMPLE 16.3

Unified Curriculum: Activity Evaluation

Name of the Activity:

Materials Used in the Activity:

1. Which of the children participated in the activity?
2. Which of the provided materials were used?
3. Which of the provided materials were not used?
4. Did the children request or get additional materials? If so, what were the materials?
5. How long did the children work with the activity?
6. Did the children return to the activity after leaving it?
7. What modifications would be needed if the activity were to be more successful?

8. What kinds of investigations did the children pursue?
9. Did the children experience any difficulty in using the materials? If so, what? What changes could be made?
10. What modifications might be needed for children with handicapping conditions?
11. Did the investigations of the children suggest any new activity ideas? If so, what are they?
12. Would you recommend that this activity be used again? Why or why not?

LEARNING ACTIVITY 91

Unified-Curriculum Evaluation Checklist

Purpose: The purpose of this activity is to develop a checklist for use with a specific unified-curriculum activity.

Procedure:
1. Develop a unified-curriculum experience that is appropriate for children of three, four, or five years of age.
2. After the activity has been planned, develop a checklist that could be used to evaluate the experience.
  a. Include in the checklist some items that would be used to evaluate the children who are participating in the activity.

  b. Include in the checklist some items that would be used to evaluate the activity itself.
3. Carry out the activity with a small group of children. Use the checklist that you developed to evaluate the activity.
4. Now, evaluate the checklist. Which items would you keep and which would you delete or change in some way? Why are those changes needed?
5. On the basis of your checklist, how would you evaluate the success of the unified-curriculum activity? What changes would you make as a result of your evaluation?

Within the use of investigative behaviors and problem solving, children can be evaluated on the development of an ability to observe, classify, use space relations, determine simple cause and effect, and make and test predictions, as well as the other types of process skills. In all cases, the process skills should be evaluated in terms of the child's ability to use the process within the context of an activity.

Finally, evaluation within the combined curriculum should include the evaluation of the broad concepts developed as a part of the curriculum. Children's ability to use patterning, work with graphing, consider number, or compare and contrast need to be evaluated. Once again, these concepts need to be evaluated in the context of activities rather than on worksheets or skill sheets that are divorced from the activity context. Example 16.4 shows a checklist for evaluating patterning as a mathematical skill and Example 16.5 shows a checklist for assessing the process skills used in a science activity.

Evaluation of the Activities

Evaluation in the combined curriculum should also include an evaluation of the activities that are being used as a part of the curriculum.

First, activities should be evaluated on the basis of whether they integrate science and mathematics into a single combined entity that utilizes skills and concepts from both areas. The activities that are selected for discovery teaching or for a centers approach should allow children to utilize the science process skills as a part of a mathematics activity and the mathematics concepts as a part of a science activity. Ideally, the activities should make no differentiation between science and mathematics, but should fully combine the two areas.

Second, activities should be evaluated on the basis of the open-endedness and flexibility that are afforded by the activity to the student. The more flexible the activity and the more open-ended the activity, the greater chance the student will have to exercise problem-solving skills and develop investigative abilities.

Third, activities should be evaluated on how they contribute to the child's ability to investigate and the child's understanding of the environment in which he or she lives.

Finally, activities should be evaluated on their developmental appropriateness. The activities should allow the children to use the thinking skills available to them at that point in time. However, a slight mismatch in thinking skills is also appropriate, particularly at the first- and second-grade levels where the transition from preoperational to concrete operational thought is being made. Children should be challenged to use their developing abilities so that their thinking skills are extended and developed. Example 16.6 shows an evaluation form that could be used for a combined-curriculum activity and Example 16.7 shows a center sheet sample for an activity.

Evaluation of the Teaching Strategies

Evaluation of teaching should include attention to the flexibility shown by the teacher. The teacher's flexibility determines the variety of investigations that will occur and the degree to which children feel free to investigate in broad areas. Additionally, teaching strategies should be evaluated for their developmental appropriateness. Teaching strategies should be matched to the developmental level of the children involved in the lesson. Therefore, appropriate strategies are those that emphasize hands-on activities, child-directed investigations, and discussions that allow children to describe their activities and findings. The evaluation of centers needs to consider the degree to which children participate in the activities of the centers, the means for updating and maintaining the centers, and the method selected for monitoring who uses the center, as well as the success of the activities themselves. Finally, evaluation of the teaching strategies should consider the degree to which the strategy combines mathematics and science and allows the integration of those areas into the entire curriculum.

Evaluation Techniques

A variety of evaluation techniques are appropriate to the combined curriculum. Informal teacher observation continues to remain an important part of the evaluation of the combined curriculum. Informal evaluation can give the teacher clues about the effectiveness of the procedures used for monitoring center use, as well as the kinds of materials that children require for their independent investiga-

EXAMPLE 16.4

Defined Curriculum: Checklist for Patterning

Child's Name

Type of Patterning	Abby	John	Tamika	Maria	Felipe			
1. Copied a pattern with two alternating shapes								
2. Constructed a pattern of two alternating shapes								
3. Extended a pattern of two alternating shapes								
4. Copied a pattern with three shapes								
5. Constructed a pattern with three shapes								
6. Extended a pattern with three shapes								
7. Copied a pattern of four shapes								
8. Constructed a pattern of four shapes								
9. Extended a pattern of four shapes								
10. Recorded a pattern by drawing shapes used								
11. Recorded a pattern by using symbols other than shapes								
12. Described pattern orally								
13. Constructed a pattern from an oral description								
14. Created a new pattern								
15. Developed a circular pattern								

EXAMPLE 16.5

Combined Curriculum: Checklist for Process Skills

Title of Activity:

Date of Activity:

Child's Name

Process Skill	Abby	John	Tamika	Maria	Felipe			
1. Made observations								
2. Recorded observations								
3. Communicated with members of working group								
4. Communicated with others in class								
5. Kept written or pictorial records of the activity								
6. Classified objects consistently								
7. Used numbers by counting								
8. Used numbers by measuring								
9. Used space relations in describing results								
10. Used space relations in determining time								
11. Made logical predictions								
12. Tested predictions								
13. Made multiple inferences								
14. Made logical inferences								
15. Drew conclusions from the activity								

EXAMPLE 16.6

Combined Curriculum: Activity Evaluation Form

Activity:

Date:

1. Was the activity developmentally appropriate?
2. Did the activity combine the science and mathematics areas in purposeful ways? How could the level of integration of the two areas be increased?
3. Which science process skills were used in the activity? How could process skill use be increased?
4. Which mathematical concepts were used in the activity? How could mathematical concept use be increased?
5. What opportunities for problem solving were included in the activity?

6. Were opportunities available in the activity for children to work in small groups or alone?
7. What materials were used in the activity? Were any materials requested by the children that were not provided?
8. Did the activity work as expected? If not, what changes need to be made?
9. Were opportunities available for additional exploration by the children? How could the opportunities for additional investigations be increased?
10. What contribution did the activity make to the children's understanding of the environment?
11. Did the children in the class seem to enjoy the activity?

EXAMPLE 16.7

Combined Curriculum: Center Sheet

Activity: Investigating Seeds

Directions:
1. Take one of the egg cartons of seeds.
2. Dump the seeds into a pile on the table.
3. Look carefully at the seeds. Write down at least three ways in which the seeds are different from one another.
4. Classify your seeds using one of the ways they are different.
5. Count the seeds in each of the groups.

6. Make a graph of your seeds to show which group has the most seeds and which group has the fewest seeds.

Ways seeds are different:
1.
2.
3.
4.
5.

Graph of the seeds:

---

tions. Informal observations can also help the teacher to determine general areas of problems in understanding of concepts or use of skills.

Informal teacher observation is good for determining general areas of strength and weakness. More formal types of teacher observation are needed for determining the child's development in the use of process skills or the attainment of mathematical concepts. In this case, anecdotal records in which specific incidents and successes are detailed are helpful. A continuous anecdotal record allows

the teacher to determine the areas that are developing rapidly and the areas that are developing more slowly. Such a record also allows the teacher to develop activities that will aid a particular child or small group in attaining desired skills.

The anecdotal record can be effective in tracing the development of a particular child, but is cumbersome in looking at the total development of a class. In looking at a class, the use of a checklist is far more appropriate. The checklist can detail the skills and concepts that are being attended to through the activities and provide a record of all children in the class and their success in developing those skills and concepts. Study of the resulting checklists allows the teacher to determine areas of particular strength and weakness for a particular class and whether selected activities have accomplished the desired goals. The checklist should provide enough detail to enable the teacher to locate areas of strength and weakness, but should not be so detailed that students have no flexibility in their activities and investigations.

Finally, the combined curriculum, particularly when a centers approach is used, allows for individual work from children. Students can produce a record of their activities within centers that can be evaluated according to the stated center objectives. Such records should be an integral part of the activity rather than an evaluation section tacked on to the activity to provide a written record that can be evaluated.

As with the unified-curriculum pattern, certain types of evaluation remain inappropriate for the combined-curriculum pattern. In particular, pencil-and-paper tests of specific concepts and skills are inappropriate to the child in the combined curriculum. Although there are concepts and skills that are emphasized in the curriculum, the development of those concepts and skills is strongly dependent on the child's developmental level and activities. Consequently, it cannot and should not be assumed that every child will reach a particular concept at the same point in time. Pencil-and-paper tests are based on the assumption that all children learn all things at the same rate and that they can demonstrate their knowledge in the same manner at the same time. There is no level at which this assumption is more invalid than at the early-childhood level.

If pencil-and-paper tests constructed by the teacher are inappropriate to the combined curriculum, then standardized tests are even more inappropriate to the combined curriculum. Standardized tests assume not only that all children in a class learn all things in the same way and at the same rate, but that children everywhere learn in the same way and at the same rate. Standardized tests also assume that children at the preoperational and early concrete operational levels are able to demonstrate their knowledge through written formats. Standardized tests are inappropriate methods for evaluating the preoperational or concrete operational child, as well as invalid means for evaluating the combined curriculum. Standardized tests tend to evaluate subject-matter areas as discrete entities: There are specific tests for mathematics, science, language, social studies, and reading. Such differentiation into discrete subject-matter areas violates the concept of the combined curriculum, which treats subject-matter areas as overlapping and combined.

EVALUATION IN THE DEFINED CURRICULUM

Evaluation of the Children

The evaluation of the children in the combined curriculum will need to give attention to the attainment of specific content and skills within the areas of science and mathematics. Since the activities selected for the teaching of science will require the children to use specific science process skills, and since the development of those skills began in the first and second grades, children can now be evaluated on their ability to use specific science processes. The use of activities and process skills in the defined curriculum is geared toward the development of particular bits of science-content information. Therefore, children also can be evaluated on their understanding of that content. Within the quantitative curriculum, certain concepts are being developed in children and so the attainment of those concepts can be evaluated through problem-solving situations just as the attainment of computation skills can be evaluated through the application of those computation skills.

The objective of the evaluation of students within the defined curriculum is to determine the strengths and weaknesses of the child within the areas predetermined by the curriculum. Areas of identified weakness may require additional experiences with the information or may require structured remediation. Where areas of weakness are identified, the reasons for the weakness should be determined. A child's developmental level should always be taken into consideration when weaknesses are identified. If developmental readiness is the cause of a weakness, the child should not be

LEARNING ACTIVITY 92

Process-Skill Evaluation Checklist

Purpose: The purpose of this activity is to develop a checklist to evaluate the process skills used by children in a combined-curriculum activity.

Procedure:

1. Develop an activity for the combined curriculum that focuses on science process skill use.
2. After the activity has been planned, develop a checklist that could be used to evaluate the activity.
   a. Include items that evaluate the use of the process skills by the children.
   b. Include items that evaluate the activity itself.
3. Carry out the activity with a small group of first- or second-grade children. Use the checklist to evaluate both the children and the activity.
4. Now, evaluate the checklist. Which items would you keep and which would you delete or change in some way? Why are those changes needed?
5. On the basis of your checklist, how would you evaluate the success of the combined-curriculum activity? What changes would you make as a result of your evaluation?

---

expected to attain the concept in question. Areas of strength may require additional experiences to strengthen understanding or develop additional concepts and skills.

Evaluation of children at the early-childhood level is not for the purpose of labeling children as failures. Instead, areas of weakness should always be assessed for causes and the child should be assisted in turning the weakness into a strength. Example 16.8 shows a checklist for the evaluation of science process skills and Example 16.9 shows a checklist for an arithmetic computation skill.

Evaluation of the Activities

The first consideration in the evaluation of activities is an evaluation of the purposefulness of the activity. Activities that lead to the desired objectives should be retained, while activities that are included more for the sake of activity than for attainment of objectives should be deleted.

Activities should also be evaluated in terms of their developmental appropriateness. Children at the third-grade level should be in the early stages of concrete operations and the activities selected should reflect the thinking skills available to the child at this level. Since the activities reflect the content of the curriculum, the content being taught by the activity should be evaluated for developmental appropriateness as well.

Activities should also be evaluated for the degree of problem solving they allow. Activities should encourage children to think for themselves, solve problems, and apply information in a wide variety of situations. Activities that appear to be too narrowly focused can be rewritten to allow for more thinking and problem solving.

Finally, activities should be evaluated according to their type. A variety of kinds of activities and approaches should be seen in the classroom. If activities all appear to be of the same type, duration, or format, then some consideration needs to be given to reworking activities or finding new ideas to provide variety. Example 16.10 shows an assessment for a science lesson, while Example 16.11 shows an assessment for a mathematics lesson.

Evaluation of the Teaching Strategies

A part of the evaluation of teaching has already been considered under the idea of evaluating activities. The teacher should first look at the variety of teaching strategies being used in the classroom. Too much reliance on one or a few types of strategies should be reviewed and the kinds of strategies being used extended to allow for greater instructional variety. All children do not learn in the same way and all subject matter does not lend itself to the same techniques; therefore, the teacher should

EXAMPLE 16.8

Defined Curriculum: Process-Skill Checklist

Activity:

Child's Name

Process Skill	Martina	Joe	Fred	Katy	Bob		
1. Made observations							
2. Recorded observations							
3. Shared observations with other students							
4. Communicated results orally							
5. Communicated results in writing							
6. Communicated results pictorially							
7. Used numbers—counting							
8. Used numbers—computing							
9. Used measurement							
10. Made logical inferences based on the activity							
11. Made multiple inferences based on the activity							
12. Drew a logical conclusion from the activity							
13. Described system used in the activity							
14. Described interactions used in the activity							
15. Described cause-and-effect relationships in activity							
16. Made predictions							
17. Tested predictions							
18. Used classification during an activity							
19. Developed own system for classification							
20. Used time measurements during an activity							

EXAMPLE 16.9

Defined Curriculum: Mathematics Checklist

Topic: Subtraction of whole numbers

Child's Name

Skill	Enrico	Joel	Jan	Katy	Emma			
1. Demonstrated knowledge of basic subtraction facts								
2. Subtracted one-digit number from two-digit number, no regrouping								
3. Subtracted one-digit number from two-digit number, with regrouping								
4. Subtracted two-digit number from two-digit number, no regrouping								
5. Subtracted two-digit number from two-digit number, with regrouping								
6. Subtracted two-digit number from three-digit number, no regrouping								
7. Subtracted two-digit number from three-digit number, with regrouping from tens to ones only								
8. Subtracted two-digit number from three-digit number, with regrouping from hundreds to tens only								
9. Subtracted two-digit number from three-digit number, with regrouping in both hundreds to tens and tens to ones								
10. Subtracted two-digit number from three-digit number, with regrouping across zero in tens place								

EXAMPLE 16.10

Defined Curriculum: Science-Lesson Assessment

Lesson:

1. Did the activity directly address the lesson objective? If not, what changes are needed?
2. Was the lesson developmentally appropriate?
   a. Content?
   b. Process?
   c. Teaching strategy?
   d. What could be done to make the lesson more developmentally appropriate?
3. Materials
   a. What materials were used in the lesson?
   b. Were additional materials needed?
   c. What substitutions could be made?
4. Process Skills
   a. Which of the following process skills were used?

   _____ observation   _____ prediction
   _____ communication   _____ conclusion
   _____ classification   _____ interaction
   _____ use numbers   and systems
   _____ space/time   _____ cause and
   relations   effect
   _____ inference

   b. How could additional process skills be included in the lesson?

5. Teaching Strategies
   a. Which teaching strategies were used in the lesson?
   b. Were the teaching strategies appropriate to the content of the lesson?
   c. How could the teaching strategies be changed to make the lesson more effective?
6. Questions
   a. Which levels of questions were used in the lesson?

   _____ knowledge   _____ analysis
   _____ comprehension   _____ synthesis
   _____ application   _____ evaluation

   b. How could the variety of questions used in the lesson be increased?
7. Activity
   a. What problems were encountered in doing the lesson's activity?
   b. Was the content information easily determined from the activity?
8. Were opportunities for problem solving and creativity part of the lesson? How could such opportunities be increased?
9. Should the lesson be used again? Why or why not?

EXAMPLE 16.11

Defined Curriculum: Mathematics Lesson Assessment

Lesson:

1. Did the activity directly address the lesson objective?
2. Was the lesson developmentally appropriate?
   a. Content?
   b. Teaching strategies?
3. Mathematics Content
   a. Which of the following skills were used in the lesson?

   _____ addition   _____ division
   _____ subtraction   _____ numeration
   _____ multiplication   _____ counting

   b. Which of the following mathematical concepts were used?

   _____ place value   _____ patterning
   _____ sets   _____ measurement
   _____ number   _____ classification

4. Teaching Strategies
   a. Which teaching strategies were used?
   b. Were the teaching strategies appropriate to the content?
   c. How could the teaching strategies be changed to make them more appropriate to the lesson?

EXAMPLE 16.11 Continued

5. Materials
   a. What materials were used in the lesson?
   b. What could be done to increase the use of manipulatives in the lesson?
6. Questions
   a. Which levels of questions were used in the lesson?

   _____ knowledge   _____ analysis
   _____ comprehension   _____ synthesis
   _____ application   _____ evaluation

7. Were opportunities for problem solving and creativity part of the lesson? What could be done to include more of such opportunities?
8. Should the lesson be used again? Why or why not?

---

use a variety of strategies matched to the children and the content information.

Evaluation of the teaching strategies should also include consideration of the success of the lessons in terms of child understanding and the degree to which problem-solving and critical-thinking skills are included in the lesson. This form of lesson evaluation requires that the teacher look back at the evaluation of the children and determine from the results of that evaluation the success of the teaching strategy.

Evaluation Techniques

The types of evaluation techniques available for use in the defined curriculum are even more numerous than the variety available for use in the combined curriculum. Teacher observation is declining in usefulness and appropriateness at this level. Informal evaluation is most frequently used to determine general areas of strength or weakness during a lesson so that the teacher can make changes in the lesson while it is occurring.

Formal evaluation through the use of checklists remains appropriate in determining a child's ability to use specific process skills and problem-solving strategies. Once again, the use of such checklists should be in the context of activities rather than divorced from the context.

Formal evaluation at the level of the defined curriculum is now extended to the use of pencil-and-paper formats. Reading and writing are becoming more developed as methods of communication at the third-grade level. Consequently, written formats can now be used in assessing the child's level of understanding of science-content informa-

tion and arithmetic-computation skills. However, pencil-and-paper tests should not become the only or even predominant form of evaluation for the child at the third-grade level. For many children, written tests of information are still developmentally inappropriate. Children who are unable to demonstrate their knowledge through the use of a formal pencil-and-paper evaluation should be provided with alternate ways of demonstrating their knowledge. Some children may be able to demonstrate their understanding by discussing a topic with the teacher, solving a computation problem while the teacher watches and listens, drawing a picture, or demonstrating through the use of materials. When children need to use alternative methods for showing their comprehension, the teacher should provide those alternative methods. The purpose of evaluation is to determine the child's level of understanding and skill and the child should be given every opportunity to do so. Examples 16.12 and 16.13 show teacher-constructed pencil-and-paper tests for science and mathematics, respectively.

At the defined-curriculum level, standardized tests become somewhat more appropriate. Such tests can give clues as to how a particular group of children measures up to predetermined standards. However, standardized tests should be used with considerable caution. Standardized tests measure only a small part of the attainments of children: those that they can demonstrate by selecting a particular response. Consequently, reading skills may interfere with the child's performance. Also, and more important, the standardized test may not reflect adequately the curriculum in which the child has participated. Indeed, the child may be

EXAMPLE 16.12

Defined Curriculum: Science Pencil-and-Paper Test

1. In the chart below, write two examples of animals that fit into each category.

   Fish   Amphibian   Reptile   Bird   Mammal

2. Match the characteristics to each group of animals by drawing a line between the characteristics and the groups.

Group	Characteristic
Mammal	1. Has feathers
Bird	2. Breathes through gills its entire life
Reptile	3. Lives in water when young and on land as an adult
Amphibian	4. Feeds milk to its young
Fish	5. Dry and scaly to the touch
	6. Has a smooth skin and feels cool
	7. Lives its entire life in water
	8. Has fur on its body

3. What kind of animal do you think makes the best pet? Why?

4. Draw a picture of an animal that is part fish, part bird, and part mammal. Label the parts.

EXAMPLE 16.13

Defined Curriculum: Mathematics Pencil-and-Paper Test

1. Use your ruler to measure the length of each of these lines in centimeters. Write the length on the line.

   _____

   _____

   _____

   _____

   _____

2. Use your ruler to draw lines that are each of the following lengths.
   a. 6 centimeters
   b. 9 centimeters
   c. 1 centimeter
   d. 7 centimeters
   e. 3 centimeters

3. How could you measure the length of the following line?

   _____

4. Which is longer: a meter or a centimeter?

5. Which would you use to measure each of the following things: a meter or a centimeter?
   a. your height
   b. the length of your nose
   c. your teacher's height
   d. the length of the classroom
   e. the width of your fingernail
   f. the thickness of your math book
   g. the height of the school

6. Write your first and last name, then measure how long it is.

tested on information at the third grade that is not included until the fifth grade in the curriculum of the school and may not be tested on information that is included at the third-grade level. If standardized tests are used, interpret the results in terms of the children being tested and the curriculum being taught rather than in terms of numbers and norms.

PORTFOLIO ASSESSMENT

The forms of evaluation discussed to this point have been concerned with assessing individual activities and individual children at a particular point in time. The purposes have been to determine the success of an activity, to determine whether changes are needed in an activity, and to ascertain a child's performance based on the stated objectives of the activity or curricular pattern. One major difficulty with point-in-time assessment is that it does not show a child's progress over an extended period of time. In order to determine how a child progresses over time, assessment should:

1. encompass the whole child, including physical, social, emotional, and mental development;
2. involve repeated observations from which patterns of behavior and development can be discerned;
3. occur continuously over time so that the child's individual course of development becomes evident;
4. utilize a variety of information from different sources; and
5. be organized in a manner that allows for easy comparison of the child's work at various times.

One way of organizing information in order to accomplish these principles of evaluation is the use of a portfolio.

Definition

An assessment portfolio is a collection of a child's work, efforts, achievements, and progress over a period of time. The development and compilation of the portfolio involves both the child and the teacher. The assessment portfolio provides a comprehensive, longitudinal view of student performance. Unlike individual assessments, the portfolio helps to integrate instruction and assessment since the examples included are most likely to be examples of on-going work rather than artificial situations designed specifically for assessment purposes. The portfolio provides students, teachers, parents, and administrators with essential information about a child's progress in various classroom activities, as well as information about the kinds of activities occurring in the classroom. And, since the portfolio is longitudinal in nature, it provides a means of tracking individual progress and forms a basis for evaluating the quality of a child's overall performance rather than performance in a single area without demonstrating the relationship of that area to others.

Components of the Portfolio

Because the portfolio assesses progress over time, it must be longitudinal. Collection of a portfolio over only a few days or weeks is inappropriate because it will reveal little about a child's development. To be meaningful, the samples in the portfolio must represent the entire period in which the child is enrolled in the program. The portfolio should be regularly checked to assure adequate documentation. An assessment portfolio includes a wide variety of materials. These materials include, but are not limited to, the following kinds of items:

1. *Work samples* make up a major component of the portfolio. These include things such as student's writing and drawing, photographs of student projects and students at work, copies of journal pages, tape recordings of children reading their own work or discussing various topics, and video recordings of special events and presentations. Work samples result from classroom activities and are an integral part of those activities.
2. *Systematic observations* also form a part of the portfolio. These are observations made by the teacher as a child participates in a lesson or activity. The observations should reflect a variety of settings and times of day. Check-

LEARNING ACTIVITY 93

Mathematics-Skill Evaluation Checklist

Purpose: The purpose of this activity is to develop a checklist for use in evaluating the learning of a mathematics concept.

Procedure:

1. Plan an activity that focuses on a mathematics concept within the defined curriculum.
2. After the activity is planned, develop a checklist that could be used to evaluate the activity.
   a. Include in the checklist items that will allow evaluation of the students.
   b. Include in the checklist items that will allow evaluation of the activity.

3. Carry out the activity with a small group of first- or second-grade children. Use the checklist to evaluate both the activity and the students.
4. Now, evaluate the checklist. Which items would you keep and which would you delete or change in some way? Why are those changes needed?
5. On the basis of your checklist, how would you evaluate the success of the combined curriculum activity? What changes would you make as a result of your evaluation?

LEARNING ACTIVITY 94

Developing a Science Test

Purpose: The purpose of this activity is to develop a pencil-and-paper test that could be used to evaluate science content and process skills.

Procedure:

1. Select a chapter from a third-grade-level science textbook. Read the text and the activities.
2. Develop a test that could be used to evaluate the content and process skills that are developed in the chapter.
3. After developing the test, consider the following questions:

   a. What levels of Bloom's taxonomy are represented in the questions that are listed?
   b. What changes in the test would you make to reflect more of the levels of the taxonomy?
   c. What modifications would be needed in order to accommodate children who are at risk?
4. Rewrite the test to include the changes that you suggested. Include alternate formats that might be needed by children at risk.

LEARNING ACTIVITY 95

Developing a Mathematics Test

Purpose: The purpose of this activity is to develop a pencil-and-paper test that could be used to evaluate mathematics concepts and arithmetic skills.

Procedure:

1. Select a chapter from a third-grade-level mathematics textbook. Read the text and the activities.

2. Develop a test that could be used to evaluate the mathematics concepts and arithmetic skills covered in the chapter.
3. After developing the test, consider the following questions:

LEARNING ACTIVITY 95 Continued

a. What levels of Bloom's taxonomy are represented in the questions that are listed?

b. What changes in the test would you make to reflect more of the levels of the taxonomy?

c. What modifications would be needed in order to accommodate children who are at risk?

4. Rewrite the test to include the changes that you suggested. Include alternate formats that might be needed by children at risk.

---

lists related to a lesson's or activity's objectives are helpful in making systematic observations.

3. *Anecdotal records* are included within the portfolio. These are recordings of factual, nonjudgmental observations of a child participating in an activity or lesson. Anecdotal records are particularly useful in documenting interactions with other children and spontaneous investigations by individuals or groups.

4. *Checklists or inventories* included in the portfolio are easy ways of recording a child's progress. These are especially appropriate when the behaviors to be observed can be anticipated, when there is a sequence of behaviors showing changes in ability to use a skill or concept, or when it is not necessary to record the quality or quantity of the performance. The observations made with a checklist or inventory should be based on regular activities rather than on specially constructed or contrived activities. For example, in observing a child's ability to classify, a checklist can be used to determine whether the child classifies all of the objects, whether classification is based on a single characteristic, whether classification is based on multiple characteristics, and whether the child can reclassify objects based on a new characteristic or set of characteristics.

5. *Rating scales* can be included in the portfolio when a behavior has several different aspects or components. Each behavior is rated on a continuum from the lowest to the highest level and is marked off at certain points along the scale. A rating scale can be used to observe a child's work with other children in mathematics or science investigations. For instance, the rating scale could consider whether a child always works alone, always works with others, or falls into intermediate categories such as "sometimes works with others" or "frequently works with others."

6. *Interviews* can be included in the portfolio and are an effective and easy means of gathering information. An interview involves asking children direct questions and recording the responses. Open-ended questions are best for eliciting responses. Interviews in which the child is working with science or mathematics materials can reveal a child's understanding of a particular mathematical concept or science process skill.

Items Specific to the Mathematics and Science Areas

The science and mathematics section of the portfolio can include a wide variety of items. The following list gives some of the possibilities:

1. photographs of the child engaged in the use of mathematics manipulatives or involved in science activities,

2. charts on which the child has recorded data from activities or investigations,

3. work samples showing understanding of science or mathematics concepts through drawings or writings,

4. work samples showing ability to use computation skills in mathematics,

5. taped interviews of the teacher and child discussing mathematics or science topics or of the child demonstrating solutions to mathematics or science projects,

6. predictions and results sheets from estimation activities in mathematics or science investigations,

7. anecdotal records of the child's problem-solving experiences,
8. checklists showing the development of the ability to use science process skills,
9. observations of the use of measuring tools in mathematics or science,
10. charts showing choices of activities from mathematics or science centers,
11. anecdotal records on group or individual work on mathematics or science projects,
12. photographs of completed science projects, including collections and models,
13. a log of science or mathematics books read or looked at, and
14. a list of the kinds of mathematics materials selected for use.

Activities, spontaneous investigations by children, and the general curriculum of the program will provide additional ideas for items to include in the portfolio.

Using the Portfolio in Evaluation

Once the portfolio has been assembled, the teacher uses the information to evaluate the child's achievement. Appropriate evaluation compares the child's present work to her or his earlier work. The portfolio should never be used to compare one child's work to that of another child. The use of the portfolio should also be consistent with the curriculum established by the school and the teacher, as well as with developmental expectations.

In order to assess the child, the teacher looks at examples of work and notes areas of strong progress and areas of weaker progress. The teacher can then determine whether the child is participating in activities that will allow for progress in weaker areas. If the child is participating in such activities, then the teacher needs to give particular emphasis to those areas of weakness. If the child is not selecting activities that will strengthen weak areas, the teacher needs to assess the child's current status and make available activities that are at a level that will allow the child to progress. However, the developmental level of the child must always be taken into account when assessing areas of weakness. For example, a kindergarten child who places two objects in a group, changes characteristics, then groups two more cannot be considered weak

in classification when he or she is actually demonstrating developmentally appropriate behaviors.

Finally, in discussing the child's progress with parents, the teacher should not only display and discuss the materials included in the portfolio, but also be able to compare the child's work to the goals and objectives of the program.

SUMMARY

As with all of the aspects of the program for the early-childhood-education level, the type of evaluation should be matched to the child being evaluated. The type of evaluation also should be matched to the type of curricular pattern in use. Evaluation should consider both the evaluation of children and the evaluation of the teaching strategies being used.

At the level of the unified curriculum, the predominant types of evaluation of children are teacher observation and anecdotal records. The curriculum experiences should be evaluated in terms of the general knowledge that is developed.

At the level of the combined curriculum, the type of evaluation is extended beyond teacher observation to some of the results of the center activities and checklists of specific accomplishments. Activities within the curriculum are also evaluated for their appropriateness and success.

At the level of the defined curriculum, teacher observation decreases in importance as more formal methods of evaluation are emphasized. Activity results, arithmetic computations, and even pencil-and-paper tests can now be used. However, no one form of evaluation should become predominant, especially the use of tests. When tests are used, there should be alternatives to the pencil-and-paper format so that students who are not yet able to communicate effectively in written form have other opportunities to demonstrate their knowledge. Activities and teaching strategies should also be evaluated. Evaluation of activities can include the success of the activity, as well as an evaluation of the variety of teaching strategies and activities used in the total program.

Finally, the evaluation used in the classroom can be assembled into an assessment portfolio that will allow the teacher to evaluate a child's progress over time. The portfolio provides not only longitudinal documentation of development, but also a variety of assessments on which to base educational decisions.

Vocabulary Terms

Anecdotal Record: an informal assessment technique in which the teacher makes observations of children in particular settings.

Assessment Portfolio: an evaluation technique based on a collection of children's work and other forms of formal and informal assessment collected over a long period of time.

Checklist: an assessment device in which a prepared list of behaviors is used to assess student progress.

Evaluation: a formal or informal means used to assess a child's performance.

Longitudinal Assessment: a means of evaluation in which observations and samples of work are collected over a long period of time and then used to assess an individual child's progress through time.

Pencil-and-Paper Test: a formal means of evaluation in which the child is asked to respond in writing to specific questions.

Standardized Test: tests that have been developed and normed outside of a particular school or classroom and that are used to determine a child's progress as compared to a wide variety of other children.

Teacher Made Test: a test designed by the classroom teacher as an assessment of a child's progress within the classroom curriculum.

Teacher Observation: an informal means of assessment in which the teacher observes a child and makes notes in the form of an anecdotal record or a checklist.

Worksheet: a prepared means for students to collect information from an activity or for students to respond to specific problems or questions.

Study Questions

1. How does evaluation differ in the unified, combined, and defined curricula?
2. What reasons are there for evaluating differently in each of the curricular types?
3. Why is a pencil-and-paper test the most inappropriate form of evaluation at the early-childhood level?
4. How does a checklist differ from an anecdotal record?
5. Many parents are concerned with test scores and grades. How would you convince parents that these traditional forms of evaluation are inappropriate for young children?
6. What are some of the reasons for evaluating teaching strategies and activities, as well as children?
7. How does portfolio assessment differ from more traditional forms of assessment?
8. What advantages does portfolio assessment have over traditional forms of assessment?
9. While discussing a portfolio with parents, the mother of the child comments that work displayed in the room seems far more advanced than that done by her child. How would you respond to this parent?
10. While discussing a portfolio with parents, the father of the child comments that it is fine to look at how the child has progressed from the beginning of the year to the end, but that in the "real world," competition is more important. He wants to know how his child is doing in comparison to the other children in the classroom. How would you respond to this father?

BIBLIOGRAPHY

Albert, E. 1978. Development of the concept of heat in children. *Science Education* 62:389–99.

Allen, K. E. 1980. *Mainstreaming in early education.* Albany, N.Y.: Delmar.

Almy, M. C. 1970. *Logical thinking in second grade.* New York: Teachers College Press.

Alvermann, D. E., L. C. Smith, and J. E. Readence. 1985. Prior knowledge activation and the comprehension of compatible and incompatible text. *Reading Research Quarterly* 20:420–36.

American Association for the Advancement of Science. 1989. *Project 2061: Science for all Americans.* Washington, D.C.: American Association for the Advancement of Science.

Ames, G. J., and F. B. Murray. 1982. When two wrongs make a right: Promoting cognitive change by social conflict. *Developmental Psychology* 18:894–987.

Anastasiow, N. J., and G. P. Mansergh. 1975. Teaching skills in early childhood programs. *Exceptional Children* 41:309–17.

Anderson, J. R. 1985. *Cognitive psychology and its implications.* New York: Freeman.

Andre, T., and G. D. Phye. 1986. Cognition, learning and education. In *Cognitive classroom learning,* edited by G. D. Phye and T. Andre. New York: Academic Press.

Anselmo, S. 1987. Are children learning to think in school? *Alabama Journal* 29:17–19.

Arnold, D. S. 1975. An investigation of relationships among question level, response level, and lapse time. *School Science and Mathematics* 73:591–94.

Aschner, M. J. 1961. Asking questions to trigger thinking. *National Education Association Journal* 50:44–46.

Bauch, J. P. (Ed.) 1988. *Early childhood education in the schools.* Washington, D.C.: National Education Association.

Baust, J. A. 1981. Spatial relationships and young children. *Arithmetic Teacher* 26 (no. 1):17–21.

Beadle, P. 1973. A self directing laboratory. *Science and Children* 10:22–24.

Beaty, J. J. 1990. *Observing the development of the young child.* 2d ed. Columbus, Ohio: Merrill Publishing Company.

Beaty, J. J. 1986. *Observing development of the young child.* Columbus, Ohio: Merrill.

Beckman, P. J., and J. P. Burke. 1984. Early childhood special education: State of the art. *Topics in Early Childhood Special Education* 1:19–32.

Benner, S. M. 1992. *Assessing young children with special needs.* New York: Longman.

Berhow, B. F., and D. Foughty. 1978. A kindergarten science program for handicapped children: Adapting existing curricula. In *Proceedings: A working conference in science education for handicapped students,* edited by H. Hofman. Washington, D.C.: National Science Teachers Association.

Berk, L. E. 1985. Why children talk to themselves. *Young Children* 40 (no. 5):46–52.

Biber, B. 1984. *Early education and psychological development.* New Haven, Conn.: Yale University Press.

Bills, F. L. 1971. Developing creativity through inquiry. *Science Education* 55:417–21.

Black, J. K. 1981. Are young children really egocentric? *Young Children* 36:51–55.

Blank, M., and S. J. White. 1986. Questions: A powerful but misused form of classroom exchange. *Topics in Language Disorders* 6:1–11.

Bloom, B., and L. Sosniak. 1981. Talent development vs. schooling. *Educational Leadership* 39:86–94.

Bloom, B. S. (Ed.) 1956. *Taxonomy of educational objectives. The classification of educational goals. Handbook I: The cognitive domain.* New York: David McKay.

Blosser, P. E. 1975. *How to ask the right questions.* Washington, D.C.: National Science Teachers Association.

Boyd, E., and K. D. George. 1973. The effect of science inquiry on the abstract categorization behavior of deaf children. *Journal of Research in Science Teaching* 10:91–99.

Bredderman, T. 1982. The effects of activity-based science in elementary schools. In *Education in the 80's: Science,* edited by M. B. Rowe. Washington, D.C.: National Education Association.

Bredekamp, S. (Ed.) 1987. *Developmentally appropriate practice in early childhood programs serving children from birth through age 8.* Washington, D.C.: National Association for the Education of Young Children.

Briggs, L. J. 1977. Developing the strategy of instruction. In *Instructional Design,* edited by L. J. Briggs. Englewood Cliffs, N.J.: Educational Technology Publications.

Brody, G. H., and Z. Stoneman. 1981. Selective imitation of same age, older, and younger peer models. *Child Development* 52:717–20.

Buckleitner, W. 1991. *High/scope survey of early childhood software.* Ypsilanti, Mich.: High/Scope Educational Research Foundation.

Buhker, C. 1983. The social behavior of children. In *A handbook of child psychology,* edited by C. A. Murchison. New York: Russell and Russell.

Burns, M. 1985. The role of questioning. *Arithmetic Teacher* 32:14–16.

Bybee, R. W., and P. A. Hedricks. 1967. Teaching science concepts to preschool deaf children to aid language development. *Science Education* 56:303–10.

Campbell, K. C., and F. D. Arnold. 1988. Stimulating thinking and communicating skills. *Dimensions* 16:11–13.

Cannings, T. R., and S. W. Brown. 1986. *The information age classroom: Using the computer as a tool.* Irvine, California: Franklin, Beedle, and Associates.

Caplan, T., and F. Caplan. 1983. *The early childhood years: The 2 to 6 year old.* New York: Putnam.

Carey, S. 1986. Cognitive science and science education. *American Psychologist* 41:1123–30.

Carlson, G. 1976. Location of a point in Euclidian space by children in grades one through six. *Journal of Research in Science Teaching* 13:331–36.

Cartwright, S. 1988. Play can be the building blocks of learning. *Young Children* 43 (no. 5):44–46.

Cazden, C. B. (Ed.) 1981. *Language in early childhood education.* Washington, D.C.: National Association for the Education of Young Children.

Cliatt, M. J. P., and J. M. Shaw. 1985. Open questions, open answers. *Science and Children* 23:14–16.

Coble, C. R., and P. Hounshell. 1978. Science learning centers. *Science and Children* 11:11–13.

Coie, J. D., K. A. Dodge, and H. Coppotelli. 1982. Dimensions and types of social status: A cross age perspective. *Developmental Psychology* 18:557–70.

Copeland, R. W. 1984. *How children learn mathematics.* 4th ed. New York: Macmillan.

Copeland, R. W. 1979. *Math activities for children.* Columbus, Ohio: Merrill.

Copple, C., I. E. Siegel, and R. Saunders. 1979. *Educating the young thinker: Classroom strategies for cognitive growth.* New York: Van Nostrand Reinhold.

Correro, G. 1988. Understanding assessment in young children. *Developing instructional programs K–3.* Jackson, Miss.: Mississippi Department of Education.

Cowen, E. L., A. Pederson, H. Babigian, L. D. Izzo, and M. A. Trost. 1973. Long-term follow-up of early detected vulnerable children. *Journal of Consulting and Clinical Psychology* 41:438–46.

Cowen, J. D., K. A. Dodge, and H. Coppotelli. 1982. Dimensions and types of social status: A cross-age perspective. *Developmental Psychology* 18:557–70.

Cratty, B. J. 1986. *Perceptual and motor development in infants and children.* Englewood Cliffs, N.J.: Prentice-Hall.

Damon, W. 1984. Peer education: The untapped potential. *Journal of Applied Developmental Psychology* 5:331–43.

Damon, W. 1983. *Social and personality development.* New York: Norton.

Davidson, J. 1989. *Children and computers together in the early childhood classroom.* Albany, N.Y.: Delmar Publishers.

Dempster, A. A. 1987. An exchange of views on the place of reading in science instruction. *Journal of Reading* 27:583–84.

Denham, S. A., M. McKinley, E. A. Couchoud, and R. Holt. 1990. Emotional and behavioral predictors of preschool peer ratings. *Child Development* 61:1145–52.

Dettrick, G. 1977. Conceptual development of projective spatial relationships within the concrete operations period. *Research in Mathematics Education in Australia* 1:47–66.

DeVries, R., and L. Kohlberg. 1987. *Constructivist early education.* Washington, D.C.: National Association for the Education of Young Children.

Dick, W., and L. Carey. 1985. *The systematic design of instruction.* 2d ed. Glenview, Ill.: Scott, Foresman.

Dick, W., and R. A. Reiser. 1989. *Planning effective instruction.* Englewood Cliffs, N.J.: Prentice-Hall.

Dillon, J. T. 1982. The effect of questions in education and other enterprises. *Journal of Curriculum Studies* 14:127–52.

Dinkheller, A., J. Gaffney, and E. Vockell. 1989. *The computer in the mathematics curriculum.* Santa Cruz, Calif.: Mitchell Publishing.

Dodge, K. A., G. Petit, J. McClaskey, and M. Brown. 1986. Social competence in children. *Monographs of the Society for Research in Child Development* 51: (2, serial no. 213).

Dodge, K. A. 1983. Behavioral antecedents of peer social status. *Child Development* 54:1386–99.

Duckworth, E. 1979. Either we're too early and they can't learn or we're late and they know it already: The dilemma of applying Piaget. *Harvard Educational Review* 49:297–312.

Dyson, A. 1987. The value of "time off task": Young children's spontaneous talk and deliberate text. *Harvard Educational Review* 57:396–420.

Dyson, A. 1988. Appreciate the drawing and dictating of young children. *Young Children* 43:25–32.

Eaton, J. F., C. W. Anderson, and E. L. Smith. 1983. When students don't know they don't know. *Science and Children* 20:6–9.

Elkind, D. 1987. *Miseducation: Preschoolers at risk.* New York: Alfred A. Knopf.

Engle, B. 1990. An approach to assessment in early literacy. In *Achievement testing in the early grades: The games grown-ups play,* edited by C. Kamii. Washington, D.C.: National Association for the Education of Young Children.

Ennis, R. H. 1982. Abandon causality? *Educational Researcher* 11:25–27.

Ennis, R. H. 1973. On causality. *Educational Researcher* 2:4–11.

Erickson, G. L. 1980. Children's viewpoints of heat: A second look. *Science Education* 64:323–36.

Erickson, G. L. 1979. Children's conceptions of heat and temperature. *Science Education* 63:221–30.

Falk, J. H., W. W. Martin, and J. D. Balling. 1978. The novel field trip phenomenon: Adjustment to novel settings interferes with task learning. *Journal of Research in Science Teaching* 15:217–28.

Falkof, L., and J. Moss. 1984. When teachers tackle thinking skills. *Educational Leadership* 42:4–9.

Fauvre, M. 1988. Including young children with "new" chronic illnesses in an early childhood education setting. *Young Children* 43:71–77.

Finley, F. N. 1991. Why students have trouble learning from science texts. In *Science learning: Processes and applications,* edited by C. M. Santa and D. E. Alvermann. Newark, Del.: International Reading Association.

Finley, F. N. 1985. Variations in students' prior knowledge. *Science Education* 69:697–705.

Fisher, K. M., and J. I. Lipson. 1986. Twenty questions about student errors. *Journal of Research in Science Teaching* 23:783–803.

Forgan, H. W., and C. T. Mangrum. 1989. *Teaching content area reading skills.* 4th ed. Columbus, Ohio: Merrill.

Franks, F. L. 1975. Educational development in primary schools: An introductory science laboratory for young blind students. *Education of the Visually Handicapped* 7:97–101.

Gabel, D. 1984. An exchange of views on the place of reading in science instruction. *Journal of Reading* 27:585.

Gall, M. 1984. Synthesis of research on teacher questioning. *Educational Leadership* 42:40–47.

Gallahue, D. 1982. *Developmental movement experiences for children.* New York: Wiley.

Gallini, J. K., and M. E. Gredler. 1989. *Instructional design for computers.* Glenview, Ill.: Scott, Foresman.

Gelman, R. 1979. Preschool thought. *American Psychologist* 34:900–905.

Genishi, C. 1988. Children's language: Learning words from experience. *Young Children* 44:16–23.

Genishi, C. 1987. Acquiring oral language and communicative competence. In *The early childhood curriculum: A review of current research,* edited by C. Seefeldt. New York: Teachers College Press, Columbia University.

Glickman, C. D. 1981. Play and the school curriculum: The historical context. *Journal of Research and Development in Education* 14:1–10.

Goffin, S. G., and C. Q. Tull. 1988. Encouraging cooperative behavior among young children. *Dimensions* 16:15–18.

Goldston, D. B., and C. L. Richman. 1985. Imagery, encoding specificity, and prose recall in 6-year-old children. *Journal of Experimental Child Psychology* 40:395–405.

Grace, C., and E. F. Shores. 1992. *The portfolio and its use: Developmentally appropriate assessment of young children.* Little Rock, Ark.: Southern Association of Children Under Six.

Greenberg, P. 1990. Why not academic preschool? *Young Children* 45:70–80.

Griffin, S. 1990. Go fishing to teach respect for nature. *Dimensions* 16:8–9.

Hanline, M. F. 1985. Integrating disabled children. *Young Children* 40:45–48.

Harris, A. C. 1986. *Child development.* New York: West.

Hartup, W. W., and S. G. Moore. 1990. Early peer relations: Developmental significance and prognostic implications. *Early Childhood Research Quarterly* 5:1–17.

Hazen, N. L., and B. Black. 1989. Preschool peer communication skills: The role of social status and interaction context. *Child Development* 60:867–76.

Hendrick, J. 1988. *The whole child: Developmental education for the early years.* 4th ed. Columbus, Ohio: Merrill.

Hendrick, J. 1980. *Total learning for the whole child.* St. Louis, Mo.: Mosby.

Hiebert, J. 1981. Children's thinking. In *Mathematics education research: Implications for the 80's,* edited by E. Fennema. Alexandria, Va.: Association for Supervision and Curriculum Development.

Hill, P. S. 1987. The function of the kindergarten. *Young Children* 42:12–19.

Hogan, J. R., and W. E. Shall. 1973. Coordinating science and mathematics. *Science and Children* 10:7.

Holliday, W. G. 1991. Helping students learn effectively from science text. In *Science learning: Processes and applications,* edited by C. M. Santa and D. E. Alvermann. Newark, Del.: International Reading Association.

Holman, C. 1990. *Young children and computers.* Ypsilanti, Mich.: High/Scope Educational Research Foundation.

Holtzman, M. 1983. *The language of children.* Englewood Cliffs, N.J.: Prentice-Hall.

Howes, C. 1988. Peer interaction of young children. *Monographs of the Society for Research in Child Development* 53: (1, serial no. 217).

Hoyt, J. 1978. Adapting science in disabled learners. In *Proceedings: A working conference in science education for handicapped students,* edited by H. Hofman. Washington, D.C.: National Science Teachers Association.

Hunkins, F. P. 1972. *Questioning strategies and techniques.* Boston: Allyn and Bacon.

Hymel, S., E. Wagner, and L. Butler. 1990. Reputational bias: View from the peer group. In *Peer rejection in childhood,* edited by S. R. Asher and J. D. Coie. New York: Cambridge University.

Inhelder, B., and J. Piaget. 1964. *The early growth of logic in the child.* London: Routledge and Kegan Paul.

Irwin, D. M., and M. M. Bushnell. 1980. *Observational strategies for child study.* New York: Holt, Rinehart, and Winston.

Johnson, D. W., and R. T. Johnson. 1987. *Learning together and alone: Cooperative, competitive, and individualistic learning.* Englewood Cliffs, N.J.: Prentice-Hall.

Johnson, R. 1987. *Approaches to early childhood education.* Columbus, Ohio: Merrill.

Kamii, C. K. 1982. *Number in preschool and kindergarten.* Washington, D.C.: National Association for the Education of Young Children.

Karnes, M. 1983. *The underserved: Our young gifted children.* Reston, Va.: The Council for Exceptional Children.

Kemple, K. M. 1991. Preschool children's peer acceptance and social interaction. *Young Children* 46 (no. 5):47–54.

Kimche, L. 1978. Science centers: A potential for learning. *Science* 199:270–73.

Kostelnik, M. J., L. C. Stein, A. P. Whiren, and A. K. Soderman. 1988. *Guiding children's social development.* Cincinnati: South-Western.

Kupersmidt, J. B., J. D. Coie, and K. A. Dodge. 1990. The role of poor peer relationships in the development of disorder. In *Peer rejection in childhood,* edited by S. R. Asher and J. D. Coie. New York: Cambridge University.

Kurdek, L. A., and R. Lillie. 1985. The relations between classroom social status and classmate likability, compromising skill, termperament and neighborhood social interactions. *Journal of Applied Developmental Psychology* 6:127–57.

Ladd, G. W. 1990. Having friends, keeping friends, making friends, and being liked by peers in the classroom: Predictors of children's early school adjustment? *Child Development* 61:1081–1100.

Ladd, G. W. 1988. Friendship patterns and peer status during early and middle childhood. *Journal of Developmental and Behavioral Pediatrics* 9:229–38.

Ladd, G. W. 1982. Promoting children's prosocial behavior and peer relations in early childhood classrooms: A look at four teacher roles. *Dimensions* 12:6–12.

Ladd, G. W. and J. M. Price. 1987. Predicting children's social and school adjustment following the transition from preschool to kindergarten. *Child Development* 58:1168–89.

Ladd, G. W., J. M. Price, and C. H. Hart. 1988. Predicting preschoolers' peer status from their playground behaviors. *Child Development* 59:986–92.

Larkin, J. H., and H. A. Simon. 1981. Learning through growth of skill in mental modeling. In *Proceedings of the third annual conference.* Berkeley, Calif.: Cognitive Science Society.

Laurendeau, M., and A. Pinard. 1962. *Causal thinking in the child.* New York: International Universities Press.

Lawson, A. E., and J. W. Renner. 1975. Relationships of science subject matter and developmental levels of learners. *Journal of Research in Science Teaching* 12:347–58.

Lindfors, J. W. 1987. *Children's language and learning.* Englewood Cliffs, N.J.: Prentice-Hall.

Linn, M. C., and R. W. Peterson. 1973. The effect of direct experiences with objects on middle class, culturally diverse, and visually impaired young children. *Journal of Research in Science Teaching* 20:183–90.

Lipson, M. Y. 1982. Learning new information from text: The role of prior knowledge and reading ability. *Journal of Reading Behavior* 14:243–61.

Long, N. T. 1973. Science curriculum improvement study (SCIS): Its effect on concept development and manipulative skills in visually handicapped children. *Dissertation Abstracts* 34:1738A.

Machado, J. M., and H. C. Meyer. 1984. *Early childhood practicum guide.* Albany, N.Y.: Delmar.

Maher, C. A., and A. M. Martino. 1992. Teachers building on students' thinking. *Arithmetic Teacher* 39:32–37.

Mayer, R. E. 1987. *Educational psychology: A cognitive approach.* Boston: Little Brown.

McClintic, S. V. 1988. Conservation—a meaningful gauge for assessment. *Arithmetic Teacher* 35 (no. 6):12–14.

McNamee, A. S. 1987. Museum readiness. *Childhood Education* 63:181–87.

Meisels, S., and D. Steele. 1991. *The early childhood portfolio collection process.* Center for Human Growth and Development. Ann Arbor, Mich.: University of Michigan Press.

Meyer, L. A. 1991. Are science texts considerate? In *Science learning: Processes and applications,* edited by C. M. Santa and D. E. Alvermann. Newark, Del.: International Reading Association.

Meyer, L. A., L. Crummey, and E. A. Greer. 1988. Elementary science textbooks: Their contents, text characteristics, and comprehensibility. *Journal of Research in Science Teaching* 25:435–63.

Meyer, R. E. 1983. What have we learned about increasing the meaning of science prose? *Science Education* 67:223–37.

Meyers, B. K., and K. Maurer. 1987. Teaching with less talking: Learning centers in the kindergarten. *Young Children* 42:20–27.

Miller, G. A., and P. M. Gildea. 1987. How children learn words. *Scientific American* Sept.:94–99.

Miller, P. H. 1983. *Theories of developmental psychology.* New York: Freeman.

Morado, C. 1986. Prekindergarten programs for 4 year-olds: State involvement in preschool education. *Young Children* 41:69–71.

Murray, F. B. 1972. Acquisition of conservation through social interaction. *Developmental Psychology* 6:1–6.

National Association for the Education of Young Children. 1988. *Statement on standardized testing of young children 3 through 8 years of age.* Washington, D.C.: National Association for the Education of Young Children.

National Association for the Education of Young Children. 1986. Position statement of developmentally appropriate practice in programs for 4- and 5-year-olds. *Young Children* 41:20–29.

National Association for the Education of Young Children and Early Childhood Specialists in Departments of Education. 1991. *Guidelines for appropriate curriculum content and assessment in programs serving children age 3 through 8.* Washington, D.C.: National Association for the Education of Young Children.

National Council of Teachers of Mathematics. 1989. *Curriculum and evaluation standards for school mathematics.* Reston, Va.: National Council of Teachers of Mathematics.

National Council of Teachers of Mathematics. 1981. *Professional standards for teaching mathematics.* Reston, Va.: National Council of Teachers of Mathematics.

Northwest Regional Educational Laboratory. 1991. *Alternative program evaluation ideas for early childhood education programs.* Portland, Oreg.: Northwest Regional Education Laboratory.

Norton, D., D. and Janke. 1983. Improving science reading ability. *Science and Children* 20:5–8.

Osborn, J. D., and D. K. Osborn. 1983. *Cognition in early childhood.* Athens, Ga.: Education Associates.

Padilla, M. J., K. D. Muth, and R. K. L. Padilla. 1991. Science and reading: Many process skills in common. In *Science learning: Processes and applications,* edited by C. M. Santa and D. E. Alvermann. Newark, Del.: International Reading Association.

Palincsar, A., and A. Brown. 1984. Reciprocal teaching of comprehension-fostering and comprehension-monitoring activities. *Cognition and Instruction* 1:117–75.

Pappert, S. 1980. *Mindstorms: Children, computers, and powerful ideas.* New York: Basic Books.

Paris, S. G., and M. Myers. 1981. Comprehension monitoring, memory, and study strategies of good and poor readers. *Journal of Reading Behavior* 13:5–22.

Parker, J. G., and S. R. Asher. 1987. Peer relations and later personal adjustment: Are low accepted children at risk? *Psychological Bulletin* 103:357–89.

Parsons, A. S. 1988. Integrating special children into day care programs. *Dimensions* 16:15–19.

Pasche, C. L., L. Gorrill, and B. Strom. 1989. *Children with special needs in early childhood settings.* Menlo Park, Calif.: Addison-Wesley.

Paulson, F. L., P. R. Paulson, and C. A. Meyer. 1991. What makes a portfolio a portfolio? *Educational Leadership* 48:60–63.

Pellegrini, A. D. 1988. Elementary school children's rough-and-tumble play and social competence. *Developmental Psychology* 24:802–806.

Pellegrini, A. D., and C. D. Glickman. 1990. Measuring kindergartners' social competence. *Young Children* 45 (no. 4):40–44.

Peterson, N. L. 1987. *Early intervention for handicapped and at-risk children.* Denver: Love Publishing.

Piaget, J. 1975. *The child's conception of the world.* Totowa, N.J.: Littlefield, Adams.

Piaget, J. 1973. *Psychology of intelligence.* Totowa, N.J.: Littlefield, Adams.

Piaget, J. 1972. *Judgment and reasoning in the child.* Totowa, N.J.: Littlefield, Adams.

Piaget, J. 1972. *The child and reality.* New York: Grossman.

Piaget, J. 1972. *The child's conception of physical causality.* Totowa, N.J.: Littlefield, Adams.

Piaget, J. 1967. *The language and thought of the child.* 3rd ed. London: Routledge and Kegan Paul.

Piaget, J. 1965. *The child's conception of number.* New York: Norton.

Piaget, J., and B. Inhelder. 1974. *The child's construction of quantities.* London: Routledge and Kegan Paul.

Piaget, J., and B. Inhelder. 1967. *The child's conception of space.* New York: Norton.

Piaget, J., B. Inhelder, and A. Szeminska. 1960. *The child's conception of geometry.* London: Routledge and Kegan Paul.

Poest, C. A., J. R. Williams, D. D. Witt, and M. E. Atwood. 1990. Challenge me to move: Large muscle development in young children. *Young Children* 45 (no. 5):4–10.

Poest, C. A., J. R. Williams, D. D. Witt, and M. E. Atwood. 1989. Physical activity patterns of preschool children. *Early Childhood Research Quarterly* 4:367–76.

Pope, M., and J. Glibert. 1983. Personal experience and the construction of knowledge in science. *Science Education* 67:193–203.

Poser, G. J., K. A. Strike, P. W. Hewson, and W. A. Gertzog. 1982. Accommodation of a scientific conception: Toward a theory of conceptual change. *Science Education* 66:211–27.

Putallaz, M., and J. Gottman. 1981. An interactional model for children's entry into peer groups. *Child Development* 52:986–94.

Roberts, N., R. C. Carter, S. N. Friel, and M. S. Miller. 1988. *Integrating computers into the elementary and middle school.* Englewood Cliffs, N.J.: Prentice-Hall.

Roedell, W. C., N. E. Jackson, and H. B. Robinson. 1980. *Gifted young children.* New York: Teachers College Press, Columbia University.

Roff, M., S. B. Sells, and M. Golden. 1972. *Social adjustment and personality development in children.* Minneapolis: University of Minnesota.

Rogers, D. L. 1990. Are questions the answer? *Dimensions* 19:3–5.

Roth, K. J. 1986. *Conceptual change learning and student processing of science texts.* (research series no. 167). East Lansing, Mich.: Michigan State University, Institute for Research in Teaching.

Rowe, M. B. 1974. Relation of wait-time and rewards to the development of language, logic, and fate control. Part II—rewards. *Journal of Research in Science Teaching* 11:291–308.

Rowe, M. B. 1974. Wait-time and rewards as instructional variables: Their influence on language, logic, and fate control. Part I—Wait time. *Journal of Research in Science Teaching* 1:81–94.

Rubin, J. H., and B. Everett. 1982. Social perspective-taking in young children. In *The young child: Reviews of research* 3, edited by S. G. Moore and C. R. Cooper. Washington, D.C.: The National Association for the Education of Young Children.

Ryan, E. D., G. W. Ledger, and K. A. Weed. 1987. Acquisition and transfer of an integrative imagery strategy by young children. *Child Development* 58:43–452.

Santa, C. M. and Alvermann, D. E. (Eds). *Science Learning: Processes and applications.* Newark, Del.: International Reading Association.

Santa, J. L. 1977. Spatial transformation of words and pictures. *Journal of Experimental Psychology: Human Learning and Memory* 3:418–27.

Scarlett, W. G. 1983. Social isolation from agemates among nursery school children. In *Early childhood development and education,* edited by M. Donaldson, R. Grieve, and C. Pratt. New York: Guilford.

Schickendanz, J. A., M. E. York, I. S. Stewart, and D. A. White. 1990. *Strategies for teaching young children.* 3rd ed. Englewood Cliffs, N.J.: Prentice-Hall.

Schickedanz, J. A., S. Chay, P. Gopin, L. L. Sheng, S. Song, and N. Wild. 1990. Preschoolers and academics: Some thoughts. *Young Children* 46:4–12.

Shade, D., and S. Haugland. 1990. *Developmental evaluations of software for young children.* Albany, N.Y.: Delmar Publishers.

Shaw, T. J. 1983. The affect of a process oriented science curriculum upon problem solving ability. *Science Education* 67:615–23.

Shepard, L. A., and J. L. Smith. 1988. Escalating academic demand in kindergarten: Counterproductive policies. *The Elementary School Journal* 89:135–45.

Shuell, T. J. 1987. Cognitive psychology and conceptual change: Implications for teaching science. *Science Education* 71:239–350.

Skrupskelis, A. 1990. Going places with young children. *Dimensions* 16:3–7.

Slavin, R. E. 1980. Cooperative learning in teams: State of the art. *Educational Psychologist* 15:93–111.

Slovin, H. 1992. Number of the day. *Arithmetic Teacher* 39:29–31.

Smart, M., and R. C. Smart. 1982. *Preschool children: Development and relationships.* 3d ed. New York: Macmillan.

Smith, C. A. 1982. *Promoting the social development of young children: Strategies and activities.* Palo Alto, Calif.: The Magfield Publishing Company.

Smith, J. C. 1956. *Outdoor education.* Washington, D.C.: National Education Association Publications.

Smith, L. D., J. E. Readence, and D. E. Alvermann. 1984. Effects of activating background knowledge on comprehension of expository text. In *Thirty-third tearbook of the National Reading Conference,* edited by J. A. Niles and L. A. Harris. Rochester, New York: National Reading Conference.

Smith, R. F. 1988. Wheels and things: Developing preschool science learning centers. *Dimension* 17:10–12.

Smith, R. F. 1987. Theoretical framework for preschool science experiences. *Young Children* 34:56–61.

Sobel, M. A., and E. M. Maletsky. 1988. *Teaching Mathe-matics.* 2d ed. Englewood Cliffs, N.J.: Prentice-Hall.

Southern Association on Children Under Six. 1990. *Developmentally appropriate assessment.* Little Rock, Ark.: Southern Association on Children Under Six.

Sproatt, R. H. 1984. Developing a positive self-concept in the young child. *Dimensions* 12:19–21.

Stafford, G. 1980. *Developing effective classroom groups.* New York: A & W Publishers.

Stewart, J. 1982. Two aspects of meaningful problem solving in science. *Science Education* 66:731–49.

Sumpton, M., and E. Luecking. 1960. *Education of the gifted.* New York: Ronald Press.

Swazuk, D. 1978. Mainstreaming physically handicapped students. In *Proceedings: A working conference in science education for handicapped students,* edited by H. Hofman. Washington, D.C.: National Science Teachers Association.

Talton, C. F. 1988. Let's solve the problem before we find the answer. *Arithmetic Teacher* 36:40–45.

Theil, R. P., and K. D. George. 1976. Some factors affecting the use of the science process skill of prediction by elementary children. *Journal of Research in Science Teaching* 13:155–56.

Tobin, K. 1987. The role of wait time in higher cognitive level learning. *Review of Educational Research* 57:175–213.

Trabasso, T., and P. van den Broek. 1985. Causal thinking and the representation of narrative events. *Journal of Memory and Language* 24:612–30.

Trawick-Smith, J. 1990. Give and take: How young children persuade their peers. *Dimensions* 19:22–24.

Tudge, J., and D. Caruso. 1988. Cooperative problem solving in the classroom: Enhancing young children's cognitive development. *Young Children* 44:46–52.

Victor, E. 1974. The inquiry approach to teaching and learning: A primer for the teacher. *Science and Children* 12 (no. 2):23–25.

Vlug, H. 1978. Science education for the deaf. In *Proceedings: A working conference in science education for handicapped students,* edited by H. Hofman. Washington, D.C.: National Science Teachers Association.

Waters, E., and L. Sroufe. 1983. Social competence as a developmental construct. *Developmental Review* 3:79–97.

Webb, L. F., and D. H. Ost. 1975. Unifying science and mathematics in elementary schools: One approach. *Arithmetic Teacher* 22:67–72.

Weikart, D., L. Rogers, and C. Adcock. 1971. *The cognitively oriented curriculum.* Urbana, Ill.: University of Illinois.

West, C. K., J. A. Farmer, and P. M. Wolff. 1991. *Instructional design: Implications from cognitive science.* Englewood Cliffs, N.J.: Prentice-Hall.

White, B. P., and M. A. Phair. 1986. It'll be a challenge!: Managing emotional stress in teaching disabled children. *Young Children* 41:44–48.

Woerner, J. J., R. H. Rivers, and E. L. Vockell. 1991. *The computer in the science curriculum.* Watsonville, Calif.: Mitchell Publishing.

Wolfinger, D. M. 1989. Developing mathematics understanding in young children. *Dimensions* 18 (no. 1):5–7.

Wolfinger, D. M. 1988. Mathematics for the young child—not arithmetic. *Arithmetic Teacher* 36 (no. 6):2–3.

Wolfinger, D. M. 1984. *Teaching science in the elementary school.* Boston: Little, Brown.

Wolfinger, D. M. 1982. The effect of science teaching on the young child's concept of Piagetian physical causality: Animism and dynamism. *Journal of Research in Science Teaching* 19 (no. 7):595–602.

Wolfle, J. 1989. The gifted preschooler: Developmentally different but still 3 or 4 years old. *Young Children* 44:41–48.

Wollman, W., B. Eylon, and A. E. Lawson. 1980. An analysis of premature closure in science and developmental stages. *Journal of Research in Science Teaching* 13:155–56.

Wright, M. 1980. Measuring the social competence of preschool children. *Canadian Journal of Behavioral Science* 12:17–32.

Ziemer, M. 1987. Science in the early childhood curriculum: One thing leads to another. *Young Children* 42:44–45.

INDEX